New Working-Class Studies

New Working-Class Studies

Edited by
John Russo
and
Sherry Lee Linkon

ILR Press
an imprint of
Cornell University Press
Ithaca and London

First published 2005 by Cornell University Press
First printing, Cornell Paperbacks, 2005

Printed in the United States of America

*Library of Congress Cataloging-in-Publication Dat*a

New working-class studies / edited by John Russo and Sherry Lee Linkon.
    p. cm.
  Includes bibliographical references and index.
  ISBN 0-8014-4252-4 (cloth : alk. paper) — ISBN 0-8014-8967-9 (pbk. :
alk. paper)
  1. Working class—Research—United States.   2. Working class—Study
and teaching—United States.   3. Working class—History—Study and
teaching—United States.   I. Russo, John, 1946–   II. Linkon, Sherry Lee,
1959–
    HD4824.5.U5N49 2005
    305.5'62'0973—dc22   2004030151

Cornell University Press strives to use environmentally responsible
suppliers and materials to the fullest extent possible in the publishing
of its books. Such materials include vegetable-based, low-VOC inks
and acid-free papers that are recycled, totally chlorine-free, or partly
composed of nonwood fibers. For further information, visit our website
at www.cornellpress.cornell.edu.

Cloth printing   10 9 8 7 6 5 4 3 2 1
Paperback printing   10 9 8 7 6 5 4 3 2 1

To Tillie Olsen and Joyce and Hy Kornbluh

Contents

Acknowledgments

New Working-Class Studies is a collaborative project that has developed over the past decade out of the efforts of many individuals around the country. At the first conferences sponsored by the Center for Working-Class Studies at Youngstown State University, we met many individuals who were interested in working-class life and culture but who felt isolated, worried that no one else shared their perspective. Over time, that group of academics, artists, and activists has developed an ongoing interdisciplinary conversation that has now become a new academic field. This book reflects their creativity, enthusiasm, and dedication, and we thank them for their inspiration.

This book was made possible by a grant from the Ford Foundation and the support of Youngstown State University. At a time when New Working-Class Studies was just emerging, Ford and YSU believed in the idea and in us. Janice Petrovich, Margaret Wilkerson, and Gertrude Fraser of the Ford Foundation had confidence in the center's work and in this book. Jim Scanlon, former provost of YSU, gave his full support for creating something new at a time when universities were cutting programs. His initial support has been sustained by our current provost, Tony Atwater, and YSU's president, David Sweet, who instinctively understood that working-class studies was central to the university, its students, and the community. Our deans, Barbara Brothers, Robert Bolla, and Betty Jo Licata, have been consistently supportive.

Several colleagues have provided important advice and encouragement, especially Jack Metzgar, Tim Strangleman, Michael Zweig, and Jefferson Cowie. Our contributors have been responsive and thoughtful, sharing their ideas, listening to ours, and helping us learn as we worked with them. We thank Fran Benson, Nancy Ferguson, and the staff of Cornell University Press for their encouragement and editorial assistance. Our graduate student intern, Lacey Kogelnik, provided essential assistance with editing and formatting the manuscript. We are grateful every day for the fine work and generous spirit of Patty LaPresta, our administrative assistant, who helps make our working lives easier and more fun.

JOHN RUSSO
SHERRY LEE LINKON

Youngstown, Ohio

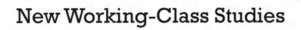

New Working-Class Studies

What's New about New Working-Class Studies?

John Russo and Sherry Lee Linkon

Although the study of the working class has a long history and deep roots, over the past decade scholars have focused on working-class life and culture with renewed interest. Equally important, recent work has raised new issues, new approaches, and new challenges. This book provides a wide-ranging exploration of both the roots and the new directions that are shaping the emerging field we call "New Working-Class Studies." The essays illustrate the ways in which new working-class studies is at once rooted in existing disciplines and innovative in the ways it integrates multiple disciplines and uses different kinds of materials. This approach allows some clear themes to emerge, such as the emphasis on interdisciplinary approaches and the centrality of cultural representations as sources for understanding working-class experience. Simply put, this volume aims to create an intellectual meeting ground. By pulling together essays that approach this new field in different ways, *New Working-Class Studies* allows readers from different perspectives to reflect on both the intellectual traditions that make new working-class studies possible and the innovative new work that is shaping its future.

Foundations of the Field

New working-class studies builds on foundations laid in several core fields. These foundational fields provided important models that suggested useful approaches and essential concepts, but then they either moved away from a focus on working-class life and culture or never fully developed an approach that took the working class seriously. Working-class studies owes much to these foundational areas, and we see important opportunities for building on these fields by refocusing on class.

Perhaps the most important foundation for new working-class studies is labor studies, which traces its history to the early twentieth century and programs such as the Bryn Mawr Summer School for Women Workers. As Dorothy Sue Cobble has noted, these early forms of worker education emphasized culture—art, literature, philosophy, music—as avenues for worker self-activity and expression.[1] While this early approach may have carried some taint of paternalism in the notion that elite educators should enlighten working women about the arts and culture, it also celebrated worker culture as valuable, engaging, and significant. In 1932, Myles Horton and Don West founded the Highlander School, offering grassroots, "popular" education focused on fighting for economic and social justice and understanding the value of the experiences and insights of "ordinary people." By the middle of the twentieth century, labor studies, and especially worker education programs, had moved toward more practical, utilitarian approaches that emphasized specific union skills, such as contract negotiations and handling grievances. The cultural approach to labor studies has resurfaced periodically, as in the work of Paulo Freire and his followers, who focused on putting worker culture at the center of labor education as a means of fostering empowerment and activism. For new working-class studies, these cultural approaches offer important models for linking the academic study of working-class history and culture with activism and education, not only of unionized workers but of K-12 and college students who come from working-class backgrounds. In addition, labor studies exemplifies the possibility of linking academic work with political organizing by working-class communities and groups.

Labor history also provides foundational ideas and approaches for new working-class studies. Much American labor history has focused on the history of organized labor, offering a model that takes seriously the history of work, workers, and working-class organizations. Yet, as David Roediger reminds us, much of this work has championed the perspective of white, male, native-born workers. By the 1960s, however, labor historians had embraced the (then) new social history, putting everyday working-class life and culture at the center of historical analysis. Such scholarship built on models offered by E. P. Thompson's *Making of the British Working Class* and the History Workshop movement, which Tim Strangleman discusses here, and by Herbert Gutman and his colleagues at the American Social History Project. The latter developed a widely used alternative history text, *Who Built America?*, and, more recently, a host of online materials aimed at dramatically changing the way American history is taught by emphasizing cultural materials and working-class experience. This approach laid the groundwork for a number of key analyses of working-class leisure culture, such as Roy Rosenzweig's *Eight Hours for What We Will* and Kathy Peiss's *Cheap Amusements.*[2]

Along with emphasizing class as an aspect of culture, social historians emphasized issues of race, ethnicity, and gender. Yet, ironically, as Elizabeth Faue argues here, the rise of social history ultimately led many labor historians to focus on race and gender and to downplay class, while others focused on the racism and sexism of the white working class. Indeed, by the mid-1990s, it seemed to some that the phrase "working class" operated as code for talking about white men, as in Roediger's groundbreaking study *The Wages of Whiteness.* As Roediger notes in the afterword to the second edition of that book, he had approached his study of the history of class and race with a "white blind spot." Although his book focuses on the intersection of race and class, the working class he studied was clearly white and male. Black slaves were not seen as part of the working class, either by Roediger or, equally important, by the white workers he studied. Nor were women included. At the same time, as Faue and Phillips note in their essays here, a new tradition of women's labor history and African American labor history emerged during the late 1980s and early 1990s. Although the people and movements studied in these works were almost always working class, such scholarship has tended to focus on how their working lives and communities were shaped by gender and race, not by class. Thus, "working class" came to be read as by definition white, male, racist, and sexist, while issues of gender and race eclipsed attention to class consciousness and class organizing.

For other labor historians, as Faue points out, the 1990s saw a return to a focus on unions as institutions, a move away from social history altogether. For new working-class studies, labor history provided a variety of models of how to study working-class life; yet that field ultimately moved away from a focus on class and put race, ethnicity, and gender at the center of its work. In addition, although some historians ventured beyond the traditional boundaries of their field to consider leisure and popular culture, few engaged extensively with materials, methods, or ideas from other fields. So even as scholars in other fields drew on labor history for their work, labor history itself remained a subfield of history.

Yet interdisciplinary approaches have long been central to the study of working-class life and culture. Within the United States, American studies provides a rich model of multi- and interdisciplinary scholarship and teaching, and by the 1960s, the field had turned away from its earlier emphasis on consensus and nationalism to explore a much more critical, contested model of American culture. At the heart of the new approach was the American studies mantra, "race, class, and gender." With a few notable exceptions, such as Michael Denning's *Mechanic Accents: Dime Novels and Working-Class Culture in America,*[3] class was rarely given prominence (though often mentioned). In the late 1990s, when a small group of American studies scholars formed a working-class studies caucus, very few of the hundreds of papers presented at the annual American Studies Association conference gave class primary attention. This was true even as the organization elected two prominent scholars of working-class culture, Paul Lauter and later Michael Frisch, to the association's presidency. As in other fields, race, ethnicity, gender, and sexuality took center stage.

In part, this reflected the American adaptation of British cultural studies, which modeled interdisciplinary scholarship that focused on everyday life, pop culture, and identity studies, especially class issues. The American version, however, focused largely on media studies and on race, gender, ethnicity, and sexuality. Again, and despite the strong model for working-class studies offered by the Birmingham school, class became the element that was named but was rarely the focus of research or teaching. Cultural studies and American studies offered important models for using popular and everyday culture, for asking questions about how individuals and groups negotiated complex identities, and for connecting power with identity, politics, and cultural practices. Yet even when these fields attended to class, many humanities scholars and graduate students who were interested in working-class life and culture still felt homeless and isolated.

At about the same time, and indeed as part of the same historical and social developments, multiculturalism came to the fore in American academic culture. Emerging out of liberal politics and the civil rights movements of the 1960s, over the next three decades critical analysis of race, class, gender, and sexuality found a home in most colleges and universities. By the early 1990s, scholars in many disciplines focused their research on issues of difference and identity, and this became a dominant approach in many fields. New courses were developed, both within traditional disciplines and in new programs and departments that focused on race, ethnicity, and gender. Campus, professional, and national projects began to provide grants and institutes to help faculty develop courses and teaching strategies for integrating multiculturalism into the curriculum. General education programs began to include required diversity courses. Attention also expanded beyond the traditional categories of race, gender, and ethnicity to encompass globalization, postcolonial studies, border studies, and other variations. Despite conservative critiques, multiculturalism flourished. Although multiculturalism may not have created the dramatic changes that some hoped for, it has had a powerful influence on higher education.

Yet, as in labor history, American studies, and cultural studies, despite the habit of naming class as one of the elements of diversity, few of these programs focused on working-class life and culture. Indeed, when we submitted a proposal to the diversity curriculum project of the American Association of Colleges and Universities in 1995—which asked "Will the working class be invited to the diversity banquet?"—we learned that ours was the only one out of more than eighty proposals to emphasize class. Looking at university bulletins around the country, one might find hundreds of departments, programs, and courses in black studies and critical race studies, ethnic studies, gender and women's studies, and sexuality studies but only three centers specializing in working-class studies, and relatively few courses in working-class history or culture. Somehow liberal and leftist politics and the social movements of the 1960s led to an academic culture that pays relatively careful attention to race, ethnicity, sexuality, and gender but views class as somehow already covered, much the way some academics once said that we didn't need to have women's studies programs because we already studied women in "regular" courses.

Recently, a new version of multiculturalism has emerged that emphasizes the intersections among multiple categories of identity and culture. Yet most of these programs define their focus as the intersection among race, ethnicity, and gender, leaving class out of the equation, even though the people studied are often working class. Students and scholars alike resist studying class, in part because class is a difficult concept to discuss, both personally and intellectually. These discussions create discomfort both for those from working-class backgrounds, who may feel ashamed that their families were not more successful, and those from more privileged families, who may resist recognizing their own privilege. Intellectually, conversations about class must take into account multiple definitions of class as well as changes in social and economic structures at the end of the millennium and the beginning of a new one. Others resist on a more political basis, fearing that working-class studies is too close to "whiteness studies," or that it is really a way of claiming space in the conversation for white, working-class, straight men. For others, talking about class may complicate discussions of the marginalization of people on the basis of race or gender; after all, looking at class differences reminds us that some people of color are in positions of privilege relative to others. For still others, lingering fears remain from earlier "red scare" periods when leftist scholars whose work focused on class were vulnerable to repression both in society at large and in the academy.

Although the reasons are no doubt complex, in multiculturalism as in other foundational fields class often gets short shrift. Yet despite this, multiculturalism, cultural studies, American studies, labor history, and labor studies provide useful models for the interdisciplinary study of working-class culture, experience, and the social politics of power. Equally important, in these areas as well as a few key disciplines individual scholars have led the way with innovative models of scholarship and groundbreaking work in teaching and organizing. Although individual scholars have always studied class, work, and working-class culture, during the 1990s several notable examples of interdisciplinary work that highlighted working-class culture and the intersections of class with race and gender laid the groundwork for the development of new working-class studies.

In labor studies, several important examples have pointed the way toward a more engaged, political, and interdisciplinary approach to labor education. As early as the 1980s, Andy Banks, Jack Metzgar, and John Russo began arguing for an "organizing model of unionism" that would focus on fostering working-class consciousness and a sense of ownership and capability.[4] At the same time, labor educators such as Elise Bryant and Joyce and Hy Kornbluh modeled an approach that put workers' culture, stories, and experiences at the heart of worker education and labor organizing. A decade later, Bob Bruno and Lisa Jordan, both at that time working for the Labor Education Service of the University of Illinois, designed an innovative model for worker education. Illinois History Works used storytelling, music, film, and audience engagement to teach the history of the American labor movement.[5] Such work also opened up the possibility of linking labor studies and labor organizing with scholarship and teaching by faculty in American studies, literature, and other academic fields.

In labor history, David Roediger's *The Wages of Whiteness: Race and the Making of the American Working Class* and Robin Kelley's *Hammer and Hoe: Alabama Communists during the Great Depression* modeled new approaches to examining the intersection of class, work, and race, a theme that has always been central to new working-class studies. Alessandro Portelli reexamined oral history, suggesting new ways of thinking about how working-class people describe their lives and experiences. Portelli also modeled cross-cultural working-class studies with significant work on both Italian and American workers. Michael Frisch offered another innovation in labor history in his collaboration with photographer Milton Rogovin, *Portraits in Steel,* a book that combines oral histories with powerful photographs of steelworkers, male and female, white and black. As with labor studies, these examples demonstrated ways of studying working-class experience that put workers' voices, memories, and perspectives at the center.[6]

The themes of memory and identity have also been explored in some of the most important innovations to emerge out of American studies. As does Denning's *Mechanic Accents,* George Lipsitz's *Rainbow at Midnight: Labor and Culture in the 1940s* and his popular culture study, *Time Passages,* model interdisciplinary approaches that use popular culture as a key resource in studying working-class culture. Late in the 1990s, Nan Enstad's *Ladies of Labor, Girls of Adventure* demonstrated the value of studying class as culture, as well as the intersection among cultural practices, representations, and working-class consciousness.[7] In all of this work, intersections among class, race, gender, and ethnicity are central, as are representations, especially popular culture—movies, music, television, and popular literature. Analysis of representations has become one of the dominant approaches to the study of working-class culture.

Although the national conversation about multiculturalism generated little work that focused primarily on the working class, multiculturalism provided the impetus for several key organizing projects that helped to make new working-class studies possible. Youngstown State University's 1995 proposal to the "Diversity and Democracy" project of American Association of Colleges and Universities (AAC&U) argued that class should be a central element in the study and teaching of diversity. The AAC&U's support helped make possible the formation of the Center for Working-Class Studies at YSU, the first such center in the country. The Ford Foundation provided additional support to the CWCS, through its Education and Scholarship program, whose goals are "to increase educational access and quality for the disadvantaged, to educate new leaders and thinkers, and to foster knowledge and curriculum supportive of inclusion, development, and civic life."[8] In part because of the CWCS's success, additional centers and projects have been established that focus not only on class but also on its intersections with race and gender. The Center for African-American Women and Labor at the University of Maryland, directed by Sharon Harley and also funded by Ford, supports research by individual scholars and symposia that explore how African American women's work has been shaped by cultural constructions of race, class, gender, and family. The Center for the Study of Working Class Life at SUNY–Stony Brook, a social-science-oriented program developed by Michael Zweig, has sponsored faculty colloquia and national conferences. A consortial center in Chicago, cosponsored by several universities there, offers an annual series of public programs, including poetry readings, education projects, and exhibits.

Beyond these developments in the foundational fields, several disciplines have produced key work that models new ways of thinking about and studying the working class. In literary studies, for example, many view Paul Lauter's 1980 essay "Working-Class Women's Literature" as *the* foundational work, offering for the first time the idea that literature by working-class writers mattered. In the early 1990s, collections of literature and essays appeared, most notably Janet Zandy's two anthologies, *Calling Home* and *Liberating Memory*; the poetry anthology *Working Classics* edited by Nicholas Coles and Peter Oresick; and a series of collections and single-author works published by Larry Smith's Bottom Dog Press. Other scholars published key studies of working-class literature, such as Constance Coiner's *Better Red: The Writing and Resistance of Tillie Olsen and Meridel Le Sueur* and Laura Hapke's *Labor's Text*. By the end of the decade, Coiner, Lauter, Zandy, and the collaborative team of Renny Christopher and Carolyn Whitson had all published essays that offered defining theories of working-class literature.[9]

Researchers and teachers of composition have long understood that class background, perhaps even more than race or ethnicity, shapes students' attitudes toward and uses of language. As Renny Christopher discusses here, advocates such as Ira Shor and Mike Rose have argued for pedagogical approaches that address the needs of working-class students, for whom college can seem an alien place. Shor's *Empowering Education* and Rose's *Lives on the Boundary* offered early explorations of how class shapes educational experiences and how higher education creates obstacles for working-class students.[10] The Working-Class Special Interest Group and Working-Class Students Listserv of the National Council of Teachers of English were among the first organizations to form within any discipline with a focus on working-class issues. Other caucuses and organizations have since formed in American literature, American studies, and film studies, suggesting a strong interest among humanities scholars in working-class life and culture.

One of the hallmarks of new working-class studies is its focus on how class and place are mutually constitutive, a trend that reflects the influence of geography on the field. As Don Mitchell argues here, labor geography has developed over the past two decades, emerging out of the Marxist and postmodern approaches of key figures such as David Harvey and Doreen Massey. In the 1990s, Mitchell's own work, especially his study of how the California landscape shapes and is shaped by migrant labor, *The Lie of the Land,* and an anthology edited by Andrew Herod, *Organizing the Landscape,* demonstrated the deep connections between the organization of space, labor politics, and the everyday lives of working-class people.[11] Mitchell was named a MacArthur Fellow in 1998, and his award helped to fund the People's Geography Project, a national collaborative effort that is developing studies of place written by and reflecting the experiences of working people.

No discussion of working-class life and culture would be possible without the formative ideas from three social sciences: sociology, anthropology, and economics. While sociologists have long examined class as a concept, arguing about how to define class and why it matters, a few key scholars have contributed ideas and approaches that make new working-class studies possible. A number of sociologists have explored ways of defining class and analyzed how it functions, from Max Weber through Erik Olin Wright. But while many of these have focused on defining class categories, the most useful sociological models for new working-class studies are those that focus on class formation, class conflict, and the intersections between race and class. A former steelworker and union organizer, sociologist Stanley Aronowitz has published a series of essential works along these lines. From his early study *False Promises* to his 2003 book *How Class Works,* Aronowitz has explored the meaning and practice of class with a consistent focus on the real lives, attitudes, and experiences of working-class people. William Julius Wilson developed sharp analyses of the links between race, class, and economic structures in his 1996 study, *When Work Disappears: The World of the New Urban Poor.*[12]

Anthropology contributes essential concepts about and strategies for studying culture as lived experience. Ethnography, especially, demonstrates the possibility of learning about culture from the inside, through participation, observation, and interviews. Although anthropologists have not necessarily focused their attention on class, they remind us of the importance and the difficulty of moving beyond one's own frame of reference in order to understand how culture works. This understanding has been especially useful for academics that do not come from working-class backgrounds, because it reminds us of the class biases that we may bring to this work. In recent years, however, a number of cultural anthropologists have applied this approach to the study of work and class. In books such as Kathryn Marie Dudley's *The End of the Line: Lost Jobs, New Lives in Postindustrial America,* Maria Kefalas's *Working-Class Heroes: Protecting Home, Community, and Nation in a Chicago Neighborhood,* and Dimitra Doukas's *Worked Over: The Corporate Sabotage of an American Community,* cultural anthropologists, like many geographers, show how the experience and meaning of being working class is grounded in everyday life, in human interactions, and in the relationship between work, place, and community.[13]

As Michael Zweig notes in his essay here, class and economics are closely intertwined. After all, the foundational idea of classes being formed by the means of production and by the different, competing interests of people who play different roles in production comes from economics. Economists have explored how class works, though with somewhat more focus on economic structures and processes than on culture and experience. Thus, economics plays a central role in new working-class studies, even though the field moved away from class-based analysis for much of the twentieth century. Yet Zweig's own 2001 book, *The Working-Class Majority: America's Best Kept Secret,* suggests a return to class-based economics. He uses economic analysis to argue for a model of class that links socioeconomic structures with power differences based on work and production. As Zweig notes, reading class in this way reminds us that the majority of Americans are working class and therefore have enormous potential for political power.[14]

These various threads are now coming together in landmark books that provide introductions and overviews of new working-class studies, texts that are—like this volume—helping to define the central questions, approaches, and insights of this emerging field. The first of these volumes is Janet Zandy's 2001 collection, *What We Hold in Common: An Introduction to Working-Class Studies,* which reprints articles from a 1995 issue of *Women's Studies Quarterly* together with a range of new pieces that show how the field is growing. Zandy's collection includes a section of essays and poems representing working-class voices, examples of course syllabi, and brief critical articles that illustrate the field's development. More recently, Michael Zweig's collection, *What's Class Got to Do with It? American Society in the Twenty-first Century,* includes eleven articles based on presentations from the 2002 "How Class Works" conference at SUNY–Stony Brook. The articles Zweig selected for the volume reflect several discussions that are central in the field, including the relationship between class, gender, and race; class in a global economy; and class and education. Contributors include scholars and activists from labor studies, literature, psychology, and other fields. These two books represent the diverse range of scholarly work in the field, but they also demonstrate that new working-class studies is generating interest among readers for whom the field suggests strategies for connecting scholarly work with social justice activism.[15]

Why did all of this work develop over the past two decades? This might seem ironic, since the image most often conjured by references to "working class" is of the blue-collar industrial worker, exactly the kind of worker most likely to have been displaced by late twentieth-century economic restructuring and deindustrialization. Yet Alessandro Portelli reminds us that working-class culture remains even when work disappears. Indeed, even as work is changing dramatically, almost half of Americans continue to identify themselves as working class.[16] In part because of this, although new working-class studies has a strong interest in both the history of the industrial working class and the experiences of displaced workers, the field has resisted simple nostalgia. For new working-class studies, dramatic changes in work raise new and significant questions about class in general and working-class culture specifically. New structures and kinds of work and the fact that working-class people are less likely than ever to belong to unions call for new ways of studying working-class life, culture, and politics. These historical and economic developments make clear that working-class culture does not exist only in the workplace, and that class conflict is not limited to the "traditional" working class. This leads to questions about how class works in both communal and individual experience, how people make sense of their class position, and how consciousness of class might lead to collective action.

New Working-Class Studies

While this brief history helps to position new working-class studies in a broad landscape of intellectual activism, it leaves unanswered the key question: "What's *new* about new working-class studies?" Clearly building on and learning from the interdisciplinary, socially critical intellectual traditions of the last thirty years, new working-class studies incorporates theories and methods from these foundational areas without privileging any single approach. New working-class studies brings together scholars, artists, activists, and workers from a variety of perspectives, disciplines, and theoretical schools. Yet within this broad and inclusive framework, new working-class studies has developed several important patterns that differentiate it from earlier approaches to the study of class. Indeed, one distinguishing feature is that it draws on such varied intellectual roots and embraces diverse and even contradictory ideas about how class works, why it matters, and how we can best understand it.

Perhaps the most striking and central difference from previous efforts is that we put the working class, in all its varieties, at the center of our work. New working-class studies is not only about the labor movement, or about workers of any particular kind, or workers in any particular place—even in the workplace. Instead, we ask questions about how class works for people at work, at home, and in the community. We explore how class both unites and divides working-class people, which highlights the importance of understanding how class shapes and is shaped by race, gender, ethnicity, and place. We reflect on the common interests as well as the divisions between the most commonly imagined version of the working class—industrial, blue-collar workers—and workers in the "new economy" whose work and personal lives seem, at first glance, to place them solidly in the middle class. In the twenty-first century, perhaps more than ever before, defining who is or is not working class is a slippery, complex task, and class as a concept carries multiple, contradictory, and complementary meanings. Understanding that class is a homograph (a word that has multiple, shifting, contested meanings), new working-class studies takes as its mission not the struggle among scholars and theorists to reach agreement about what class is but rather the exploration of how class works, as both an analytical tool and a basis for lived experience.

Within the field, individuals adopt several different positions about how to define class. Some use traditional Marxist models that define everyone who works for a wage, who does not own the means of production, as working class. Others focus on social status and factors such as education, lifestyle, and self-definition in determining class position. Still others emphasize the uses of class and the working class in contemporary political and popular language, and how these linguistic patterns influence people's responses to their class situations. For many in the field, these approaches are not mutually exclusive but rather complementary. New working-class studies almost always begins with some combination of the power relations associated with work, political struggle, and lived experience, grounding the study of how class works in the lives, words, and perspectives of working-class people, and using these as the foundation and location for analyses of systems of power, oppression, and exploitation. Attention to discourses of class, whether in popular culture, the arts, or political activism, is also central to this work. As Jack Metzgar argues here, the vernacular of class plays a key role in whether people will act in their own class interests, so we must pay attention to language and images as well as economic and social structures. What unites this work, regardless of which of these approaches an individual scholar or artist might find most persuasive or useful, is that working-class people and their lives take center stage.

It is in part because of this interest in the lived experience of working-class people that new working-class studies has been so influenced by representations that provide access to working-class voices and perspectives. To a large extent, this means collecting and studying representations that capture the voices of working-class people, such as oral histories, songs, poems, and personal narratives. In her essay here, Rachel Rubin shows very effectively how much we can learn about working-class experience and perspectives by listening to popular music. Yet in many cases, these representations also reflect efforts by the media to capitalize on the working class as an audience, something popular music also illustrates clearly. Representations can also rely at least partially on the framing efforts of academics who collect and make available oral histories. So representations can tell us much not only about how working-class people view the world and their own experiences but also about how the working class is seen by the media, the academy, and in contemporary culture at large. On some level, perhaps, scholars in working-class studies, even (and, in some cases, especially) those who come from working-class backgrounds, are very conscious of their own class privilege and the potential problems involved in studying the working class from the outside. We recognize that we must study and use these materials thoughtfully, respectfully, and without romanticizing the working class. One way of putting working-class people at the center of new working-class studies is to make working-class voices a primary source for the study of working-class life.

While putting working-class people and culture at the heart of its work, new working-class studies does not privilege class over other aspects of identity or social processes. Some leftist scholars have argued that class should be the center of discussion because it was the most important category of analysis, the one that should, in theory, supersede all divisions and provide a source for unity across boundaries of difference or location. In contrast, new working-class studies puts class at the center because we see class as deeply interwoven with other formative elements of society—race, gender, work, structures of power—and because we see class as the element that is often least explored and most difficult to understand. As bell hooks suggests:

> Class is still often kept separate from race. And while race is often linked with gender, we still lack an ongoing collective public discourse that puts the three together in ways that illuminate for everyone how our nation is organized and what our class politics really are. Women of all races and black people of both genders are fast filling up the ranks of the poor and disenfranchised. It is in our interest to face the issue of class, to become more conscious, to know better, so that we can know how best to struggle for economic justice.[17]

New working-class studies argues that class should be taken as seriously as race and gender, given as much critical attention, questioned as deeply, and brought into not only academic but also public discussions about identity, difference, and cultural politics. Thus, we see new working-class studies as closely allied with other emerging approaches to what Bonnie Thornton Dill calls "intersectional studies," work that analyzes how multiple social categories work together. Yet, as Dill acknowledges, few of these intersectional projects put class at the core of their work because American culture so powerfully resists talking about class.[18] New working-class studies recognizes that the common interests of class can bring together people who view themselves as competitors, yet we also recognize the very real divisions that have shaped, for example, white working-class racism. The unifying potential of class will always remain as mere possibility unless discussions of race, gender, and ethnicity become central to class-based organizing.

New working-class studies attempts to develop strategies for making sense of the complex mosaic of class, race, gender, and ethnicity, both intellectually and politically. This work takes many forms, from historian Kimberley Phillips's study of the community life of black workers and their families who migrated from Alabama to Cleveland to the novels of Afro-Caribbean writer Agymah Kamau, which explore how class and race together shape experiences of community life and immigration for the residents of a fictional Caribbean island.[19]

As this comparison suggests, new working-class studies takes many forms, not all of them traditionally academic. It is as involved in the creation of representations as it is in the study of them. For example, the study of film in new working-class studies includes not only explorations of how the working class has been portrayed in film, such as in the work of Stephen Ross,[20] but also, as Tom Zaniello suggests here, the consideration of filmmaking itself is a way of studying class. The significance of new working-class studies in fostering the creation of representations can also be seen in the growing interest in working-class poetry that Jim Daniels documents here. The cultural work pursued by the Bread and Roses Project of Service Employees International Union 1199, for example, which sponsors a variety of arts projects, exemplifies the intellectual goals of new working-class studies.[21] Bread and Roses and other organizations have sponsored photographic exhibits that allow audiences to see the lived experiences of working people. In newspapers and magazines, we've seen greater attention to working-class people, through stories of displaced workers, for example, and in the equal attention given to working-class victims of the 9/11 bombings in the series of obituaries in the *New York Times*. Both Elizabeth Faue and Renny Christopher mention autobiographies as key *sources,* but we would argue that memoir is also an important *form* of new working-class studies. Many of the scholars active in the field come from working-class backgrounds, and their own stories offer valuable insight into how class works and how it does and does not change as individuals gain education and professional identity. Among the foundational works for the field have been anthologies of personal essays by working-class academics and cultural workers, such as *This Fine Place So Far from Home* and *Liberating Memory*.[22] Texts like these illustrate how new working-class studies combines personal reflection, storytelling, and class analysis.

In part because of the influence of geography on the field, new working-class studies also offers a model for studying class that links the local with the global. Much of the most interesting and innovative work in the field examines how class works in particular places and times, suggesting the importance of paying attention to how working-class culture is shaped by location. Class identity and solidarity are closely tied to place, because the forms and structures of work, the way class intersects with ethnicity and race, and the language of class are shaped by the industries that tend to dominate particular places. Thus, Jeff Crump's study of the relationship between class, race, and community in midwestern towns where

Mexican workers were brought in to work in packinghouses highlights different tensions than those identified by Mary Romero in her study of Chicana domestic workers in the Southwest. Studies of deindustrialization have identified common threads about the undermining of class identity when industries close, yet the local situation examined by Kathryn Marie Dudley in *The End of the Line* differs in significant ways from what we found in our *Steeltown U.S.A.: Work and Memory in Youngstown.*[23]

It may seem ironic, but this attention to how class is geographically grounded is closely associated with a growing interest in cross-cultural and global analyses. Yet given the connection between the movement of work and a number of key tensions in working-class culture and experience, this should not surprise us. Not only do commonalities of class connect the varied local experiences that new working-class studies explores, as Alessandro Portelli argues here, but local communities are all being affected, albeit differently, by a global change in economic and political structures. More concretely, the loss of jobs that challenges working-class culture in one place may be directly related to the growth of manufacturing, often in the form of sweatshops, elsewhere. One of the most interesting trends in new working-class studies is the development of studies that view the working class as both local and global. For example, Jefferson Cowie's *Capital Moves: RCA's Seventy-Year Quest for Cheap Labor* follows one company's movement of its production across the United States and finally to Mexico, identifying significant commonalities, including the way women workers in all four communities resisted being seen as simply "cheap labor."[24] As this kind of work suggests, place and locality matter, in part because communities are connected in ways that may not at first be obvious. Understanding these intersections and issues is especially important today, as the United States and the world face a period of massive social and economic disruption, increasing class stratification, and political uncertainty. Identity seems more fluid than ever; community is fragmenting; national cultures are being challenged; and globalism is growing in ways that are often troubling. Perhaps more than ever before, we must come to understand the connection between race, class, gender, and sexuality and the root causes of social, economic, political, and educational problems.

What is new about new working-class studies, then, is its approach: a clear focus on the lived experience and voices of working-class people; critical engagement with the complex intersections that link class with race, gender, ethnicity, and place; attention to how class is shaped by place and how the local is connected to the global. Rather than embracing any single view of class, new working-class studies is committed to ongoing debates about what class is and how it works. New working-class studies is multidisciplinary as well as interdisciplinary; it provides a site for conversation and opportunities for collaboration among scholars, artists, activists, and workers representing a wide range of approaches. New working-class studies is about working-class people, but it also involves working-class people as full participants. Ultimately, new working-class studies is not just an academic exercise. Rather, we strive to advance the struggle for social and economic justice for working-class people. Put differently, those active in new working-class studies constantly ask ourselves two questions: For whom are we engaged in this work? What does it mean to be a socially responsible academic? As many others have said before us, our role must be not merely to interpret the world but to change it.

PART ONE

NEW WORKING-CLASS STUDIES AT THE INTERSECTIONS

Working-class life and experience is shaped by the complex interactions among class, race, gender, place, and other categories. Defining clearly how class, race, and gender intersect and pursuing scholarship that examines multiple aspects of identity and power is challenging, difficult work. As David Roediger points out in his essay, " 'More Than Two Things': The State of the Art of Labor History," exploring more than two categories at one time requires creative approaches to research and writing. As the four essays in this section suggest, expanding our scholarly assumptions by considering new kinds of evidence and rethinking some core ideas can help us meet this challenge.

Elizabeth Faue, in her essay "Gender, Class, and History," argues that the study of working-class history should emphasize the relationship between cultural identity and work. Faue traces the ways that labor historians have engaged with working-class culture and consciousness, suggesting a logical connection between the social history of the 1960s and New Working-Class Studies. Yet, she notes, the field has lost touch with class, as some scholars focus greater attention on race and gender while others focus on the institutional history of unions. Faue calls for a return to a more interdisciplinary, intersectional approach to labor history, and she suggests that studying the lives of working women, through biographies and memoirs, offers a rich opportunity to make such a move.

Roediger examines the difficulties of juggling more than two categories of cultural identity in any single project, and he suggests that doing so requires interdisciplinary work. He sees opportunities for enriching historical analysis by using literary texts, which can capture effectively the complexity of working-class experience. Roediger illustrates his argument by discussing the poetry of Sterling Brown, whose poems tell stories that show clearly how class, race, and gender operate together and in tension with each other.

In her essay, " 'All I Wanted Was a Steady Job': The State and African American Workers," Kimberley Phillips argues that expanding the definition of work to include public sector employment, especially in the military, can help scholars gain a deeper understanding of how class has worked for African American men in the twentieth century. Phillips positions her analysis in the context of existing scholarship on African American labor, and she shows that we can gain new insights into how class and race intersect by viewing familiar history differently.

Alessandro Portelli advocates cross-cultural analysis as a tool for understanding both the common experience and the cultural differences of working-class culture internationally. Equally important, he argues for the centrality of workers' voices as a tool for understanding how class works. He shows how listening to the stories of laid-off industrial workers in Ypsilanti, Michigan, and Terni, Italy, provides insight into how class is shaped by place as well as by global economic forces. In all four of these essays, scholars work with sources outside of their home disciplines, and they ask critical questions about how to define the subject of working-class life and culture.

1

Gender, Class, and History

Elizabeth Faue

Since the new social history revived the questions of class mobility and collective action in the 1960s, labor and working-class historians have integrated a range of innovative approaches, social and cultural theories, and research methods.[1] Cultural Marxism and engagement with labor struggles inspired many historians of the working class to break with the intellectual legacy of the Wisconsin school of labor history. The goal was to explore the working-class past beyond the institutional labor movement, the formal labor market, and electoral politics. Historians of the working class moved from the study of labor leaders and institutions toward history written "from the bottom up." They probed the impact of industrialization on families, explored the changing forms of working-class protest and working-class community, analyzed the shifting strategies of labor unions, and revealed the past of unorganized and nonunion workers as well. Work became paired with society and culture, politics with ethnicity and religion. If working-class culture mattered, so too did the workplace, which remained for many the birthplace and touchstone of American class consciousness.[2]

The labor struggles of the 1960s and 1970s were not, however, the only political movements that shaped the new working-class history. The civil rights movement and the women's movement stimulated new scholarly research. Addressing the silences of mainstream accounts and the new social and labor history, women's and African American historians raised questions about gender and racial politics for labor and the working classes. The issue was not only about sex and racial discrimination but also how labor historians consistently neglected or underplayed race and gender as analytical categories. As late as the 1990s, many labor and working-class historians remained committed to an understanding of class consciousness and class politics that was public, production-centered, and predominantly white and male. Faced with feminist analysis and critical race theory, some labor historians reasserted the importance of the state and workplace struggles.[3] Others charged that feminist scholarship, with its emphasis on language and identity, was responsible for the declining significance of class in historical research. Ill at ease with subjective and cultural understandings of class, many saw gender analysis, cultural history, and postmodern theory as being subversive of class politics. Turning their sights to labor, law, and politics, they trumpeted neoinstitutionalism as a solution for the perceived woes of labor history.[4]

Turning away from cultural history meant that labor historians neglected the new initiatives in working-class studies that emerged in the 1990s, but this was not the only retreat. Studies of class mobility, family structure, community, and industrialization—which had sparked the new labor history—declined in favor of a renewed institutional focus. Sociologists, on the other hand, redirected their attention to working-class politics and experience. They revitalized the study of social movements and the process of bureaucratization, explored deindustrialization and working-class family life, and probed questions of class identity.[5] While literary scholars explored the "laboring of American culture,"[6] labor historians examined, instead, union politics and the state. The exception remained in the areas of race and gender history, where proliferating studies of working-class whiteness and masculinity developed alongside the new institutionalism.

These developments left labor and working-class history at a disadvantage when working-class studies emerged fully as a field. Using literary and ethnographic means to explore the working-class past, not historical methods, working-class studies surfaced not as a flowering of the social and cultural history of workers—as one might have predicted in 1975—but in studies of working-class literature, sociology, and anthropology. Its epicenter, the Center for Working-Class Studies at Youngstown State University, focused much of its energy on the cultural and political expressions of class in studies modeled more closely on American studies and women's studies than on social history. Until recently, labor historians have shown little interest in the center's conferences. This essay seeks to redress that absence.

The New Labor History

The past forty years has seen a revival of labor and working-class history and a reorientation from its roots in institutional economics toward a more social and cultural history of labor. Inspired by cultural histories of British labor (especially the work of E. P. Thompson and Eric Hobsbawm) and the cultural anthropology of Clifford Geertz, working-class historians in the United States set out to unearth the meaning of working-class ritual and protest, to study working-class communities, and to record working-class political history. Foremost among its practitioners were David Montgomery, Herbert Gutman, David Brody, and Alice Kessler-Harris.[7] As a generation of new labor historians, they were collectively committed to studying history at the grassroots, a move inspired by historical sociology, the French *Annales* school, and a revitalized vision of progressive history. At the outset, the new labor and working-class history adopted a focus on local and community history as a means of accessing the working-class past. Further, following Thompson and Hobsbawm, it tapped the interdisciplinary font of historical sources, including folk songs and hymns, folklore and local ritual, oral histories, city directories, and census returns.

In the new labor history, race and ethnicity played important but contradictory roles in the formation of an American working class.[8] Ethnic and racial communities bound together workers in ways that made possible the labor struggles of the past two hundred years. Before the Civil War, slave communities also provided support for informal resistance and open rebellion against the slave regime. While some workers had abolitionist instincts, the possibility of slave labor replacing free labor caused many workers and farmers to oppose the employment even of free blacks. Slavery served both black and white workers as the great trope of oppression. Labor republicanism and successive labor movements saw unfree labor not only as a legal condition of servitude but also as dependence on the wage system.[9]

During the late nineteenth and early twentieth centuries, waves of immigrants entered the wage labor market in ways that renewed the experience of and resistance to industrialization. Their ethnic loyalties were the source of collective strength and also division. While immigrant communities often harbored oppositional politics, ethnic conflict undermined interethnic working-class solidarity. The tight ethnic bonds among both native-born and foreign-born workers precluded unified protest. Skilled workers, who successfully organized labor and fraternal unions, assumed that low-skilled foreign-born workers stood as obstacles to the labor movement's ends. Craft fraternity, not class solidarity, was the key to staving off the symbolic and the real threat of dependence.[10]

Only in the twentieth century, as workers came to share common cultures and unions in mass production industries developed new strategies, did ethnic divisions cease to undermine class consciousness. After the defeat of mass working-class protests during and after World War I, militant trade unionists and radicals recognized the role that ethnic and racial division had played in strikebreaking and union decline. The racially inclusive (and even, to an extent, gender egalitarian) ideology of the CIO and leftist politics gave rise to the massive union movement of the 1930s and further union gains during World War II. Even so, the legacy and practice of racial hostility remained a chief obstacle to working-class unity. By the 1960s, with the resurgent civil rights struggle, the rise of the women's movement, and significant shifts in the labor force and industry, the labor movement was faced with new challenges. Much of the hostility toward minority and women workers remained, but so too did renewed employer resistance and restrictive labor laws. Labor historians, from Stanley Aronowitz to the new generation of women historians discussed below, explored how race, ethnicity, and gender disrupted and complicated the simple story of industrial union success that was the hallmark of institutional labor history.[11]

Women, Gender, and Labor

The last thirty years have been a time for discovering and recovering women's working-class past. Early in the century, the Wisconsin school of labor history implicitly argued that women in the labor force were a problem to be solved. Either women workers would be incorporated into the labor movement through participation (parallel to their integration into the polity through suffrage) or they and the labor movement would be the losers. Unorganized women workers threatened to undermine the industrial democracy that progressives sought to build. Women had to be encouraged to join labor unions and discouraged from doing dangerous, poorly paid, or physically depleting work. As women entered the labor force in ever-greater numbers in the 1960s and broke down gender barriers to full participation in society, they represented the best hope and greatest obstacle to labor movement stability and growth. In many ways, the influx of women into government employment, clerical and service work, and unionized occupations during the twentieth century fulfilled that hope. The feminist movement, which created a new politics of work for women, also gave rise to a new feminist labor history.

During the 1960s, as social history began to take center stage, studies of women workers and women of the working classes played a new and important role in revitalizing labor history. First, some labor historians who had their origins in the Old Left brought to bear a historical interest in "the woman question" to women's history. Marxist historian Philip Foner, a pioneer of the new women's and new labor histories, brought out his comprehensive institutional labor history of women in the United States in 1979. Other labor historians published important overviews of women and work and women and the labor movement. These surveys helped to bring together older economic studies of women and work, revealed significant events and trends in working women's history, and began the exploration of sex discrimination and gender conflict in the labor movement and in the workplace. In *Out to Work,* to use the best-known example, Alice Kessler-Harris wove a strong narrative of women's struggle against low wages and poor working conditions at the workplace against the background of legal, cultural, and familial constraints on women's ability to work and their right to waged employment.[12]

The next wave of studies addressed the white and male bias of labor and working-class history by exploring the labor movement's long-standing exclusion of women workers. These studies probed the racial, ethnic, and sex-based policies of the Knights of Labor, the American Federation of Labor, the Industrial Workers of the World, the Congress of Industrial Organizations, and other national as well as local unions. Historically, women's participation and treatment in labor and working-class organizations hinged on the social and political context of class. The proportion of women in the labor force and their employment in critical industries; the economic interests of employers and labor unions; the role that community played in labor organizing and the presence of supporting working-class political institutions; and the level of ideological and political commitment to equality—all served to either expand or limit the opportunity for working women to join the labor movement, protest, and engage in collective bargaining.

These studies paid scant attention to questions of class subjectivity and to the linguistic and symbolic systems that underwrote and rationalized discrimination against women and their secondary place in working class political and social organizations. Still, they raised issues about domestic ideology and its impact on class politics, analyzed the sex segregation of the labor force and sex typing of occupations, and located gender conflict in workplace competition and occupational practice. If working women's history in the 1970s and early 1980s shared the institutional bent of much labor history, there was a telling difference. For feminist scholars, exploring the identity, values, and prejudices of working-class communities and organizations demanded attention to the subjective and gendered dimensions of working-class culture. Women's labor historians considered the private as well as the public, the informal as well as the formal, and the community as well as the workplace as appropriate domains for their research. They revealed the character of male-female relations, the strengths and limitations of working-class family solidarity, and the outlines of class identity for women, particularly in connection to ethnic, racial, religious and political allegiances.[13]

Influenced by the new social history, women's labor historians used another approach to get at the gendered character of class solidarity and protest. Using the community study as a platform to address the division of labor and the basis of class solidarity, historians explored the underpinnings of gender segregation and sex discrimination in the workplace, sexual hostility at work, and women's exclusion from and secondary citizenship in labor unions and working-class political organizations.[14] Community studies provided historians with the advantages of in-depth detailed analysis and perspective on long-term trends. At the same time, community studies, whether of an important national conflict or a revealing local history, allowed historians to tell stories, uncover the lost working-class past, and populate the historical landscape with gendered class subjects.

One of the important contributions of community studies was asking how class and gender were together embedded in social and cultural life. In writing about the local arrangements of class, it was necessary to integrate workers, whether women or men, into their cultural and political contexts in ways that institutional studies often avoided. Further, writers of working-women's history had to document the past of working-class men as well as women, because local histories were often either nonexistent or poorly documented. This practice drove home the lesson that gender was a relational category and that women's history had to be written in relation to men's, just as men's history requires knowing women's.

Family, the crucible of class consciousness and of gender identity proved to be a contested arena for and complicated source of class politics. Exploring the bases of women's collective action, women's labor historians found that families and households shaped the conditions under which both women and men mounted protests and called strikes. Scholars further noted differences by industry, division of labor, work organization, and community. Asking what constituted loyalty and allegiance, solidarity and community, within the working class, they found that in workplace and community, "solidarity," "working class," "politics," and "struggle" often were perceived as masculine, a definition that sometimes served as an obstacle to more inclusive class action.[15]

This point was driven home by the concurrent development of studies of women's occupations and the gendering of work culture. Building on the argument that class identities were rooted in the workplace, women's historians looked at occupations, crafts, and skills that were in part defined by the sexual division of labor. First, in women's occupations such as nursing and clerical and sales work, they found a remarkable similarity between traditional ideas about women and the rationalization of work in female terms. In clerical occupations, which had once been the domain of young men seeking to make it in business, the demand for workers and the mechanization of labor (through the typewriter, for example) transformed office work. It stratified job categories along sex lines (accountants were male, bookkeepers female; office managers often male, secretaries, typists, and file clerks female) and created new management rationales for keeping clerical wages low and creating barriers to advancement and promotion for women workers. Sales work similarly created gender-specific positions and work cultures that reinforced gender ideals. Nursing, like elementary school teaching, was defined as a women's profession. Responding to new demands for hospital nursing care and to cultural ideas about women's nature, professional nurses viewed the assignment of tasks, the pay scale, and the professional horizons through the lens of conservative gender ideology. Second, in sex-segregated service and manufacturing work, women's work culture often provided an outlet for excluded workers. It sometimes also gave rise to women's independent unionism, as it did in waitressing. In cigar making, a once male-dominated and skilled craft, women were relegated to industrialized and low-skill work, which made them the target of skilled workers' hostility and excluded women from full participation in unions.[16]

Cultural studies of work and gender among women led to parallel developments in the understanding of men and labor. The issue had first arisen in historian David Montgomery's studies of workers' control, which focused on the male occupations of ironworker and machinist. He argued that the ideal of manly work drove skilled workers' politics and culture. Their identity as masculine craft workers sparked an alternative and oppositional stance toward employers and emphasized the role of skill. Taking manliness at face value meant, however, that the subjective and gendered understandings of the links between manliness and class politics remained unexplored. Moreover, Montgomery did not consider the corrosive impact of the skilled crafts identifying work with masculinity and defining class solidarity as a set of fraternal—explicitly male and white—bonds.[17] The new gendered labor history did.

In a series of discrete but related studies, women's labor historians examined how craft union practice and bureaucratic unionism excluded women in express and subconscious ways. In working-class struggles where both men and women had a stake in the outcome of bargaining, women's protest and demands were seen as less central, necessary, or worthy. Working-class voices were male, even as they relied on women and children to rationalize men's wages in terms of family need. Workingmen often argued that women's demands were the territory of individual and private luxury (pin money); workingmen's demands, on the other hand, were legitimated as class protest. Ironically, the study of family budgets suggested that men automatically claimed the lion's share of discretionary income. Women were much less likely to claim extra food and clothing, spending money, or small luxuries such as tobacco and reading material. These case studies underwrote how looking at women and gender could change and deepen our historical understanding of class, but at the same time there was a central tendency to downplay, devalue, and undermine women's needs compared to men's.[18]

In its initial phases, women's labor history addressed how working women's experience differed by race as well as how racial division and competition affected the female labor force and unionization. In documentary histories and historical surveys of race, gender, and work, women's historians sought to find the patterns of racial difference among women, trace the combined effects of sex and racial discrimination, and find the structural and cultural underpinnings of women's social inequality.[19] A major subject was domestic service, in which over one-third of all women workers were employed in the nineteenth century. Foreign-born women were specifically recruited as servants in northern cities, at least until the 1920s; African Americans in the South and Latinas in the West and Southwest dominated regional labor markets in domestic service. In each case, the tensions between women employers and women workers surfaced as an important component of working-class life and labor. Women of all races competed with one another for service jobs during the Great Depression, despite the growing importance of clerical and sales work.[20]

Cooperation and competition among women of different races became another area of inquiry for women's labor historians. Particularly significant were those periods, such as the 1930s, when women competed within a scarce and narrowing labor market. Despite economic pressures, sex-segregated jobs remained male- or female-dominated during the Great Depression, with substitutions only at the margins of industrial work, in professions such as teaching and in government employment. In these areas, it was men who made gains in the 1930s. Among women of different races, however, the Great Depression and later World War II caused division and competition, especially for the rare jobs in which women could find skilled, well-paid employment. During the economic crisis, white women were sometimes given employment otherwise consigned to the poorest minority women. This competition had a debilitating impact on race relations among women and limited union organization and unified collective action.[21] Recent work in labor history on race and working-class whiteness has influenced women's labor history. The idea that racial identity informed the relations between the races and affected women's perceptions of themselves, their co-workers and neighbors, and their class politics has only recently generated historical studies.[22]

New Institutionalism

By the 1990s, despite significant strides in integrating gender, many labor historians steered clear of the questions of gender and class subjectivity and directed their attention instead to neoinstitutional studies of labor unions. Some engaged with other fields in a critical reevaluation of labor movement practice while others focused on the state in regulating labor relations or providing for social welfare. One question was how the late-nineteenth-century legal order constrained labor's economic and political action and protected employers against liability.[23] The answer focused on the interaction between state and capital and the limited ability of labor to secure economic and political gains because of judicial conservatism.

Another group of studies considered the character of twentieth-century labor relations, especially the Wagner National Labor Relations Act of 1935 and the post-World War II labor compact.[24] They addressed an expanded state and liberalized judiciary and asked whether the labor movement benefited or lost from legal sanctions and state supervision of labor relations. In large part the issue was whether a centralized and increasingly bureaucratic labor movement and the newly powerful federal state that emerged from the Great Depression guaranteed union success or undermined workers' capacity to control working conditions, organize new areas within the economy, and respond to the political and economic challenge of organized employers.

A third strand of new institutional studies, stimulated by the new women's history, examined protective labor legislation and the scant welfare provisions for working women. The contradictory character of labor laws that offered minimal protection for the poorest workers and yet restricted women from many better-paying and more skilled jobs remained the major finding.[25] Finally, renewed interest in the state brought with it studies of working-class and especially labor movement politics, a trend that marginalized local studies in favor of studies of the federal bureaucracy, presidential administrations, and national political campaigns.[26]

Each of these strands proved fruitful in working out the political and economic parameters and legal and social constraints within which workers and unions operated. At the same time, the emphasis on courts, political parties, and union contracts marginalized the history of nonunion workers during the conservative 1980s and 1990s, a period that witnessed aggressive employer campaigns for union decertification, a wave of deindustrialization and plant relocation, and intensified globalization that moved the majority of manufacturing businesses outside the continental United States. These trends accelerated the decline in union membership and union density.[27] In delineating the institutional environment of working-class life, historians contributed to understanding formal working-class politics but did not connect them to capital movements and political campaigns that created a labor force decidedly more female, minority, and nonunion than it had been in the heyday of the old institutional labor history.

Limited by scarce resources and subjected to the cyclical nature of seasonal and regional markets, workers in the twentieth century had little access to the state and little recourse beyond it. Voluntary associations offered working-class men and women the only means of shelter from the consequences of occupational disease, industrial accidents, poverty, and unemployment. Facing police hostility, labor injunctions, and criminal prosecutions for union organizing and public protest, workers often shied away from the collective action that was their major form of political redress. How such restrictions shaped working-class identity and consciousness—the subjective meanings of class for men and women, families, and communities—fell outside the purview of a labor history concerned only with the institutional and formal expression of class politics. As a result, labor history remained only tangentially related to the new field of working-class studies when it emerged in the 1990s.

Labor History and Working-Class Studies

The rise of working-class studies as a scholarly and political endeavor is the subject of other essays in this volume. As it gained greater visibility, there was one great absence. Because labor historians were engaged in studying institutional struggles, they little considered how their interests connected to the new interdisciplinary field. There were, however, two areas of labor history that seemed to connect. Influenced by women's and African American studies, labor historians of women and minority workers explored the subjective experience of class and sought to define what class politics meant. These historians argued that labor and working-class historians had to reexamine how class, race, and gender shaped political language, social practice, and collective identity. Everyday life, popular culture, and consumption were as integral to class identity as formal politics and thus important in understanding the working-class past. As a group, we argued that class consciousness was not only the product of workplace interactions but was rooted fundamentally in families, households, and communities.[28] Questions about the emotional lives of the working class, its political representation and self-representation, and distinctive life histories—neglected even in the heyday of the new social history—resurfaced.

Historians laid the groundwork for these developments in studies that explored the lives of urban working-class women. Located at the intersection of labor, immigration, urban, and women's history, these books drew connections between class and gender identity and the new consumer culture. Amusement parks, dance halls, movie theaters, and music venues as well as changes in housing and employment increased the range of activities and the amount of time men and women spent together. In response, middle-class reformers sought to protect young working women from the dangers of the modern city. Their efforts were often thwarted by working-class women's sense that wage work and the new heterosocial world of leisure offered them autonomy and adventure. New patterns of sexual behavior among men and women in heterosexual and same-sex relationships followed, with tremendous consequences for working-class families and communities.[29]

The study of gender and racial identities thus became central to new ways of understanding and conceptualizing class, writing the biographies of those engaged in working-class political and cultural struggle, and connecting with interdisciplinary scholarship on the working class. In effect, labor history scholarship that dealt with class definition, socialization, expression, mobility, and identity offered the opportunity to reopen the central narrative of labor history, making possible connections between it and working-class studies.

One arena in which these connections seemed clear was working-class gender identity, representation, and language. Joan Scott's work on gender, language, and politics, primarily engaged with English and French labor history, had a significant influence in the United States as well. Scott prompted feminist labor historians to explore how class politics was filtered through the lens of gender. Working-class protest spoke in the symbolic language of gender, using male images, clothing, and words to convey a sense of militancy, strength, and solidarity, while it demonized workers and state authorities with feminized images of fat employers, subversive class traitors, and brutal police. Women workers who were on strike chose among the symbols of modernity, femininity, and masculinity to broadcast their own sense of self. They represented new forms of politics infused with consumer culture, liberated sexuality, and personal independence. Finally, because working women faced complicated and complex sources of oppression and inequality, research on gender identity brought out how women did not experience life only in gendered terms but in the multiple facets of racial, cultural, occupational, and familial identities. These findings had real and positive consequences for understanding both working-class family lives and women's workplace politics.[30]

The understated theme of many new studies of gender and class was how women workers expressed their indigenous and class-specific version of politicized womanhood, sometimes characterized as working-class, or industrial, feminism. Echoing earlier work on the connections between feminism and labor organization in the early twentieth century, women's historians sought to locate where gender and class politics met and how they influenced or impeded women workers in the workplace and community struggles of the twentieth century. Other historians took on the sex segregation and sex discrimination that characterized women's labor force experience and their participation in and/or exclusion from the labor movement. Their work took seriously women's attempts to create autonomous means and independent institutions to improve their working and home lives. Finally, the passage of affirmative action and equal pay legislation in the 1960s energized the efforts of women in the labor movement and in women's organizations to improve women workers' jobs and lives. Tracing these changes and how they affected women's experience within labor unions required new institutional studies. These studies, however, paid important attention not just to the institutional possibilities but also to the subjective meanings of women's gains and losses in the labor force.[31]

Recent contributions in the history of workers include a series of pathbreaking labor and working-class biographies that expand our knowledge of what class, gender, and labor meant in the twentieth century. In doing so, they echo developments in working-class studies that have used personal narratives and biographies to open up questions of working-class subjectivity. Earlier labor historians had capitalized on the biographical impulse by writing the biographies of countless labor leaders and following their institutional moves and political strategies. More recent working-class biography, however, has opened the doors to asking questions about the social and cultural contexts of working-class lives and the intimate aspects of social relations among the working class. The harsh realities of poverty and injustice that workers often had experienced as children, the ethnic and racial character of working-class community and labor organization, the relationship between familial and sexual choices on the one hand and one's politics on the other are themes that have surfaced in recent labor biography. Significantly, so too have the intimate connections and personal contexts for class activism and labor solidarity.

Men and women in working-class biography are treated unequally. Men's emotional lives often are neglected or simply noted and unexplored. Although biography allows private stories to emerge in narratives of public achievement, labor historians seem reluctant to ask how Samuel Gompers's patriarchal manner or Walter Reuther's personal life affected labor politics. The biographies of laboring women, however, have paid far greater attention to sexuality and individual identity.[32]

Although the private lives and emotions of working-class men and women frequently are absent from institutional labor history because of the reticence and privacy of ordinary men and women, working-class memoir brings us into the heart of gendered class identity. In Cheri Register's *Packinghouse Daughter,* to use a recent example, incorporating questions about how her family came to arrive in the working class from economic circumstance, personal misfortune, and family predilection allows us to see the contingency of class identity and politics. The book further underlines how uncertainty and aversion to risk were key characteristics of working-class and poor lives. Memoirs of contemporary class experience introduce other subjects, from ethnic and cultural contexts for class politics and the material expression of working-class lives to an insider's view of class mobility and its impact on individual personalities and collective politics.[33] In these memoirs, gender plays a significant role in laying down the parameters of class identity, defining the possibilities for and constraints on class politics, and relaying the import of gender for class solidarity.[34] Reading these and the memoirs of labor and political radicals, one begins to understand the intimate ties and personal connections that nurtured individual working-class men and women and served to infuse their class struggles with the sustaining power of family and community.[35]

The development of New Working-Class Studies in the 1990s has offered an implicit challenge to, and an explicit model for, labor historians. As an interdisciplinary field that emphasizes social and cultural approaches to understanding class, it suggests the narrowness of institutional studies that isolate class within the workplace and formal politics and present a truncated view of working-class lives. Yet, working-class studies also bears a strong resemblance to the ambitions and achievements of the new labor history that emerged in the 1960s. It recaptures the sense of class as a complex phenomenon that is found in locations outside the factory and the union hall and expressed in ways apart from union membership and the skilled work of white males. Labor historians could profitably learn from its use of narrative, its analysis of framing, and the organization of materials to understand the subjective meanings as well as the objective conditions of class. Further, many of those associated with working-class studies have shown substantial commitment to current labor struggles and work with working-class communities and labor unions, in ways that institutional labor historians promote. Interest in culture and gender has not depoliticized working-class studies.

The full integration of labor and working-class history into the field of working-class studies requires historians to research and write more subjective, interdisciplinary, and cultural accounts of the working-class past. In many ways, it calls for us as labor historians to return to the vision of the *Annales* school and the new working-class history—that is, to write the history of ordinary people, of working-class men and women, in all its dimensions. That is a tall, and quite probably impossible, order. And yet, the new social history of the 1960s had as an unwritten assumption that the recovery of the working-class past was a collective, not an individual, endeavor. No single study could hope to cover or interpret all of the working-class past. Of necessity, the breadth of class experience has required cooperative and collective endeavors; and the new working-class studies confirms that.

At the same time, there are perspectives on class identity and categories of experience—the most important of which is gender—that cannot be ignored in any study. The findings of the last forty years of work in labor history suggests—even demands—that gender and class (and, we also know, race) be seen as interlocking and interconnected categories. Our understandings of class, work, community, and politics are bound up in cultural expectations about gender and articulated in gendered language. Gendered language often harbors class dimensions as well. Language thus does not trump experience so much as give it form and meaning, and labor historians would do well to find ways to incorporate both language and gender in their work.

Despite gains in scholarship, women workers have continued to be relegated to the back rows and chapter margins of the labor movement and labor history. If devaluing gender in labor history in part resulted from the Left's rejection of cultural analysis, it is time to recognize that resisting gender, culture, and subjectivity kept labor and working-class historians from fully participating in the emergence of working-class studies. Drawing on what we now know of the subjective lives and identities of working-class women and men, it might be possible to regain that ground and contribute to a growing field of scholarship in which class, along with race and gender, is central. The gendering of labor history makes it possible to reimagine the working-class past in ways that are compatible with working-class studies. It promises to enrich not only labor history but working-class studies as well.

2

"More Than Two Things": The State of the Art of Labor History

David Roediger

This essay originated as an attempt to bring together the emerging field of working-class studies with existing work in what has been called "whiteness studies." If organized under a one-dimensional heading such as "whiteness studies," however, such recent scholarship would have precious little to offer. The best critical studies of whiteness written over the two decades—works by Alexander Saxton, Matthew Jacobson, Cheryl Harris, Allan Bérubé, Theodore Allen, Bruce Nelson, Linda Gordon, Neil Foley, Thandeka, Maurice Berger, Toni Morrison, Karen Brodkin, and Noel Ignatiev among others—are not narrowly focused on whiteness, nor even on race.[1] They take up questions of gender, class, representation, sexuality, and much more. Such scholars have never attempted to constitute "whiteness studies" as a field, separate from labor history and ethnic studies. Indeed, the "whiteness studies" label is the invention of detractors, who use it to cast critical studies of whiteness as narrow, race-obsessed, politically correct, and, above all, trendy and ephemeral. Writers studying white identity, on the other hand, almost all emphasize debts to a long tradition of scholarship, artistry, and agitation whose leading figures—W. E. B. Du Bois, Ida B. Wells, James Baldwin, Leslie Marmon Silko, and others—certainly illuminated white identities, but who studied life and history in all of its complexities.[2] Since working-class studies will prosper insofar as it too avoids compartmentalizing the experiences of working people, I want to discuss whiteness as one of many identities and social positions that labor historians have attempted to see in their dialectical relationships. No claims are made regarding the superiority of labor historians studying "whiteness." We historians do not have secret knowledge that is necessary to penetrate, or to represent, those relationships. Indeed, the open-to-the-arts interdisciplinarity of working-class studies may give it a better chance to develop the complexity that we all need. In any case, we are much in search of models, and this essay proposes that those models might come from a consideration of creative writers, and specifically of the poet Sterling Brown.

My point of departure is a despairing after hours conversation among participants at a superb graduate student conference on labor history at the University of Iowa. Reflecting on the conference's attention to studying race, gender, and class together, the students offered a bleak prognosis. They worried that writing about those three axes of inequality and identity in what Rose Brewer has called their "simultaneity" is not just difficult but probably impossible.[3] Not only did the necessary mastery of secondary literatures seem daunting, but the organizational problems also appeared insurmountable. Workers were to be discussed in their relationships with several other classes, with (a variety of) other races, and with at least one other gender. Categories themselves shifted with time, and workers' lives deserved to be set also in labor processes, labor markets, international migrations, regions, communities, and religious identities. The tasks being proposed for them—and they noted that we older folks proposing the tasks had not carried them out in our own work—conjured up images of matrices, not of practicable dissertations, let alone of readable books.

The conversation brought me up short because of a blithe optimism that I had projected onto such younger scholars and because of a near Whiggish faith in the progress of labor history as a field. My own research trajectory had buttressed the latter faith. After early work on white labor's struggle for more leisure and, separately, on the history of slavery, I had attempted to study class and race together. Like most historians of whiteness in the United States I had come to the subject via the study of class. It was easy then to imagine the simple addition of gender as another "factor" in working-class history. Having read drafts of Tera Hunter's book manuscript, later to appear as *To 'Joy My Freedom,* just before going to Iowa, I strongly suspected that such an additive process would be "easier" for a new generation of scholars who had matured intellectually reading fine works that paired the study of race and class, of gender and class, and of race and gender.[4] Certainly there were obstacles—at the Organization of American Historians meetings just before the Iowa conference a senior labor historian had taken me aside and to task, for "airing the dirty laundry" of labor by emphasizing the troubled conjuncture of "white" and "worker" in the identities of a segment of the working class. And, of course, the calls for the study of race, gender, and class together had hardly been printed before they were ridiculed as mere posturing and political correctness.[5] Nonetheless, the possibilities seemed as great to me as the difficulties did to the students. My response to them was therefore both categorical and unconvincing: "We know that race, gender, and class can be studied together, and in books which do not ignore all else, because it has been done." With Hunter's book not yet in print, my supporting examples came from genres that provoked further disquiet in the room: If creative writers can capture the simultaneity of race, class, and gender, I argued, so must we historians be able to do so. Reread Toni Morrison and Herman Melville for tutelage and for inspiration. "But they," came the apt reply, "can make things up."

In many ways, things have profoundly changed in the few years since the 1996 Iowa conference. Not only can one now point to Hunter's award-winning book as a realized model, but the shelf of studies considering class, race, and gender has grown to formidable proportions. In the very recent past, for example, studies such as Julie Willett's *Permanent Waves,* Linda Gordon's *The Great Arizona Orphan Abduction,* Elsa Barkley-Brown's work on Richmond, Virginia, Tiffany Patterson's wonderful manuscript on Zora Neale Hurston as a student of the lives and loves of Afro-southern workers, Evelyn Nakano Glenn's *Unequal Freedom,* Venus Green's *Race on the Line,* and Robert Lee's treatment of white labor, gender, and Chinese exclusion in *Orientals* have joined earlier classics such as Vicki Ruiz's *Cannery Women, Cannery Lives* and George Lipsitz's *Rainbow at Midnight* in showing that the difficult is both possible and fascinating.[6]

Nonetheless, any discussion of the relationships among working-class studies, critical studies of whiteness, and U.S. labor history must take into account the continuing problem of moving toward the simultaneous consideration of multiple social identities and social positions such as those of class, gender, and race. "Nobody," the critic and theorist Edward Said once tersely pronounced, "is only one thing." The great labor folklorist Archie Green has echoed, expanded, and proletarianized Said's observation. Green has held that if asked who they are, those whom we unproblematically cast as "workers" might go far down a list before fixing themselves with that label: American, drag queen, juggler, member of the middle class, Elvis impersonator, low rider, born-again Christian, Samoan, my kid's mom, trekkie, slam poet, Little League coach, and feminist might all come first. Such multiplicity does not make class even a modicum less important, but it does relocate class within an ensemble of social relations, identities, and dreams. It reminds us that the young Marx's discussions of socialism as transcending capitalism's reduction of infinitely varied human qualities to mere "labor" ought to be viewed not only in the context of a utopian future but also in the here and now. Frederick Cooper has recently observed that in the early industrial period "Class struggle . . . was largely about avoiding being made into a class, about avoiding becoming generic sellers of labor power but retaining a bounded, culturally rooted sense of difference and particularity." In a very different way, this is also true of late capitalism. Every day capital's logic seeks to reduce humanity to labor, and every day workers refuse and resist being so diminished. More ominously, the identities workers embrace sometimes, as in the case of whiteness, set them apart from the rest of humanity and ultimately from their own full humanity.[7]

Labor history in the United States was founded in a refusal to pay attention to the sorts of insights Said and Green generate—a refusal that replicated the narrowed vision of the craft and caste unionism of the American Federation of Labor. Particularly to be avoided was any sustained consideration of the implications of labor's adopting the identities of an oppressive racial group as its own. Thus, the foundational text of labor history, *History of Labor in the United States,* by John R. Commons and his associates in the Wisconsin school, exults:

> The anti-Chinese agitation in California, culminating as it did in the exclusion law of 1882, doubtless was the most important single factor in the history of American labor, for without it the entire country might have been overrun by Mongolian labor, and the labor movement might have become a conflict of races instead of classes.

In abjuring the consideration of white workers' racial consciousness, even in discussing a campaign for racial exclusion, the Wisconsin school defined an extreme boundary of its tendency to see the history of labor as the unfolding of the logic of craft unionism. Utopian dreams, in such a view, originated largely from reformers outside of labor's ranks, and workers' rich cultural lives scarcely merited note.[8]

One of the great, if halting and precarious, triumphs of working-class history centers on an ability to transcend this narrow heritage. Building on the work of such predecessors as Caroline Ware, W. E. B. Du Bois, and Philip S. Foner, the "new labor history" (now itself thirty-five years old!) has positioned itself to respond at least a little to Green's remarks.[9] If we have seen some retreat from Herbert Gutman's insistence on exploring workers' culture in all its variety, and a conscious recentering of trade union history, we have also witnessed the maturation of scholarship in which workers dream, sing, dance, keep faith, read, and rebel. Nan Enstad's *Ladies of Labor,* Peter Linebaugh and Marcus Rediker's *The Many-Headed Hydra,* Robin Kelley's *Hammer and Hoe,* and Peter Rachleff and Beth Cleary's studies of race, class, and puppetry would stand among works having pride of place here.[10] If by "state of the art" we mean the scholarship best carving away calcified boundaries, such works would join those mentioned above as pioneering in the treatment of the simultaneity of race, class, gender, and more, and in defining a cutting edge in labor history, one which can greatly inform and enrich working-class studies.

If, however, we take the "state of the art" to mean the more pedestrian place where most of our work is currently situated, the best that we can say is likely that the field can now speak to Said's, but not to Archie Green's, point. That is, excellent studies teach us that labor is more than one thing, but not necessarily more than two things. We now possess a wonderful set of books and articles treating race and class, another on class and gender, another on class and ethnicity, another on class and sexuality, and still another on class and religion, for example.[11] To note that such studies tend to be based (like my own work) in dyads is not to minimize their substantial contributions, nor to suggest that such approaches are incompatible with the best in pathbreaking scholarship. Works such as Neil Foley's *The White Scourge,* for example, or Bruce Nelson's *Divided We Stand* might be counted as "race and class" scholarship, but they are anything but narrow. In the former, three racial positions are successfully placed in class contexts; in the latter, the sophistication with regard to the role of the labor process in shaping segmentation within the working class, which has long marked studies of labor and gender, finds its way into the study of labor and race.

Nonetheless, the continued predominance of "Noah's Ark" (always in pairs) approaches to working-class history bears emphasis. Both the hard-won insights developed by such approaches, and the difficulties at times in moving beyond them, lead us back to the origins of working-class studies history in deeply reductionist and inegalitarian paradigms. Unlike, for example, the history of the American West or (post) colonial history globally, working-class history in the United States tends not to reflect on its originary moments, its mentors, and its archive. Were the Whiggish scenario I had propounded at Iowa the whole story of the progress and the state of the field, such an agonizing over origins would scarcely matter. With the scholarship divided between sophisticated and even more sophisticated studies, we could just wait for further progress. However, the recent and well-received calls for labor history to eschew both literature and the study of power and language; the broaching of the idea that the old labor history was right about the wonderful achievements of labor in the 1890s (with no mention of the triumphs of caste and craft unionism coming out of that decade); the shrill attacks on scholars writing about race, gender, and class together; and the reassertion of trade-union centeredness in working-class history all argue against such a progressive narrative for the field. Above all, the lack of passionate objection to such trends suggests that the "state of the art" also includes disquieting elements and the real possibility of the emergence of a "new, old labor history."[12]

In the rest of this essay I want to give "state of the art" a more productive twist, emphasizing its last word. The one thing I got right at Iowa was the emphasis on the use of interdisciplinary models and, in particular, of insights from creative writers. Indeed, the possibilities for interaction between working-class history and literature have perhaps never been better. Naomi Wallace's gender-bending, race-changing masterpiece on packinghouse labor, *Slaughter City,* and Mark Nowak's provocative poetry on race, class, memory, and steel both include a scholarly apparatus directing readers to books by labor historians. (In Wallace's case, the bibliography has been incorporated into programs when the play is performed.) If a certain methodological conservatism walls off labor history from literature, the emergence of working-class studies as an interdisciplinary field largely pioneered by scholars of culture and class offers great opportunities to transcend parochialism.[13] In any case, the exemplary "state of the art" works described above are almost all deeply marked by consistent engagement with the arts and literature, at the level of content and, at times, of form. Ruiz's *Cannery Women* repeatedly draws key evidence on the complexities of multiple identities from songs and poems; Kelley probes race, class, and religion through sacred and secular music; Lee's *Orientals* rests on a culturally aware American studies methodology; Lipsitz begins *Rainbow at Midnight* by considering Marilyn Monroe, Hank Williams Sr., and Chester Himes as World War II workers. Barkley-Brown grounds her methodology in the arts of jazz and quilting; Enstad's access to the dreams of shirtwaist strikers comes in large part via dime novels; Gordon and Hunter offer key scenes drawing on the techniques of dramatists and novelists—filling in details and speculating as to consciousness. In *Many-Headed Hydra,* Linebaugh and Rediker incorporate Shakespeare's *The Tempest* centrally and come closer than any other work to replicating the ability of Du Bois (himself a prolific creative writer) to make history rise to the level of poetry. Moreover, the author of the best historical study of whiteness, Alexander Saxton, first made his mark as a novelist.[14]

Therefore, I want to suggest that we might not look only to the historians of today but also to a long line of creative writers as our models. To underscore that point, and because almost any excuse is good enough to revisit his inspired verse, I offer sixty- to seventy-year-old poetry by Sterling Brown as the "state of the art" where the study of multiple identities and locations within the U.S. working class is concerned. Brown, the great critic, collector of slave narratives, literary historian, folklorist, and blues poet, was born in Washington, D.C., in 1901. A careful student of history, Brown wrote poems on Nat Turner, on slavery and emancipation, and even on the record of traitors in African American struggles. The poems to be considered come from the Great Depression, a time when Brown gained some celebrity as a poet and then lost it, in part because his complex working-class characters always exceeded the formulas of socialist realism and the homilies of Popular Front Americanism.[15]

In "Break of Day," Brown writes about the violence associated with the hate strikes and terror undertaken by white southern railway craftsmen bent on driving African Americans from jobs as brakemen and firemen. From the early twentieth century such a reign of terror had cost blood. With the coming of new technologies that made the fireman's job easier, cleaner, and safer, and with the Depression putting all jobs at more of a premium, pogroms designed to remove black workers increased, resulting in the murders of ten workers in the early 1930s. In the poem "Big Jess," a black fireman on the Alabama Central is shot dead when a mob stops the train on which he was crossing Black Bear Mountain. Some engineers, whether because of personal bonds, paternalism, or the knowledge that black workers could be made to perform tasks that white firemen would not, maintained ties with individual African Americans and preferred to work with them, although the railway brotherhood aggressively promoted color bars. Big Jess of the poem, a "man in full," apparently has formed close homosocial bonds with the engineer under whom he worked. Just before the murder, that engineer had let Jess "talk on the whistle" of the train, greeting his "sweet hipted Mame" and their son. Such bonds could not prevent Jess's killing, and Mame was left "waiting for the whistle" heralding Jess's projected breakfast-time return. It would never come: "The grits are cold, and the coffee's boiled over / But Jess done gone, baby he done gone."[16]

Brown's 1932 poem "Scotty Has His Say" could serve as an epigraph for Hunter's brilliant study of domestic servants and laundry workers in the New South. In the poem, as in *To 'Joy My Freedom,* nobody is only two things. Black women's laboring bodies are never reduced to just that, recuperation of body and spirit through dance is vital, and resistance takes varied subterranean forms. The male voice of the poem continually warns: "whuh folks, whuh folks; don' wuk muh brown too hahd!" and promises retributions ranging from "I gonna sprinkle goofy dus' / In yo' soup tureen" to "I'll put a sprig of poison ivy / In yo' B.V.D.s." The concluding lines offer the narrator's rationale for defending his partner:

> 'Cause muh brown an' me, we'se champeens
> At de St. Luke's Hall:
> An yo' cookin' and yu' washin'
> Jes ain't in it, not at all.[17]

In the late 1930s, Brown published a series of poems on interracial labor struggles that likewise help to define the state of the art in limning the multiple identities of working people. The most celebrated of them, "Sharecroppers," appeared in Alan Calmer's 1939 collection *Get Organized: Stories and Poems about Trade Union People.* The plural title of "Sharecroppers" introduces the story of an individual sharecropper, beaten, shot, and left to die by his landlord and "some well-armed riff-raff," who presumably are the other sharecroppers in the poem's title. While brutalized, he maintains a manly bearing thoroughly conditioned by race and class. He also keeps the secrets of the union activity that provoked the mob. Finally, alone,

> He gave up one secret before he died:
> "We gonna clean out dis brushwood round here soon
> Plant de white-oak and de black-oak side by side."

In "Mr. Danny," the formidable, many-sided, and deeply gendered forces arrayed against such a planting of solidarity are tellingly rehearsed. The poor-white title character of the poem has "got a goat to ride." Rhyming "ride" with "satisfied,"

Brown shows how the pitifully meager benefits of whiteness shaped the miserable satisfaction of some impoverished white men:

> Dirty as sin, an' hookworms
> Pluggin' away inside,
> Bats in his belfry flappin' around,
> But he got a black goat to ride.[18]

The powerful verses of "Colloquy (Black Worker and White Worker)" and of "Side by Side" repeatedly transgress the color line as the logics of both interracial, homosocial solidarity and of division are articulated. "Colloquy" begins with a white worker seemingly reaching out to an African American worker: "It's been a long time since we got together, Sam." Sam's reply comes quickly: "A long time? I don't know when we did befo'." Perhaps it was when whites stoned him as a kid. Ultimately, even as he recalled a history in which "De whites stood together on top of ar shoulders / An give it to us in the neck," Sam shook hands on mutual opposition to common bosses. In "Side by Side," Brown showed that John Cracker and Joe Nigg share much:

> Your shanty is shaky, John, the roof is leaky,
> The same wind whistles through yours and Joe's.

But it is the wives who take the first tentative, grounded steps beyond segregation. They

> Sometimes cross the railroad divide
> Ignore the whistle that blows far away,
> The smudge of smoke down the line,
> Forget sometimes and talk.

The two come together because one "knows what to do for sick children" and the other "has a new way to fix up greens."[19]

Returning to these brief verses by Brown affords us several insights. His attention to a wide variety of working-class identities, even and especially as he moved toward Marxism and attempted to write a poetry of labor unity, provides proof against the foolish charge that attention to race, class, and gender reflects contemporary obsessions, ahistorically exported into the past by politically correct scholars unversed in how class organizations actually took shape. Brown's poetry reflects his familiarity with rough and tumble social processes but, as Mark A. Sanders's astute *Afro-Modernist Aesthetics and the Poetry of Sterling Brown* puts it, Brown shows exactly how and why white "blindness" could devastate class initiatives.[20]

Brown's insistence on moving beyond the two-ness of race and class also matters greatly as we consider our tasks. Even in the stark context of job competition and white terror in "Break of Day," gender remains central. The murder victim's fatherhood and manhood not only mean that his death leaves a tremendous void but they also provide vital clues concerning what may have bonded the white engineer to him. Brown's emphases contrast sharply with those of the most recent, and sometimes useful, major study of Black railway labor, Eric Arnesen's *Brotherhoods of Color.* That book, despite its title, does not include *gender, manhood, masculinity, family, marriage,* or *brotherhood* in its index and misses the richly gendered meanings of railroad work so searchingly examined in Paul Taillon's forthcoming study. The interracial exchanges by women, outlined in "Side by Side," still largely await their historians, despite excellent recent work on gender and the color line.[21]

Brown further offers a model for how we think and write about the divisions born of multiple identities, especially divisions among workers based on race. In part, the artist's attention to tone, so foreign to the training of most historians, serves Brown well in writing of murderous racial divisions. Sanders writes of the tragic tone of "Break of Day" in a manner connecting it to the greatest 1930s historical work, W. E. B. Du Bois's *Black Reconstruction,* a volume anchored by its avowed insistence that the retreat of white workers from alliance with blacks and the "counterrevolution of property" following the Civil War constituted a "tragedy which beggared the Greek."[22] Like Du Bois, Brown's tragic tone utterly transcends the limits of what the British Marxist critic Raymond Williams calls "liberal tragedy," with its emphasis on timeless flaws and individual failings. Indeed, in their historico-poetic works Brown and Du Bois presage the rehabilitation of tragedy as a social form that Williams identifies with Bertolt Brecht's later works. In his tragic mode, Brown utterly avoids the preachy, the weepy, and the histrionic. The brutality of the murder is "conspicuously absent" in "Break of Day," Sanders writes, adding, "The speaker simply presents the skeleton of events and allows them to gain cathartic impetus, not so much from the sense of singular tragedy, but from the fatiguing sense of repetition." Brown's is a "tragedy of community and condition as much as an individual tragedy." Another critic has written that Brown's art exemplifies the wisdom of the injunction that the poet should not shout but rather should seek to elicit a "desire to shout" among readers.[23] That's not a bad goal for working-class studies as it tackles questions regarding divisions and multiple identities within the working class.

Like Du Bois, Brown insisted on placing the possibility of interracial class alliances within the context of a real and bloody record of white workers' failure to see that they shared a common poverty with the black workers whom they "rode." Brown never shied away from such history, but he did dissent from the view that the repetition of such history under new conditions was a matter of fate. The capsulized history offered by the "poolroom philosopher" in "Side by Side" was for Brown a part of the story but not necessarily its end:

> Po' whites is the cue ball, nigger the eight-ball
> Cue-ball knocked the eight-ball sprang in the pocket,
> Then scratch itself: so eight-ball and cueball
> Both in the pocket, and the game is done.[24]

Unity, for Brown and for Du Bois, always had to emerge from the self-activity and moral decisions of struggling women and men, who were prayers, dancers, mothers, and pool players as well as workers. Solidarity had a better chance of emerging if the past of racial oppression was fully broached. The observation of the critic Matthew Lessig—that in "Sharecroppers" Brown's work "risks opening deeply rooted racial divisions at the same time that it seeks to forge interracial class bonds"—describes a contradiction that, as Lessig appreciates, Brown embraced as a productive one.[25] For Brown, facing multiplicity and division was part and parcel of forging bonds. There is much for us to learn from such views.

Brown's emphasis on the multiple identities of working people shows why both those who narrowly defend "whiteness studies" and those who subject it to hidebound criticism are destined to rehash caricatures rather than to recast debates on race and class. While Brown is certainly a critically important student of whiteness, as Sanders observes, he was unwilling to constitute white racists as the central and simple subjects of his imaginative inquiry. Brown's poetry consistently crosses color lines, seeing race, like gender and class, as a relationship. The New Working-Class Studies can afford to do no less.[26]

3

"All I Wanted Was a Steady Job": The State and African American Workers

Kimberley L. Phillips

Wearing sharp-creased khakis and spit-polished shoes, seventeen-year-old Arthur Rucker boasted to his friends that the army provided more than they could possibly find in their small Indiana town. "The army," he said, "got better schools, offers travel and career training that will make your country head swim." He especially waxed eloquent about his new uniform: "The U.S. Army provides these sharp threads to its men—dig me!" Fourteen-year-old Willie Ruff listened to Rucker's stories about army life with rapt attention. Born in northwest Alabama, Willie Ruff had recently migrated to Evansville, where his father had not found steady work. Hungry, Willie forged his father's signature and enlisted in the army in late 1945. Over the next four years, the teenager received regular meals, warm clothing, a high school education, and superior training in music that made him a master French horn player in the renowned army band. Willie Ruff also received dependent benefits that allowed him to provide for his younger siblings, including their medical care. After he was accepted at Yale in their music program, Ruff received an honorable discharge in 1948.[1] His reasons for turning to military employment were not unusual for young African American men in the immediate aftermath of World War II. He and other African Americans chafed under the continued policies of segregation, but he welcomed the educational benefits, health care, and a steady wage the army offered.

Willie Ruff departed the military just as blacks began to enlist in record numbers, suggesting much about the increased importance of military employment after World War II. Between 1948 and 1973, the military employed over one-third of the black male population, with a significant portion of this population made up of voluntary enlistments.[2] The overrepresentation of blacks in the military, combined with a similar history in public sector civilian employment, means that a significant portion of African Americans have labored outside industrial and traditional service occupations. Why is it that despite its obvious drawbacks as work—especially during wartime—Uncle Sam's military became the largest single employer of black folk?

Post-World War II draft policies have been rightly criticized for biases against poor men, especially poor men of color. Yet since 1950, blacks have volunteered and reenlisted at twice the rate of white men. While historians have ably demonstrated the racial and class biases of the draft, this half century of blacks' high volunteer rates has yet to be fully explained.[3]

On the one hand, the post-World War II migration from the South to urban centers in the North failed to yield significant economic, social, or political gains for the majority of African Americans, and a disproportionate number of young men were pressed into the military, whether through the draft or voluntary enlistment. Faced with restricted economic and educational opportunities, many black men reluctantly enlisted in the military "as the only thing left to do."[4] At the same time, many African Americans considered enlistment as a critical employment opportunity when wage work became unstable and scarce. Autobiographies, memoirs, biographies, oral histories and narratives, along with abundant evidence from organizational records and print culture, convey that African Americans' decisions to enter military service were shaped by struggles for work, mobility, education, and unfettered access to public space.[5] This overwhelmingly young, male, and frequently undereducated population viewed the military as a means to escape segregation; to have solid steady work, wages, and job training; and to receive better education for themselves and their families. Black men living in urban areas, where the completion of high school did not readily translate into occupational mobility or access to higher education, turned to the military to help them define and decide their destinies. Any consideration of black working-class life after 1945 must include an understanding of the military's far-reaching impact.

Unlike the rich outpouring of scholarship on blacks' efforts to move into southern, northern, and midwestern industrial labor after 1910, the dramatic expansion in the state and federal governments as employers of black Americans has garnered relatively little attention from historians of the black working class.[6] During World War II and since, state and federal governments have provided significant, albeit uneven, employment opportunities to African Americans. Blacks' gains in civilian federal employment have been especially significant on military bases in southwestern and southern states and in agencies that provide social services (including the U.S. Postal Service).[7] It is particularly noteworthy that labor historians have not considered voluntary military enlistment as wage work or as a calculation in African Americans' understanding of labor opportunities. Reiterating a claim that scores of other African Americans have made since World War II, Debra Dickerson recounted why she joined the Air Force in 1980: "All I wanted was a steady job and an escape route out of the inner city."[8]

As Dickerson suggests, if we want to understand African American working-class history, we must consider how military work has offered an ambivalent but nonetheless alternative path for African Americans in search of steady work, equal wages, occupational mobility, and maintenance of their households. Adding military employment to the landscape of African American labor and working-class history deepens and complicates our study, extending our attention beyond industrial and service work to the often contradictory opportunities that military work has offered. This reflects, in part, the effort New Working-Class Studies has made to expand "labor history" to consider "work" in much broader terms, not simply as waged labor but as all kinds of work in a variety of settings, along with the broader social and cultural conditions that shape working-class life. Even more important, examining the reasons why so many blacks chose to enter the military after 1948 can help us understand how African Americans have understood economic opportunity, class mobility, and the obstacles they faced in achieving these aspects of the proverbial American Dream.

The expanded importance of military work can be understood most clearly by positioning it in a broader history of the labor experiences of African Americans. Over the past decade, nuanced studies have documented the expansion and contraction of black workers' presence in industrial jobs and unions in the twentieth century. Most of this new scholarship has focused on the work experiences of blacks in heavily unionized occupations such as railroad work,[9] and the coal,[10] steel,[11] auto, and meatpacking industries.[12] Providing critical insight into the constructed and contingent roles race has played in shaping blacks' access to wage labor between 1910 and 1950, these studies consider both the contested relationships of black and white workers and the machinations of employer and state policies in structuring and maintaining racial hierarchies. The civil rights movement and the expanded role of the federal government in workers organizations form important backdrops to these studies.[13] Studies of black labor in newer industries, such as oil and paper,[14] and groundbreaking studies on black workers in farm labor, domestic work, and service occupations (which includes telephone operators, retail workers, and clerical workers) have demonstrated that the movement of blacks into industrial work has been uneven and overwhelmingly gendered.[15]

In addition to labor studies' traditional concerns with the shop floor and labor organizations, recent studies have considered black workers in the complex relationships of families, communities, and organizations that have shaped responses to, and experiences in, the workplace.[16] Influenced by critical race and feminist theories, these studies have considered how gender—and other historically constructed identities—have shaped calculations of work, household, and community needs.[17] Throughout decades of labor organizing, black workers and their communities expanded their role in civil rights struggles, making class central to calls for equality in every area of their lives.

Between 1940 and 1950, the economic and educational gains African Americans in the South experienced coincided with an unprecedented migration out of the South to urban centers in the West, Northeast, and Midwest. Careful consideration of employment and education data partly explains this conundrum. When compared with similar economic gains of whites in this period, black wage gains remained far lower. In 1950, for example, African Americans had half the median income of whites in the South, and by 1960, according to various studies, "black males were relatively worse off" than they had been in the previous decade.[18] Blacks' migration emerged as a collective and individual response to limited economic and educational opportunities in the segregated South.[19]

More than 2.5 million blacks migrated out of the South from 1940 to 1965, exceeding the migration of the period from 1910 to 1930. This later migration, as with the earlier movement of African Americans, had a general cohesiveness. Each year in the second wave, 5 to 6 percent of the black population left the South for cities in the Northeast, West, and Midwest. In its early phase, male migrants between the ages of sixteen and twenty-four predominated. By the close of this migration period, the sex ratio became more balanced and included children, as migrants made locations outside the South their permanent homes.[20]

In the postwar years, blacks' migration out of the South appears to have been equally motivated by personal choices and by responses to segregation.[21] After World War II, as black Southerners pushed for integration of schools, public spaces, and the political process, they encountered massive white resistance.[22] This backlash may have encouraged many blacks to consider migration, but many made the choice to leave based on assessments of opportunities elsewhere. In addition to individual economic motivations for this widespread and protracted migration, other personal and collective reasons fueled black out-migration. The mechanization of agriculture in the South after the 1930s freed children from farm labor, making it possible for more African American children to attend school for sustained periods of time. Unable to secure employment with occupational mobility, these same children left the South for employment elsewhere.[23] Just as the earlier generation desired greater freedom from segregation, post-World War II migrants had similar goals. Wartime surveys, for example, revealed that high numbers of black soldiers intended to migrate from the areas where they had been inducted.[24]

In the long-established black communities of Philadelphia, New York City,

Cleveland, and Detroit, chain migration resumed during World War II and continued afterward. As in the earlier period, family and friends played critical roles in providing information and resources about employment, housing, schools, and social life. Even when unemployment began to rise in many cities, African Americans expressed a desire to live and work around familiar people. In 1948, Willie Ruff moved to New Haven, Connecticut, from Alabama to be near his mother and siblings. He recalled that the dense presence of kin "made me feel so much at home that it seemed like Alabama again."[25] The prewar phenomenon of dramatically increasing black settlement in cities with an established black community remained a pattern in the 1950s and 1960s. West Coast cities, such as Seattle, San Diego, and Los Angeles, had relatively small populations of African Americans before World War II; these populations quadrupled after the war and saw further growth as a result of black soldiers and sailors deciding to settle in the city and surrounding areas.[26]

Once they settled in these cities, African Americans' occupational status and educational opportunities stagnated. Sociologists, economists, political scientists, and historians agree that in the period between 1950 and 1980, blacks' economic mobility and gains showed two consistent patterns: a significant portion saw economic gains while another portion showed marked deterioration in their economic status. Along with the larger historical context of racial oppression, declining employment opportunities in heavy industry, such as steel in Pittsburgh and Cleveland and auto manufacturing in Detroit, impeded lasting gains in African Americans' economic stability.[27]

As two generations of black workers "shattered the rigid color bars"[28] and gained access to new occupations and union leadership, few could ensure their children would have access to jobs at all. Tens of thousands of jobs were lost in the period between 1954 and 1965, many of them in urban industries. Whatever progress blacks had made in acquiring jobs in old and new industries, these advances were dwarfed by the periodic layoffs and loss of jobs all together. This history of deindustrialization and only marginally improved economic opportunity, along with struggles over integration generally, created the conditions that made military service attractive.

Willie Ruff enlisted in a segregated army, but he witnessed the beginning of its slow integration. Through pressure and necessity, the army implemented a hodgepodge of integrated units and bases, all-black units with black or white officers, and segregated bases. Despite a policy of segregation, the army did not appear eager to remove African Americans from its ranks. Faced with the prospect of peacekeeping and restoring stability to Europe and Asia after the war, the U.S. military quickly agitated for a continued draft and a large standing military. As the military turned to creating a peacetime force, it confronted a generation of young men hardly eager to stay enlisted. Equally problematic, the segregated military was a costly endeavor in terms of resources and training given to black troops.[29]

The military's official commitment to segregation precipitated sharp and highly organized protests from African Americans. Beginning in 1940 and continuing after the war, black soldiers and veterans, civil rights leaders, activists, and organizations maintained constant pressure on the War Department to abolish segregation in the military. As Congress considered the creation of a draft and continued segregation of the military, black leaders supported A. Philip Randolph's call for widespread civil disobedience, including a massive march on Washington. Randolph called for black men to refuse draft notices.[30]

Alarmed at rising black protest and the challenge that segregation posed to foreign policy (as in the ability of the United States to oppose Communist oppression in other countries while denying rights to black people at home), President Truman issued Executive Order 9981, which called for the desegregation of the military. Short on details for implementation, the order nonetheless stipulated that all members of the armed services would receive "equality of treatment and opportunity . . . without regard to race, color, religion, or national origin."[31] In the months following the order, only the Air Force began to fully integrate. When the Korean War began, most army units remained fully segregated, and only concerted pressure by African Americans, including a well-publicized investigation of racial bias in courts-martial procedures by NAACP legal counsel Thurgood Marshall, led to the army's desegregation by 1955. Full desegregation of bases dragged on into the next decade.[32]

The military services' crablike moves toward full integration received widespread attention in black America. In the pages of the black press, especially the monthly mass magazines, black soldiers testified that they had received equal and steady wages and access to benefits such as health care.[33] During the Korean War, numerous articles, reports, and photo essays suggested that, unlike World War II, black participation in combat had "relaxed the color line."[34] Investigations later challenged these claims, yet the *perception* within black America was that integration of the military had occurred rapidly and "without incident."[35] Accounts in mainstream publications with a predominantly white readership made similar assessments. In May 1956, *U.S. News and World Report* asserted: "The biggest single blow against segregation in the United States has been struck by the Armed Forces."[36] In these popular depictions of an integrated military, gone were the complaints about work as "Jim Crow slaves." Instead, photo essays portrayed black men and women in skilled work as technicians, nurses, and in combat units.

These popular perspectives extended to all aspects of military life. Numerous photo essays included accounts of black military personnel and their dependents touting integrated base housing, schools, and recreation, claims few could make in civilian communities.[37] Despite reports of discrimination in housing and education off-base, James C. Evans, civilian assistant and liaison to the NAACP, noted with some confidence that, through "a considerable amount of documentation," integration of the military services "ha[d] moved faster and more solidly than many of its most optimistic proponents had anticipated."[38] African American civilian employees on southern military bases, too, experienced an end to policies of segregation.[39] Although the segregated military had been perceived as a threat to U.S. efforts to lead as the most powerful democratic nation, by 1960 the integrated military overseas was pitched as its best ambassador. The author of one article concluded: "Through integration, our mighty defense machinery, with all its potential for destruction, is sowing seeds of brotherly love and understanding among Americans."[40] These policies of full integration in all aspects of the military services found widespread support from civil rights organizations and African Americans more generally.

The June 24, 1948, Selective Service Act required all men between the ages of eighteen and twenty-one to register for the draft. The law also abolished the racial quota system. Black enlistments increased, as did enlistments overall, and few men were inducted between late 1948 and early 1950.[41] This high volunteerism, fueled by a recession, stalled as the Korean War led to the drafting of 1.5 million men between 1950 and 1953; African Americans made up nearly one-quarter of these new troops, with half of this population still voluntary enlistments. After the war ended, black enlistments in the army remained over 13.5 percent (compared with 11 percent of the population as a whole). Their voluntary enlistments remained close to, or over, 10 percent until 1965, when the percentage of black enlistments rose to 14 percent, steadily climbing to well over 20 percent by the 1970s.[42]

The limited economic opportunities of African Americans played a greater role than the desegregation of the military in shaping the post-1948 trend of increasing black enlistment. The armed forces benefited from African Americans' location at the bottom of the social, political, educational, and economic ladders. Rubin "Hurricane" Carter was one of these men faced with little economic opportunity.

In 1953, having recently escaped from a New Jersey juvenile detention home, Carter joined 150 other African American men from the Philadelphia–New York City area and "boarded the Army Special," a segregated train bound for basic training in Columbia, South Carolina. Not one of the black men had been to the Deep South. While white recruits "relaxe[d] in comparative luxury, the black men crowded into "a decrepit old cattle car . . . like sardines."[43] After their arrival, the men were "taken to two trucks and prodded in like cattle." After the end of basic training, Carter was sent to Fort Jackson, Kentucky, where he found a military in transition. Integrated units trained together and he found himself calling cadence, infusing the parade of male bodies with pride and dignity in a "bebop style." He described his ability to order white men around as nothing less than a miracle: "I'm saying that my pride, my individual pride was all that I ever had in life.

Stronger than dirt, mightier than the sword, more satisfying than sex, than life, is pride!"[44] This newly integrated world that Carter inhabited on base included his introduction to boxing, which catapulted him into the elite ranks of soldier-athletes. In addition, he discovered black soldiers practicing Islam. These intertwined elements created a haven that provided him with education, camaraderie, and skills. Carter left the army with mixed feelings that came from his witnessing the possibilities it provided him and the slow process of its integration.

In the aftermath of the Korean War, African American men continued to volunteer at high rates. While tens of thousands of African Americans chose the military as a source for employment, many conveyed that their choices were shaped by struggles for work, mobility, education, and access to public space. This overwhelmingly young, male, and frequently undereducated population viewed the military as a means to have steady work and wages, better their education, and acquire job skills.

African Americans made calculated decisions about enlistment. In 1961, then Jimmy Hendrix enlisted in the army rather than wait for his "call up" into the infantry (called "ground pounders" in black neighborhoods). "I didn't have a cent in my pocket," he recounted, "and I walked into the first recruiting office I saw and went into the Army."[45]

Other incentives pushed Hendrix toward enlistment. He had been arrested several times on charges of auto theft and feared he would end up in jail. Few young black men in his neighborhood of southern migrants had opportunities outside of the military, and too many ended up in prison.

The racial and class biases of the Selective Service System in the 1960s created a working-class military with a disproportionate percentage of black men. Between 1964 and 1973, 2.2 million men were drafted into the military and 8.7 million enlisted in order to minimize the impact of the draft on their individual choices. Many more men potentially eligible for the draft—16 million—did not serve because they were able to avoid it. Through complicated policies, men found numerous ways to receive exemptions prior to the Vietnam War, but the period from 1964 to 1973 stands out in the history of U.S. conscription because of the class, racial, ethnic, and regional biases that dictated who served in the military and, in particular, in Vietnam.[46] Those who were drafted or enlisted were poor (25 percent) or working class (55 percent). The draft lottery established in late 1969 was intended to "produce a representative cross-section of draftees," but it failed to do so. College students continued to seek and receive deferments until 1971; many young men with connections and the economic means received physical exemptions. Only troop withdrawals from Vietnam slowed draft calls to a crawl.[47]

The overwhelming majority of men who served in the military during this period volunteered. Why? The answer is at once obvious and complex. A careful examination of black unemployment rates during the 1960s reveals a correlation between military enlistment, race, and class. As jobs became scarcer, especially in northern cities, black men joined the military in disproportionate numbers.[48] Joblessness for young black men between sixteen and twenty-four rose between 1954 and 1980, with a dramatic rise between 1967 and 1975; the gap between these rates and those for similarly aged white men increased, too. Black urban high school graduates were less likely than any other group to gain access to northern colleges, and few had the means to attend historically black colleges. In this period, especially outside the South and in urban areas, black college attendance rates stagnated. Men without access to higher education showed the greatest gaps in occupational choice, mobility, and income.[49]

Unable to attend college and pushed out of employment viewed as critical to the war, both circumstances that led to draft deferments, these men volunteered as a means to control their fate. Better to take matters in their own hands then be left to the vagaries of wartime.[50] Many African Americans, believing they would eventually receive draft notices, volunteered in order to "give themselves a choice." Military studies suggested that nearly half of those who voluntarily enlisted in 1969 did so believing that if they didn't, they would soon be drafted.[51] Raised in East St. Louis, Illinois, Harold Bryant enlisted in the army in 1965 after having to leave college eight months earlier: "I had went to college for a semester at Southern Illinois University at Edwardsville, but the expenses had gotten too much for my family." He found work as a sheet metal assembler at McDonnell Aircraft. Bryant's friends had been drafted into the Marines, a fate he viewed as less than desirable. "I enlisted in the Army to stay out of the Marines," he said.[52]

Many black men viewed enlistment in the military as an economic opportunity. Surveys, including one conducted by the National Opinion Research Center in 1964, found that almost twice as many blacks as whites, 37 percent to 21 percent, gave "self-advancement" as their primary motive for enlisting.[53] Recruiters promised these men that they would receive critical new job skills, access to higher education, and better wages than they might in civilian employment. Many men found such claims to be unfounded.[54] Observers of the military took great pains to claim that "the most spectacular increases in the opportunities of Negroes during the past generation have occurred in the armed forces."[55] At the height of the Vietnam War, military researcher Richard J. Stillman asserted that the numerous news stories about black war heroes demonstrated that "[c]learly life is more equal for the Negro in the armed forces than in civilian communities. Here he can forget the problems of race and receive good pay, patriotic fulfillment, and society's recognition." He characterized the high enlistment and reenlistment rates of black soldiers as evidence of blacks' job satisfaction: "Negroes have a 49.3-percent reenlistment rate, compared with 18.5 percent for whites."[56]

Despite such claims, blacks in the armed forces expressed no greater patriotism or belief that the military provided them with significant opportunities than did whites. Overall, about one-quarter of black soldiers believed that the military provided greater economic, educational, and social advantages than civilian life; two-fifths believed civilian and military opportunities were about the same; two-fifths believed civilian life offered greater opportunities. When region, rank, education, and time in service were taken into account, black men from urban areas with a high school education or better tended to see the military as a place of opportunity. Those soldiers who had been in combat in Vietnam showed a greater commitment to the military than those who had not. Indeed, black men with more than four years in the military had greater advancement in rank and pay than those with less than four years. In some airborne units, which received higher pay, African Americans comprised 40 percent of the volunteers; similarly, promises of higher pay and rapid advancement propelled many black men to volunteer for combat.[57]

Hidden in these scattered wartime studies was important information about black men's understanding of economic opportunities in urban areas. The military, not civilian employers or educational institutions, provided steady work and wages, especially at the height of the Vietnam War. Higher enlistment rates suggest that, as a group, black male migrants no longer viewed the city as a place of economic opportunity. Rural and southern blacks viewed the military as less advantageous than civilian employment, partly because the military did not provide training that translated to civilian life; many nonetheless viewed their own mobility as (unfortunately) linked to enlisting in the armed forces.[58] Such assessments coincided with black soldiers' militant responses to inequities in the draft, job and housing discrimination, and efforts by the government to end black radicalism. "Saigon and Harlem," wrote one reporter in 1968, "are two fronts of the same war."[59] That same year, black reenlistments dropped from the previous year's 66.5 percent to 31.7, and desertions, riots, and other forms of insubordination rose.[60] The downward trend in black reenlistment did not continue, however; black reenlistment rates rose above 45 percent by 1970.

These fluctuations occurred as policy analysts and politicians began to debate the merits of an all-volunteer military. Blacks' higher enlistment and reenlistment rates caught the attention of those proposing a volunteer military. Attentive to the correlation between black unemployment rates and enlistment rates, some feared that in a strong economy and without the incentive of the draft, blacks would not enlist. Others speculated that an all-voluntary force might be an all-black military. One proponent of ending the draft concluded that the military could attract more whites by "raising wages." Ignoring the relatively lower wages that many black men earned generally, he claimed that African Americans reenlisted "because of the military's lack of discrimination" and "because the present low wages are more attractive to Negroes than whites." He conceded that "the employment market forces at work" propelled blacks into the military; he nonetheless remained optimistic that a "predominantly Negro" service would be impossible: "There wouldn't be enough Negroes to fill it. Negroes tend to have a higher rejection rate than whites."[61] In the discussions and calculations, planners concluded that unemployment would continue to encourage black enlistment in disproportionate numbers, but higher pay and more stringent standards would make the military as competitive as any civilian employer.

As the post-Vietnam War economy faltered and entered a protracted recession, the military became an all-volunteer force in 1973. The proportion of African American enlistees, which included an increasing number of black women, grew to over 21 percent overall, and close to 29 percent in the army by the time of the first Gulf War in 1991. During the Clinton administration, the military began to downsize, and black enlisted personnel had higher rates of involuntary separation from the services. These cuts began in 1992, when the U.S. economy was entering its fourth year of recession. Alarmed at African Americans' declining access to the military, policy analysts noted that "the Armed Forces have served as a de facto jobs program for black Americans. The military, which offers decent entry level pay, job training, and financial assistance for college, is the closest that many poor blacks come to finding an economic ladder."[62] Other observers suggested that black politicians and civil rights leaders, "if [they] really had [their] people's best interests at heart, would fight against proposed cuts in military manpower and recruitment." Citing evidence that "a greater proportion of blacks serve in medical, administrative and functional support, and service support occupations than in combat specialties," conservatives asserted that the sharp defense cuts would impede black economic progress: "Hundreds of thousands of blacks have used the military to escape the ghetto. The armed services provide opportunities to ambitious blacks who are thwarted in civilian life."[63]

The military has continued to represent itself as an important jobs program for African Americans and as an alternative to civilian employment. Such claims, however, rest on the complicated calculus that has shaped blacks' decisions to enlist since 1945. As in the 1960s, few observers of military policy have advocated expansion of civilian jobs programs, better funding for schools, increased access to higher education, a national health insurance program, affordable child care, or an increase in the minimum wage. Comprising over 30 percent of the women in uniform, black women have cited military benefits as the driving force behind their high enlistment and reenlistment rates. For both men and women, the cost of higher education remains prohibitive, and the military offers alternative means of obtaining funding to go to college.[64]

Military employment remains an uneasy choice, however. Long before the expanding U.S. economy of the 1990s went into recession during the Bush administration, military wages had already stagnated. A significant number of enlisted personnel have turned to food stamps.[65] Nonetheless, military benefits, when compared to the limited benefits of service and low-wage civilian employment, remain significant. That so many African Americans continue to choose the military over civilian employment and higher education demonstrates the barriers many continue to face in the job market. As in the 1960s, enlistment in the military is a calculated opportunity, made out of hope and necessity. It is a choice that has required consideration of individual, family, and community needs not easily found in civilian employment. As working-class studies considers work more broadly, along with the social and cultural conditions that shape work experiences, nontraditional employment such as military service needs to be examined.

4

"This Mill Won't Run No More": Oral History and Deindustrialization

Alessandro Portelli

Ypsilanti, Michigan, is also known as Ypsitucky, for the Kentucky migrants who came to this industrial town to work and live during World War II and afterward. In my oral history work in Harlan County, Kentucky, I interviewed several who came back: "Detroit? Cold weather and cold people" (Bill Jint); "Detroit? All those buildings, they stifle your view" (Annie Napier).[1] I wanted to talk to someone who had stayed. Bill Winters, a significant figure in Ypsilanti politics, has lived there for over fifty years, although he visits Harlan County often. From Harlan, he still has some of the accent and the firm union consciousness, even after retirement. We met in the Bomber Café, where everyone seemed to know him.

It's a historic restaurant, he told me with pride.[2] The photos of airplanes and yellowed newspapers on the walls explain the name: half a mile from here, the factories built the planes that fought in World War II. ("Oh," I told Winters, "so you're the ones that made the planes that tried to kill me when I was two years old in Rome.")

The photographs and the pride reminded me of Bruce Springsteen's song "Youngstown": "These mills they built the tanks and bombs that won this country's wars." And in the story Bill Winters told me I recognize the working-class patriotism—we worked hard and well, we built perfect machines, we're the ones who made America great—that is such an important and ambiguous part of working-class identity in the United States.[3]

I thought of this working-class pride often after September 11, 2001. The images of the bomber planes in Ypsilanti sent me back to the classic photographs of Mohawk steelworkers, sitting dangerously in the middle of sky and eating their lunch during the construction of the Empire State Building. It was hardly mentioned after the tragedy of September 11, but those two arrogant towers were the work of human hands. While putting together a radio program on music and literature in the United States, I was struck by how often the image of towers occurs in working-class music, coupling pride with a complaint or protest about the lack of respect for the workers that built them: "Once I built a tower to the sun, brick and rivet and lime / Once I built a tower, now it's done—brother, can you spare a dime?" (the 1932 classic by E. Y. Harburg and Jay Gorner); "When towers of steel rose from out the plains / Did you see my hands working there?" ("Song of My Hands," a 1940s song by Bernie Abel); "You made their railroad rails and bridges, you ran their driving wheels / And the towers of their Empire State are lined with Homestead steel" (Tom Russell, "U.S. Steel," 1997).[4]

A couple of weeks later, as a guest speaker at a technical high school in Terni, in Umbria, central Italy, I talked about my visit to Ypsilanti. Like Youngstown and Detroit, Terni is a factory town, a steel town created and kept going primarily to build cannons and armor plates for warships. The students, slightly bored at first, perked up when I said the words "steel mill." They will do some other work—mostly industry related, though—but all of them have a grandfather, a father, or an uncle who worked in a steel mill, or an older brother who still works in what is left of them; and many had a grandmother, a mother, or an aunt who knew the textile mill from the inside.

I told them about Bruce Springsteen's "Youngstown," a song about the short and violent life of the Industrial Revolution. He sings about the finding of the iron ore in 1802, the birth of the factory, the generations who worked there, the wars they worked for and fought—and then the end, the closing of the factory: "Now sir, you tell me the world's changed / Once I made you rich enough / Rich enough to forget my name." Then, I read from an interview with Umberto Catana, a steelworker from their hometown: "My grandfather was a farmhand. . . . He was a farmhand, because we've always been poor luckless folks. Then, my father came to work at the mills, in 1911. After he retired, I went, and now I have my son there. It's a chain of poor luckless folks. My father was a carpenter; I worked in iron carpentry; my son is working at the penstocks—I guess they'll get rid of him, too, because they're going to shut them down, sell them off, too."[5]

All the students knew about Springsteen, and some had heard "Youngstown," but no one had recognized that the story the song tells is the same as that of their own town. In both Catana's narrative and Springsteen's song there is a sense of how short-lived the Industrial Revolution was—if it can all be contained in one family's memory, in the lines of one song. One wouldn't know it from history books, where it seems to have lasted as long as the Middle Ages.

This, of course, is no news in the United States, where the memory of the wilderness and its early settlement is still vivid in many communities. Coal mining families in Harlan County, Kentucky, tell stories that range from that of the first family that settled Cranks Creek where they were attacked by the bear that lived there before them, to the coming of the lumber mills, the railroad, the mines, and on to their demise. Mildred Shackleford had retained very precise information about her first ancestor in Harlan County, a Revolutionary War veteran who moved to the county. And now they're witnessing the demise of the world whose making they can still remember.

In Italy, though, where beginnings are supposed to be lost in the mists of time, the sense of excitement that accompanies the beginning of modern industry is even more vivid—and less recognized in the dominant historical record. No book, for instance, tells stories like the one of Umberto Martinelli, whose father came from the village of Massa Martana to work in the foundry in the 1880s.[6] When he went back, he told the folks at home, "You won't believe this, but where I work iron flows like water!" They were witnessing a miracle—indeed, they were *part* of the miracle, they were making the miracle happen.

That pride and excitement has been carried down through the generations. These stories and songs convey the intensity of the experience of those who were shaped by it, in a beautiful hell of fire and soot and flowing steel. It may be a chain of poor luckless folks, but it's also the red thread than keeps their lives together. We must keep this in mind when we try to understand the pain of losing that world, a world that no longer has any place for them or for the next generations.

Springsteen's song and Catana's narrative both portray the betrayal these men and women feel when they find themselves abandoned, ignored, even despised, after being used. Bruce Springsteen sings: "We sent our sons to Korea and Vietnam / Now we wonder what they were dying for." A Terni steelworker, Settimio Piemonti, broke into the office of the company president and told him: "My father drove the oxen that broke the ground where the mills were built; I put in forty years in the factory; how come now there's no place for my son?"

Workers from Terni and Detroit speak similarly about being abandoned. Ida Szarbella was a Terni textile worker: "My father worked there for forty-eight years. And so did my grandfather; he was hired when they were building the mills, in 1884. When I retired, after twenty-five years, they gave me no recognition." In Tom Russell's "U.S. Steel," he sings, "My wife stares out the window with a long and lonely stare / She says you killed yourself for thirty years but no one seems to care."[7] The song describes the workers' last meal at Homestead, the same factory where in 1892 another generation of workers had fought the Pinkertons who came to break their strike. "There's silence in the valley, there's silence in the street / There's silence every night here among these cold-white sheets," Russell sings. At some point U.S. Steel also bought some of Terni's steel mills, and later sold them to a German conglomerate.

In the United States, when this intergenerational chain of work breaks, it is felt less as a political and economic loss and more as an existential catastrophe, a deep wound to identity, pride, self-esteem. "They used to call us working class," sings country-rocker Pete Anderson, "now we ain't working anymore." What will they be called? Will they have a name now that the mills don't run anymore?[8]

This question is even more painful for Italian workers, who have been educated to think of themselves—the working class as embodied in the factory workers—as the vanguard of history, the standard-bearers of all forms of progress. The loss of a name is an apt metaphor for the sudden disappearance of the working class from political discourse once the proletarian revolution is no longer on the agenda. Interviews in Terni reveal the puzzlement of workers when they no longer hear themselves described as the producers and the protagonists but as remnants of a bygone age—and even as parasites, whose jobs in a factory that is losing money are retained at the expense of taxpayers. In the 2001 elections in Italy, no party had anything in its platform concerning work and the workers. So abstract has the very existence of actual workers become that the right-wing candidate, Silvio Berlusconi, Italy's richest man, could plaster the country with huge billboards claiming that he would be a "worker-president" (*un presidente operaio*). He meant that he would work hard, but his language (*operaio* means "industrial worker") showed that the very image of the working class could be appropriated by its opposite once it has been abandoned by its former representatives. Ten years ago, Berlusconi's claim to incarnate the working class would have been laughed off the TV screens; in 2001, he won by a landslide.

The songs and the stories about the closing of the mills are about silence, emptiness, defeat, disappointment—and anger. They respond to the implied message to displaced workers: "You built a tower, now you're a beggar; you made the guns and planes, and they don't even remember your name; you lined the towers with steel, and then they sent you off with a shake of the hand and didn't notice that your hand is stiff with work-induced paralysis." From Springsteen's "My Hometown" to Si Kahn's "Aragon Mill," the songs echo the same sense of emptiness and silence that forms the refrain of "U.S. Steel": "This mill won't run no more." A folk song from Calabria, which I heard sung by homeless construction workers in Rome, says: "I toiled so hard to build a castle, and I thought it would be mine; but when it was done, finished and beautiful, the keys were wrenched from my hand."[9] Sometimes it's a plea, sometimes a warning: the last lines of "Song of My Hands" says that "my hands made your machines, they can stop them, too."

I asked the students in Terni this question: Bruce Springsteen sings the story of the Youngstown mills and their workers. How come there is no artist in Italy to sing the story of the factories of Terni? To my pleased surprise, a girl objected, and mentioned two classic protest songs, Paolo Pietrangeli's "Contessa" and Francesco Guccini's "La Locomotiva." Yet, neither relates to this history. While "Youngstown," "U.S. Steel," and "Aragon Mill" are about ordinary people today, "Contessa" is a powerful revolutionary anthem and "La Locomotiva" is an epic narrative of events of a century ago, and in both songs workers are imagined rather than perceived. The students have never heard of other classics, such as Gualtiero Bertelli's "Nina," which told the same story as Springsteen's "The River" a generation before: "Remember, Nina, how long it took us to finally go to bed and make love together?"—and now, "now, Nina, you're expecting, and I'm out of a job."[10] They had never heard of Lucilla Galeazzi, born and raised in Terni's working-class neighborhood, who has sung the songs of their steelworker and textile worker fathers and mothers all over Europe.

Italian popular culture—as well as much political and academic culture—has always had a hard time imaging workers as persons rather than as a class, as individuals rather than as symbols. Thus, it has a hard time understanding that the worker's political plight is also deeply personal—and remembering that they still exist even when proletarian revolution is no longer imminent. Too many "workerist" ideologists of the 1960s and '70s have forgotten the workers as quickly as the rich man in Youngstown. They, too, are part of this maddening silence.

Whatever we think of the historical role of workers *as a class* today, workers as individual people are still very much in existence. This is where oral history becomes necessary. All its tools, from the individual life story to the face-to-face individual interview, remind us that we do not deal only with ideas and statistics but with bodies and minds as well. No matter how reduced their ranks, no matter how uncertain their collective historical role, or how changed the forms of their work, workers are very much a presence in the contemporary world. The social and physical presence of the working class, in other words, outlives its myth—and sometimes myth and presence join again, as when three million people demonstrated in Rome against the repeal of job-security laws in 2001.

One of the problems with working-class politics, at least in the Italian Left, was that workers seemed to be important and interesting only *as* workers and as the revolutionary class—basically, only eight hours a day and five days a week, barring overtime. Oral history makes us aware that the culture of workers is more complicated than their political role. The life-story approach reveals that work, no matter how important it has been in their lives, was still only a part of them: the biography of the ordinary worker begins before the factory and continues after it. Hearing their stories, it becomes easier to perceive workers as complex individuals whose lives have many facets. Virtually all the steelworkers I interviewed in Terni had other interests, ranging from painting to hunting, from carving wood to making music. Dante Bartolini, my most important inspiration in the 1970s, had been a steelworker, a partisan, an herb doctor, a singer, a poet, a storyteller, a skilled hog killer, and a barman. His revolutionary working-class conscience was the result of all these aspects of his personality and experience.

The perception of the working class as made up of individuals, enriched by their complex lives and multiple identities, is one important lesson the Italian Left can learn from U.S. working-class studies and from U.S. popular culture. On the other hand, U.S. scholars and workers have much to gain by learning to think critically of the identification between class and nation, an identification that too often helps shift the blame for the workers' plight onto other workers in other parts of the world. A poem posted in an exhibit of working-class photography and poetry that accompanied the conference in Youngstown described poignantly the despair of a laid-off auto worker, ending with a barb against "you intellectuals with your foreign cars." After I read it, for the first time in my life I was moved to write a poem and stick it to the wall:

> One hundred and fifty two workers
> Committed suicide
> After being laid off
> From the Fiat automobile factory
> In Turin.
> I guess it serves them right
> For making foreign cars.

As I looked at the photographs on the walls of Ypsilanti's Bomber Café, I thought that no one ought to pay for a sense of identity and presence by killing himself with pneumoconiosis or silicosis in the coal mines of Harlan County or in the kilns of Pittsburgh, or Youngstown, or Terni. "My father laid bricks at the Martin ovens; actually he died at fifty-seven, he got azotaemia, he got all these factory diseases," Antonio Ruggeri, a disabled steelworker, told an interviewer. "My father died in it, my grandfather died in it, I can only hope I won't die in it, too."[11] And no one ought to die from making planes and warships, guns and bombs, to kill other people.

But I was also thinking that things went the other way around. The workers have become invisible and irrelevant, yet work-related illnesses are still rampant, and the guns and the bombs are with us more than ever. I guess it's another miracle of the postindustrial age.

PART TWO

DISCIPLINARY PERSPECTIVES

New Working-Class Studies involves multiple disciplines and often engages scholars in interdisciplinary work, and the field is also bringing discussions of class, and especially working-class, experience into other disciplines. In some cases, the result is a new set of questions, while in others this growing attention to working-class culture asks scholars to return to and reexamine earlier ideas in their fields. The three essays in this section reflect on how three core disciplines have contributed and responded to the development of new working-class studies.

Paul Lauter has been writing about working-class literature since the 1960s, long before the rise of new working class studies. Yet as he suggests in his essay, questions about what constitutes working-class literature, whether it should be studied, and why it matters remain unresolved in literary studies. Lauter offers his theory of working-class literature, using poems by Kenneth Patchen and Elizabeth Bishop to raise questions about theme and perspective.

Perspective is also central to working-class geography. As Don Mitchell argues in "Working-Class Geographies: Capital, Space, and Place," geographers have been wrestling with issues of class and power for several decades, but thinking about landscapes in terms of power and economics is different from a working-class geography. Mitchell advocates an approach that examines the politics of space and place from the perspective of working-class people, looking not only at how landscapes limit workers' power but also at how working-class people act to shape and use the landscape.

For some fields, focusing on class is a new approach, but as Michael Zweig suggests in "Class as a Question in Economics," scholars in his field might benefit from a return to approaches that have been set aside. Economics, after all, has long been central to class analysis. More important, he suggests, class analysis provides a tool that can help economists understand more fully the different interests and behaviors of capitalists and workers. According to Zweig, new working-class studies reminds economists of the importance of including class and the lived experience of working-class people in their analyses. It can also help to make economics more visible and available to scholars in other disciplines, and it can also infuse economics with insights and approaches from a wide range of other disciplines.

5

Under Construction:
Working-Class Writing

Paul Lauter

Anyone who thinks about working-class culture immediately faces definitional problems, especially in the United States: What do you mean by "working class"? And how does culture inflect a designation whose meanings generally are derived from economic and power relationships? Or, to reduce the question to its simplest terms, what's distinctive about working-class culture, and particularly working-class literature?

This is very familiar and in many ways rocky territory. In the years before World War I, the question might have been formulated by cultural critics as "Do [sometimes "Why do"] workers write, or want, poetry?" Or, among bourgeois writers, "What do *we* have to know about *them?*" During the 1930s, the question might have emerged as "How might proletarian writing foster the revolution?" Later, in the 1960s, Raymond Williams distinguished working-class from bourgeois culture by associating the latter with individualism and the former with collectivity.[1] Whatever the merits of that binary, he also proposed that working-class culture is given expression not so much in works of the imagination as in organizational forms—for example, in unions and council houses.

Many critics of the 1960s and '70s, including Martha Vicinus, Dan Tannacito, Igor Webb, and myself, regarded that idea as narrow and inaccurate, certainly in American experience. On the other hand, we worked from limited sets of working-class literary expression.[2] Moreover, like earlier critics and many working-class writers, we emphasized primarily the *functions* of working-class literary expression, especially for social protest. Our concern was not, as in some cold war and recent theory, to pose a distinction between presumably "authentic" expressions of working-class life—in oral testimony, for example, or in informal genres such as letters—and the radical fictions that writers on the left constructed about working-class life. Nor were we deeply engaged with the few worker-writer groups then taking root in Buffalo and San Francisco.

But the flourishing of self-defined working-class writing during the past two decades has called into question all such limiting definitions. Writers who see themselves and call themselves "working class" have been composing in every available genre, in a great variety of styles, and with many different objectives. To some extent they have pressed past the definitional issue toward a kind of "I know it when I see it" approach. And they have forced scholars and anthologists more systematically to pursue the project of recovering working-class expression from earlier moments. Still, the definitional problem continues to haunt.

That should be no surprise, for a similar issue threads through cultural work in other categories of identity and analysis, and part of the new vitality of working-class writing has had to do with matters of identity.[3] Working-class writers force us to ask: How do the distinctive *experiences* of working-class communities and their particular cultural traditions shape the forms and characteristics of literary expression? How do these change over time and as the conditions of life and of cultural production them-selves change? What, in short, is the difference between working-class writing (and music and visual arts) and that produced by, addressed to, consumed in, or concerned with other classes? To be sure, there are no hard and fast lines between working-class art and other cultural forms; there are, rather, tendencies, directions, what we might call "centers of gravity," and it is these I will try to sketch in what follows.

When I began stumbling down this road, I used as a starting point two excellent short poems, one by Kenneth Patchen and one by Elizabeth Bishop. Considering these works together is useful, since class is itself a term of comparison and con-trast. Taken together, these poems give us an initial platform to see how class sen-sibility gets expressed in language, in imagery, in the details—in other words, in the very formulation of the experiences that constitute class as a lived reality. I find the term "sensibility"—though one might use "culture"—helpful because it persists in many ways over time and despite changes in one's material class posi-tion. Sensibility is not the leftovers of one's origins, managing a faint corporeal-ity at the margins of imaginative life, but rather the intellectual templates we carry with us and in terms of which we interpret experience. So, to begin with Patchen's "The Orange Bears" and Bishop's "Filling Station":

The Orange Bears

The Orange bears with soft friendly eyes
Who played with me when I was ten,
Christ, before I'd left home they'd had

Their paws smashed in the rolls, their backs
Seared by hot slag, their soft trusting
Bellies kicked in, their tongues ripped
Out, and I went down through the woods
To the smelly crick with Whitman
In the Haldeman-Julius edition,
And I just sat there worrying my thumbnail
Into the cover—What did he know about
Orange bears with their coats all stunk up with soft coal
And the National Guard coming over
From Wheeling to stand in front of the millgates
With drawn bayonets jeering at the strikers?

I remember you would put daisies
On the windowsill at night and in
The morning they'd be so covered with soot
You couldn't tell what they were anymore.

A hell of a fat chance my orange bears had![4]

Filling Station

Oh, but it is dirty!
—this little filling station,
oil-soaked, oil-permeated
to a disturbing, over-all
black translucency.
Be careful with that match!

Father wears a dirty,
oil-soaked monkey suit
that cuts him under the arms,
and several quick and saucy
and greasy sons assist him
(it's a family filling station),
all quite thoroughly dirty.

Do they live in the station?
It has a cement porch
behind the pumps, and on it
a set of crushed and grease-
impregnated wickerwork;
on the wicker sofa
a dirty dog, quite comfy.

Some comic books provide
the only note of color—
of certain color. They lie

upon a big dim doily
draping a taboret
(part of the set), beside
a big hirsute begonia.

Why the extraneous plant?
Why the taboret?
Why, oh why, the doily?
(Embroidered in daisy stitch
with marguerites, I think,
and heavy with gray crochet.)

Somebody embroidered the doily.
Somebody waters the plant,
or oils it, maybe. Somebody
arranges the rows of cans
so that they softly say:
ESSO-SO-SO-SO
to high-strung automobiles.
Somebody loves us all.[5]

The primary contrast here is, of course, that between working-class life observed from the inside and from the outside. Between the orange bears "who played with me when I was ten" and "Do they live in the station?" The same kind of contrast might be made, say, between the view of working life Melville recounts in *Moby Dick* and that in his story "The Tartarus of Maids," between a "squeeze of the hand" and the marked paper that the narrator of "Tartarus" follows through the paper-making machines. Or the differences between most of the "industrial" novels of the turn of the twentieth century and a book more directly out of working-class life, such as Robert Tressell's *The Ragged-Trousered Philanthropists.*[6] But this is, I think, the least interesting and resonant of the contrasts in these poems. On the other hand, since many if not most extended texts—especially fiction—about working-class experience were in the past written by people from different class sensibilities, this kind of distinction can be useful, not so much to establish authenticity as to account for the qualities and limitations of a certain angle of vision. For example, Elizabeth Stuart Phelps's outlook limits what she can understand and portray about working-class organization, indeed about the inner qualities of working-class life, in *The Silent Partner.*

To return to my poems: what is initially interesting is how each deals with—or rather uses—dirt, flowers, and other fragments of experience. There are at least three issues here: the details one chooses; the priority or emphasis one gives them; and the particular terms, the language, in which one registers the details and thus responds to them. Details, priority, language—these, it seems to me, together with the context in which one places these elements, inscribe what I'm calling class sensibility. For example, Patchen emphasizes details of industrial violence, with its disorder, injury, and death, in language familiar to those who work in steel: "rolls," "seared," "slag." Such lines record the lived experiences of men in the Mahoning Valley; such diurnal details of industrial life become the common coinage of the male working-class sensibility that informs Patchen's poem. Moreover, because these accumulated details come first in the poem, they establish the experiential context in which the speaker's reading of Whitman and his observations of dirt and flowers are set. The coal dust that stinks up the coats of the orange bears and the soot that covers the daisies are in that respect continuous with the experience of industrial accidents and decay. And the accidents and decay are as quotidian as the dirt and the soot. The dirt and soot are, one might say, here expressions of class violence as well as of working-class consciousness about it.

Igor Webb points to a comparable passage in *The Ragged-Trousered Philanthropists* that describes the pain and frustration experienced by an apprentice boy trying to push a heavily loaded cart up a hill:

> Selecting a distant lamp-post, he determined to reach it before resting again.
>
> The cart had a single shaft with a cross-piece at the end, forming the handle: he gripped this fiercely with both hands and, placing his chest against it, with a mighty effort he pushed the cart before him.
>
> It seemed to get heavier and heavier every foot of the way. His whole body, but especially the thighs and calves of his legs, pained terribly, but still he strained and struggled and said to himself that he would not give in until he reached the lamp-post. . . .
>
> The cart became heavier and heavier. After a while it seemed to the boy as if there were someone at the front of it trying to push him back down the hill. This was such a funny idea that for a moment he felt inclined to laugh, but the inclination went almost as soon as it came and was replaced by the dread that he would not be able to hold out long enough to reach the lamp-post, after all. . . . He was just able to stick it and guide it so that it ran into and rested against the kerb, and then he stood holding it in a half-dazed way, very pale, saturated with perspiration, and trembling.[7]

The passage, painfully expressive in itself, becomes a kind of symbol of the broader qualities of work life with which the book deals. Similar passages characterize many working-class fictions, ranging from the killing beds of Upton Sinclair's *The Jungle* to the scalding scene in the casings department near the end of Tillie Olsen's *Yonnondio*.[8] Indeed, they are a fixture of working-class texts—just as scenes from the fields and cabins were fixtures of slave narratives—because they embody experiences of particular kinds of work, because they convey the qualities of that experience to an audience mainly unfamiliar with it, and because they establish the context within which other events accrue meaning. And because, as Studs Terkel put it in the introduction to his book *Working,* "This book, being about work, is, by its very nature, about violence—to the spirit as well as to the body. It is about ulcers as well as accidents, about shouting matches as well as fistfights, about nervous breakdowns as well as kicking the dog around. It is, above all (or beneath all), about daily humiliations."[9]

By contrast, Bishop begins with dirt observed: "Oh, but it is dirty!" And in observed dirt the poem continues: "all quite thoroughly dirty." Indeed, the abstraction *dirty* occurs four times, as does *oil* or *oily,* apart from *grease* and *greasy.* These details are not directly associated with forms of work that produce grime but combine "to a disturbing, over-all / black translucency." The phrase has the effect, I think, of aestheticizing the grease, oil, and dirt; indeed, here they are linked up with beautiful objects, a wicker taboret, a "hirsute begonia," and a doily embroidered with "marguerites." These unusual words—*taboret, hirsute* (rather than hairy), *marguerites* (rather than daisies)—help lift the experience being described *out* of the dailiness of the filling station and into a realm of detachment and irony. It is from that perspective that Bishop can conclude the poem with what might be thought of as an embroidered motto: "Somebody loves us all." That ironic, oddly detached conclusion contrasts sharply with the sadness and rage conveyed by the language, content, and even the structure ("had" at the very end) of Patchen's last line: "A hell of a fat chance my orange bears had!"

I want to look a little more at what I have categorized as "context." Underlying Patchen's absorption with industrial violence is the tangibility of work and of class conflict as central elements of working-class experience. Others have argued that a concern for class as a central social phenomenon itself marks working-class writing, just as a concern with race supposedly marks African-American writing. But that, it seems to me, is a claim deeply enmeshed in identity politics. Toni Morrison has argued that much of *white* American writing is obsessed by race, as is shown precisely by its suppression.[10] So I want to suggest that it is not a concern for class, as such, that marks working-class writing—after all, class is as much an obsession of Scott Fitzgerald and Mary McCarthy. It is, rather, a steady awareness of class conflict over work and the control of workplaces as deeply determinative of the whole of life that marks much working-class writing. Take, for example, a poem by John Gilgun:

> *Counting Tips*
>
> for Janet Zandy
>
> My mother came home from work,
> sat down at the kitchen table
> and counted her tips, nickel by nickel,
> quarter by quarter, dime by dime.
> I sat across from her reading Yeats.
> No moonlight graced our window
> and it wasn't Pre-Raphaelite pallor
> that bleached my mother's cheeks.
> I've never been able to forget
> the moment she said—

interrupting *The Lake Isle of Innisfree*—
"I told him to go to hell."
A Back Bay businessman
had held back the tip, asking,
"How much do you think you're worth?"
And she'd said, "You can go to hell!"
All evening at the Winthrop Room she'd fed
stockbrokers, politicians, mafioso capos.
I was eighteen, a commuter student at BU,
riding the MTA to classes every day
and she was forty-one in her frilly cap,
pink uniform, and white waitress shoes.
"He just laughed but his wife was there
and she complained and the boss fired me."
Later, after a highball, she cried
and asked me not to tell my father
(at least not yet) and Ben Franklin
stared up from his quarter
looking as if he thought she deserved it,
and Roosevelt, from his dime, reminded her
she was twenty years shy of Social Security.
But the buffalo on the nickel, he—
he seemed to understand.[11]

The setting is a working-class kitchen; the issues, money and power. But it starts "My mother came home from work" thus textually intruding that restaurant and its class conflicts into "home" with her. It is her work that interrupts "The Lake Isle of Innisfree," whose lines well stand as the contrast to restaurant and kitchen:

I will arise and go now, and go to Innisfree,
And a small cabin build there, of clay and wattles made;
Nine bean rows will I have there, a hive for honey bee,
And live alone in the bee-loud glade.[12]

Uh, huh! In Gilgun's mother's kitchen, bean rows do not spring up nor bee hives appear, hanging sweetly in the glade. Rather, a husband's anger threatens, Franklin stares disapprovingly from the biggest money—quarters—in her collection of tips, and only the hunted buffalo seems to understand. The working-class home is no refuge from the operations of the bourgeois economy. The differing tensions between the husband and wife in the restaurant and the ones in the home also mark class-based power disparities. And the details—the work scene of the Winthrop Room, the frilly cap and pink uniform, the MTA—register the specific elements of work life that shape working-class sensibility. Even the sequence of particulars represents working-class sensibility within the poem: it begins, and ends, with the need for counting tips (over against reading Yeats); and "I told him to go to hell," here the expression of class resistance, the equivalent in Patchen of clashing with the National Guard, becomes the exasperated pivot around which the action revolves.

The contrasts with Bishop's filling station are again instructive, for the only actual work we hear of going on there are embroidering, watering the plants, and arranging the cans of oil—the creation of beauty, in short. Nothing wrong with that—indeed, creativity is an often-suppressed quality of work, especially given the alienated labor produced by capitalist discipline. But these do not determine the central features of the service station—oil, dirt—that Bishop focuses in on. Whereas the mills and conflict over them are at the heart of Patchen's story, fouling the crick, stinking up the bears' coats, blackening the daisies, omnipresent, more inescapable than death, more powerful than god, indeed, "God Job," as Olsen's Jim refers to it in *Yonnondio,* or "Job," capitalized, as Pietro di Donato's Geremio calls it in *Christ in Concrete.*[13]

The physical experience of "Job" or labor, including all its pleasures and dangers, are virtually inescapable in working-class writing. Elmo Mondragon presents his work as a poet in terms that root that craft in his and his father's carpentry:

> My craft is the emotions. The ship I build
> Is intended for starry nights and open water.
> Nights where barefoot sailors stand and wonder
> How will it end? Will we ever see the earth again?
> The drift beneath our feet carries us to our deaths
> And to blossom teeming shores beautiful beyond our imagination.
> It is the work of my hands.
> Carpenter hands my father gave me
> Call to every piece of work.
> To the fruit and labor of this earth:
> Here, rest here, in my palms.
> Each strike, every flail, a tenderness.
> I will build, will strike and shape
> Will nudge and nestle to their peak
> The startled doves of your emotion.
> I will take your breath away.[14]

Here, in contrast to the Bishop poem, the creation of beauty becomes an explicit expression of working-class activity, the craft of the worker coming—in a marvelous play on the word *craft*—to be at one with the object of his creation. What takes our breath away is the godlike power of unalienated labor to create, to carry us to that "blossom teeming shore beautiful beyond our imagination."

Still, it is often not so much work itself as the lives, the people for whom working is central, that give working-class literature its distinctiveness. This may seem like a truism, but it registers a vital dimension of working-class creativity: that is, the idea that those whose lives are overwhelmingly shaped by work—not, say, by romance, nature, or art—are significant subjects. Or, as Langston Hughes frames it in his poem "Johannesburg Mines":

> In the Johannesburg mines
> There are 240,000 natives working.
>
> What kind of poem
> Would you make out of that?[15]

We may take it for granted that labor and the people who do it are fit subjects for all art, not just low comedy (think Bottom in *Midsummer Night's Dream*), but not only is that a relatively recent innovation, it is one often ignored in practice, especially in popular culture. "Nine to Five" is the exception as a song, or as a subject, not the rule. Indeed, I'd argue that one of the primary characteristics of "industrial" fiction in the late nineteenth and early twentieth centuries was to place working-class life at least somewhere on the screen. Certainly that is a main function of Upton Sinclair's *The Jungle* as well as Jack London's *People of the Abyss* and his wonderful story "The Apostate."[16] Such works address themselves consciously to a middle-class audience presumed to be unfamiliar with the realities of working-class experience. Even proletarian fiction of the 1930s, however, functions in part as a guide through the unknown:[17] a book such as William Attaway's *Blood on the Forge* (1941) relates the ordeal of black workers imported by steel managers from the South to break strikes, while Thomas Bell's *Out of This Furnace* (1941) offers the differing history of central European immigrants to the steel towns of western Pennsylvania. The very title of Tillie Olsen's poem "I Want You Women Up North to Know" (1934) expresses the notion that speaking the truth about industrial oppression will lead to change.[18]

If from certain perspectives, the European fictions of writers such as Henry James served as quasi guidebooks for aspiring bourgeois travelers, so working-class texts take us, whatever our own class origins, into spaces we are unlikely to have visited. Unless, that is, we were part of Sister Monica's "Field Trip to the Mill, 1950" described by Patricia Dobler in a poem by that name:

> And the three warning whistle blasts
> the blazing orange heat pouring out
> liquid fire like Devil's soup
> doesn't surprise her—she understands
> Industry and Capital and Labor,
> the Protestant trinity. That is why
> she trembles here, the children clinging
> to her as she watches them learn their future.[19]

Most industrial processes, much less the experiences of working in them, have been as remote for readers outside a particular industry—whether steel, the phone company, fish canning, the diner kitchen—as are the electronic or economic realities to which terms such as "bytes" and "derivatives" refer.

To return again to Bishop's poem: its "external" view introduces another issue. It clearly does not provide space for a working-class voice, hardly even an active presence except to the extent that the invisible hand that crochets and arranges oil cans is there. But is that so very different from other, more "internal" compositions? To be sure, when Susan Eisenberg composes "Poems from the Construction Site" (the subtitle of her second book),[20] she largely speaks out and out of her own working-class experience. But is that the only form of authenticity? When Meridel Le Sueur, anxious about her middle-class position, wrote about "Women on the Bread Line" or of *The Girl,*[21] a farm girl, waitress, and finally organizer, are these not working-class texts? To be sure, Le Sueur herself decried what she saw as her own bourgeois individualism, but it seems to me that what is critical is less the expression than the *creation* of working-class sensibility in texts. Oddly, perhaps, I come around to T. S. Eliot in this connection, at least to the extent of agreeing that a poet has not so much a personality to "express" as a medium to use.[22] Here I suspect that I may part company with those who extol authenticity of expression over precision of execution. We wouldn't buy that in tools and dies; why then in poetry? An emphasis on expression, after all, makes a kind of essentialist assumption, namely, that working-class sensibility is simply *there* and needs only to be recorded. Whereas, I think that working-class sensibility is always under construction through the language, details, sequences of a wide variety of texts, including, in its way, Bishop's.

What needs to be recognized is less the class origins than the differing qualities of excellence of many working-class texts in speaking to, and certainly for, a particular audience, one largely distinct from that which would be impressed and even moved by Eliot's startling images or his allusions to Dante, Marvell, or Thomas Middleton. In the past, much working-class verse, especially the song, has constituted variations on texts well-known to the audience. What is remarkable—and fun—was not the surprise of a simile like "the evening is spread out against the sky / like a patient etherised upon a table." Rather it had to do with how a well-known character like "Casey Jones, The Engineer" becomes "Casey Jones, The Scab"; or the hymn "We Are Climbing Jacob's Ladder" becomes "We Are Building One Big Union." Or "Which Side Are You On" and "Hard Times in the Mill" are cleverly recast to serve new purposes in a new time with a new audience: "And before I be a slave / I'll be buried in my grave / And go home to my lord / And be free" is transformed into "For I'll fight for my right / To be free."

Nor is the issue literary allusiveness itself: after all, Patchen's reference to the Haldeman-Julius editions is deliberately evocative and, in a sense, literary; Gilgun's poem is a response to and commentary on Philip Levine's "You Can

Have It."[23] As explicitly intertextual is H. H. Lewis's wonderful "Parody Written in Pottersfield":

> The punchclock clinks the end of working day,
> The lordly "super" from the curb de-parks,
> His wearied hirelings homeward flock away,
> Leaving the world to Mammon—and to Marx.[24]

The literary assumptions here may mostly mark the striking changes over the last seventy years in the culture of working-class consumers at least of verse. However that might be, my point is that we need always to consider the inescapable literariness of what is involved in the second term of our subject, "working-class *writing*." The act of writing does *not*, in my view, declass a person, but it does bring into play certain disciplines and a set of cultural traditions different from those that govern, say, interactions on the shop floor, at the supermarket, or even in the Allentown kitchen.

There are two issues here, one having to do with the tension between working-class collectivity and the individualism of writing; the other with what constitutes the "literary." In her "Hanging In, Solo (So What's It Like To Be the Only Female on the Job?)," Susan Eisenberg makes explicit, if only half-seriously, the connection between the individual experience and the collective meanings embedded in it.

> On the sunshine rainbow days
> womanhood
> clothes me in a fuchsia velour jumpsuit
> and crowns me with a diamond hardhat.
> I flare my peacock feathers
> and fly through the day's work.
>   Trombones sizzle
> as my drill glides through cement walls
>   through steel beams
> Bundles of pipe rise through the air
> at the tilt
>   of my thumb.
> Everything I do
>   is perfect.
>
> The female of the species
> advances 10 spaces and
> takes an extra turn. . . . [25]

But collective implications are here a conclusion whereas for Raymond Williams they represent a starting point, a distinctive way of coming to understand the world, a sensibility, that is.[26] It does not seem to me that, in form at least, Eisenberg's move from individual to general is altogether different from that in, say, Keats's "Ode on a Grecian Urn." To see that is to see a certain tension, always already implicit in the act of creation, between the consummate individualism of that act and the very real sense of collective spirit of working-class culture toward which Williams's formulation points. It is that tension about which Le Sueur wrote feelingly and on which many other writers of the '30s seemed to impale themselves. And it is, I think, one feature of a good deal of working-class writing today, from the essays of working-class academics to tense poems such as Tom Wayman's "The Country of Everyday: Literary Criticism," which begins with the electrocution of a young foreman, and poses "every poet who considers the rhythm / of the word 'dark' and the word 'darkness' " against "a crew . . . balancing high on the grid / of a new warehouse roof, gingerly taking the first load of lumber / hauled thirty feet up to them."[27] Part of what is at play here resembles the dilemma with which Hawthorne contends in the "Custom House" introduction to *The Scarlet Letter:* Is writing a legitimate calling for an American man? Another part of the tension resides in the separateness of the poet considering his linguistic choices, over against the "crew" working together to build. That anxiety persists in a great deal of working-class writing. It is an anxiety having to do with the differences between core working-class values—solidarity, care for craft, a certain social conservatism—and those of the dominant capitalist culture—profit motives, measuring by market values, the wage labor system, selfish individualism[28]—within which Americans have lived. It is a product of feeling somehow alien in one's very own nation.

With respect to the question of what is "literary," the debates of the last thirty years about which works might be admitted to a literary canon really concern the definition of that term. In the past, part of the difficulty in gaining attention for working-class writing had to do with its forms and expressive styles. As Martha Vicinus put it in 1974, "We currently exclude street literature, songs, hymns, dialect and oral storytelling, but they were the most popular forms used by the working class."[29] More recently, forms have included testimonial writing, interviews and other oral forms, as well as more commercial songs, such as those of Bruce Springsteen, Billy Joel, Charlie King, Larry Penn, and Ani DiFranco. With the emergence of cultural studies, with the broadening of serious study to a much greater textual diversity, and with working-class writers using the full range of literary forms, this problem has partly faded. But only in part, for reasons having to do both with the force of history on working-class culture and the imperative of "use."

Perhaps more so with working-class literature than with other forms of writing, history is a looming presence that seems to "date" texts. If the 1905 poetry of Colorado miners or the debates about "proletarian" literature seem faded to us, that may well be because the particular conditions—if not really the basic issues—out of which they arose and to which they spoke no longer obtain. That, in turn, may be a result of the functional character of much working-class culture. In the first half of the nineteenth century, as I have mentioned, one significant form was that of the slave narrative, designed to win adherents to the cause of abolition and to accepting the full humanity of black people. Such designs on the reader produced certain designs of the texts. Around the turn of the twentieth century, as Dan Tannacito showed, the poetry written and published by Colorado miners sought to articulate "class values," build solidarity, celebrate working-class heroes and heroines, and excoriate scabs, Pinkertons, and other traitors and lowlifes. Such songs were written neither for the market nor for posterity; rather their value was in the "immediate use made of" them by their "local audience" of workers and sympathizers.[30] Songs and ballads like those composed by Joe Hill, Ralph Chaplin, and other IWW activists (e.g., "Casey Jones," "The Preacher and the Slave," "Solidarity Forever") served similar functions in rallies and on picket lines during that period. In the 1930s and '40s, most of the proletarian fictions that dealt with working-class life were formulated to play roles in the class conflict then perceived to be coming to a revolutionary—or at least radical—moment. For example, the many novels about the 1929 textile strike in Gastonia, North Carolina, and elsewhere in the South and Northwest were, as Walter Rideout demonstrated some years ago, part of a wide effort among leftist intellectuals to win adherents to socialist or communist politics.[31] These novels protested the conditions of labor, the alienation of the production line, and the intimidation, violence, and humiliation that undermined the dignity of working people.

Working-class writers have thus been faced with another tension between keeping their eyes on the prize—the political positions to which they would bring their readers—and the literary tactics they have at their disposal. To be sure, they are hardly alone in this: antiwar poets of the 1960s such as Robert Bly, Denise Levertov, and Galway Kinnell, or poets affiliated with other social movements such as civil rights or Brown Power or feminism, likewise have written with social goals in mind, as is the case with works such as June Jordan's "Poem About My Rights" or Rodolfo "Corky" Gonzales's *I Am Joaquín/Yo Soy Joaquín* or Joy Harjo's "The Woman Hanging from the Thirteenth Floor Window."[32] But "use" is not a category widely cultivated in the study of literature. When I was in graduate school, I was taught that a teacher had two primary responsibilities: that of a scholar, to establish a text; and that of a critic, to explicate it. More recently, that agenda has broadened to include theorizing and historicizing. Still, I've seldom heard literary people talk about the "usefulness" of a creative text; indeed, bourgeois aesthetic theory has worked to obliterate "function" as a category of analysis, relegating that category to ethnography or the study of design. That may be a result of the relatively broad margins of bourgeois life and of the arts that grow from and express it; the wider the margins, the less insistent the imperative for usefulness. It may derive from the deeply political separation of aesthetics from politics that was enshrined during the cold war when "use" was dismissed as equivalent to the presumption of the American Writers Congress that art should be a "weapon."

But it may also have to do with the real difficulty of conceiving how a specific work might have functioned in a specific historical moment, especially for those unfamiliar with social and political activism. In his film *Napoleon,* Abel Gance created a wonderful scene to suggest the inspirational and ideologically unifying potential of a work of art, in this case the "Marseillaise." The creator of the song, Claude Joseph Rouget de Lisle, arrives in Paris with his military comrades to present it to the Directorate. Danton seizes upon the song as a means for articulating the revolution's ideology, and he sets the writer upon a balcony to sing and teach it, as copies are passed out to the multitude. Gradually the song spreads through the crowd, taken up even by those who do not read, until it swells into a gigantic current of enthusiasm and unity. The scene is, of course, a largely fictional, though fundamentally truthful, instance of the use of verse. It is easy to grasp. But it is by no means easy, particularly in academic contexts, to understand why people might stand up at meetings and sing "Oh, Freedom" much less "Hallelujah, I'm a Bum," or why workers, after long and arduous days laboring at their jobs, might join writing groups, like those of the John Reed clubs in the 1930s or the worker-writer groups of the 1970s and '80s.

All the same, just as poor peasant societies create a cuisine that uses every scrap of animal or plant for food, so working-class writers use whatever opportunities present themselves to pursue the issues of class conflict, the oppression of labor, the corruption of institutions such as home and school, the fundamentally undemocratic character of corporations, and other concerns. Their objectives have included stirring the masses to action, as it might have been put by Joe Hill, Woody Guthrie, Florence Reece, Sara Ogan Gunning, Pete Seeger, or other activist songwriters. They have included efforts, like those of H. H. Lewis or Tillie Olsen, to enable readers to make sense of the fragmented, contradictory experiences of working-class life. They have involved explicit arguments for socialism, giving people heart for the struggle, as in *The Jungle* and in many of the proletarian texts of the 1930s and '40s. They have also involved valorizing the lives of particular working-class people, as in Jeanne Bryner's "For Maude Callen: Nurse, Midwife, Pineville, N.C., 1951" or Judy Grahn's "common woman" poems such as "Ella, in a square apron, along Highway 80."[33]

This tension over ends and means has surfaced periodically. For 1930s and '40s writers such as Le Sueur, Olsen, Robert Cantwell, Clara Weatherwax, and even Patchen it had to do with their deployment of modernist literary techniques in works directed in significant measure to an audience of working people.[34] That audience was widely presumed by critics (though not by these writers) to be unsympathetic to or even obtuse about literary modernism—at least in the forms familiar from Eliot, Pound, and Stein. Writers like Le Sueur and Olsen were subjected to criticism having to do with the supposed political consequences of their stylistic innovations.[35] Other writers, such as Mike Gold and Mike Quin, placed a premium on composing in very direct, even journalistic prose, presumed to be more accessible to a wide readership. The debates over style involved both politics and the question of an author's relationship to his or her audience. The political issues are outside the scope of this chapter and in most respects peripheral to the current concerns of working-class writers, though the relationship between working-class literature and explicitly socialist literature is rich and intriguing.[36]

But the question of audience remains fraught. I have argued that class conflict and the everlasting presence of work itself are generally thematized in working-class writing. And I have suggested that details, language, even allusions in working-class writing are drawn from the mainly commonplace experiences distinctive to working-class life, modulating over time as those particularities do. I've argued, too, that working-class literature has had, in general, a significant functional, instructive component often related to the political objectives of working-class movements.[37] But can it be defined by its audience? Who buys the chapbooks and the small zines in which such writing largely emerges? Is working-class culture defined by the mass-market television programs popular in working-class communities? Are the distinctions once drawn by critics such as Dwight Macdonald between "popular" and "mass" culture still relevant?[38] Such questions seem to me more in play today than they have been for many years, and that may have to do with the fact that class itself, as a living concept and an analytic tool, has once again come to be relevant in American discourse. In the recent past, we can observe a dialectical relationship between the emergence of, say, feminist politics and the flourishing of women's writing. Similar dialectical processes have marked the evolution of political consciousness and of creative writing in black, Latino, and Asian American communities. Movements generate audiences; audiences foster writers; writers forward movements. The question of the relationship between working-class creativity and its audience, then, is no settled matter but always, and necessarily, under construction.

6

Working-Class Geographies: Capital, Space, and Place

Don Mitchell

> Given . . . that its geographical organization seems to make a difference in the way that capitalism works, the question that must be raised is this: how might different groups, with different sets of interests seek to manipulate this geographical organization to their own benefit and to the disadvantage of those with whom they may be in conflict? . . . The production of space and landscapes must be seen not just as secondary to the social relations of everyday life but as highly political acts that are central to it.
>
> Andrew Herod, *Labor Geographies*

The League of Revolutionary Black Workers was founded in Detroit in 1969 by activists affiliated with the Dodge Revolutionary Union Movement (DRUM) then active in the auto (and other) industries, in an effort to expand the struggle from the shop floor to the community.[1] One of the league's achievements was to push struggle into the realm of popular culture, seeking to make laborist politics a social movement, just as the old radical unions had (unions such as the Industrial Workers of the World, the Communist unions of the 1930s, and the radical elements that were at the heart of the CIO before their expulsion). To this end, the league produced a remarkable film called *Finally Got the News* that showed how the exploitation of *blacks* in the United States was the exploitation of *workers* in the United States. They showed how the intersection of race and class was deeply structured by geography, a geography that did not necessarily respect national borders but that was nonetheless closely attuned to ethnicity. The League of Revolutionary Black Workers drove home this point in a striking scene that showed a series of white businessmen sitting at their desks. Over this montage was a rap by Ken Cockerel, a league activist:

> They give you little bullshit amounts of money—wages and so forth—and then they steal all that shit back from you in terms of the way they have their other thing set up, that old credit-stick-'em-up gimmick society—consumer credit—buy shit, buy shit—on credit. He gives you a little bit of money to cool your ass and then steals it all back with shit called interest, which is the price of money. They are motherfucking, non-producing, non-existing bastards dealing with paper. . . .
>
> He is in mining! He went to Exeter. He went to Harvard. He went to Yale. He went to the Wharton School of Business. And he is in "mining"! It is these motherfuckers who deal with intangibles who are rewarded by this society. The more abstract and intangible your service, the bigger the reward.
>
> What are stocks? A stock certificate is evidence of something which is real. A stock is evidence of *ownership*. He who owns and controls receives—profit!
>
> This man is fucking with shit in Bolivia. He is fucking with shit in Chile. He is Kennicott. He is Anaconda. He is United Fruit. He is in mining! He's in what? He ain't never produced anything his whole life. Investment banker. Stockbroker. Insurance man. He don't do nothing.
>
> We see that this whole society exists and rests upon workers and the whole mother-fucking society is controlled by this little clique which is parasitic, vulturistic, cannibalistic, and sucking and destroying the life of the workers everywhere; and we must stop it because it is—evil![2]

This view of the geography of capitalism from the streets has more than the ring of truth about it. It links the institutions of local working-class life—from the loan sharks to the more legit rent-to-own stores to the loan officers at banks—that make living on workers' wages possible to the way capital moves around the globe to seek out new opportunities for profit. It shows who is alienated by and who benefits from the geography of capital. Along with other images in the film, the scene shows how the geographical organization of capitalism is fundamental to its operation. And it shows how geographical organization isn't just natural but is made—and therefore can be unmade.

The academic discipline of geography has been trying to catch up with Cockerel and the League of Revolutionary Black Workers ever since. And, perhaps, it is finally in a position to begin to show how the league was right in its analysis. In coming to that position the discipline of geography has made itself critical to the New Working-Class Studies.

Radical Geography and the
Geography of Capitalism

Geography seems an unlikely home for radical analysis. For much of its modern history it has been marked by either an almost sycophantic relationship to state power or by an intellectual and political isolationism. That changed rapidly beginning in the late 1950s, first with what came to be called the "quantitative revolution"—marked by the use of positivist research methods and elaborate statistical models—and then even more intensely as a new generation of scholars linked their research and teaching to activist movements. In the process—and in tandem with the development of feminist, antiracist, and other radical geographies—geographers began to develop a full, complex theory of the geography of capitalism.

Rejecting neoclassical theories of economic location that examined how firms selected locations for economic activity by weighing a set of "factors of production"—land, access to raw materials and markets, labor—geographers radicalized in the 1960s showed how geographies of environment, class difference, gender and sexuality, and race were all central to the shifting "shape" of capitalism and the worlds it defines. Such a geography of capitalism was rooted in a more expansive turn to social justice in the discipline.

William Bunge, for example, had been one of the high priests of the "quantitative revolution," writing an influential if controversial and highly mathematical codification of spatial science and neoclassical location theory. Eventually published as *Theoretical Geography,* Bunge's PhD dissertation sought to work out the mathematical, often geometric, "laws" governing the structuring of spatial relationships. Bunge took a job in the geography department of Wayne State University in Detroit and was quickly radicalized by the uprisings on the streets and in the factories around him. He took his skills as a "spatial scientist" to the streets, founding the Detroit Geographical Expedition in the Fitzgerald neighborhood. Using the tools of mapping and spatial analysis to expose the gross inequalities that constructed an urban geography that was literally deadly for poor and black residents, he used geographic knowledge—a sort of streetwise science—to empower rather than further colonize impoverished Detroit residents. Bunge and his colleagues exposed a radically different economic landscape than the one prophesied by neoclassical location theory, a landscape of deprivation, racism, and the scarring power of corporate and elite control. It was a landscape of power—a kind of power that neoclassical theory simply could not account for. It was built on the backs of an exploited, racially divided working class, but it was also built for the benefit of the "parasites" that Ken Cockerel talked about at the end of his rap. The economic landscape was, in Bunge's terms, a "geography of revolution."[3]

Though Bunge was eventually hounded out of the discipline of geography—and out of the United States—for his revolutionary actions, his Detroit Geographical Expedition and his radical commitment to constructing landscapes of social justice have remained key models for activist-scholars ever since. He showed that a focus on poverty and on the fates of the most oppressed in imperialist, racist, capitalist society had to become and remain our focus if we were ever to create what he later called a "geography of survival."[4]

Like Bunge, the geographer David Harvey had cut his teeth on the "quantitative revolution" and, like Bunge, had been one of its prime codifiers. Harvey's *Explanation in Geography* is a massive, thorough, and still influential examination of the philosophical roots and implications of positivist theories in geography. After completing that book, Harvey left his native England for a position at Johns Hopkins University in Baltimore. And, again, like Bunge, he was radicalized by the politics of the streets and the massive riots that shook the city. In the aftermath of the riots that tore through Baltimore in the wake of Martin Luther King Jr.'s assassination, and working within the ongoing antipoverty activism that he quickly allied himself with, Harvey was forced to ask whether social justice had a geography, and if it did, how it was produced. The result was the remarkable book *Social Justice and the City.* In this book, he explores various "liberal formulations" of social justice (e.g., the distributional theories of justice associated with John Rawls) before finding them inadequate to the task of explaining the systematic geography of oppression he witnessed in Baltimore.[5]

Harvey therefore turned to Marxist theories of exploitation and oppression and explored what he called a series of "socialist formulations" of social justice. This effectively announced the arrival of a sophisticated Marxism in geography. *Social Justice and the City* may not have been much to the liking of what radicals called "establishment geographers," but it found a ready audience among an increasingly sympathetic cohort of younger geographers. In 1969 a new journal—*Antipode: A Radical Journal of Geography*—was founded by students and faculty at Clark University in Massachusetts. *Antipode* served as a lively forum for the debate, experimentation, and polemic that accompanied the construction of an anti-establishment geography. Radical geographers were beginning to read widely not only in Marxism but also in existential and phenomenological philosophies, socialist feminism, anarchism, and the emerging environmental literature. And not only reading: early radical geography was closely linked to the array of activist movements of the time.[6]

Activist links were vital, but so were theoretical advances. For understanding the geography of the economy, this meant discovering how "contemporary geography is not a *by-product* of the structure of capitalism, but an integral component of the capitalist mode of production."[7] Any emancipatory or liberatory theory or social movement had to understand this point. Indeed, Harvey argued that theories of justice and oppression could not be understood outside a more general theory of capitalist development and change. For this reason, he argued, geography had to become Marxist, and Marxism had to become geographic.[8] While Harvey's main goal was to write a theory of capitalist urbanization and urban consciousness, he found that to do so he first had "to write a treatise on Marxian theory in general, paying particular attention to the circulation of built environments, the credit system and spatial configurations." The result was perhaps the most important book in post-World War II geography, *The Limits of Capital*. *Limits* reworks Marx's theories of capital circulation to show what happens when spatial relations are placed at the center of these theories and why it is necessary to do so.[9] It is impossible to understand what geographic theory can *add* to Ken Cockerel's intuition about how capitalism creates and destroys working-class lives without understanding at least some of what Harvey argued in *Limits*—and what he didn't.

Capitalist Circulation and the Making of the Economic Landscape

In *The Limits to Capital,* Harvey argued that while *production*—the subject of volume 1 of Marx's *Capital* and the site for the production of value—was important, a more thorough theory of capital *circulation* was necessary, since value was only value when it was "value in motion." Within a theory of circulation, *production* was a problem to be solved, not a starting point, since production required that at least some value be "fixed," or frozen, in the machines, land, buildings, and the bodies of laborers that make production possible in the first place. But value fixed in place is not value-in-motion, and so it is, by definition, capital devalued. Or at the very least, since it is fixed in place for some relatively long period of time, it is subject to the risk of devaluation by, among other things, technological innovation elsewhere, the collapse of markets, obsolescence, or labor unrest. At the root of capitalist production of value is a contradiction: for capital to circulate, some value must be fixed in place, thereby increasing the risk that this capital may not be realized as value.

This contradiction cannot be overcome in capitalism; it can only be displaced. Harvey shows that the credit system—including the consumer credit Ken Cockerel complains about—has developed in part to address this contradiction, to organize its constant displacement. Some kinds of credit—what Marx calls "fictitious capital"—are a claim on future surplus value; fictitious capital is the promise of value realized in the future. Fixed capital can circulate ahead of itself (as it were) in the form of paper or electronic representations of its future realization. Such advance circulation of the potential to realize surplus value only forestalls, and certainly deepens, the potential for crisis, since now the stakes are raised and the burden of crisis is shifted into others' hands. In the credit system, the ever-present possibility that values encapsulated in commodities might not be realized is delayed. But this delay means that effective demand—the desire and ability to make good on surplus value *already spent*—becomes a serious social problem (rather than just a problem limited to individual capitalists or firms).[10]

Such an analysis has at least two important implications for working people, their families, and their communities. The first concerns location, and the second concerns workers' roles as both producers and consumers. Taken together, the two outline a critical and contradictory working-class geography.

Location, Harvey argues, is perhaps best explained through a theory of rent. He shows that though a holdover from precapitalist social practices, rent in capitalism has become a means for adjudicating the circulation of value through land, and for the distribution of surplus value in particular places. Location affords producers certain advantages and disadvantages (as neoclassical location theory suggests). All other things being equal, location closer to a market, on particularly fertile soil, or at the source of coveted raw materials provides owners or users of land with the ability to capture a greater amount of surplus value. In essence, they are awarded "excess profit." Owners of locationally advantaged land, therefore, can appropriate increased rent. And to the degree that such locational advantages are relatively permanent, owners can also attract greater capital investment, and especially greater investments in fixed capital (such as soil improvement, more advanced production facilities, or more expensive housing). Such advantages also bring with them spillover effects onto neighboring lands, which in turn create agglomeration effects: increased investment (and rent) at one location can make increased investment (and rent) at a second location sensible.[11]

But since this investment—this gamble on the advantages of location—is an investment in fixed capital, it is subject to the threats and risks noted above. The drive for technological innovation that is part of the accumulation imperative of capitalism means that any place and its built environment (all that fixed capital wrapped up in buildings, roads, and so forth) is vulnerable to devaluation through the development of new methods of production, improved transportation systems, or the creation of locational advantages elsewhere. Moreover, fictitious capital—interest-bearing capital—seeks the greatest return, and in land markets that means "promot[ing] activities on the land that conform to the highest and best uses, not simply in the present, but also in anticipation of future surplus value production."[12] This means that the realization of assumed future values tied up in the fixed capital of one location might very well get invested in another area, perhaps in a new production facility that outcompetes the factory that gave rise to the fictitious capital in the first place, leading to that factory's devaluation and perhaps its closure. Under capitalism, the construction of a built environment—a city or town or neighborhood or factory—might undermine its own reason for being. In capitalism, deindustrialization and capital flight *make sense.* Geography is thus central to the very functioning of capitalism, not just incidental to it.

This brings us to the second point—the role of workers as both producers and consumers. As George Henderson has memorably shown, workers' bodies themselves are a central—and contradictory—site for the accumulation of capital. Quoting volume 2 of *Capital,* Henderson argues:

Unless capital does away with the human body, it will always face the "natural limitations of the labor-power itself" as a barrier to increased rates of production. Workers are the sites of biological processes and energy flows for which capital has only partial solutions (e.g., robotics). They are themselves obstacles to capitalism. Bodies persist. That they are *waged* bodies is a capitalist solution. That they are waged *bodies* is a capitalist problem.

Waged bodies—working people—are a capitalist problem because they have wills, needs, desires, and biological limits and they often—willfully—stand against the needs of capital. Such a capitalist problem, however, has a typically capitalist solution: "The inability to fully substitute for the bodily reproduction of the workers and labor power has come to occasion a whole realm of capitalist production for consumption and reproduction, the realm of capitalist-produced commodities that are sold and bought *for* reproduction (food, housing, etc.)."[13] Workers and their communities, in this sense, are critical to the ongoing circulation of capital. Money must move into—and out of—the hands of workers, even as it must be frozen in the built landscape of houses, churches, shopping centers, bars, restaurants, parks, and all the other things that make life, including working-class life, possible.

Such a circulation of capital roots working people in place. Not only does this give a worker "a little bit of money to cool your ass," as Cockerel put it, but it also provides both the foundation for, and the means of producing, a geographical landscape of social reproduction. This landscape is a significant site of social struggle—over who will pay for it, what it will contain, who controls it, who belongs in it, and who does not. In that sense, the landscape itself helps establish the value of labor power, for as Marx put it, "in contradistinction . . . to the case of other commodities, there enters into the determination of the value of labor power a historical and moral element"—a historical and moral element that is *given* in the landscape itself. For if the spatial arrangement of the landscape requires, for example, workers to commute by car, then that must be factored into the value of labor power. Or if, as in the Detroit that Bunge mapped, a landscape of dilapidated housing, broken or absent playgrounds, and disinvestment in schools for some working-class residents is taken as *normal* (if it is not successfully contested), then the cost of labor power can be driven down. So too, of course, can the cost of labor power be driven up through struggle over the built environment.[14]

If a contradiction of mobility and fixity defines *capital,* it also defines *labor.* Labor power "is the only commodity that can bring itself to market under its own steam." The "mobility of labor" may thus be understood as an aspect of the freedom of labor under capitalism, a freedom that is deeply ironic, since working people have no choice but to sell their labor-power: "The freedom of the labourer to move is converted into its exact opposite. In search of employment and a living wage, the labourer is forced to follow capital wherever it flows." Indeed, "the more mobile the labourer, the more easily capital can adopt a new labour process to take advantage of superior locations."[15]

And yet the completely free mobility of labor would undermine capital. The inability to maintain a reserve army in specific locations would create an upward pressure on wages, decrease the ability of locally rooted firms to compete in larger-scale labor markets, and thus cause rapid declines in the rate of profits. This explains occasional business support for unemployment benefits, welfare supports, and so on, which can help to root a reserve army in place. At a larger scale, this need to balance the mobility and immobility of labor helps explain the remarkably contradictory border policies that most wealthy nation-states develop.[16]

Harvey argues that for workers, though, geographical mobility can have quite different meanings. Among other things, mobility can be an escape from oppression or simply a move to a place where a better life may be possible. Mobility can be a means not only to survive but to thrive. Such mobility also can be a double-edged sword, since it can lead on the one hand to "disruption of traditional support mechanisms and ways of life," and, on the other, "the networks of personal contacts, the support systems and the elaborate coping mechanisms within family and community, institutional protections, to say nothing of the mechanisms of political mobilization, can all be built up through creative efforts of workers and their families into islands of strength and privilege within a sea of class struggle."[17] This building up of strength and privilege can be both progressive and regressive: progressive in fomenting working-class solidarity that can help workers win a relatively better way of life; regressive in its potential exclusivity (the history of the white working-class in Detroit has been both).

Mobility—or really control over the *conditions* of mobility—is thus an aspect of class power and struggle. Understanding the intersection of location, place, and mobility in relation to the logic of capital circulation allows us to understand how both social and political contradictions and social and political power are rooted in place and space. Focusing on the circulation of capital, as Harvey urged, opens up new questions about the changing geographies of class within which we live.

Socialist Feminism and the Geography of Social Reproduction

Throughout *Limits* workers remain relatively undifferentiated and abstract. There are only the smallest hints as to what role "historical and moral elements" such as gender, race, and nationality might play in class geographies. Feminist geographers have challenged the disembodied theories of capitalism Harvey presented. As Vera Chouinard argues, socialist feminist work in particular "demonstrated that the reproduction of class inequalities and power in capitalist cities and regions cannot be understood in isolation from gendered social divisions and forms of oppression." Linda McDowell earlier raised questions about standard geographical and social divisions between public and private, the worldly and domestic, and work and home, and focused on the critical role of *reproduction* in capitalist production. The home was reconceptualized as a place of work, within which divisions of labor both structured and were structured by complex interactions with the market, with changing local and extralocal labor conditions, and so forth. The home was not so much a retreat from the realm of capitalist production and circulation as a part of the web of social relations that gave shape and substance to patriarchal capitalism: the home was both a site for the circulation of capital *and* a lived space. Key questions in understanding gendered divisions of labor and geographical space interrogated "why and which areas of reproduction become socialized and which become privatized." In particular, "production and reproduction" had to be understood "as *part of a single process*" under capitalism.[18]

"Reproduction" is a key mediating term between the structure of capitalism and the agency of workers, their families, and their communities. "The maintenance of the working classes," Marx argued, "is, and ever must be, a necessary condition to the reproduction of capital." He continues: "But the capitalist may leave its fulfillment to the labourer's instinct of self-preservation and of propagation."[19] While workers may have considerable agency in their own reproduction, Marx misses at least three key dynamics. First, processes of reproduction are shot through with gender relations; second, the reproduction of individuals and classes has always been a key site of state regulation and private meddling; and third, reproduction is a field for capitalist accumulation (as Henderson intuited). Reproduction, that is, is always *social* reproduction. And the historical and geographical development of changing relations of social reproduction is exactly what McDowell was thinking of when she asked us to turn our attention to questions of what, in the house and in other sites for reproduction, has been socialized and what has been privatized.

Processes of reproduction are every bit as geographically uneven and contradictory as the processes of production and capital circulation. In fact, the geographies of production, circulation, and reproduction are necessarily linked. To give only one example, as Kristin Nelson has shown, the historical development of domesticity for some classes of women (part of the process of class reproduction) later helped to create locally defined female surplus-labor pools in the suburbs. These pools in turn helped lure back office and manufacturing firms to suburban locations, so as to take advantage of women whose commute times (and thus the scale of their labor market participation) were constrained by gendered responsibilities for child care and education. To put this another way, the reproduction of a certain *male* class of workers—and the whole social and geographical infrastructure that made that reproduction possible—helped also to produce a *female* class of workers or potential workers. More generally, the unevenness of historical practices of social reproduction is critical to evolving *spatial* divisions of labor. To point to an obvious example, the migration of (mostly male) agricultural laborers from Mexico to the United States has not only displaced the costs of reproduction (from the California fields to Mexican villages, for example) but has also been fundamental to the production and reproduction of a class of female workers in the maquiladora zones of northern Mexico.[20]

These gendered dynamics of social reproduction significantly complicate the geography of capitalist circulation that Harvey outlines. Value circulates differently through men and women's hands, and this difference is not innocent. Rather, it is contested and is itself reproduced, thereby transforming the social geographies of class and capital. In this regard reproduction is always a problem to be solved, rather than the fact that Marx thought could be assumed. As Cindi Katz puts it:

> Social reproduction is the fleshy, messy, and indeterminate stuff of everyday life. It is also a set of structured practices that unfold in dialectical relation with production, with which it is mutually constitutive and in tension. Social reproduction encompasses daily and long-term reproduction, both of the means of production and the labor power to make them work.

Within capitalism, social reproduction requires, in fact, not just that generic labor be reproduced but "reproduction of the labor force at a certain (and fluid) level of differentiation and expertise." Social reproduction is thus "historically and geographically specific . . . its contours and requirements . . . the outcome of ongoing struggle." As Katz goes on to make clear, understanding the *restructuring* of social reproduction requires understanding how *agency*—the agency of the state, of corporations, of working-class men and women, of social movements, of managers—is constantly being restructured and differentiated across space and within places. What people *can* do varies by geography.[21] How else is it possible to say of a corporate executive in urban America, "He's in mining"?

Restructuring, Scale, and the Fate of Working-class Places

To put all the above in stark terms: Social reproduction, like production and circulation, *takes place*. Place is the locus of struggles over which structures and whose agencies will predominate. And places themselves are not only differentiated by the "inner logic" of capitalism and the associated contradictions that Harvey examined but by ongoing struggles over reproduction that are rooted in gender (and race and nationality).

Such a common-sense statement relies on a significant theoretical development in geography. In 1984, shortly after Harvey published *Limits*, two other important books appeared: Doreen Massey's *Spatial Divisions of Labour* and Neil Smith's *Uneven Development: Nature, Capital, and the Production of Space*. Both helped frame debates about the geographical nature of economic (and social) restructuring and the fate of working-class places. Massey argued persuasively that

> new spatial divisions of labor (forms of economic uneven development) are thorough re-workings of the social relations which construct economic space. . . . They are more than just new patterns of employment, a kind of geographical reshuffling of the old pack of cards. They represent whole new sets of relations between activities in different places, new spatial forms of social organization, new dimensions of inequality and new relations of dominance and dependence. Each new spatial division of labour represents a real, and thorough, spatial structuring. It marks a new form of regional problem; and more basically it marks not a new re-organization of relations *in space,* but the *creation of a new space.*

To make such an argument, Massey had to focus on the *particularity* of socio-spatial relations even as they were often conditioned through more general processes. "Local uniqueness matters," she argued. It matters both because geographical variety is not just an outcome—"it is integral to the reproduction of society and its dominant social relations"—and because the restructuring of economic relations has constructed a highly complex geography where "enormous variation" exists within every region and every locality.[22] The map of social relations cannot be drawn in broad strokes—a prosperous Sunbelt and a declining North, for example—because new spatial divisions of labor are uneven at all scales, from the neighborhood where Ken Cockerel confronted the check-cashing and short-term loan businesses, all the way up to the global, where men "in mining" conduct their affairs.

To capture the dynamics of the processes through which spatial divisions of labor—and thus places—are structured and restructured, Massey argued that "the structure of local economies can be seen as a product of the combination of 'layers,' of the successive imposition over the years of new rounds of investment." Existing socio-spatial relations provide the foundation upon which new relations must be formed. Further, "if a local economy can be analysed as the historical combination of layers of activity, those layers also represent in turn the succession of roles the local economy has played within wider national and international spatial structures." The point, Massey argued, was that "layers of activity" developed out of the already existing "local" characteristics as they combined with forces and processes operating at wider scales.[23]

Alan Warde suggested that Massey's formulation offered a highly productive "geologic" metaphor. As a geologist studies the sequencing, composition, and morphology of rock layers in order to reconstruct the geological history of an area, the geographer could examine the layers of economic and social structuring as each provided the context for (and was transformed by) the next. A very complex process of sedimentation is at work. As Massey put it, "The layers of history which are sedimented over time are not just economic; there are also cultural, political and ideological strata, layers which also have their local specificities. And this aspect of the construction of 'locality' further reinforces the impossibility of reading off from a 'layer of investment' any automatic reverberations on the character of a particular area."[24]

The invocation of "locality" in the previous sentence turned out to be quite important. In the ten years after *Spatial Divisions of Labour* was published a cottage industry—and accompanying chorus of debate—developed around trying to understand the role of "locality" (that is, place) in urban, regional, and industrial restructuring. In turn, this work was central to understanding place-based and more extensive working-class geographies. The result was a growing understanding of how class-based places have, in fact, become more, not less, important in a world being restructured through what we now call "globalization."

But to see why, we need to turn to the second influential book published in 1984, Smith's *Uneven Development*. Smith's goal, working through a deeply philosophical, theoretical, and political Marxism, was to show how the "spatial fix" that Harvey argued was so critical to any mode of production (and its changes) was itself wrapped up in a dual production of *nature* and *space*. Echoing both Marx and Harvey, Smith argued in *Uneven Development* that "the production of nature (and of space) is accomplished by the continual, if never permanent, resolution of opposing tendencies toward the *geographical equalization and differentiation* of the conditions and the levels of production. The search for a spatial fix is continually frustrated, never realized, creating distinct patterns of geographical unevenness through the continual seesaw of capital."

On the one hand, capitalism produces nature and associated geographical spaces broadly appropriate to its needs. Nature and space are both conditions for and outcomes of production and the reproduction of social life. On the other hand, the division of labor (no matter how simple or detailed) "is the historical basis of the spatial differentiation of levels and conditions of development. The spatial or territorial division of labour is not a separate process but is implied from the start in the concept of the division of labour." Smith shows that the dialectical relationship between uneven development and territorial divisions of labor results in and from the dual, contradictory tendency toward geographical equalization (e.g., through the mobility of capital and labor, the equalization of wage rates, the determination of rents) and geographical differentiation (the detailed divisions that allow one capital to capture more relative surplus value than another).[25]

The dual tendencies toward equalization and differentiation express themselves through what Smith calls "the 'seesaw' movement of capital":

> If the accumulation of capital entails geographical development and if the direction of this development is guided by a rate of profit, then we can think of the world as a 'profit surface' produced by capital itself. . . . Capital moves to where the rate of profit is highest (or at least high). . . . The mobility of capital brings about the de-

velopment of those areas with a high rate of profit and the underdevelopment of those areas where a low rate of profit pertains. But the process of development itself leads to the diminution of this higher rate of profit.[26]

Hence the "seesaw." This is what it means for an executive to be "in mining": his job is to bring about transformations in the geographical landscape that benefit him and his company.

Yet we can also see what the seesaw motion of capital means for workers. Underdevelopment and disinvestment may make all kinds of sense to a man "in mining," but to the miners it can mean the destruction of a livelihood and of the places in which they live. It makes little difference to the miners that the seesaw motion means that investment might eventually return, for by then they will be gone, or dead, or skilled in ways wholly inappropriate to the new round of investment.

In neoclassical economics, and in the economic fantasy world that occupies the cheerleaders of globalization, such a seesaw motion is efficient, and over the long term and over the whole of economic space it will lead to a more "efficient" economy. But "the long term" and "the whole of economic space" imply an argument about the geographical and temporal *scale* of development and disinvestment. For Smith, understanding uneven development requires understanding how geographical scale is produced. Smith argues that scale—from the body and home to the globe—does not simply naturally exist but is socially produced by (among other things) the tension between equalization and differentiation.[27]

Scale is the crucible within which practices of economic and political cooperation and competition are forged: scale defines the extent across which particular rules governing the economy are relevant. U.S. labor law, for example, establishes the states as the appropriate scale for governing many aspects of organization (e.g., cooperation between often competitive workers), even as capital operates at national and international scales. Moreover, practices operating at one scale—the regional or global, say—can have profound, and profoundly differential, impacts at other scales—such as the city or neighborhood. Scale is a way of not only thinking about but also analyzing the reasons for winners and losers in the capitalist economy.

In this sense, "locality" (a scale) is produced through processes of uneven development operating at other scales. The fate of places in capitalism is often well beyond the power of those places to determine. At best, in this view, they may be able to "capture" investment for their locality rather than seeing it go somewhere else. The recent history of this process is obvious enough as place after place has offered tax, rent, environmental, and wage incentives to footloose capital, in a competitive, seemingly zero-sum game as the scale at which capital operates seems to grow ever larger. And working people, to the degree they are rooted in place, seem always to be at a disadvantage, as their jobs are sold out from under them, their places of business relocated, and, perhaps, new industries requiring different skills take their place.

The details and the contradictions of these processes are highly complex. Influenced by Massey's arguments about changing spatial divisions of labor, and taking seriously the notion that sedimented histories of locality are critical to the shape and experiences of economic restructuring, at the end of the 1980s the Economic and Social Research Council in Britain sponsored a "localities initiative" called "Changing Urban and Regional Systems in the UK" (CURS). The CURS initiative traced the differential impact and explored the specific processes of restructuring in seven localities in England. This project, and others like it, drew immediate criticism from a number of geographers, sparking what came to be known as the "locality debates." These debates concerned issues such as the proper ways to engage in theoretical abstraction, the legitimacy of using empirical case studies as exemplars of more general change, the role of Marxist theory in geography, and the rise of postmodernism. The outcome was a realization that, in understanding economic restructuring and uneven development, different practices—the circulation of capital through production systems, the development of geographically "stretched" commodity chains, or the ways that places sell themselves in a global "location market"—must be understood through the metric of scale. Places and locations could no longer be studied as if they were somehow on their own. Instead, they had to be understood within a much more complex geographical context that was structured at all scales, from the most local (the bodies of specific workers) to the most global (flows of capital between global currency markets).[28]

As a result, Massey changed her metaphor: places were not so much (or only) sedimented constellations of social relations but were instead best understood as nodes in a network, governed by what she called a "power geometry"—exercises of power that had (at least metaphorically) a topological structure.[29] Perhaps the metaphor here is not so much geology as manifold physics. Boundaries between places are porous, open, constantly shifting. Or, in Smith's terms, the production of scale is always ongoing; that is, restructuring is constant.

All this may seem a long way from the immediate concerns—the geographies of injustice in urban America—that first animated radicals such as Bunge and Harvey, even if it is not disconnected from them. Even so, what is most remarkable about the intellectual ferment of geography in the 1980s was how much *people* disappeared from geographical theorizing about capitalist economic development and change. While Ken Cockerel could not have been clearer as to why capitalism was evil—because of what it did to *people*—geographers lost sight of that, to a large extent, as they constructed a highly sophisticated geography of capitalism. Geography remained radical, but its politics focused more on social process than on people.

Toward a Labor Geography

This critique was perhaps most forcefully lodged by Andrew Herod. He argued that for all that was good in radical economic geography, it was hollow at its center because it was so capital-centric. It too often ignored the workers—the "embodied labor power"—that should have been at the heart of any radical theory of capitalist production and change. Beginning in the early 1990s, Herod entered a series of pleas for placing labor, and especially laborers, at the center of geographical analyses of capitalism. At one level this was a fairly straightforward call for assuring that workers and their organizations would be taken seriously as active agents in the making and remaking of economic geographies. The implications of such a move are vast. Not only are theories of economic geography at stake but so too are theories about the making of political, social, and cultural geographies. Herod argued that a truly labor-oriented geography would recognize that:

> The production of space in particular ways is not only important for capital's ability to survive by enabling accumulation and the reproduction of capital itself, but it is also crucial for workers' abilities to survive and reproduce themselves. Just as capital does not exist in an aspatial world, neither does labor. The process of labor's self-reproduction (both biological and social) . . . must take place in particular geographical locations. Given this fact, it becomes clear that workers are likely to want to shape the economic landscape in ways that facilitate this self-reproduction.[30]

Such shaping is always political, but it is also deeply embedded in social and cultural practices, and thus what may appear from an economic point of view to be workers actively working against their own best interests appears from other points of view to be perfectly logical.

Herod argues that we must always seek to understand how workers have vested, and often contradictory, interests "in making the geography of capitalism in some ways and not others." He lays out five key arguments. First, even if workers are "bound within the confines of a capitalist economic system, the production of the geography of capitalism is not the sole prerogative of capitalism." Second, "the social actions of workers relate [among other things] to their own spatial visions of a geography of capitalism that is enabling of their own self-reproduction and survival." Third, because different groups of workers will have different (and differently located) interests and spatial visions, "labor" cannot be understood "as an undifferentiated mass"; it is rather a divided and struggled-over social formation. Fourth, because groups of workers and factions of capital are each trying to construct "spatial fixes" to the specific problems and contradictions that each faces, "*it is the conflicts over whose spatial fix . . . is actually set in the landscape that are at the heart of the dynamic of the geography of capitalism*"; struggle determines. But, fifth, the ordinary and extraordinary struggles of workers both produce and are constrained by geographical scale: "the scale at which power is to be exercised may be vigorously fought over, for example, when workers with different agendas argue whether it is the provision of local or national labor agreements that should take precedence in any particular situation."[31]

Herod first formulated his arguments while working on his PhD at Rutgers University where he was a student of Neil Smith. There were several of us there at the time (including Rebecca Johns, Leyla Vural, and myself) who sought to develop what has since come to be called a "labor geography." Each of us started with workers' lives and worked toward understanding the broader political geography of labor struggle, particularly in the United States but also overseas. Herod's work focused primarily on the institutional practices of labor unions, showing how workers and their organizations struggle over and produce the scales of capitalism. Johns uncovered the geographies of international labor solidarity at a time when campaigns such as the antisweatshop movement were only beginning, trying to understand the geographical conditions that make international solidarity possible (or not).

Vural and I turned more to "cultural" questions. Vural sought to understand the geographies of unionism as a social movement and way of life, focusing particularly on the historical geography of the International Ladies Garment Workers Union in New York. I took as my focus the geographical landscape, exploring how California's agricultural landscape was constructed through struggles by the Industrial Workers of the World in the 1910s, by Mexican, Japanese, Filipino, and other ethnic unions of the 1920s, and by the contending AFL and Communist unions of the 1930s. Against these unions, and against all the unorganized agricultural workers of the state, stood the rural vigilantes of the era, the state agencies called into existence to explain and ameliorate class struggle in the fields, and the growing power of agricultural corporations. I argued that the very shape, the very *look,* of the California landscape was a result of workers' struggles to make a living in it and of the efforts of capital and the state to stanch those struggles in a manner appropriate to their own (often differentiated) needs.[32]

Working a few years later, Ruth Wilson Gilmore examined in her Rutgers dissertation how political and economic crisis in the United States created surpluses of labor, land, and state capacity that were eventually absorbed through the development of what she calls a "post-Keynesian" prison-industrial complex. She argued that the insertion of prisons into the "de-laborized" landscapes of California's Central Valley recapitulated in new forms traditional labor-capital relations: they created new kinds of "factories in field." In turn, the incarceration of a largely black and Latino male surplus labor population in rural California has had dramatic effects on working-class communities in Los Angeles and elsewhere.[33]

In all this work at Rutgers, economic geographies were examined in the context of gendered, racist, and nationalist practices. The insights of socialist feminism were indispensable. From it we learned that the writing of geography is always political, and we saw ourselves engaged in a political project. As Herod has written, constructing labor geographies is

> a political argument . . . about whose interests economic geographers and other social scientists choose to understand and represent. The social production of knowledge is a political process. Conceiving workers as simply factors of production or 'variable capital' is to tell the story of the making of economic geographies through the eyes of capital. . . . [But] it is also possible to tell the story of the making of economic geographies through the eyes of workers.[34]

We were not alone. Students and faculty members in a number of other universities (UC Berkeley, Clark, Iowa, Queen's University in Ontario, Ohio State, Minnesota, Johns Hopkins, and the Open University in England) also turned their attention to the range of historical and contemporary struggles facing workers. In Britain, researchers focused on the transformation of union power in the wake of Thatcherism, the ways that labor was policed during the 1984 coal strike, the movement against plant closures, and, in line with the locality debates, the fate of working-class places in the new neoliberal world.[35]

Nor were we working in a disciplinary vacuum. Though grounded in the theoretical debates that have animated radical geography, most of the work in the new labor geography also draws heavily on research and ideas from industrial relations, labor and social history, radical economics, feminism, and cultural studies, even as it contributes to them. Politically and empirically, labor geography is primarily concerned with putting flesh—and social will and intentionality—on the theoretical bones of radical geography, refocusing radical geography with two main goals: showing how people make their own geographies, even if not under conditions of their own choosing (to paraphrase Marx); and showing what this making of geography *means* to the people who do it. This is an ambitious project, and it is beset by all manner of theoretical and political difficulties. Yet it is an important project, for without it we cannot even come close to figuring out what might constitute a socially just geography—which was the impetus for the radical geography movement. Nor, without it, can we begin to see—or to understand— how a man "in mining" can have so much power, control so much wealth, and decide the fate of places such as Detroit, even though "he don't do nothing."

. . . and Working-Class Geographies

Ken Cockerel died at age fifty. Both his wife and his son became city council members in Detroit, the latter becoming central to debates over living-wage ordinances. One of Cockerel's comrades in DRUM and the League of Revolutionary Black Workers, General Baker, was blackballed from the auto industry for his organizing. When he got work at Ford under an assumed name, he was ratted out by a police informer. He eventually worked his way back inside and some thirty years on he now works the midnight shift at the blast furnace at Ford. He told me that he works that shift in part because it gives him time for political organizing. He remains committed to the racial and class struggle that has defined his life and given shape to contemporary Detroit. But he is also clear that these struggles are linked to larger ones: they cannot be separated from more global struggles against capitalism and oppression. Detroit exists within and as part of a globally uneven and dynamic system, and understanding the geographical opportunities and constraints that system creates is vital to its revolutionary transformation. Or, as Baker puts it:

> We learned a fundamental lesson that the most important place we occupied in society in Detroit in 1967 and 1968 was at the point of production. Now, that estimate didn't just fall out of the sky, it was a practical assessment of the situation we were confronted with to figure out how to move. That's how we proceeded to carry out the work inside of the plants.
>
> We had conditions then that don't exist today. Back in the early '60s, the plants were stable. They stayed in one place. We didn't have massive plant closings. Today, you have international unions and union leaders in collaboration with the company. If you get a militant person elected at a local, that plant closes and the work is sent somewhere else, just because of the politics of the person at that local.
>
> ... We've got a different situation than we were confronted with then that needs different analysis and estimates of how we carry out the struggle.[36]

Geography matters. That is, social struggle requires constant analysis of changing social and spatial relations. The *place* of struggle, as Baker makes clear, is always vital, and always changing. It is central to how workers make and remake the spaces of capitalism, and how they seek to transform them.

Geographic approaches to working-class places and working-class struggles show that class and class practices can only be understood as part of a web of social identities—race, gender, sexuality, citizenship. But as General Baker, Ken Cockerel, and the other members of the League of Revolutionary Black Workers make clear, the obverse is also true: to understand oppressions of race, gender, and other markers of identity, one has to pay close attention to class. And class, as we have seen, is necessarily marked by geographically complex patterns, textures, and strategies. Working-class histories and geographies—the geographies of capitalism—are complex, contradictory, and confusing. There is still much to be learned about them.

Yet surprisingly, and the merits of the new labor geography notwithstanding, geographers have shied away from developing a robust working-class geography that understands the relationship between space, place, and power in all its historical complexity. In part this is because labor geography has developed most directly out of economic geography, and as a response to a set of specific and often technical concerns that include the spatial divisions of labor and the role of location in the global economy. With a few notable exceptions, it has not been well linked, for example, to historical geography, which has strong connections to social history.[37] But perhaps as important in this underdevelopment is the adoption by many proponents of new labor geography of crippling "anti-essentialist" notions about class: notions that go beyond the obvious point that class solidarity and identity is an achievement rather than a thing to assume that class has no objective basis in reality. At best, this argument suggests, we can only examine different groups of workers in different social settings; we cannot see them as a unified class. What gets lost is the degree to which it is the process of living an objective relation (to the means of production, for example) that gives rise to the *differences* that make working-class geographies so complex and class solidarity so difficult.[38]

Geography thus needs a much fuller, even more materialist, approach to working-class geographies than it has so far developed. It needs to begin developing more firmly grounded theories of identity, while showing how space, place, and the geographies of power are central to these because they are determinant, in so many ways. Radical geographical analyses of capitalism have been enormously insightful; the development of a labor geography has been an important step toward beginning to understand working-class geographies. The task now is to develop these insights with not just "labor" or "laborers" but *working people* at the center of analysis.

Such a shift might allow us finally to begin to realize the goal David Harvey set out for geography twenty years ago, a goal that is applicable to the whole of working-class studies:

> The geography we make must be *a peoples' geography,* not based on pious universalisms, ideals, and good intents, but a more mundane enterprise that reflects earthly interests and claims, that confronts ideologies and prejudice as they really are, that faithfully mirrors the complex weave of competition, struggle, and cooperation within the shifting social and physical landscapes of the twentieth [and twenty-first] century. The world must be depicted, analyzed, and understood not as we would like it to be but as it really is, the material manifestation of human hopes and fears mediated by powerful and conflicting processes of social reproduction.
>
> Such a peoples' geography must have a popular base, be threaded into the fabric of daily life with deep taproots into the well-springs of popular consciousness. But it must also open channels of communication, undermine parochialist world views, and confront or subvert the power of dominant classes or the state. It must penetrate the barriers to common understandings by identifying the material base to common interests. Where such a material base does not exist, it must frankly recognize and articulate the conflict of equal and competing rights that flows therefrom. To the degree that conflicting rights are resolved through tests of strength between contending parties, so the intellectual force within our discipline is a powerful weapon and

must be consciously deployed as such, even at the expense of internalizing conflicting notions of right within the discipline itself.[39]

These, finally, will be geographies sufficient to describe and explain the worlds Ken Cockerel and General Baker knew—and worked so hard to make just.

7

Class as a Question in Economics

Michael Zweig

The refusal of modern economics to address issues of class contains a double irony. First, class is demonstrably a central feature of economic life. What's more, class was well recognized in the writings of Adam Smith and other founders of economic analysis. From Smith's eighteenth-century writing in the early days of capitalism to John Maynard Keynes's twentieth-century analysis of the Great Depression and the steps required to alleviate it, economic theory has included explicit treatment of class as an important feature of the economy. But from the late nineteenth through the twentieth century, especially during the second half of the twentieth, the scope and subject matter of economics changed in ways that rendered class irrelevant and drove it from the discipline.

The main intellectual feature of this change was the near-total focus on the market as the proper subject matter for economics as an academic discipline, coupled with the reduction of "the market" to a mechanism for the organization and regulation of production and consumption in the presence of scarcity. The main technical feature that accompanied this new focus was the dominance of formal mathematical modeling as the method for exploring individual and business behavior in market activity, and the effects of those activities on market outcomes.

Reducing the field of economics by separating the market as a mechanism from the economy as a set of social relations has weakened the connections between economics and the other social sciences (except insofar as the reduction of other disciplines to mathematical modeling has also taken place). This reductionism has also, by definition, masked the power relations that shape the rules by which markets operate and drive market outcomes.

To assert and investigate the place of class in economics is to acknowledge its place in the economy itself. Classes are not sterile categories into which we fit people according to some checklist of characteristics intrinsic to the individual. Classes are dynamic social creations that emerge in the interactions among people that are established when goods and services are produced. These in turn have consequences for income, wealth, and the distribution of output across the population, which double back to influence patterns of production.

Most people in the United States are working class[1]: men and women, skilled and unskilled, blue-, white-, and pink-collar, in all industries and from all nationalities and races; people who have little control over the pace and content of their work, who are no one's boss, who answer to the discipline and needs of their employers on the job. They form a class because they share a relationship with another class, the capitalist class, those who exercise power by controlling the operations of the businesses that employ the working class. In the United States the working class is 62 percent of the labor force; the capitalists are 2 percent.

The popular view is that most Americans are "middle class." Usually this connotes some sense of lifestyle reflected in stable employment and the ability to consume an array of goods and services beyond the bare minimum for survival, albeit through ever-increasing consumer debt. Looking at class in terms of power, however, we discover a working-class majority. The middle class are those professionals, supervisors, and small-business owners whose positions of economic authority are between those of the working class and the capitalists, and who have mixed and contradictory experiences—sometimes akin to workers, sometimes reminiscent of capitalists. In the United States the middle class constitutes 36 percent of the labor force.

Class becomes relevant when we reassert the traditional scope of economics as the study of social processes that govern production, exchange, and distribution. This is especially so when we understand class primarily as a matter of power rather than income or lifestyle. The operations of power in economic relationships are often indicators of class dynamics and often go a long way toward determining market outcomes. Let's look at some examples from various aspects of the economy to illustrate the point.

Wages and Profits

Adam Smith wrote *An Inquiry into the Nature and Causes of the Wealth of Nations* in 1776 as a sharp polemic against the power of the merchants and the monopoly protections they were afforded by kings.[2] Smith's central point was that wealth has its origins in the *production* of goods, not in trading them. His insights into the division of labor, self-interest, and the power of competition demonstrated how markets might stimulate and regulate production, thereby sustaining growing wealth in an orderly society.

When Smith insisted that all wealth is created in production and focused on the division of labor as the foundation of increasing productivity, he both emphasized and explained the special importance of *labor* in the production of wealth. Smith was clear that *all* value has its origin in the work of productive laborers: "The value the workmen add to the materials, therefore, resolves itself . . . into two parts, of which the one pays their wages, the other the profits of their employer. . . . He would have no interest to employ them unless he expected from the sale of their work something more than what was sufficient to replace his stock."[3] Smith saw that the capital accumulating in the hands of business owners came not from the owners' actions but exclusively from the productive efforts of their workers. Smith and other pioneering political economists accepted this class structure as a fact of economic life and commented explicitly on the differences in interests between the class of owners and the class of workers.

Today an appreciation of the importance of class in the economy is very much associated with Karl Marx. But, as we have seen, class in modern economics predated the publication of Marx's *Capital* by nearly a hundred years. In 1852, four years after the *Communist Manifesto* appeared, Marx described his contributions to theories of class:

> And now as to myself, no credit is due to me for discovering the existence of classes in modern society or the struggle between them. Long before me bourgeois historians had described the historical development of this class struggle and bourgeois economists the economic anatomy of the classes. What I did that was new was to prove: 1) that the *existence of classes* is only bound up with *particular historical phases in the development of production,* 2) that the class struggle necessarily leads to the *dictatorship of the proletariat,* 3) that this dictatorship itself only constitutes the transition to the *abolition of all classes* and to a *classless society.*[4]

In *Theories of Surplus Value, Capital,* and other writings, Marx elaborated classical political economy and took its class analysis of production to new and, for capitalists, threatening places.[5] At the same time, by the late nineteenth century the Industrial Revolution was in full swing and capitalism was consolidated as a social system, having destroyed feudalism in England and much of Europe and slavery in the United States.

In 1870, in the context of these new conditions, three economists, working independently in three countries, set out a radically different way of understanding economic behavior. The "marginalist revolution" expounded by Stanley Jevons in

England, Karl Menger in Austria, and Leon Walras in Switzerland rooted the decision making of businesses and households in a common desire to derive the maximum possible profit or pleasure with given available resources. To accomplish this supposedly natural and universal human desire, they proposed that people behave in such a way as to equate the additional benefit gained from any economic action with the additional cost incurred in taking that action. That is, people act to equate the marginal (extra) benefit with the marginal (extra) cost of employing another person, producing another unit of output, or buying another unit of any product for consumption. Instead of the investigation of long-run economic growth at the heart of classical economics, the new approach took available resources as given and investigated how these scarce resources might best be allocated to competing possible purposes.[6]

Marginalism, however, did not come to dominate economics until three decades had passed. There is no substantial evidence that its founders deliberately set out to create something new in an explicit attempt to answer Marx or defend capitalism from its critics, but the new approach did come into prominence in part because it gave its advocates a handy cudgel to take up against Marx's theory of exploitation. It did this by simply changing the subject, disregarding the dynamic problem of economic growth and capital accumulation in favor of a static problem of allocation. The new marginalist economics also challenged the method developed by classical economists, from Smith to Marx, which had dominated economics for over a hundred years. As British economist Ronald Meek put it:

> In value theory the new trend was marked in particular by the emergence of a subjective theory of value based in one way or another on "utility." . . . The primary attention in the theory of value was shifted from the relations between men as producers to the relation between men and goods. And in the theory of distribution which gradually developed, quite largely on the basis of the inspired hints of the three founders themselves, the tendency was in the same general direction—towards the notion that the socio-economic relations between the classes which supplied land, labor, and capital had nothing essentially to do with the respective rewards the market process afforded them.[7]

The marginalist revolution denied that power relations among classes, in particular between the capitalist and working classes, had any bearing on wages, profits, or the distribution of the nation's output between labor and capital. To replace these relationships among people, the marginalists proposed the relationship between people and products, or simply relationships among products—how much additional output will result from the application of an additional worker, how much additional output will result from the application of another piece of capital equipment.

The marginalist revolution affected all aspects of economic analysis, including its implications for our understanding of the determinants of wages and profit. In a nutshell this dispute centers on the answer to the question: Are workers paid wages in accordance with how much they produce, or in relation to what it takes to produce *them?* Smith and the classical economists proposed the latter and held that wages were paid in amounts just adequate to allow workers to buy what they need to be able to work and to raise a new generation of children who will enter the workforce to take their place at death or retirement—what might be called a "subsistence wage," not necessarily set in biological requirements for mere survival, but in the norms of a reasonable life workers are able to establish in conflict with employers.

In contrast, for the marginalists a worker's wage corresponds to the value of the product the worker produces (on the margin). The new doctrine proposed a uniform theory for the compensation of all "factors of production," as classes came to be called—labor, capital, and land. Each of these factors receives compensation, whether called wages or profit or rent, in the amount of the value of output produced by the last unit of that factor applied as an input for production. As each factor of production makes its own contribution to additional output when additional units of it are applied, the owners of the factors—workers, capitalists, and landowners—receive their respective shares of the total.

When the marginalists broke with the classical understanding that capitalists pay wages to sustain workers while taking profits from the workers' production, they obliterated class distinctions. Instead, they treated everyone as an equivalent economic actor, differentiated only by name and specific function, each trying as any other to get the best possible return for what its owner sells in the market, each realizing a return based on the same rules of marginal productivity. As economist and historian of economic doctrine Joseph Schumpeter put it, referring to the formulations of John Stuart Mill and others in the later years of the classical tradition but in terms appropriate to the marginalists as well: "Social classes were not living and fighting entities but were labels affixed to economic functions (or functional categories). Nor were the individuals themselves living and fighting beings; they continued to be mere clotheslines on which to hang propositions of economic logic."[8]

In marginal productivity theory, profit as a return to capital arises in response to the marginal product of capital, the amount of extra output created by an additional amount of capital seeking a return. But this return to capital is devilishly hard to calculate using marginal productivity theory.[9] And beyond theoretical difficulties, as a practical matter no necessary connection exists between increases in the productivity of labor and increases in real wages. In the twenty-five years following World War II American workers did receive wage increases more or less in line with improvements in productivity, but after 1973 the relationship ended.

For the next thirty years (except for three years at the end of the 1990s) labor productivity went up while real earnings fell.[10]

In other words, workers' ability to capture for themselves a share of their own increased production led to dramatic increases in working-class living standards in the two and a half decades following 1945. This was also, and not coincidentally, a period of comparatively strong union power and influence. By the middle of the 1970s, however, union power had eroded to such an extent that power relations between labor and capital changed qualitatively.[11] Business leaders and their political allies pressed their advantage, resulting in a thirty-year decline in working-class living standards and further erosion of union strength. The increases in labor productivity that underlay continuing economic growth after 1973 went entirely to capital, and then some, as evidenced in the widening inequality of income and wealth characteristic of American (and global) experience that accompanied lower real wages over the period.[12]

This history suggests that wages are not, as the marginalists would have it, determined by productivity. Rather, wages provide workers with the ability to buy the living standard they need, according to the culture and expectations of the time. When the working class is strongly organized it can win increases in real wages and living conditions (which must be supported by the actual capacity to produce the goods and services involved). When workers are weakly organized, living standards decline, with lower wages, fewer benefits, longer working hours, less stable employment, and all the other features of working-class life manifest since the 1970s.

But where unions continued to exercise power in this period, concessions were limited and gains sometimes won, even during the George W. Bush administration. In 2003, the Communications Workers of America (CWA) was able to win the restoration of twenty-three hundred jobs at Verizon in New York State by demonstrating to an arbitrator that the layoffs violated the collective bargaining contract that Verizon had with CWA.[13] In the public sector, Transport Workers Union Local 100, representing over thirty-four thousand workers in the New York City transit system, credibly threatened a strike toward the end of 2002 (although it would have violated state labor law) and won major gains in health funds, important changes in discipline procedures, and modest wage increases in a climate of general budget crisis.[14]

It is well documented that unions and collective bargaining improve the wages, benefits, and working conditions of their members compared with similar workers not in unions.[15] Union protection for workers also improves their productivity, the quality of the products they produce, and other measures of business activity. The one business measure that suffers from union presence is profit.[16]

As these and other examples attest, economists' ability to understand what drives the distributions of income and wealth requires our integration of class into the analysis. To be useful for the purpose, class in economics should convey the "living and fighting entities" in Schumpeter's formulation, not the ever-present "labels affixed to economic functions." Considering class as a power relationship contributes to this approach.

Globalization and International Trade

In the recent era of neoliberalism, "the market" has taken on talismanic power in international economic relations. In the story promoted by the U.S. Treasury, the International Monetary Fund, and think tanks boosting capitalism since the end of the cold war, every social good will follow the implementation of unrestricted markets in countries around the world.

But in the international economy, as much as in any domestic one, markets are structured by class power and generate differential outcomes for different classes. The neoliberal revolution in international economic affairs, which began in the early 1970s and gained strength through the 1980s and 1990s, paralleled the rise of free-market ideology in the guidance of the domestic U.S. economy. In both arenas the economic architecture changed from what had emerged after World War II. Instead of institutions and policies based on a Keynesian understanding of market limitations and the need for government action to stabilize the economy, preference went to a more aggressive reliance on "free" markets.[17] Matching these changes in macroeconomic and regulatory policy were changes in labor market practices to improve "flexibility," which always meant weakening unions and exposing workers more nakedly to the power of employers to fire people, reduce wages and working conditions, and in other ways reduce the living standards of working people.

The results internationally have matched the results we have seen in the United States. In country after country, inequality has increased because of policies imposed by the IMF and the U.S. Treasury. Growth rates have gone down instead of up. Hunger has become more, not less, widespread. The forcible end of subsidies for vital consumer goods has led to the absolute impoverishment of tens of millions of people. Meanwhile, a relative handful of people in every country, plugged into the new relationships in the role of capitalists, have done fabulously well.[18]

Economists understand that trade between countries can help create conditions for the production of greater wealth, mainly because trade allows for specialization, which in turn enhances productivity. This is as much the case for trade between the United States and Mexico as it is for trade between Texas and New York. But economists also understand that there is no way to tell from the market alone how the gains from trade will be *distributed.* Just as increased productivity can increase the incomes of workers, capitalists, or both in varying degrees, so the gains from international trade can go to one country, the other country, or both (and within each country to different classes). The distribution of gains from trade, whether international or domestic, is the result of the relative power of the traders.

David Ricardo, the British economist and government official of the early nineteenth century, is most closely associated with developing the theory of gains from international trade, having invented the notion of "comparative advantage" to explain the phenomenon. In his famous empirical example, repeated in most introductory economics textbooks, England should specialize in the production of cloth, Portugal in wine. Rather than each country producing both to satisfy its own needs, both countries could be better off if England produces less wine and more cloth, exporting its surplus cloth to Portugal in exchange for the additional wine the Portuguese can produce if they move resources away from the production of cloth. Allowing this specialization, supported by trade, will result in more of each good being produced with no additional resources used—a powerful result and strong impetus to trade.

Ricardo's theory explained the empirical fact that England exported cloth to Portugal, from which it also imported wine. But it turns out that this arrangement was not the simple result of unregulated market forces responding to comparative advantage in the two countries. As Harry Magdoff has pointed out, this trade pattern had its origins in the more-than-two-hundred-year relationship between England and Portugal that preceded Ricardo's observation. In this history, England was the dominant economic force, supported by military power none could effectively challenge. The English forbade the Portuguese from producing cloth to challenge their own exports and encouraged the Portuguese to develop wine production for export as a way to undermine the French, who were rivals of the English.[19] The market does indeed operate as a technical mechanism to allocate resources and organize trade, but it cannot be understood outside the context of the social power that operates through it. Class analysis is central to this contextual approach.

We see the same dynamics at work in the imposition of the neoliberal trade regime on the twenty-first century world economy. The United States, principal champion of "free trade," relies shamelessly on all manner of trade restrictions that favor special business interests at home, ranging from billions of dollars in farm subsidies paid out each year (most of which go to a small fraction of farm owners, the largest in the industry[20]) to tariffs to protect the steel industry. They include the special last-minute exemptions to "free trade" in the North American Free Trade Agreement (NAFTA) negotiated by President Clinton to protect the citrus and sugar growers of Florida and Louisiana in order to gain treaty ratification votes from their representatives in Congress. Yet union attempts to secure worker protections through enforceable labor standards written into the trade agreements are regularly dismissed as the pleadings of special interests violating the principles of "free trade."

Even as class forces within the United States shape the rules and patterns of market activity, the United States operates as an imperial power to impose arrangements favorable to U.S. capital worldwide. The national security strategy enunciated by President George W. Bush in September 2002 made plain that the United States would intervene anywhere on earth, with unilateral military force when necessary, to secure the interests of investors seeking favorable market conditions.[21]

American military doctrine is developing to match these ambitions. U.S. Air Force General Howell M. Estes III, commander in chief of the North American Aerospace Defense Command and United States Space Command, in 1997, explained that the purpose of U.S. weapons in space was "dominating the space dimension of military operations to protect U.S. interests and investment." Putting this mission into historical perspective, he stated, "Military forces have evolved to protect national interests and investments—both military and economic. During the rise of sea commerce, nations built navies to protect and enhance their commercial interests. During the westward expansion of the continental United States, military outposts and the cavalry emerged to protect our wagon trains, settlements, and railroads. The emergence of space power follows both of these models."[22]

The implications of neoliberal globalization for inequality are well known to our strategic planners: "Although unlikely to be challenged by a global peer competitor, the United States will continue to be challenged regionally. The globalization of the world economy will continue, with a widening between the 'haves' and 'have-nots.' "[23] The haves and have-nots of colloquial parlance reflect the capitalist and working classes that appear in a more rigorous analysis of the capitalist system and its global operations.

Class, Ideology, and the Real World of Production and Exchange

Is class an ideological category meant to import value judgments and subjective controversy into an otherwise scientific, objective investigation of markets characteristic of contemporary economics? I would say no, but also yes.

First, class has significant explanatory power when it comes to the market, no matter what one's beliefs. What we have seen above with respect to wages, profits, and the global economy emerges again in studies of public finance, regulatory policy, fiscal and monetary policy, health and health care systems, and a host of other subjects in economics. This is why we cannot dismiss class as an ideological category dragged into the field to satisfy the preferences of economists motivated by left-wing political aims.

Understanding the importance and function of class in the economy does not obviate the need to know in detail about market operations. Marx understood the need to analyze the market and acknowledged the role of supply and demand, but in their social context. For him, and sometimes for the classical economists whose work he devoured in the British Library as he wrote *Capital,* the social context was essential; and class relations were a significant element of that context.

Still, to the degree that marginalist analysis shapes technical procedures (linear programming, for example) that help us produce more efficiently, there is gain to be had for any class in power. As Ronald Meek put it: "We should remember what it is that the economists and calculators are trying to do. They are trying, in essence, to *economize*—to make the best possible use of the scarce resources at man's disposal. It has always puzzled me that this kind of aim should be regarded almost as an ultimate value when it is pursued in art, literature, and music, and yet as somehow sordid and ignoble when it is pursued in the ordinary business of life."[24] Producing as much as possible using given resources; allocating a limited budget to purchase a collection of goods and services that convey the highest possible level of satisfaction to the purchaser; choosing among alternative methods of production so as to conserve resources to the greatest degree possible and still satisfy the production target: such problems yield to the economist's techniques. But this type of problem hardly exhausts the issues people confront when experiencing the economy as an engine of production and distribution. And even within the narrow range of maximization problems of the sort just described, class plays a significant role in understanding the choices different people make and the economic constraints they live within.

It is telling that marginalist analysis takes as given people's preferences and constraints. They are simply facts, as is the desire to maximize in the first place. This brings us to the other side of the question: whether class is an ideological import into economics.

Economists tend to uphold the division between what is called "positive" and "normative" economics.[25] The former deals with "what is," the latter with "what ought to be." Economists, like anyone else, have personal preferences for how the world should be ordered and how economic resources should be used. These preferences might be expressed in such statements as "More economic equality is better than less" or "Only people who can afford it should have access to basic health care" or "No one should pay more than 20 percent of their income for housing." These normative statements about the economy are legitimate value judgments, but the economist has no special or professional standing to assert them (or their opposites)—in these matters the economist's opinions have equal weight with those of any member of society.

Positive economics, on the other hand, is the special province of the economist. It involves knowledge of the workings of the market as an objective matter. "If the price of a product goes up, people will demand less of it" or "Cutting taxes for low-income people will result in greater demand, everything else unchanged" are examples. The point of the distinction is to assert that the tools of "positive economics," devoted to a study of the market mechanism, are the proper subjects of economics. The findings are available to people of every political and ideological persuasion, but those persuasions themselves have no place in economics per se. Rather, they are the subject matter of politics, philosophy, psychology, or some other field. Economics should focus on the facts of market laws, the objective functioning of the market mechanism. Values have no place in this inquiry. Following along these lines, the introduction of classes and class conflict into the model breaks the barrier, introducing politics and (at least implicitly) value judgments into economics.

As tempting and intuitive as the distinction between positive and normative may seem, however, it is not complete. The "laws" of the market are totally dependent on such value-laden assertions as "the primacy of the individual as an independent decision maker" and the proposition that "personal happiness derives from the possession of goods and services made available in the market." Introducing class into the picture is no more and no less ideological than resisting its introduction in favor of individualism.

More broadly, the assertion that there are significant "facts" preceding and independent of theories used to explain them is also unsatisfactory. As the historian E. H. Carr has shown, of all the various "facts" and "events" and "behaviors" and "dates" that swirl through our experience, we consider particular facts, events, behaviors, and dates interesting, important, and ripe for investigation because they correspond in some way to a theoretical framework we bring to the world. "Fact" and "theory" are inseparable, each meaningless without the other.[26]

When British prime minister Margaret Thatcher asserted that only individuals exist and that "society" is a fiction (let alone classes within society), she was making an ideological statement central to the theory and practice of neoliberal economics. It is normative to its core because it seeks to defend the individual against what are taken to be inappropriate restrictions imposed through government power and regulation.

How starkly different are these sentiments than those spoken by Ronald Meek, on the occasion of his appointment as chair of the economics department at Leicester University in 1964:

> Man is at last beginning to master the machine [that is, the market] which has hitherto controlled his economic destiny. . . . First, by preventing the machine from operating at all in certain important fields where he thinks that decisions ought to be consciously and purposefully made; and second, by taking action to ensure that the results which the machine produces in the remaining fields coincide with his aims.[27]

As a practical matter, we have seen in the Great Depression of the 1930s—and in the predatory and destructive behavior of unregulated capital throughout the history of capitalism—that the market as a mechanism often breaks down. What's more, we have concluded that these breakdowns are socially dysfunctional and cause unwanted suffering, whether through mass unemployment or the loss of pensions for Enron workers or the price gouging of California residents by deregulated energy companies in 2001. When Meek spoke about people learning to "master the machine" he was talking about the assertion of social limits on private behavior, especially the behavior of capitalists, and taking out of the market arena altogether some "important fields" of human welfare such as health care and housing.

Meek's 1964 comments came at the high point of social democratic economic policies in England, and in Europe and the United States as well (that was the year of the Great Society and the War on Poverty). The priorities implied are not only value laden, they are practical only in the presence of a working-class social force capable of mustering the political capacity to limit the authority of capital and the primacy of markets. Such force was at play in Europe from the latter part of the nineteenth century and in the United States from the 1930s. The degree to which Meek's economic thinking now seems far away marks the shifts in power between the working and capitalist classes in the intervening years.

Class undoubtedly carries ideological freight as well as explanatory power into economics. But in acknowledging the significance of class in economics, there is no need to accept the transcendent revolutionary significance Marx gave to the working class. This part of Marx's contribution to class analysis is still an open empirical question; the answer is yet to be determined in history. But capitalist history to date confirms the persistence and deep importance of class in almost all aspects of the capitalist economy.

We can also safely conclude that class forces contribute to shaping history. No individual or class controls history; there is no predetermined outcome to the historical process. But capitalists organize to influence events in their interests, whether through political lobbying, research centers, or trade associations, to say nothing of using the armed might of the state domestically and internationally. The working class, too, can create organizations to identify and advance its interests and shape the future of the country. Economics is inescapably caught up in this class conflict.

"Class" is an intellectual category that reflects a social reality concerning economic power. But power is complex and shapes many aspects of people's lives. Race and gender are among other intellectual constructs that concern life-shaping power relations. Class, race, and gender are different but not wholly separate;[28] there is no experience of class that is not inflected by race and gender, and no experience of gender or race that is not inflected by class. A serious investigation of class must bring with it investigations of race and gender as well.

Something as complicated as class cannot be understood with the tools of any single discipline. As the field of working-class studies shows, class is germane to inquiries throughout the social sciences and humanities. Working-class studies will develop through discipline-specific investigation, but also through interdisciplinary conversations and cross-references.

Attention to class in economics is vital to the discipline itself, as we have seen, but the economist's treatment of class can contribute to other fields of study. In particular, economics locates class in the production process. In doing so, economists tend to ground discussions of class in the material world. The origins of class in production suggest an objective basis for politics and history and a material aspect to culture.

PART THREE

REPRESENTATIONS

New Working-Class Studies places working-class people, their voices, experiences, and perspectives, at the center of its research, teaching, and activism. Stories, images, songs, oral histories, and poems created and used by working-class people provide access to this working-class perspective. In studying representations of, by, and for the working class, scholars ask not only how working-class people represent themselves but also how they are represented. The four essays in this section examine representations created by working-class people, as well as representations created for and about them.

In "Work Poetry and Working-Class Poetry: The Zip Code of the Heart," poet Jim Daniels traces the attention to work experience and the straightforward language that marks contemporary poetry about work and working-class life. At the same time, he provides an overview of the growing body of working-class poetry, reviewing key anthologies, journals, and individual writers' work.

Tim Strangleman's "Class Memory: Autobiography and the Art of Forgetting" also looks at texts created by workers. He uses the popular British genre of memoirs about railway work as a case study to argue for the value of working-class autobiography as a tool for understanding both the day-to-day experience of working-class people and the nature of work. He also suggests that workplace autobiographies provide a counterbalance to studies of "the end of work" that too often devalue work itself. For Strangleman, part of the promise of new working-class studies is its attention to workers' voices.

In "Filming Class," Tom Zaniello examines popular, documentary, and alternative films that represent working-class life and culture. His survey includes representations of union activism in Hollywood movies as well as several documentaries on coal miners' labor struggles. He concludes that Hollywood's approach to working-class culture is mixed, but he sees greater complexity and sympathy in alternative films, including documentaries and the emerging body of alternative media, though these reach far smaller audiences. Despite the unevenness of these representations, Zaniello argues that film is not simply a good tool for understanding class but that it is also an important form of new working-class studies.

Popular music, as Rachel Rubin argues, is both created by and used by working-class people as part of everyday life. In " 'Working Man's Ph.D.': The Music of Working-Class Studies," Rubin suggests that popular music can help us gain insight into how people form identities based in work, how working-class people form and understand their own class consciousness and class struggle, and how class intersects with race, gender, and religion. She also reminds us that we should not only read popular representations but also consider how they are created within the context of both lived experience and the business of popular culture. As Rubin suggests, representations reflect working-class perspectives, but their creation and use is also a social practice that is often mediated by individuals and corporations that are not working class.

8

Work Poetry and Working-Class Poetry: The Zip Code of the Heart

Jim Daniels

The writer Richard Price said that where you're from is "the ZIP code for your heart."[1] This essay will examine recent work and working-class poetry in anthologies and textbooks, journals, and books by individual poets, discussing how this poetry is establishing a sense of place for writers and readers—a "home" in the world of literature, a zip code for the places of work and the influences of work on our lives as individuals, and on our larger society, a home where the poems can be discussed, recorded, and *felt*.

As a poet who has often written about work and working-class issues, I have been collecting whatever poetry I can find on the subject of work for over twenty years. In 1981, I moved to Pittsburgh to take a job teaching at Carnegie Mellon University. In December of that year, I gave my first public reading in town at the University of Pittsburgh. Someone got up during the question and answer session and (1) said that what I was writing was not poetry, (2) said he was appalled that I was teaching, and (3) accused me of flaunting my working-class genitals.

What happened next is a story for another time, but that evening proved to me that a bias against poetry about work in general, and working-class subjects in particular, exists in our country. I have amassed my personal collection of working-class poetry because of my personal interest as a reader and writer and my need to feel part of a larger community that values writing about our daily working lives. Since I am a poet, I write this essay *as* a poet, rather than a scholar. Poetry about work and class has been around in various forms for a long time, and it is not my objective to cover that entire history. I cannot even adequately cover the recent history. So much has been published in recent years, I cannot possibly discuss every significant poet, and I'm sure I'm simply not familiar with some important working-class poets, so I apologize in advance for any glaring omissions. My strategy is not to single out individual poets to the exclusion of others but rather to use excerpts from individual poems to illustrate various aspects of work and working-class poetry, and provide evidence of the energy and momentum that has kicked this poetry into another gear in the last twenty-five years.

Work poetry is written about a job, regardless of whether that job is blue collar, white collar, whatever. Working-class poetry, on the other hand, does not necessarily have to be *about* work—a lot of it deals with the effects of being working class on family life, relationships, and so forth, outside of the workplace. All work poetry is not working-class poetry, and vice versa, though the lines between them are blurred. I prefer to keep them blurred; it's no coincidence that a lot of working-class poetry is also work poetry. Any writing that engages in examining what we do for a living in a serious way is a valuable addition to our literature, and any hairsplitting over what's working-class and what's work poetry is counterproductive to the larger political impact of legitimizing work as a subject for serious examination in our poetry. This essay is about both because the impulse driving work poetry—to look at work from the insider's point of view—is similar to the impulse driving working-class poetry: to lift the veil, the curtain behind which our culture has often placed work and the lives of workers.

In the past, poetry was often seen as a pastime of the leisure class, and indeed a great deal of contemporary poetry still seems more concerned with leisure time activities and an emphasis on language at the expense of content and clarity. Work and working-class poetry is *about* something, and that necessarily makes it more connected to many other academic fields—history, sociology, economics, and so forth. And, certainly, issues of race and gender are important in any discussion of work and working-class poetry. As part of the larger field of working-class literature, this poetry is contributing to a more public discourse on the subjects of work and the working class.

Of course, most poets write about other subjects besides work. A work poem doesn't have to be written by someone currently doing that job in order to be "authentic," in order to be a good poem. We cannot create the authority for poems from outside the page. Poems have to reach out to an audience through the richness of detail and attention to poetic technique, regardless of an individual's work background, though the detailed imagery in the best work and working-class poetry is more often remembered than imagined, and in recent years more poetry has emerged directly from insiders, those who have done or are doing the work they're writing about.

The danger exists of putting poets into categories as a way of dismissing them.

Some poets embrace the designation "working-class" poet, while others reject that label. Here, I am going to look at poets who have written about work and class to varying degrees; it's up to them what they call themselves. What is clear is that there are more of them—of us—than ever before, and that work and working-class poetry is having a major impact on our literature.

A clear sense of a developing movement began in the early 1980s and has now established itself to such an extent that the hole in our literature is very slowly being filled. Why the relative boom in working-class poetry? The poet, anthologist, and essayist Tom Wayman explains it this way in his book *Inside Job: Essays on the New Work Writing:* "The increased access to post-secondary education since World War II, plus the growing awareness of some professionals that their work world shares aspects in common with many other types of employees, has resulted in the emergence of writers able to depict actual daily work in our society and the effects this work has on the range of human activities and attitudes on and off the job."[2]

Although this poetry has nudged its way into many mainstream publications and has achieved broader recognition in the poetry community, it continues to be excluded from many discussions of contemporary poetry in academic circles and publications. Rather than belabor these critical discussions, I prefer to acknowledge and celebrate the large body of work that has appeared in the last twenty-five years. I have broken the work down into three categories: publishers and anthologies, books by individual poets, and journals and special issues. Although this essay is organized around resources for finding this poetry, within and across the sections, I have tried to identify major themes and common threads found in work and working-class poetry.

Publishers, Anthologies, and Journals

One common element among work and working-class collections is that they tend to be published in small presses, and thus they do not often get widespread national distribution. As a result, anthologies have made a major contribution to the awareness and study of work and working-class poetry, gathering work from small-press publications and giving it more exposure and keeping it in print longer. Some of the heroes of this movement are anthologists such as Tom Wayman, Peter Oresick and Nicholas Coles, and Janet Zandy, who have collected and preserved the work of many small-press poets. Their anthologies are more likely to be used in working-class literature courses than are individual volumes, and certainly they have a longer shelf life than any journal.

A passion for the writing is most clearly seen in small presses, which are often run by one dedicated individual. Other heroes of work and working-class poetry are such editors and publishers of small presses as Larry Smith (Bottom Dog

Press), John Crawford (West End Press), M. L. Liebler (Ridgeway Press), Howard White (Harbour Publishing), and others who continue to find and publish the poetry of work and working-class poets. While Smith, through his own stories, poems, and memoirs, and Liebler, through his poems and music with the Magic Poetry Band, make significant contributions through their own creative work, their commitment to publishing the writing of work poets has had a major impact on the literature.

Certain publishers such as Bottom Dog Press and West End Press have specialized in publishing work and working-class themed collections and anthologies. For example, in its Working Lives series, Bottom Dog has published collections by working-class poets, including Jeanne Bryner's *Blind Horse* (1999) and Naton Leslie's *Moving to Find Work* (2000), along with anthologies and critical books about working-class writing. Singlejack Books, in San Pedro, California, published the Singlejack Little Books of working-class poetry with the explanation, "The shape and size of Singlejack Little Books is determined by the ease with which they fit into work shirt, blouse, apron or pants, and skirt pockets or purses."[3] In other words, they were designed to be read by workers.

The pioneering work of Canadian poet Tom Wayman influenced many American working-class poets who went on to produce their own anthologies. Wayman's third anthology, *Going for Coffee: Poetry on the Job,* was published in 1981 and reprinted with a new introduction in 1987, testimonial to its popularity and its place as a seminal text in what Wayman calls the "new work writing." He writes, "Overall, the new work writing is characterized by attention to detail only an insider could know, by the presentation of anecdotal narratives rather than lyrical effusions, and by a considerable use of humour."[4]

While Wayman had edited earlier anthologies of mostly Canadian poets, *Going for Coffee* included more poets from the United States, an indication that work and working-class poets across North America were beginning to find one another. For example, Wayman included poets who appeared in Robert Carson's *The Waterfront Writers: The Literature of Work* (Harper and Row, 1979), which came out of the Waterfront Writers and Artists, a group of San Francisco longshoremen.

Peter Oresick and Nicholas Coles recognized that no comparable anthology to *Going for Coffee* had been published in the United States, and they edited *Working Classics: Poems on Industrial Life* (University of Illinois Press, 1990). Wayman is quoted in their introduction, and his poems are also included in the book. The central distinction between *Working Classics* and *Going for Coffee* is that *Working Classics* focused on the working class in and out of the workplace, while *Going for Coffee* focused on work, regardless of class. *Working Classics* is a valuable resource for readers searching for poems about, for example, the home and family lives of working-class people.

Working Classics was a landmark anthology for working-class poetry in this country; until its publication, no other collection had brought together most of the central voices of working-class poetry and received such widespread distribution. It is clearly a poetry best-seller, selling approximately 8,000 copies to date—a phenomenal number considering the average print run for any book of poetry is 1,000 or 1,500. While Wayman's anthologies had wide distribution in Canada, it was often by word of mouth that poets in the United States became aware of his important collections of work poems.

The two most recent anthologies by Wayman (*Paperwork,* 1991) and Oresick and Coles (*For a Living,* 1995) reflect the economic shift from blue-collar jobs to service jobs for many members of the working class. *Paperwork* contains a section on service work, and *For a Living* focuses on nonindustrial work—"white collar, pink collar, domestic, clerical, technical, managerial, or professional."[5] As Coles and Oresick write in their introduction, "Most of the poems here were written in the 1980s and 1990s and represent predominant forms of work in the 'postindustrial' era."[6] Fifteen poets appear in both Oresick and Coles anthologies, evidence perhaps that not only are a number of poets concerned with writing about work, regardless of what type of work, but that many poets have either crossed class boundaries or shifted into service jobs in their working lives.

Some anthologies, like *The Waterfront Writers,* were generated by a small community of workers and celebrate the sense of community created through the shared interest in writing about their work. Other similar collections include *Shop Talk: An Anthology of Poetry from the Vancouver Industrial Writers Union* (Zoe Landale, editor, Pulp Press, 1985) and *Something to Say,* a collection from the Boston Worker Writers (West End Press, 1979). *Between the Heartbeats: Poetry and Prose by Nurses* (edited by Cortney Davis and Judy Schaefer, University of Iowa Press, 1995) is perhaps the most successful of these anthologies, selling over eight thousand copies and prompting a sequel, *Intensive Care: More Poetry and Prose by Nurses* (Iowa, 2003). *Nursing Times* wrote, "Quite simply wonderful. . . . Beg, steal, or borrow this book; if that fails, buy it."[7] This quote reflects the sense of excitement writing about work can generate and that there is an audience eager for literature about what we do every day. It legitimizes us to see our daily work written about, whether we are nurses, doctors, coal miners, or factory workers.

Another thematic anthology, *Coalseam: Poems from the Anthracite Region* (1996), includes the work of fourteen poets who write about coal mining. In the introduction, editor Karen Blomain says that some of the basic impulses of working-class poets are to "celebrate, condemn, and ultimately comprehend as they write. . . . It is not just the hard mining life that these pages honor. They are, in large measure, given over to the ordinariness of life, the beautiful common moments which, although they might have happened anywhere, happened there, at that particular moment, to that particular person."[8] To celebrate, condemn, and comprehend: these three Cs characterize a great deal of work and working-class poetry.

In "The Bootleg Coal Hole," from *Coalseam,* Harry Humes writes about bringing his father's lunch to the mine where he worked:

> They'd sit in the shade with their sandwiches,
> the bread smudged with dirt from hands and faces,
> while my father, good with dynamite,
> would crank a handle, and the ground would shake
> with the afternoon's work blown loose
> from the face of the vein.[9]

Humes brings the authority of witnessing to bear on his father's work in the coal
mines. Although Wayman makes a distinction between insider and outsider writing, the lines blur as to who exactly is an outsider, for the effects of labor rever-
berate throughout the lives of the workers and their circles of friends and family.
Anyone, participant or observer, who pays attention to work, to workers and their
lives, makes an important contribution to the literature of work and the working
class.

Labor Pains: Poetry from South East Michigan Workers (1991), another thematic collection, focusing primarily on auto work, is noteworthy for being edited
by Leon Chamberlain, an insider, an auto worker who spent over thirty years
working in factories before retiring, and for containing poems by Ben Hamper,
better known as the author of *Rivethead,* the memoir of working on the line at
General Motors in Flint, Michigan. This short poem from Hamper shows the
humor Wayman mentions as a characteristic of many work poems when he describes a fellow employee high on acid. Humor is often used as a release, as a
coping device, as a way to break the monotony of the work:

> didn't show up on pay day
> missed the softball showdown
> & we're assuming the worst[10]

Humor with a kick to it—the implications of a worker missing payday, no laugh-
ing matter. The humor in *Labor Pains* (and other anthologies) is often satiric, as
in Michael Stenberg's "Dances with Welders," a spoof on the film *Dances with
Wolves,* or scatological, as in Chamberlain's "A Poem Dedicated to a Real Ass-
hole."

While many poems about work focus on the dehumanizing aspects of the job
and the cruelty of the bosses, a sense of pride also emerges, not only in the content of the poems but in their rhythm and linguistic energy. In Lolita Hernandez's
"diamonds on the pads of my hands," she writes with a tough, celebratory pride
in her assembly-line job, and ironically contrasts the music of pop culture—Paul
Simon's "Diamonds on the Soles of Her Shoes"—with the hard reality of her job:

i got diamonds too . . .
on the pads of my callused hands[11]

Poems like this show defiance in the face of a "we" who either treat the workers dismissively or ignore them, reflecting in part a popular culture that often renders the working class invisible or caricatured. In Hernandez's case, she also deals with gender issues, the strength of a woman in a male-dominated profession.

Two collections, *If I Had a Hammer: Women's Work in Poetry, Fiction, and Photographs* (Papier-Mache Press, Sandra Martz, editor, 1990), and *Calling Home: Working-Class Women's Writings* (1990), focus on the perspectives of working women. Both contain a great deal of fine work poetry by women, including Sue Doro, Susan Eisenberg, Kate Braid, Meridel Le Sueur, and many others. One need only note that *The Waterfront Writers* contains no women writers to begin to see the value in these collections focusing exclusively on women.

The impulse behind many of these anthologies and individual collections of poems is to make visible the work and working-class lives that have often previously been invisible. In "Down on the Strike Line with My Children," from *Calling Home*, Donna Langston writes: "I'm down on the strike line with my children and we are not invisible to each other, to those who won't cross our lines, or to those who pass us by."[12]

The moments on strike, off the job, or out of a job resonate powerfully in the struggle to create an individual life. In Rina Ferrarelli's "I'm Standing in Line," she writes about standing in a line for unemployment compensation:

. . . the clerk
who stands at the window hour after hour
or works at a desk squeezed between desks
in a mustard-colored room
. . . .
. . . makes it feel like a handout.[13]

Another type of anthology presents the best writing from specific work or working-class journals. For example, *Overtime: Punchin' Out with The Mill Hunk Herald* (1990) contains the best work published in the *Mill Hunk Herald* magazine, a "classic grassroots worker rag," in the words of founder Larry Evans, which published twenty issues from 1979 to 1989 as "sometimes a quarterly, sometimes bi-annual, sometimes never mind."[14] The *Mill Hunk Herald* began as a Pittsburgh area steelworkers' rag and ended up as a national working-class journal, clearly making the leap from the local to a broader contributor base and readership. Readers and writers found *Mill Hunk* because they were looking for a grassroots publication accessible to workers, and it was successful in large part because it operated outside the traditional world of literature. The *Mill Hunk* published many pieces by "unknown" writers as well as more established working-class poets such as Sue Doro, Savina Roxas, Georgeann Rettberg, and Mike Basinski. The *Mill Hunk* was journalistic in its approach, and, like the articles, the poems clearly had a narrative slant to them, and an explicit political edge, as in Mike Basinski's "Priorities":

> They were going to install the safety device
> . . . .
> there was a work order in maintenance
> but there were priorities
> the faster assembly line had to be installed[15]

While the *Mill Hunk Herald* was documenting the decline of the steel industry in the East, on the West Coast the journal *Processed World* was documenting "the Underside of the Information Age—in words and scathing graphic humor, as told by those who live it." *Processed World* also published a "best of," *Bad Attitude: The Processed World Anthology* (1990). The poems sprinkled among the essays and cartoons frequently had the sting and bite of the *Mill Hunk Herald*'s poems, and featured the voice of the insider, as in Ron De La Houssaye's "Corporatania," in which he details his sense of isolation and lack of control over his work in a way very similar to that expressed by many blue-collar poets:

> I do not know how long I've lived inside Corporatania.
> It is impossible to know because we have no way
> to measure time. Personaltime tracking is considered
> unsocial activity—calendars not publiprinted now.
> . . . .
> Second daily workblock now begins: I sit,
> the terminal watches me key-in my ID.
> Quickly, it notes how long I've been away
> —"OVEREXTENDED RESTPERIOD . . . WILL REPORT"—[16]

Besides the anthologies, a few textbooks focusing at least in part on literature about work have been published in recent years. *The Art of Work: An Anthology of Workplace Literature* (Christine LaRocco, Jim Coughlin, editors, 1996) and *The Art of Life: An Anthology of Literature about Life and Work* (LaRocco, editor, 1998) are companion volumes published by South-Western Educational Publishing. Both texts include extensive teacher support materials and are designed for use in technical and School-to-Work curriculums and for English and communication courses with a workplace focus. These books include poems by Tom Wayman, James Scully, Patricia Dobler, Rina Ferrarelli, and David Budbill. *More Than a Job: Readings on Work and Society* (John Gordon, editor, New Readers Press, 1991), and, most recently, Paul Lauter and Ann Fitzgerald's book, *Literature, Class, and Culture* (Addison, Wesley, Longman, 2001), include many working-class poems as part of their examination of class in our society. These texts suggest the emergence of work as a focal point for courses in schools across the country.

In addition to collecting work and working-class poems in anthologies and textbooks, some editors and publishers have also reprinted out-of-print collections by individual poets to help keep the literature alive. For example, Chris Llewellyn's *Fragments from the Fire,* which won the Walt Whitman Award, was originally published by Penguin Books in 1987 (one exception to the small-press publications), but Penguin let it go out of print. In 1993, Bottom Dog Press came to the rescue and reprinted the book along with a new collection of Llewellyn's poems, *Steam Dummy.* When Midwest Villages and Voices published Sue Doro's *Heart, Home, & Hard Hats* in 1986, it reprinted many poems from *Of Birds and Factories,* her first collection published by People's Books and Crafts in 1983, both with Meridel Le Sueur's preface. Peter Oresick's *The Story of Glass,* originally a chapbook, was reprinted in *Definitions* (West End Press, 1990). Clearly, writers and publishers are committed to not only publishing working-class poetry but to keeping valuable working-class poetry in print.

In addition to the anthologies and textbooks, a number of literary journals have sprung up in recent years with a focus on work or working-class issues. Like the *Mill Hunk Herald,* David Josephs and Carol Tarlen's *Working Classics,* Fred Whitehead's *Quindaro, The Unrealist, Praxis,* and *Sez,* all have published quite a bit of working-class poetry. As with all small-press ventures, a journal's continued existence is tenuous at best. Although universities offer sustaining support to many literary journals, magazines that specialize in working-class issues often have to go it alone and, as a result, tend to have short lives. *The Minnesota Review,* a Marxist literary journal, and *The Progressive* continue to publish poetry that focuses on work and the working class. The *Blue Collar Review* ("a journal of progressive working class literature," editor Al Markowitz, co-editor Mary Franke) is a recent journal that has emerged to cover work and class issues. In the introduction to the winter 2001–2002 issue, the editors state, "Words are dammed up. Especially worker's words; the People who live under systems like insects live under giant tree roots. The dirt is breaking loose. The words are more than any of us can count. They must flood. They must pour. About what we really do and experience all night or all day."[17] In addition, they quote Meridel Le Sueur on the journal's cover: "The artist's duty now is to recreate a new image of the world, to return to the people their need and vision."[18] While some publications cease to exist because of a lack of resources or energy, others, such as the *Blue Collar Review,* continue to rise up to take their place.

A number of more general literary journals have devoted special thematic issues to work in an acknowledgment of its central place in our lives. Examples include *event* (with an editorial by Tom Wayman, 1982), *Pig Iron* ("Labor & the Post-Industrial Age," 1990), *Seattle Review* (1994), *Witness* (1996), and *North*

American Review (2001). The editor of *event,* Leona Gom, begins her introduction with this simple acknowledgment: "This issue of *event* deals with work, with what all but the most privileged of us do in order to survive."[19] What could be more simple, on the one hand, yet more revolutionary, on the other? The facts of our working lives are a given; it's the place of work in our literature that's been at issue.

In the *North American Review*'s special issue on "Working" (September–October 2001), the introduction states: "Since the GI Bill and accompanying opportunities afforded through higher education, America moved progressively from a blue to a white collar economy. Our contributors write about older blue collar concerns, and how they remain with us today. All of these writers honor the dignity of labor without glossing over the physical rigors of work. They do so without sentimentalizing their subject, or being condescending toward their characters."[20] Without sentimentalizing, without condescending—two other important traits of our finest work and working-class poetry.

Each of these special issues takes a slightly different slant and focus on work (*Pig Iron,* for example, focuses on the postindustrial age) but each, in its own way, has recognized and valued the poets' take on our daily work. Bob Hicok, in "What We Say," published in *Witness*'s "Working In America" issue, acknowledges a central impulse behind a great deal of work writing:

> Another poem about the things we build
> that glow and disappear, and the words
> we repeat, owning at least what we say.[21]

We own the words. They are our tools.

Books by Individual Poets

Although many poets have written an occasional poem about work, a number of collections stand out for their immersion in a particular workplace. The entire focus and concept of these books puts readers in the workplace. The cumulative effect of the poems makes these individual volumes some of the most effective and powerful examples of work and working-class poetry.

Herbert Scott's influential book of work poems, *Groceries* (1976), was one of the first volumes by an individual poet to consist entirely of poems about a work environment. Scott laid the groundwork for other poets to follow. He plunged his readers into the world of the grocery store, as opposed to touching on it in an occasional poem. The book sends the message many work and working-class poets want to send: that there's poetry in these workplaces, that the workers have lives the world needs to pay attention to, that work affects every aspect of our lives, even our dreams—*especially* our dreams. Scott spent eleven years working in the grocery business, and he clearly knows his subject matter. Through the creation of personae such as "Boss," "Butcher," and "Clerk," Scott not only captures the workplace environment but the people—the other workers—and gives them voice. As the "Boss" says,

> You want an education
> you come to the right place.
> We all got to eat.[22]

In 1988, Signpost Press published *Dream of Long Headdresses: Poems from a Thousand Hospitals* by Richard Martin. This little-known collection, based on Martin's experiences as a hospital orderly, does for hospital work what Scott does for supermarkets. Like Scott, he covers the landscape of the hospital and its various personnel, from nurses to cleaning women, from emergency rooms to cancer rooms. Through the compilation of rich, vivid detail, Martin puts us in the rooms of the sick, as in this cancer poem, "Room 212," where he describes a woman dealing with radiation treatments:

> A smile and auburn hair
> are listed as casualties.[23]

Cortney Davis (coeditor of *Between the Heartbeats*) makes nursing the focus of her own book of poems, *Details of Flesh*. Like Martin, she forces us to see patients not from the perspective of hospital visitors but through the eyes of someone who treats the patients every day. In her touching poem, "What the Nurse Likes," Davis details her observations of patients:

> I like the way men become shy.
> Even angry men bow their heads
> when they are naked.[24]

On the blue-collar side, a landmark was City Lights Books' 1980 publication of Antler's long poem, *Factory,* which focused on his work at the Continental Can Company. In this epic poem, Antler evokes the spirit of Whitman and Ginsberg while ranting and encanting for sixty-four wild pages:

> Hum-drum! Hum-drum! Hum-drum!
> I should be paid for discovering America
>   is committing suicide with factories!
> I should be paid for wondering if I'm only a defect
>   in the mass-production of zombies![25]

Unlike Scott, Antler puts his own persona at the center of this collection—"I should be paid for writing *The Infinite Autobiography of This Spot Through Eter-*

nity!"[26] He makes explicit political statements throughout the poem, indicting America and the factory for creating dehumanizing work environments. What saves the poem from becoming a simple political polemic is that Antler always circles back to the cans:

> the way the lids pour out like suicide battalions,
> the way I pretend to check for defects every so often,
> the way I shove enough in a bag like this,
> the way I fold over the top and tape it like this,
> the way the rows of 'em rise on the skid like this—[27]

Antler and other poets capture the driving, repetitious nature of the work through the use of rhythm and repetition. Peter Oresick's "The Story of Glass," from *Definitions,* takes its readers through the production of glass, from beginning to end, the rhythmic intensity of the lines pulling us through the process:

> From the holes of the earth, from
> truck, from silo, from cullet,
> from scale, batch, take, heat-wind; from
>
> heat, from ribbon, from flow, roll
> roll, from lehr, they feed the line.[28]

Christian Thomas's *Môly & Manganese* is also driven by the sounds and rhythms of factory work—particularly in his long poem, "Sprawl," as heard in these lines:

> The clatter
> of sandblasted grit
> ricocheting through
>   wheelabrator housing. . . .[29]

Yet another factory volume, Michael Casey's *Millrat,* set in a textile mill dye house, is, like Herbert Scott's *Groceries,* more concerned with creating characters and voices within the workplace, and contains poems with titles such as "the company pool," "coffee truck," "foreman," and "forklift driver," that help create a sense of the work environment. Casey's work is characterized by wry humor and understatement. "The company pool" is a long, convoluted explanation of how the company pool works:

> ya pay a dollar an a quarter ya givit ta me
> . . . .
> the dollar goes inta the home run pool

and ya don't haf ta pay the quarter
unless ya want ta
we use the Record
and we check out the runs column
on the sports page
not that this paper's always right
in fact it usually ain't right. . . . [30]

Like Casey's, the more successful individual volumes often use persona poems to help humanize the work environment and play off the physical descriptions of the work. Hearing the voices of other workers helps convey the human interplay so vital to survival in the working world. The stories we tell on the job, the oral histories and work legends, supply the raw material for many work poems, and while they often have an anecdotal quality to them, they are more than anecdote. Beneath the casual language is the depth of emotion we expect from any good poem.

In her brief foreword to Susan Eisenberg's *It's a Good Thing I'm Not Macho,* Denise Levertov mentions one of the tensions between work poetry as a kind of documentation and history and poetry as literature: "The 'ideas' in this book are firmly embedded in the 'things'; it *can* be read simply as a document that recounts what it was like to be one of the first women in America to work in building construction. But in addition one can find here the symbolic resonances that bring one back to reread a work of literature many times, long after the simple informational level has been received and stored in the mind."[31]

Certainly, a number of work and working-class poets do see *part* of their role as documentation, particularly in relation to the decline and disappearance of factories and steel mills in places such as Pittsburgh—once known as the Steel City—that now have no mills left. Peter Blair evokes this sense of loss even in the title of his Washington Prize–winning book, *Last Heat.* Many of the poems have an elegiac tone to them, not romanticizing the mills but *remembering,* and through remembering, documenting an important part of our culture so that it won't be erased or glossed over. Blair's title poem takes on this documentary tone:

. . . Drawing a long iron spoon
from the furnace notch, he pours out ten puddles
of liquid light into the dust. The steel curdles
and cools into slate-gray pucks, souvenirs
for the few old-timers who've gathered
with cameras.[32]

Like the old-timers, Blair is capturing the moment, but with words, not a camera. Nick Muska's *ELM* (Toledo Poets Center Press, 1979) takes this documentary impulse one step further by including photographs of a number of his fellow workers at Elm Storage Company, an industrial warehouse, along with the poems in which they appear.

Jeanne Bryner, an emergency room nurse, grew up in a mill town in a mill worker's family and also takes a documentary approach in many of her poems. In "How to Say It," from her collection *Blind Horse,* she documents the disappearance of the steel mill from her perspective outside the mill by focusing on the effects on the community:

> Wasn't this the center of your valley,
> the loading docks, blast furnace, smokestacks
> five times higher than your grandfather's barn?
> Wasn't this world filled with salty men
>
> like your father, buttoned in greasy coveralls,
> laced in scorched boots?[33]

Both the act of witnessing and the act of participating are important elements of contemporary work and working-class poetry. Often, the act of participating—the insider's perspective—results in lifting the veil, seeing the men and women behind the curtain working to produce every single thing we purchase. In "What the Slogan Means," from his *Right Livelihood,* David Brooks looks beneath the slogan "Beef, real food for real people" to list and identify the real people who work to package the meat, then concludes:

> . . . When someone
> says "Beef, real food for real people," I think,
> you really don't know, you really haven't
> the faintest idea.[34]

Martin Glaberman's *The Grievance: Poems from the Shop Floor,* a classic example of Singlejack Books' little books, also deals with the danger of the work. The book is laced with dark humor and wit, as in this excerpt from "Ecology" in which he responds to a fellow worker losing a finger by telling another worker not to leave it on the floor:

> . . . it could make the relief man
> uneasy
> being pointed at[35]

Many working-class poets have written about the mills and factories as a malevolent part of the American urban landscape. Particularly in cities dominated by one large industry, the workplace takes on a personality and force of its own, as in Afaa Michael Weaver's "Bethlehem":

> The mills are a gray city
> that erupted and rose from the Earth
> like varicose veins, pores puffing
> smoke into the thickened sky.[36]

Weaver's description of the mill is similar to Philip Levine's factory descriptions in "Detroit Grease Shop Poem" and other poems. Levine, a Pulitzer Prize–winning poet, is probably the best-known poet for examining his work and working-class background in much detail. Although Levine has always written about other subjects, he is often identified with work and the working-class because some of his most powerful poems have come out his early work experiences in Detroit. He speaks to the universality of work in the following lines from "What Work Is":

> We stand in the rain in a long line
> waiting at Ford Highland Park. For work.
> You know what work is—if you're
> old enough to read this you know. . . . [37]

In Tom Wayman's "What the Writing Students of Detroit State Think of Philip Levine," he discusses the irony of teaching Levine's poems to auto workers:

> Here where the entire university
> turns around the car plants: 40,000 students
> and almost all are employed,
> so there are morning classes
> for those just off nightshift, nodding asleep
> in the back rows, and for the others
> going on to work. . . . [38]

Wayman details not only the difficulty of teaching those who are working *in* the jobs Levine writes about, but also the difficulty of reaching a reading audience with poetry about work, hard work that keeps workers too busy to find time to read, even when it's poetry about both the place they live and the work they're doing.

Like Wayman's students, many work and working-class poets struggle to find time to discuss important work-related issues that affect their lives at home. Because of the strain of work and the dependence on the work to support the workers and their families, sometimes political issues were simply not discussed. Poetry, however, provides a space for aspects of work life that can be difficult to discuss, such as racism and sexism. For example, Aurora Harris explores workplace racism in her poem, "Dream 1:10–1:25 a.m., August 22, 1997":

Words between men

became rancid in stomach
when the color of his skin
was more convincing than your color
to get contracts for the firm
when Southfield was a field.

Words between men

a sour truth
of being black
in the fifties
with "white" partner.
. . . .
Whatever happened to *dream,*
Daddy? Is it out there?[39]

Discrimination and deceit also appear in Gary Soto's darkly humorous poem, "Mexicans Begin Jogging," where the boss's assumption that Soto must be an illegal immigrant forces Soto to needlessly run away when the Border Patrol arrives:

At the factory I worked
In the fleck of rubber, under the press
Of an oven yellow with flame,
Until the border patrol opened
Their vans and my boss waved for us to run.
"Over the fences, Soto," he shouted.
And I shouted that I was American.
"No time for lies," he said, and pressed
A dollar in my palm, hurrying me
Through the back door.[40]

Patricia Dobler, in "Steelmark Day Parade, 1961," from *Talking to Strangers,* acknowledges the inherent racism beneath the celebratory surface of the parade by noting the absence of blacks among the workers:

This steelmark is heraldic, new,
a steel-blue brand honoring the men
who make steel. Everyone loves it.

"But really, where *are* the Negroes?"
he asks again. Not here, not yet,
they don't exist in 1961 . . .
. . . forbidden

> to make steel or wear the steelmark
> branded on the hardhats of the town's blond men.[41]

In Dobler's poem, it is clear that the idea of "solidarity" did not extend beyond color lines.

Or gender lines. In *It's a Good Thing I'm Not Macho* (Whetstone Press, 1984), subtitled *a cycle of poems,* Susan Eisenberg divides the book into three sections: as a woman, as a mechanic, and as a woman mechanic. These divisions clearly set up tensions in the book that reflect the experiences of many women in traditionally male-dominated workplaces (Eisenberg was one of the first female apprentices in the International Brotherhood of Electrical Workers in Boston). Kate Braid, a journeywoman carpenter, also writes of being a woman in a profession dominated by men in her book *Covering Rough Ground.* Her sections, "The Birth of Buildings," "Sister in the Brotherhood," "Where She Wants to Be," and "Woman Who Knows Wood," like Eisenberg's, organize aspects of the work environment in relation to her as a person, as a woman.

To celebrate, condemn, and comprehend. Certainly, the poetry of women working in male-dominated fields involves those three things. In "Past the Finish Line," Eisenberg celebrates finishing her apprenticeship with the other women in her group:

> Where a 100-year curse had vowed
> 'no woman shall pass here'
> we passed:
> all five
>   as one.[42]

Eisenberg and Braid cover similar territory in terms of language, of comprehension—not only of the language of the job but the language of men. In "Sister in the United Brotherhood of Carpenters & Joiners of America," Braid writes:

> The men own the words
> so far.
> I learn this language
> cold, hide
> behind concrete
> learn to love
> that it is soft
> and hard at once.[43]

Like Braid, most workers, regardless of gender, have to deal with the specific vocabularies of the workplace, the encoded language and definitions that create communities. One challenge for work poets is not to sacrifice clarity by using too much work-specific vocabulary without contextualizing it for readers. In the following excerpt from Eisenberg, she lets us in on the importance of the job-specific language on her all-male worksite:

> we find, almost easily, the language
> that is common:
>   *—Get me some 4-inch squares*
>   *with three-quarter k-o's*
>   *—Need any couplings or connectors?*
>   *—No, but grab some clips and c-clamps*
>   *and some half-inch quarter-twenties.*
> Passwords.
>   *—You know what you're doing in a panel?*
>   *—Sure.*
>
> Mechanic to mechanic.[44]

In addition to being in tune with the language of the workplace, one must also be in tune with the tools themselves. Braid's sequence of poems personifying her tools, "Tool: Instrument for Getting a Grip on the World," is an excellent examination of the link between worker and tool, for workers are often alone with their tools or their machines while on the job:

> Saw is the sensitive one
> unforgiving, impatient with her own
> power so be careful.
>
> Always a talker, she chants or whines
> depending on how
> you treat her.[45]

When it comes to condemning, no other subject has prompted as much poetic outrage as the Triangle Shirtwaist Company Fire of March 25, 1911. At least three poets—Chris Llewellyn (*Fragments from the Fire*), Mary Fell ("The Triangle Fire"), and Ruth Diagon (*Payday at the Triangle*)—have written long poems or series of poems about the fire in which 146 workers, mostly women, died, many jumping from windows to their deaths because, quoting Llewellyn, "the bosses had kept the doors locked to keep out union organizers."[46] Why have three poets in a span of seventeen years felt compelled to write poetry about this great tragedy of American labor history? Partly, it's an urgent sense that we should not forget or gloss over the past, and partly it may be because sweatshops continue to exist seventy-five years later, and women continue to be underpaid and exploited in the workplace. These documentary poems are political acts of salvage and recovery in hopes that the past may not be repeated. The poems link the past and present, particularly in Llewellyn's book. In "Triangle Site: Asch Building, 1911; Brown Building, 1981," she returns us to the site of the tragedy from the perspective of the present. The task of any poet dealing with historical material is to humanize the historical figures, and each of these three poets attempts to do this. Llewellyn writes of this difficulty in "Sear":

> . . . To write about them
> yet not interfere, although I'm told
> a poet's task is to create a little world.[47]

Both Llewellyn and Diagon take on the voice of Lena Goldman, who ran a cafe near the factory.

> Garment workers from Triangle always came to my cafe.
> Each Saturday the boys and girls in groups, arm in arm
> and laughing. You'd think after fourteen hours packing
> and sewing they'd be ready to drop! But not on payday. (Llewellyn)[48]
>
> mrs. lena goldman sweeps her restaurant sidewalk
> it's closing time the girls are coming my customers
> . . . .
> girls in summer dresses speeding down heights of 80
> feet 62 thud dead girls at windows framed in flames.
> (Diagon)[49]

Each poet brings to bear her imaginative energy to put us in the place of the observer to the tragedy so that we can be as horrified as Lena Goldman.

To celebrate, comprehend, and condemn? Some work and working-class poets barely find time to breathe, like performance poet Sean Thomas Dougherty in "Labor Day," from his book *The Body's Precarious Balance*:

> A morning without work is a morning to breathe, to watch the rain clear and walk
> inside the passing voice of strangers, a dog barking, students with their bouncing
> knapsacks of books, baseball hats worn backwards, as I walk headed toward
> nowhere important, which is, of course, the most important place of all—[50]

Few poets continue to hold down working-class jobs and write poems, simply because they don't have the time to write about their work lives, busy as they are with the daily struggle to survive—the hours at work eat up a large portion of their days, and the hard work sucks away the energy necessary to write after work. Joseph Millar, author of *Overtime,* spent twenty-five years "working at a variety of jobs, from telephone repairman to commercial fisherman. . . . In 1997, he gave up his job as a telephone installation foreman . . . and teaches at Mount Hood Community College."[51] I don't think it's a coincidence that he published his first book only after taking a teaching job, an occupation that often gives poets more time and support for their writing.

On the back cover of Fred Voss's *Goodstone Aircraft Company,* the poet Gerald Locklin writes, "There are an awful lot of educated poets around, and quite a few talented ones, and an occasional poet from the working class, but there are very few talented educated poets who are still members of the working class, and of these few, Fred Voss, aerospace machinist, is one of the finest."[52] Poets like Leon Chamberlain, steelworker Timothy Russell, and butcher shop worker Arlitia Jones are more the exception than the rule. Both the emotional and physical aspects of the work take their toll, as in the following excerpt from Voss's poem, "Asleep" in which, after a long litany of the hard work they do in the aircraft factory, he comes to this despairing conclusion:

> and yet we believe that we are powerless
> as we sit in bars
> and watch the President on television.[53]

This feeling of defeat and powerlessness is a common sentiment in many work poems. Even in Hollywood. The actor Harry E. Northup, who has appeared in thirty-six films (including *Blue Collar*), has written a great deal about the acting profession. In his book *Reunions* he voices numerous complaints familiar to those in the working class—here, age discrimination and loss of benefits:

> the complaint is i am old
> no one hires me
> 25 years making a living
> no work this year[54]

> i made a modest living as an actor
> for 25 years
> last year i did not work as an actor
> this year i pay for medical and dental
> insurance[55]

This sense of powerlessness to control or have any influence over our working lives enters into all fields of work and is reflected in much work and working-class poetry. Workers are often rendered invisible in our culture, and the strain of working for someone else, and the mind-numbing routines of many blue-collar jobs in particular, create a sense of isolation that is difficult to overcome. In Millar's "Telephone Repairman," he writes of the particular isolation of that occupation, but he is also exploring the larger tension that exists in all workplaces—the isolation of the labor, as opposed to the impulse to connect to others:

> We live so much of our lives
> without telling anyone,
> going out before dawn,
> working all day by ourselves,
> shaking our heads in silence
> at the news on the radio.[56]

"We live so much of our lives / without telling anyone." Most work and working-class poets are driven to write by the narrative, storytelling impulse—to *tell* someone our lives in our poems. To tell people where we're from. To write from a place, a place where things happen, to record the stories that aren't being recorded anywhere else. Karen Blomain writes in the *Coalseam* introduction, "In the act of compiling this anthology, I realized once again the value of writing from place."[57]

But where does one find the time to write about place, to think about one's life, when, as we see in Dougherty's poem, even doing nothing becomes a luxury? Thinking about life—this is the lyric impulse. The lyric poem suggests a more leisurely examination of our lives and the world, the luxury of contemplation that many work and working-class poets struggle to obtain. One of the few working-class poets to focus on the lyric, Timothy Russell, a retired steelworker from Weirton Steel in West Virginia, often finds startling revelations in juxtapositions between the mill and the natural world. In "In Re," the sonnet that opens his Terrence Des Pres Prize–winning volume *Adversaria*, Russell describes the beauty of the world outside the mill, contrasting it with the attitude on the inside:

> White petals of the black locust flutter
> less like snow or ash than live confetti
> . . . .
> . . . And all we do is mutter[58]

Yet even in Russell's more poetic lyric, he echoes the complaint of Dougherty and others—the sense of being cut off from the world outside of work where other things are happening. The seasonal transitions are muted by the constants of the working world.

Like Russell, Arlitia Jones, who works full time in her father's butcher shop in Alaska, continues to try to balance her work and writing lives. Jones, who won the Dorothy Brunsman Poetry Prize for her first book, *The Bandsaw Riots* (Bear Star Press, 2001), uses humor in her workplace poems to capture the insider's look at customers, machinery, and, of course, meat. In "Shit Job," she performs anagram riffs on the AMPUTATION DANGER sign that she reads "a thousand times every day":

> GREAT DAMNATION!
> DANG! A PERMUTATION
> TAMPON AND GUITAR or
> PURE MAN ATTAIN GOD

Humor with an edge to it. Humor used as a survival technique:

> Anything to keep from hearing
> when he leans into your ear
> to remind you: I'd get
> a monkey to do your job,
> if I could just keep it
> from shittin' on the floor.[59]

A safety poster at the Ford plant I worked in read "Daydreams Can Cause Nightmares," but what is poetry but a form of daydreaming, dreaming while awake? And like daydreaming, poetry offers some solace for many of these poets engaged in their daily work.

In It Together

Sue Doro writes in "Muscle":

> Listen!
> This is a muscle poem.
> Its sounds are loud and can be frightening
> to untrained ears.[60]

Most literature tries to make the personal universal. As universal as possible. To be a hand reaching out to make connections. Now that we have seen a steady influx of work and working-class poetry in the last twenty to twenty-five years, there is no turning back. This poetry is not going to disappear. Yet it still exists on the margins of our literature. How do we expand the audience? What *is* the audience for work and working-class poetry? How do we train our culture's ears to listen to it? This poetry is an antidote to genteel poetic traditions, yet how do we administer the antidote? How do we get access to the patient? Part of the answer lies in our nation's classrooms, where this poetry should be taught as part of our literature—to continue creating a home for work as one of the central literary threads alongside death, love, and beauty. Part of the answer lies in getting this poetry into our workplaces, where workers can find their home(s) in our literature. The success of books such as *Working Classics* and *Between the Heart-*

beats demonstrates that poetry about the working class and work has a substantial audience.

This poetry helps create a sense of us being in it together, against those who refuse to acknowledge the impact of our *working* lives on the *rest* of our lives. We can feel this sense of connection, for example, in this excerpt from Tom Wayman:

> The sun up through a blue mist
> draws its own tide: this is the factory hour.
> As I drive east, I pass dozens like myself
> waiting on the curb for buses, for company crummies,
> for car pools; grey plastic lunch buckets,
> safety boots, old clothes. All of us pulled
> on the same factory tide.[61]

Writing a poem about the daily work you do is a political statement, whether that job is teaching college or working as a janitor, whether that job is nursing or working as a longshoreman. In Wayman's essays, he frequently makes the point that, regardless of the color of the collar, the work we do is usually controlled and evaluated by someone else: "In our culture, there is an almost pathological aversion to presenting an accurate portrayal of daily work. . . . The workplace remains a portion of our lives where we do not yet enjoy the democracy we are told is our birthright—off the job. Hence we live in a daily absurdity."[62]

The work and working-class poets discussed here share a number of common concerns as they strive toward the common goal of presenting that accurate portrayal of daily work and its effect on our lives. Through the poems, they bear witness to and participate in this world that is so often invisible in our literature, without sentimentalizing or being condescending toward the workers or the work. This often involves creating a sense of history where no written history has existed before—a defiant witnessing in the face of willful ignorance. Many of the poems seem to say, at a most basic level, we're here, and we're not going away, we're not going to be erased or ignored; we're proud of what we do, of our own survival against the machine—whatever machine that happens to be. Sometimes, racism and sexual discrimination are part of the machine the workers have to oppose, and that makes it all the more difficult, but poets do not shy away from dealing with those serious issues.

Tonally, these poems frequently use humor as a way of asserting workers' humanity in the face of often mind-numbing, repetitive labor. Even when making damning political indictments, the poets often rely on humor as opposed to preaching and polemics. Other ways of humanizing the workplace and the work experience involve using persona to bring in the voices of fellow workers, and personifying the tools, machines, and even the mills and factories themselves.

The authenticity of the poems often comes from a strong sense of detail, of concrete image. The language tends to be informal, but it often echoes workplace rhythms and job-specific vocabularies. And away from the workplace, working-class poems often rely on home and family as an emotional counterbalance to the workplace.

While these poems are often about feeling powerless and defeated, they are also often about pride and celebrating the experience of work. This central tension appears in much work and working-class poetry—to maintain human pride and dignity in the face of workplaces that often challenge that basic humanity, particularly in relation to the struggle over control of our own work environments. Many of these poems examine both the physical and psychological tolls of various jobs. Finally, the simple act of writing these poems asserts that these writers are finding time for themselves, controlled by no boss anywhere, regardless of what their present employment status happens to be.

Going through all of this work and working-class poetry, I have often felt like reading these poems aloud to somebody. They are funny, sweaty, earned poems. As Sue Doro says, they're "Muscle" poems. Poems from a place. Poems from a heart. What makes work and working-class poems *poems* are the same things that make anything a poem—the intense compression and shaping of the language to create deep emotional resonances. The time to slow down and pay attention to the world is a luxury for work and working-class poets. The straightforward quality of this poetry owes a great deal to a certain no-nonsense approach. The poets don't have the luxury of not being understood. They have something to say. They have stories to tell, and hey, listen up!

9

Class Memory: Autobiography and the Art of Forgetting

Tim Strangleman

Before becoming an academic, I spent five years as a signalman on the London Underground. At sixteen, I was thrust into a byzantine world of work populated by many and varied human beings who were united, and sometimes divided, by a long-established working-class culture. My exposure to this environment started me on the road to becoming a sociologist before I ever knew such a vocation existed. I was taught my craft by a variety of men, sometimes little older than myself but usually a good deal more senior. Many of those I worked with were from my father's or even my grandfather's generation. London Transport was defined by the seniority system, with virtually every blue-collar job, as well as a number of white-collar ones, achieved by length of service. Those who stayed the longest were rewarded with the best-paying positions. I have kept a seniority list for the whole of the grade[1] of signal worker from 1985, containing the names of 286 staff, two of whom were women. Apart from this male dominance what is also notable is the age profile of this workforce. The first entry on the seniority list dates from 1937, the last from 1984—a span of forty-eight years. Across these years new additions appear on the list almost every year, with fifty-two workers from 1937 to 1949, forty-one from 1950 to 1959, and seventy-four from 1960 to 1969. The document is a vivid reminder for me, and a historical testament for others, of the family-like quality of a workplace where individuals occupy different places in a hierarchy at different times in their working lives. At the time, I had a clear sense of being part of something larger than my immediate work group. It testified vividly to the lively work culture that I had recently joined, one I assumed would be mine for the rest of my working life.

In becoming first a railwayman and later a sociologist, I began to understand the complexity and subtlety of working-class culture, particularly the way workplace norms and values were embedded and transmitted over time. I became aware of how the collective memory of the work group was embedded within the workforce and that this memory was a live and active process, not an unchanging tradition, remote and scholarly. My socialization and training involved formal, classroom-based learning, but the informal aspects transmitted from those around me were far more important—tacit knowledge and skill that was a collective property built up within a workforce over decades. As I became an academic, I developed a research interest in trying to understand this workplace culture more fully; I have often found myself in the difficult position of trying to describe something that I am the product of in academic terms. Much of my formal research has involved oral histories of current and retired railway workers, but I have also benefited from a very large and not well-researched set of literature— the autobiographies of former workers in the industry. The sheer size and scope of railway memoir in Great Britain sets it apart from any other sector of the economy and is perhaps unique in the industrialized world. Hundreds of railway autobiographies have been published, ranging from those produced by very small publishers to the glossy products of university presses. These books are produced and consumed largely by working-class people. Indeed, publication of such an expanding range of material is only possible because of a popular market eager for more "tales from the rails."

But in drawing on such resources I became aware of the way these texts have been the object of caution or even derision by labor historians. It is the very popularity of railway autobiography that has attracted criticism from elite historians who decry both its production and consumption as superficial and nostalgic. This has been true for all kinds of working-class autobiographies. In his groundbreaking collection *Useful Toil,* John Burnett writes, "It remains true that the direct, personal records of working people have not so far been regarded as a major historical source, and the whole area of such material remains largely unexplored territory."[2] Burnett argues that professional historians have assumed that the lives of ordinary men and women were "too dull and of insufficient importance to merit recording."[3] At the same time he notes that there was no dearth of such material. By the early 1970s, researchers had identified and catalogued some 6,500 published autobiographies, as well as 2,000 diaries, of working people in Great Britain alone. Academics' reluctance to use such material is partly related, Burnett claims, to the content and style of the record. This creates a disjuncture between what the historian or sociologist "wants" and what these autobiographies provide, which is partly related to the differing class and cultural backgrounds of

FIRING DAYS

Reminiscences of a Great Western Fireman.

by Harold Gasson

Harold Gasson's *Firing Days* is a typical autobiography from a fireman and other railway operating staff. Gasson worked in the industry from 1940 until he left in 1958 for better-paid employment in the railway car manufacturing industry. Front cover of *Firing Days: Reminiscences of a Great Western Fireman* (Oxford: Oxford Publishing Company, 1973). Reproduced with permission of the Publisher, Ian Allan Publishing Ltd.

producer and user. As a former railway worker and now as an academic, I see a tremendous value in this writing, but I remain surprised by the continued reluctance of academics, particularly railway historians, to use such sources.

In exploring this paradox I want to reflect on this form of working-class literature, the autobiography of workers from the railway industry, predominately, but not exclusively, from Great Britain.[4] I want to place this genre in the broader context of working-class autobiography and examine the implications of its study and use for New Working-Class Studies. The creation, criticism, and consumption of this material not only offers useful raw material for working-class studies but also defines what this discipline is about. In essence, I want to argue for a critical generosity in our reading and writing about this source of history. New Working-Class Studies should foster dialogue about how the form and nature of autobiography allows us privileged access to working-class experience.

Class History on the Line?

The oral historian Paul Thompson once remarked that "one of the great advantages of oral history is that it enables the historian to counteract the bias in normal historical sources; the tendency, for example, for printed autobiography to come from the articulate professional or upper classes, or from labour leaders rather than the rank and file."[5] For the railway historian, however, there is no shortage of working-class accounts of work life. But where do these autobiographies come from, what are they like, and how do we work with them? The first thing to note in railway industry memoir is the tremendous variation in style and quality, but also the sheer number and range. Such is the appetite of the audience that new titles seemingly appear each week. The earliest is from 1881—Michael Reynolds's *Engine-Driving Life: Stirring Adventures and Incidents in the Lives of Locomotive Engine-Drivers.*[6] Although new books appeared throughout the twentieth century, the genre expanded greatly starting in the late 1960s. This expansion tells us much about the audience as well as the producers of the literature. The stimulus for production came from the dramatic changes in the industry during the post-World War II era. This period witnessed a substantial rationalization and closure program, technological changes (in particular the end of steam traction and its replacement by diesel technology), and a massive reduction in the workforce. These events stimulated the desire for memoirs of a time that was being lost; it also created a set of workers who were moved to write about their experience of both these contemporary changes and their earlier careers.

Most of the earlier books were written by a narrow range of workers—most notably signal staff (switchmen or pointsmen) and train drivers (engineers) and their firemen, because of the romantic aura that surrounded these workers, especially the footplatemen (engineers). The shelves of enthusiast bookshops are filled with titles such as *Bert Hooker: Legendary Railwayman, Life Adventure in Steam, 55 Years on the Footplate, Yesterday's Railwayman,* and *Railway Lines and Levers.*[7] More recent books, however, include railway memoirs by guards (conductors), station workers, control staff, and craftsmen and laborers from within the railway workshops.[8] All told, the genre reflects the depth and breadth of experience over time within the industry. Examples of railway autobiography reflect different types of work, across generations and across time, as well as space. This not only allows the careful reader access to the thoughts and experiences of individuals but also enables one to compare different types of work and to identify changes across generations.

During the 1960s, critics expressed concern about the academic standard of much of the popular histories of the railway industry. In a 1968 essay subtitled "An Essay in Nostalgia," John Kellett reviewed a selection of such histories and observed: "None of the books quotes any sources or authorities for its statements, and all have pathetic indexes. . . . In fact, it is clear that they are books intended to be wallowed in rather than read, and certainly not to be studied, to be used for convenient reference, or serve as the basis for further work."[9] This charge of romantic sentimentality or even nostalgia is a recurring one. The second substantive criticism, one that follows from the first, concerned the content of the subject matter. David Howell characterized the genre as "history written by enthusiasts and for enthusiasts": "Commentaries are often uncritical. But the limitations of this literature are often acute, neglecting the harsh experiences of company employees and ignoring the economic pressures on railway companies even before the start of serious road competition."[10]

These observations are directed at a whole range of popular writing on railways and not simply autobiography, but there have also been direct attacks on autobiography. David Wilson, in his book on the footplate grade, itself an example of popular railway history, comments: "A great number of over-romantic accounts—books, pamphlets and magazine articles—have been written about footplate life, and footplatemen themselves have contributed to this. What is perhaps most revealing about all these works is their very existence: after all there are few if any works entitled *How I Became a Capstan Lathe Operator*, or *Ace Dustbinman.*"[11]

In essence, historians are hostile to this more popular form of knowledge because of what some claim as the "fetishism" attached to hard facts. Raphael Samuel and Paul Thompson in their collection on popular and oral history, *The Myths We Live By,* note that "historians deal, by preference, with 'hard' realities—family, work and home; politics and government; church and chapel. We cleave to precise locations, dateable periods, delimitable fields of study."[12]

Some historians do not see value in these accounts in general, because of an established distaste for working-class autobiography. Railway historians also object to these sources, or at least worry about how to use them, because of the audience that brings it into being. In other words, historians have questioned the validity of railway autobiographies because their production and content are driven by popular demand from a general audience, rather than by scholarly concerns. Michael Robbins acknowledges this fact in describing these books' concentration on technology: "It is idle not to recognize that the locomotive section is the most attractive part of railway history to many readers, and these readers make publication commercially possible."[13] Kellett, likewise, acknowledges the reason for the existence of much of the literature he condemns: "They [railway enthusiasts] also help to explain the great proliferation and large sales of railway books, for no readers are more insatiable and compulsive than those who are seeking their own past."[14]

Popular history and autobiography lack legitimacy as historical documents because they are assumed to be written by and for a sentimental, nostalgic, and uncritical group who lack the sophistication and critical faculties of objective academics. It is possible, however, to arrive at a more positive reading of some railway histories in their more popular forms, particularly memoirs of working life. First, the very popularity of accounts of "life on the lines" creates an economic case for celebrating rather than critiquing their publication. Second, a careful reading of these autobiographies reveals a far more nuanced picture of working-class life than critics of the genre suggest. Although these publications are frequently nostalgic or sentimental, they are also often complex accounts of careers, reflecting the values and meanings of workers themselves.

Life on the Line

By examining a selection of studies (memoirs), looking at the way they structure their narratives of work and self through issues of socialization, generational relationship, skill, and work, we gain access to the process of being and becoming in the context of working-class life. Identity is achieved through a collective social process, not an individualistic sense of career. Almost all the texts I've studied follow a predictable pattern, offering a chronological account of working life beginning with the writer's introduction to the adult world of work. For many, this socialization began before they ever started work formally. As in other industries, many workers had relatives who were already "on the job," and this provided a kind of anticipatory socialization to work. Charles Taylor, who became a skilled craftsman in the locomotive works at Crewe in northwest England, describes this situation:

> We were a family steeped in railway tradition, living in a three-storey house at the end of a row adjacent to Flag Lane railway bridge. My bedroom was at the top, with a wonderful view of the Works Yard so that the panorama of Chain Shop, Stone Yard, Brass Finishing Shop, Wheel Shop and the Melting Furnaces became very fa-

miliar, together with the fan of sidings serving them and providing stabling for the works shunting engines.[15]

Similarly, Ken Gibbs stresses the importance of family connections to work in his book:

I was destined to follow my father, grandfather and great-grandfather into the service of the Great Western Railway at Swindon, without any thought that there could possibly be any other acceptable form of employment. . . . There was never a question of what did I want to do! I was destined to be a fitter, turner and locomotive erector like my grandfather.[16]

Gibbs discusses the totality of the institution at Swindon and the interpenetration between work and social and cultural life: "We were a railway family, in a railway street, in a railway area, an area which you couldn't leave without going under, or, with care, over a railway line, and where just about every family had at least one member who worked 'inside'."[17] These memoirs clearly show how the world of work was a very real presence in the lives of children and adolescents.

Autobiography allows us privileged access to the meaning of work in modernity. These books approach issues of industrial discipline and the work ethic with striking complexity. Many accounts describe the moral regulation that was enforced not only by supervisors but by the workers themselves. Once in the workplace, the new employee was rapidly introduced to the world of labor. Nowhere is this more graphically illustrated than in the writing of those who later became firemen and train drivers. For this grade, the bottom rung of the occupational ladder in steam days was as the cleaner. Frank McKenna describes the experience of cleaning the underside of a locomotive in Carlisle's Kingmoor shed in 1946:

Sweating with fear as well as activity I climbed up into the belly of the engine across brake hangers, stretchers and slide bars. I sat across a brake stretcher, the filth oozing through my overalls and trousers, trapped in space. For more than an hour I perched there in the darkness broken only by the spluttering of the flare lamp, almost overpowered by the sense of isolation and danger. The dankness of the cotton waste, the sickly smell of the cleaning oil and the menacing black underbelly of the boiler petrified me. . . . I had now discovered the daily ritual of the junior cleaner on the shift.[18]

Many former workers convey in a very practical way the process by which the technical aspects of labor were infused and overlaid by social forms. McKenna's first job not only taught him the technical skills of the job but also acted as a vivid introduction to a workplace hierarchy that had a moral quality to it. Everyone who began their railway careers in this department had gone through a similar induction. The allocation of work in this way is ritualistic as well as practical in that it combines the technical and the social. To fail this initial test was to effectively exclude oneself from the work group.

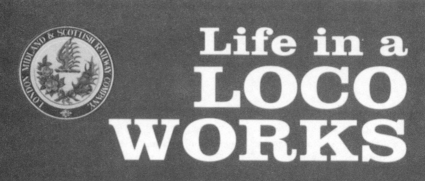

Life in a
LOCO
WORKS

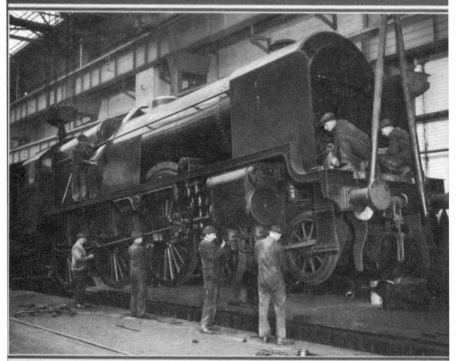

First-hand experiences of a Crewe
engineering apprentice in wartime

OPC
Charles Taylor

Charles Taylor's *Life in a Loco Works* is a reflection on his wartime work in Crewe Engineering's locomotive works and is part of a genre of writing spawned by the success of books written about more glamorous railway occupations. Front cover of *Life in a Loco Works: First-hand Experiences of a Crewe Engineering Apprentice in Wartime* (Oxford: Oxford Publishing Company, 1995). Reproduced with
permission of the Publisher, Ian Allan Publishing Ltd.

McKenna also illustrates the sense of fear and menace of the world of work, which, while important, is rarely captured by social scientists interested in the meaning of work.

This sense of work as initially an alien environment is reflected in a great variety of ways in these autobiographies. Ron Spedding, an apprentice in Shildon Wagon Works recalled his first walk to work:

> The streets were so very quiet that the steady tread of my hobnailed boots muffled by the ground frost sounded unnatural. As I proceeded, men appeared out of the shadows to move in the same direction as myself; a door would open to reveal a shaft of light and a figure silhouetted for a moment, then the door would close and the figure would move forward to join the general flow. As I approached the Works the number of figures increased rapidly, until I was surrounded by a mass of moving humanity. . . . As we entered the Works' gates the steam buzzer blew with insistent clarity, giving all present a loud reminder that another working day had just begun.[19]

Spedding's description simultaneously emphasizes the profoundly mundane and extraordinary character of many working lives. Autobiographies also capture the physical character of the workplace and the impression it makes on a new worker. Charles Taylor describes waiting to be allocated duties on his first day and the factory's assault on his senses: "We waited outside the machine shop office surrounded by the noise, smell and warmth of lathes, while away on the right showers of sparks rose from the polishing bench. It was going to be a long day."[20]

These autobiographies discuss the social aspects of work rather than simply the technical; the binary opposition that academics too readily make for intellectual purposes is not present here. They provide a real sense of the way the social and the economic interpenetrate to humanize work and in the process render it less alien. Ron Bradshaw describes his feelings about his entry into the adult world of employment: "At fifteen and a half years of age, I was quickly to learn the meaning of maturity and manhood, for here I was a lone teenager thrown into a world of adult working men, without a single person of my own age group for companionship or consolation."[21] The same writer elaborates on the socialization process in his discussion of his growing relationship with the older man who was training him as a junior signal worker:

> By the eighth day that hitherto impenetrable barrier had been conquered and Ted Cox's face broke down into a satisfied smile. With a pat on the back he announced "You'll make it lad. Now we'll show you how to write. Your script is appalling." . . . Up to then, I had secretly feared him; now I felt a conversion to almost hero worship.[22]

Such quotes frame a more complex understanding of the process of socialization and the relationship between generations in the workplace.

Important, too, is the sense of gendered relations formed here, the way masculinity at work is played out in a highly personal way, as the joint production between younger and older men. Many of the volumes I have reviewed give very practical demonstrations of this complex process, and they echo Susan Faludi's account of shipyard workers in the United States:

> As in so many blue collar jobs and union environments, old-style paternalism could easily become an exclusionary despotism. But such a system also held a capacity for nurturance through apprenticeship and it was on this that the shipyard workers came to base a viable and encompassing work life. Each successful man in the shipyard had a "father," a more experienced older man, not a relative, often not even of the same race, who had recognized his abilities and cultivated them.[23]

Understood in such a way, the terrain of masculinity and, more widely, of industrial work becomes far more diverse than is often allowed for. Workplace culture is based on norms of reciprocity between workers with intergenerational linkages. Thus, the joint production of work identity allows workers at particular stages of their working lives to draw on different but common resources. Once again, a moral order overlays these processes, which develops character simultaneously in both men.

Many of the autobiographies discuss training in both formal and informal senses. The descriptions of the way socialization and training are embedded within social relations are particularly powerful. Knowledge transmission takes the form of narrative whereby workers learn lessons from the past. The autobiography is especially good at reflecting on the process through which the author gains knowledge and later comes to see the subtlety and complexity of the process. Bradshaw illustrates this point well when he relates an incident when he made a mistake while in training:

> Joe [the qualified signalman], rather than chastise me after the visible shaking-up, was feeling sympathy but repeated the importance of observing a constant vigilance and the importance of signal arm response and track circuit indicators. He quoted the Castlecary (Scotland) accident of 18 months ago when 35 people were killed. During the ensuing enquiry a signalman was held partially to blame for incorrect observation of the indicator of a distant signal. This little episode had a sobering effect on my possible over self-confidence and was to remain a constant reminder when working busy boxes later, a truly graphic illustration of "more haste, less speed!"[24]

This example is typical of what we find in many if not all of the autobiographies. It shows how working-class culture relies on storytelling, on oral accounts, and to some extent on myth. Knowledge and understanding is embedded within social relations and is transferred through a work culture that appropriates and shapes history. Autobiography plays a crucial role in the critical appreciation of this process and the wider structures of feeling of working-class life. Autobiography offers a reflection on these processes in the context of a lifetime; it is the act of evaluation, of becoming, and embedding.

Working-Class Autobiography and New Working-Class Studies

What does the study of working-class autobiography tell us more widely about working-class life, and what are the implications for new working-class studies? Analysis of this kind of material contributes significantly to our knowledge and appreciation of working lives, and the act of studying autobiography allows us to understand the project of working-class studies. In researching working-class life through autobiography we are engaged in a process that of necessity raises a number of methodological and epistemological questions. These in turn raise important questions about what working-class studies is, or could be. To answer this last question first: for me, the potential of new working-class studies lies in its sensitivity and critical respect for its object of study, working-class life. This movement attempts to capture the meaning and experience of working-class life. For me, then, what we are engaged in is the attempt to recover memory and meaning, understood very broadly, what Raphael Samuel and Paul Thompson refer to as the "myths we live by."[25]

In many ways, this sensitivity to ordinary working lives has had a long and honorable tradition in Britain. During the 1960s, the idea of "history from below" emerged, perhaps best captured by the social historian E. P. Thompson, who famously talked about the need to "rescue" the working class "from the enormous condescension of posterity."[26] Thompson argued that social history should be conceived of as a gigantic act of reparation, a process of social remembrance in which the voices of the dispossessed and marginal were to be heard. Thompson's work and approach were influential in Britain and elsewhere, and the late 1960s witnessed the explosion of interest in history from below, or people's history, that explicitly challenged the method and subject matter of elite history. In the British context this trend solidified around the History Workshop movement, a loose band of amateur and professional historians who studied and wrote about working-class life and reported their work in a series of conferences, in working papers, and later in the highly respected *History Workshop Journal*. From its earliest beginning, the movement internalized the understanding of history in a broad and inclusive manner in opposition to a narrow elitist history. Reflecting on the movement a quarter of a century after its birth, Raphael Samuel wrote:

History Workshop started from some very simple faiths. There was in the first place the passionate belief in going directly to the sources. Since our chosen subject matters were those which high scholarship had ignored, or which fell beneath the dignity of conventional history, it was possible to pursue the quest without reference to competitors—there would not be any—or to any possible secondary literature.[27]

Along with taking seriously an expanded range of historical sources, this movement began to question working-class subjectivity and how one gained access to it in the process of understanding it. In their important collection *The Myths We Live By,* Samuel and Thompson set out a powerful case for the serious study of myths within oral history and other accounts of working-class life: "We are arguing for the universality of myth as a constituent of human experience. It lies behind any historical evidence. Hence to identify the element of myth in oral sources is certainly *not* to say that we are working with memories of a false past."[28] Samuel and Thompson go on to argue that oral histories and autobiography offer us access to a truth in both a subjective and objective sense and that it is a mistake to believe that we can jettison the one while valuing the other. Rather, these sources offer "double validity in understanding a past in which, as still today, myth was embedded in real experience: both growing from it, and helping to shape its perception."[29] This sense of history as the experience of process is crucial in understanding the importance of autobiography. The stress on the interrelationship between experience and memory gives us access to the embedding process. Class is both a product of and is structured by this embedding process, and class must, therefore, be understood through these narratives of life. To borrow Richard Sennett and Jonathan Cobb's phrase, we are examining the "hidden injuries of class" as well as what I would suggest are the hidden rewards of class.[30]

Thus, the debates in History Workshop, and more broadly the "history from below" movement, in the British context rehearsed many of the arguments about the validity of both subject matter and method that were being raised in working-class studies during the 1990s and 2000s. What is interesting and important about new working-class studies is its rediscovery of these issues at a time when academic debates about class are shifting. Over the last decade, social commentators on the left have tried to make sense of the contemporary world of work, employment, and class.[31] In many ways, American writer Jeremy Rifkin stimulated much of this debate in his book *The End of Work.*[32] Rifkin argues that work as we have known it is in terminal decline. On the one hand, new technology abolishes work, making an international division of labor truly possible for the first time. On the other, the acceleration of global market forces coupled with a reluctance by nation-states to intervene in world markets leads to a situation in which work becomes contingent and profoundly unstable. *The End of Work* provides a vivid backdrop against which other authors on the left have sought to paint their pictures of contemporary capitalism.

What is important here is that two separate but related themes emerge from this literature, both of which have important implications for contemporary class analysis. First, there is the sense that much of the contemporary world of work offers little for the working class and that this class has lost purpose and, to a large extent, agency. Workers, whether in jobs or unemployed, feel like passive victims of juggernaut capitalism. In *Work, Consumerism, and the New Poor,* Zygmunt Bauman writes that in the past "work was the main orientation point, in reference to which all other life pursuits could be planned and ordered."[33] He goes on to claim that "a steady, durable, and continuous, logically coherent, and tightly structured working career is however no longer a widely available option. Only in relatively rare cases can a permanent identity be defined, let alone secured, through the job performed."[34] Ulrich Beck sees a noticeable acceleration of this process: "The 'job for life' has disappeared. . . . Paid employment is becoming precarious; the foundations of the social-welfare state are collapsing; normal life-stories are breaking up into fragments."[35] Beck argues that the West is suffering what he terms a "Brazilianization" of work conditions and social welfare. The working class is denied any meaningful sense of agency in the contemporary world; it is abandoned by global capital and powerlessly tied to local, impoverished labor markets.

Second, this literature also questions the industrial past and in particular the ability of workers to find meaning and identity in work. Essentially, in making a bid for a utopian future or by questioning the nature of contemporary capitalism, many established and respected writers on the left degrade and demean the experience of industrial work. Stanley Aronowitz and William DiFazio, for instance, talk of the "dogma of work" to describe the beliefs of those who still wish to see full employment.[36] Similarly, André Gorz writes about the "ideology of work." He describes how society can "reclaim work" and suggests that "we must learn to make out the contours of that other society beneath the resistances, dysfunctions, and impasses which make up the present. 'Work' must lose its centrality in the minds, thoughts, and imaginations of everyone."[37] He is perhaps most critical when he talks of those who would find value in the past:

> Even in the heyday of wage-based society, that work [modern work] was never a source of "social cohesion" or integration, whatever we might have come to believe from its retrospective idealization. The "social bond" it established between individuals was abstract and weak, though it did, admittedly, *insert* people into the process of social labour, into social relations of production, as functionally specialized cogs in an immense machine.[38]

This theme is present in other commentaries. Bauman, for instance, talks of how "factories turned out many and varied commodities, but all of them, in addition, produced the compliant and conforming subjects of the modern state."[39]

Beck, too, is utopian in his assessment of the future while simultaneously critical of those who would hold on to the industrial past, what he describes as a "nostalgia for the age of full employment."[40] As in the debate over the current state of employment, in this view the working class, historically as well as in contemporary society, is robbed of any meaningful agency. The forging of identity out of industrial work is dismissed as simply nostalgia for a bygone age.

If we take these claims seriously, then we will find ourselves back in the position we were in before the advent of "history from below." Although sympathetic to working-class aspirations, the "end of work" writers ultimately portray a narrow and depressing world—one in which workers either find meaning in alienating industrial work as a result of false consciousness or realize the hopelessness of their lot and cope with it as best they can. However seemingly sympathetic these writers may be, they nonetheless replicate the narrow elitism of previous academics when discussing the working class.

New working-class studies finds itself developing in this context, but it would be wrong to see it as a movement that simply replicates the new history movements of the 1960s. New working-class studies is distinct in several ways. First, it emerges as a set of concerns at a time of tremendous upheaval in the workplace. While it is easy to dismiss the wilder claims of the end-of-work theorists, the developments of the last two decades have stimulated an interesting series of debates about the nature of employment today and during the long boom of the post-World War II era. In many ways, deindustrialization and the advent of mass unemployment have together acted as a huge breaching experiment wherein society and individuals reassess what work is and was. For me, the importance of working-class studies lies in its ability to make sense of this experience through a critical but sympathetic lens. We must avoid romanticizing and nostalgia for an industrial past and an organized working class. As Kathryn Dudley notes, "American industrial workers are also subject to the kinds of historicizing and romanticizing imagery that characterizes nostalgic treatments of more distant but nonetheless passing ways of life."[41] But, equally, we must avoid the arid account that sees the working class as now and always passive, hapless victims of impersonal structural forces. Working-class studies is the interdisciplinary interrogation and analysis of the broad working-class experience, sensitive to notions of class, race, and gender and other forms of identity. The field provides a lens through which we may understand, explain, and interpret the process of class formation and reproduction as well as the embedding of class. Perhaps the most positive aspect of a renewed interest in working-class studies is that its object and subject of study comes from and addresses working people. Working-class studies should draw lessons from the History Workshop movement and conceive of history and its study in a very catholic way. Working-class studies should become the work of many hands, not simply the domain of elite academics. Autobiography is an essential part of the process of understanding the full depth and breadth of working-class life. As Ron Spedding, one of the autobiographers heard from earlier, noted when explaining why he wrote his life story, "I think my main reason for writing this book is to place on record the daily life experienced in a factory as seen from a workman's point of view and not through the eyes of someone who sees it as a collection of buildings occupied and worked by nameless robots."[42] Using my own biography and those of others has helped me bridge the gap between being a nameless robot and an academic. Working-class studies has allowed me to explore this distance and, in the process, understand more about both working-class and academic cultures.

10

Filming Class

Tom Zaniello

Although film was the primary medium of mass culture in the first half of the twentieth century, Hollywood rarely made films about work, organized labor, or class consciousness. When workers and working-class issues did appear they were portrayed in a negative or condescending manner, so it was left to independent, inevitably documentary, filmmakers to extend the canons of social realism they inherited from the New Deal films of the Depression era. While Hollywood films usually presented a working class insufficiently powerful or not even self-conscious enough to make significant changes in society that would benefit them, documentary films began the process of reclaiming the images of working-class militancy and labor history essential to understanding the role of class in society.

Film is the ideal means of understanding class formations in general and working-class history in particular, because representations of class in film are both authentic—the visuals are accurate photographically—and problematic—ideological content may be open or suppressed. It is therefore essential to read films as texts simultaneously privileged and "thick," that is, as capable of both the erasure and the disclosure of the issues of class.

When cinema verité filmmakers began to pioneer low-cost filmmaking outside the big-budget control of Hollywood during the 1960s, they made a radical break with the old forms of Hollywood's representation of class. They in turn were followed by videographers, using the new medium (videotape) that became the dominant form of filmmaking and viewing by the end of the twentieth century. For the first time, independent directors could approach topics by using the new medium outside the control of the powerful media industry. Difficulties remained, however, with distribution and access to audiences, which are recurring problems for filming class. When the twenty-first century computer age transformed the earlier media of film and videotape into a new form, the digital, activist and innovative filmmakers were able to expand the variety of topics and radical approaches to filmmaking.

All three media, however, remain in simultaneous use today, and all three have a critical relationship with the dominant form of traditional feature filmmaking represented by Hollywood. In the field of New Working-Class Studies, those who analyze films and those who make them have had to take the measure not only of these traditional and electronic media but also of their blurred boundaries, their varying audiences, and their complicated financial infrastructure.

New working-class studies has also had a dual role in apprehending the traditional forms and their challenging offspring. On the one hand, films from all media are an essential means of comprehending the changes in work, the politics of organizing, and the assessment of the power of class in contemporary society. On the other hand, in its breakthroughs in subject matter and in the use of nontraditional forms—agit-prop films, postmodern documentaries, digital filming and satellite transmission, and "art" films—new working-class studies offers a paradigm of committed filmmaking that has much to teach film studies as it is usually constituted.

To understand the role of film, as a source for and as a form of working-class studies, we must consider three issues: (1) the power of Hollywood to set the agenda of working-class images in traditional filmmaking; (2) the way alternative or independent films have challenged that dominance; and (3) the ways new forms of filmmaking expand the sometimes narrow scope of traditional film studies.

The Power of Hollywood

Film viewers recognize Jack Nicholson's portrayal of the Teamster leader in *Hoffa* (1992), Sally Fields's role as a Southern textile worker in *Norma Rae* (1979), or Marlon Brando's turn as a small-time enforcer for racketeers in *On the Waterfront* (1954) as the defining figures of Hollywood's labor films. The films dramatize union organizing, corruption, and racism in workplaces as diverse as a textile plant, the docks, and the trucking industry, but the only images of labor that are not consistently negative appear in *Norma Rae.*

Beyond these successful films led by well-known stars, Hollywood's portrayal of labor is mostly a story of what has been missed: the great labor history drama of the Flint sit-down strike, for example, has never been re-created in a feature film, while the lives of labor heroes such as the leader of the Wobblies and the Western Federation of Miners, Big Bill Haywood, have never made it onto the screen. The lives of three of our other fascinating labor heroes and martyrs have been left to foreign production companies to film: Sweden's Bo Widerberg made *Joe Hill,* about the life and death of the Wobblies' troubadour, and Italy's Giuliano Montaldo made *Sacco and Vanzetti,* about the anarchist martyrs of the 1920s; both films were subtitled in English and released in the United States in 1971, where they found weak box office returns.

If we look at the portrayal of Appalachian miners as a case study in filmmaking both inside and outside Hollywood, budget dollars, audience share, and stereotyping are all recurring issues in both the analysis and the production of films in new working-class studies. As I demonstrate in *Working Stiffs, Union Maids, Reds, and Riffraff: An Expanded Guide to Films about Labor* (2nd ed.; Ithaca: Cornell University Press, 2003), more films have been made about miners than about workers in any other industry. Films about Appalachian miners follow much of the mainstream stereotyping of Appalachia in general, but the representation of Appalachian miners in the media is instructive as a reflection of how market forces—not just stereotyping—play an important role in new working-class studies.

The dominant image in Hollywood of the southern white working class has been that of shiftless white trash, known primarily in the 1930s as "peckerwoods" and epitomized in the novels and film adaptations of Erskine Caldwell, such as *Tobacco Road* and *God's Little Acre.* The image of the miners in this region, however, has been a little more complicated. *Harlan County War,* for example, dramatized the 1970s Brookside mine struggles on HBO/cable TV in 2000, covering an extended and violent strike by the United Mine Workers (UMWA) against Duke Power Company. It used the same material as Barbara Kopple's Academy Award–winning independent documentary *Harlan County, U.S.A.,* which used the cinema verité approach to get very close to the miners on strike and eventually to their wives and mothers who had to take over the fight when the men were enjoined from picketing. The film appeared in 1979, while the aftereffects of the struggle were still being felt, but usually it only played at film festivals or political meetings. Similarly, *They'll Never Keep Us Down,* a UMWA agit-prop documentary designed to promote the 1987 Pittston miners' corporate campaign, circulated mainly to union halls and community centers.

Despite radical differences in funding, format, distribution, and appeals, all of these projects are clearly examples of filming class. *Harlan County War,* however, cost $10 million to produce, depended in part on star power (Holly Hunter), and was made for a mass audience of millions of viewers, while the other films had very modest budgets, never circulated commercially, and appealed to a relatively narrow band of viewers that were potentially sympathetic to Appalachian workers and their families.

Holly Hunter in Tony Bill's 2000 film *Harlan County War*.

These films about the Appalachian working class, like all such films about work, organized labor, labor history, and related economic issues, play an essential but unusual role in new working-class studies. They illustrate how film functions in three traditionally distinct arenas: (1) public performance or exhibition in theaters or through electronic media; (2) labor organizing and political activism; and (3) academic study, film history, and individual research (through the Internet). *Harlan County War* reached its target viewing audience on cable TV and also circulates through videocassette rental stores; *They'll Never Keep Us Down* played a role in the Justice for Pittston Miners committee's campaign in support of a successful United Mine Workers' strike; and *Harlan County, U.S.A.* became a fixture at film festivals, eventually earning a distinctive place in documentary film histories and courses as a striking example of cinema verité ("direct cinema") filmmaking.

We cannot always make such neat distinctions, however, with many other films. The simultaneous release of videocassettes and/or DVDs when films are broadcast or showcased in theaters has erased the sharp distinction we used to make between feature films and television productions. The classic Edward R. Murrow documentary on migrant workers, *Harvest of Shame,* for example, was made only for broadcast television in 1960; it can, of course, only be seen today on videocassette. Two important documentaries on the urban working class— *Surviving the Good Times* (2000), a longitudinal study of two laid-off workers and their families in Milwaukee, and *Taxi Dreams* (2001), a portrait of immigrant taxi drivers in New York City—were both made for PBS but were almost immediately released on videocassette as well. Neither of these videocassettes is likely to find widespread distribution in rental stores, but they will most likely fill a specialty niche in academia generally and in new working-class studies in particular.

Alternative Currents

Although some distinctions between big-budget Hollywood or cable TV filmmaking and independent productions have narrowed in recent years, we should be aware that Hollywood has not addressed the evolving labor scene, especially the capitalist global village, in which corporations routinely close their American factories and "go south" to avoid union organizing. Nor does it seem to be interested in the streams of migrant labor represented by, for instance, a Mexican national who works in a maquiladora in Ciudad Juarez across the border from El Paso or who is trucked to work on a farm in California's Imperial Valley or who joins a line of day laborers in Los Angeles.

And while a unionized job is not in this worker's future, neither is his or her appearance in a Hollywood feature. This worker, by the way, has been featured in at least two important independent films made outside the Hollywood system: Ken Loach's mainly British financed *Bread and Roses* (2000), set during the Justice for Janitors campaign in Los Angeles, and David Riker's independently produced *The City* (2000), which features Latino immigrants in New York "playing themselves" as workers in sweatshops and day-labor work sites. They signal a slight erosion of the big-budget trend in which only star power guarantees access to mass audiences, as *Bread and Roses* played in a number of commercial theaters and *The City* was broadcast on PBS stations.

Historically, feature films with a labor focus have fared somewhat better on cable and public broadcast channels than in movie theaters. *The Killing Floor* (1984), a sleeper about the successes and failures of racial integration in the Chicago meatpacking industry during World War I, has been moderately well distributed on videocassette. Unlike *Harlan County War,* it has no top-ranked stars; it played on PBS stations as a pilot film in a proposed series of films about classic moments in labor history. PBS canceled the series, however, because it was too sympathetic to the workers, although the "public" corporation argued that the reason was the excessive underwriting by the United Food and Commercial Workers, the union that is the lineal descendant of the Meatpackers. The second film in the series, *Lost Eden,* on the Lawrence, Massachusetts, textile mills, was completed but never released.

On the other hand, PBS has featured the first film adaptation of a story about migrant workers from inside the experience, *And the Earth Did Not Swallow Him* (1994), based on Tomás Rivera's experiences in a Mexican American migrant family. HBO and other cable networks have also backed a number of important projects, such as *10,000 Black Men Named George* (2002), the first feature film to tell the story of organizer and political activist A. Philip Randolph and the formation of the Brotherhood of Sleeping Car Porters, the first major black union.

Although a select few feature films join traditional documentaries as films important for new working-class studies—whether in classrooms or in union apprentice programs, at labor film festivals (such as those in Rochester and Washington, D.C.), or at arts and cultural events (such as the labor arts festivals in San Francisco and at the George Meany Center in Silver Spring)—the genre of film most often screened is the documentary. Classic labor history documentaries such as *The Inheritance* (1964), on the textile industry, from the former Amalgamated Clothing Workers of America (now UNITE), or fictional re-creations of actual struggles in *Norma Rae* (on textile mill organizing) or *Matewan* (1987), an independent feature film about Appalachian mine workers, join recent documentaries about labor struggles such as both versions of *Out at Work* (1996; 1999), on the harassment of gay workers, *Secrets of Silicon Valley* (2001), on immigrant labor in high-tech industries, and *Goin' to Chicago* (1994), on black workers' migration from the South, as important ways of prioritizing contemporary struggles in labor history.

Because labor films in themselves do not constitute a distinct cinematic genre, it is not surprising that many viewers perceive documentary as somehow the only natural cinematic form for labor issues. Documentary is the film form often iden-

Silvia Goiz as Ana in the "Seamstress" episode of *The City* (*La Ciudad*) by David Riker, 1999. Photograph by Victor Sira.

Black sharecroppers arrive in Chicago during the Great Migration in *Goin' to Chicago*, a 1994 film by George King.

tified with topics of labor, in part because of the social realist documentaries of the Depression era, when unemployment, union organizing, revolutionary rhetoric, and natural disasters dominated people's lives, and documentary films employed a photojournalistic style to represent their lives.

A number of critically acclaimed documentaries with a strong labor focus have had varying degrees of success in reaching viewers. Murrow's *Harvest of Shame* (1960) is a classic of investigative journalism that was first broadcast on television, while the Maysle brothers' *Salesmen* (1969) was a breakthrough cinema verité film that was quite successful in film festivals and university film series. *With Babies and Banners* (1978) and *The Life and Times of Rosie the Riveter* (1980) offered—usually for classroom study—new strong feminist perspectives on labor history sorely missed in early documentaries. Barbara Kopple won two Academy Awards for her "purely" labor films, *Harlan County, U.S.A.* and *American Dream* (1990) on the momentous Hormel meat strike in the 1980s, an unprecedented accomplishment. Michael Moore's postmodern spoof on the chairman of General Motors, *Roger & Me,* was the first major labor-related documentary to make a profit in commercial theaters.

New working-class studies has a special interest in the work of independent filmmakers such as Barbara Kopple and Michael Moore, the two leading filmmakers in cinema verité and postmodern "guerrilla" filming respectively. Both began as underfinanced independents with their first projects (*Harlan County, U.S.A.* and *Roger & Me*) but now secure major contracts with cable TV networks and commercial distributors. Although this may make them less financially independent, their work always remains progressive and, in most cases, very close to working-class issues. Nevertheless, their styles of filmmaking are radically different, as Moore's approach often involves creating the situations he films, while Kopple immerses herself in the social and political context she explores without substantially altering its flow.

From Agit-Prop to Digital Doc

New working-class studies has begun to encompass four new arenas of media work, all of which are alternatives to dominant filmmaking because they embrace politically charged topics and create radical visions of labor and class issues. Although agit-prop documentaries may have been dismissed by film critics as "only" political documents, they are nonetheless one of a number of ways new filmmakers focus on class. Other ways include postmodern approaches to editing, the collaboration of digital videographers and subsequent satellite transmission, and even the creation of the "art" video.

Although documentaries about labor struggles and labor history have constituted a core element of working-class studies since at least the 1970s, agit-prop films represent a category of labor documentary with a special relationship to new working-class studies because they are usually part of the ongoing struggles, yet they tend to receive less exposure than traditional documentaries in academic settings and even film festivals. These films have an even shorter shelf life than standard documentaries and are rarely shown after their initial distribution.

Agit-prop films are specifically designed to organize or mobilize workers or develop community support for boycotts during a corporate campaign or to expose an injustice. Agit-prop documentaries differ from both traditional and postmodern documentaries because they do not attempt to take the "long view" of history and neither challenge the form of the documentary nor offer a balanced journalistic report. Speaking directly to an almost convinced audience of potential supporters, the most successful agit-prop films tend to focus on only one specific issue, have an attention-getting slogan or title, and suggest specific actions for the viewer to take.

In the 1930s the familiar identification of agit-prop documentaries with left-wing and pro-working-class forces become apparent in the work of the Film and Photo League, which made films that highlighted Depression-era struggles. The war years saw the rare theatrical release of an agit-prop film, *Native Land* (1942), which was based on the La Follette hearings on Violations of Free Speech and the Rights of Labor. This is more of a mock documentary as the filmmakers mix both documentary footage and restagings of incidents such as labor spying.

The next major era of agit-prop films was the 1960s, led by California Newsreel, a collective of filmmakers that believed in shooting fast, editing quicker, and distributing right away as they made films of immediate political struggles. Thus their *Black Panthers* (1968) and *San Francisco State Strike* (1969) were films of the political moment, designed to spread the word to movement organizations across the land. California Newsreel also began to mix reportage and agit-prop documentary in *Finally Got the News* (1970), a report of the revolutionary formations of black workers in Detroit's auto plants.

Even given the limitations of the form, a remarkable variety of agit-prop films have evolved, in most cases challenging either specific employers or even whole sectors of American culture. Some of the best include: *Chaos: The Movie* (1994), sponsored by the Association of Flight Attendants union, which pioneered a strategy of unannounced and selective strikes by their crews; *Mickey Mouse Goes to Haiti* (1996), the National Labor Committee's exposé of the globalization of garment work and subsequent poverty wages; and *One Day Longer* (2000), about the Hotel Employees and Restaurant Employees six-year strike in Las Vegas. The most famous agit-prop film, *The Wrath of Grapes,* was made by the United Farm Workers in 1986 to build support for their latest grape boycott. Fifty thousand copies of this film were distributed, probably the most extensive agit-prop film campaign ever, but, strangely enough, a court ordered its circulation halted because one of the interviewees had not agreed to the film's use as a fund-raiser.

In addition to these agit-prop documentaries, whose makers seek a national and even international audience, an ever increasing number of unions and related corporate campaign groups have turned to the form simply to inform their membership or other sympathetic viewers of their mission or of a specific campaign. During the Pittston miners' struggle in 1987, the Justice for Pittston Miners committee released *They'll Never Keep Us Down,* an eleven-minute review of the issues behind the strike. The Teamsters released a celebratory ten-minute video-cassette, *America's Victory: The 1997 UPS Strike,* to commemorate their success against UPS. Another typical variation on agit-prop was the International Brotherhood of Painters and Allied Trades (IBPAT) video release, *Operation Clean Brush,* a 1996 video documenting the joint donation of union labor and Sherwin-Williams paint to paint over 250 houses in the Atlanta, Georgia, Olympic neighborhood and provide job training for local unemployed people. Similarly, *Rebuilding the American Dream,* a twelve-minute United Brotherhood of Carpenters (UBC) video, outlines an agreement between the federal Department of Housing and Urban Development and UBC and IBPAT to rehabilitate public housing and provide jobs through union apprentice programs. Although these videos in some cases are unabashedly public relations pieces, they represent current social concerns among trade unionists. For future labor historians, they will also provide a virtual time machine of attitudes and projects.

Postmodern documentaries are hybrid forms, drawing freely on traditional social realism but intercutting scripted or fictional scenes as well as sequences from other films (sometimes Hollywood films, sometimes deliberately campy or absurd films) and often starring the filmmaker as an essential part of the action. Michael Moore adapted the form for network and cable TV in his two series, *TV Nation* and *The Awful Truth.* Moore's guerrilla television style involves hit-and-run filmed confrontations and creatively staged and semiscripted surprise filming opportunities. The films sometimes were chronological, but their mixed modes of pop and high culture made them seem more like MTV than Frederick Wiseman. The controversies over Michael Moore's postmodern documentary filmmaking began with *Roger & Me* and extend to his Academy Award-winning *Bowling for Columbine* and his even more controversial *Fahrenheit 9/11.* Only gradually and with reluctance did the alternative filmmaking establishment understand that his work could not be judged by the standards of social realist or cinema verité documentary filmmaking.

The Big One (1997), Michael Moore's scattershot exploration of corporate downsizing and organizing drives (especially at Borders bookstores), was the most Internet-linked labor film in recent years. Even before its fairly wide theatrical circulation, Moore was heavily involved in using and redefining cyberspace as a new forum for postmodern documentary. The Web sites for both *TV Nation* (1994–95), Moore's television series of comic exposés of American culture and industry, and for his production company directed readers to peruse the Boycott Borders site and other sites relating to union organizing. The Boycott Borders site posted a "confidential" manual, "Union Awareness Training for Borders Managers," which exhaustively documents what managers need to know about union organizing ("Employees start gathering to talk in areas that are off the beaten path"), their own employees ("Borders is a national corporation with a large pool of full-time employees who generally tend to a little left of center"), and unions in general ("Unions are businesses which survive solely on the dues of their members"). This remarkable document would not have been so readily available without the Internet; furthermore, it becomes part of the documentary network of Moore's film.

A third direction, inevitably a future component of new working-class studies, involves digital videographers who support antiglobalization campaigns. What is of particular interest is how videographers from as many as nine activist and media organizations pool their footage, edit a digital program, and send it out through satellite transmission, the Internet, or both. *Showdown in Seattle: Five Days That Shook the WTO* (1999) was a five-part video broadcast day by day during the demonstrations in Seattle from November 30 through December 4, 1999, while *Breaking the Bank: A Challenge to the IMF and World Bank* (2000) recorded the April 2000 protests in Washington, D.C., against the International Monetary Fund (IMF) and World Bank. Besides showing rousing scenes of the street protests, antic puppet figures, and police attacks, the documentaries impeach the World Bank and the IMF for their reckless policies, which exacerbate the poverty and diminishing food supplies of Third World countries.

A fourth arena of new working-class studies involves the video "art" film, primarily an apolitical form in the past. Humphrey Jennings and Paul Strand, for example, were two outstanding early filmmakers who worked with labor and other class-intensive subjects, but later crossed over to the imagistic, nonnarrative forms associated with "art" filmmaking. Strand, who directed *Native Land*, also made *Manhattan* (1921), an impressionistic study of New York City at street level, and *Redes* (also known as *The Fishermen's Nets*, 1936). Jennings's wartime films, such as *Diary for Timothy* (1945) and *Listen to Britain* (1942), attempted to define the British character during wartime in anecdotal and imagistic style.

Recently, a number of filmmakers and artists have used the "art" film to explore labor and class issues. James Benning, considered a master of avant-garde minimalist filmmaking, explored California's largest growing region in *El Valley Centro* (2001). In static, extended shots, he isolated the beauty and threat of the powerful agribusinesses, their infrastructure of irrigation canals and railroads, and the undocumented immigrant labor that keeps the system working.

Travis Wilkerson's *An Injury to One* (2003) shows an important piece of labor history rarely covered in traditional documentaries. His film offers a partly imagistic, partly narrative account of Frank Little, the Wobbly murdered by vigilantes in Butte, Montana, in 1917 because of his organizing efforts in the copper-mining region that then supplied 10 percent of the world's copper.

Combining the "art" film with music video style, Bryn Zellers's *Process: Change and Sacrifice—Inclination and the Walk through Fire* (2003) uses archival footage (from, for example, the Republic Steel massacre of workers in Chicago in 1937), performance tapes (Zellers in an asbestos suit walking through fire), and scripted scenes (a steelworker handing his son a lunchbox with a little flame within) to build an interpretation of a powerful industrial culture in its heyday and decline.

Digital filmmaking and experiments with new forms of documentary make filming class easier than ever. The record of the past in Hollywood and in independent filmmaking indicates, however, that the danger always exists that these new and important films and the struggles they define will not persist without support and effort by interested viewers, teachers, trade unionists, community organizers, and researchers. Those who struggle to understand, or even to challenge or change the status quo, have greater technical means and artistic license to do so. Filming class has of course always been technically possible for any filmmaker; new working-class studies now provides the field for such filmmaking to flourish.

Films Cited

American Dream, directed by Barbara Kopple, 1990
And the Earth Did Not Swallow Him, directed by Severo Perez, 1994
The Awful Truth, directed by Michael Moore, 2000–01
The Big One, directed by Michael Moore, 1997
Black Panthers, produced by California Newsreel, 1968
Bowling for Columbine, directed by Michael Moore, 2002
Bread and Roses, directed by Ken Loach, 2000
Breaking the Bank: A Challenge to the IMF and World Bank, produced by Independent Media Center, 2000
Chaos: The Movie, produced by Association of Flight Attendants, 1994
The City, directed by David Riker, 1999
Diary for Timothy, directed by Humphrey Jennings, 1945
Fahrenheit 9/11, directed by Michael Moore, 2004
Finally Got the News, directed by Stewart Bird, Peter Gessner, Rene Lichtman, and John Louis Jr., 1970
God's Little Acre, directed by Anthony Mann, 1958
Goin' to Chicago, directed by George King, 1994
Harlan County, U.S.A., directed by Barbara Kopple, 1977
Harlan County War, directed by Tony Bill, 2000
Harvest of Shame, directed by Palmer Williams, 1960
The Inheritance, directed by Harold Mayer, 1964
An Injury to One, directed by Travis Wilkerson, 2003
Joe Hill, directed by Bo Widerberg, 1971

The Killing Floor, directed by William Duke, 1984

The Life and Times of Rosie the Riveter, directed by Connie Field, 1980

Listen to Britain, directed by Humphrey Jennings, 1942

Long Day at Overnite, produced by the International Brotherhood of Teamsters, 2002

Manhatta, directed by Paul Strand, 1921

Matewan, directed by John Sayles, 1987

Mickey Mouse Goes to Haiti, produced by the National Labor Committee, 1996

Native Land, directed by Paul Strand, 1942

Norma Rae, directed by Martin Ritt, 1979

One Day Longer, directed by Amie Williams, 2000

On the Waterfront, directed by Elia Kazan, 1954

Operation Clean Brush, produced by the International Brotherhood of Painters and Allied Trades, 1996

Out at Work, directed by Kelly Anderson and Tami Gold, 1996; 1999

Process: Change and Sacrifice—Inclination and the Walk through Fire, directed by Bryn Zellers, 2003

Rebuilding the American Dream, produced by the United Brotherhood of Carpenters, 1994

Redes, directed by Paul Strand, 1936

Roger & Me, directed by Michael Moore, 1989

Sacco and Vanzetti, directed by Giuliano Montaldo, 1971

Salesmen, directed by David and Albert Maysles, 1969

San Francisco State Strike, produced by California Newsreel, 1969

Secrets of Silicon Valley, directed by Alan Snitow and Deborah Kaufman, 2000

Showdown in Seattle: Five Days That Shook the WTO, produced by Independent Media Center, 1999

Surviving the Good Times, produced by Bill Moyers, 2000

Taxi Dreams, directed by Joanna Head, 2001

10,000 Black Men Named George, directed by Robert Townsend, 2002

They'll Never Keep Us Down, produced by the United Mine Workers of America, 1987

Tobacco Road, directed by John Ford, 1941

TV Nation, directed by Michael Moore, 1994–95

El Valley Centro, directed by James Benning, 2001

With Babies and Banners, directed by Lorraine Gray, Anne Bohlen, and Lyn Goldfarb, 1978

The Wrath of Grapes, directed by Leona Parlee and Lenny Bourin, 1986

11

"Working Man's Ph.D.": The Music of Working-Class Studies

Rachel Lee Rubin

> My pants are ragged, but that's all right
> I've got five dollars and it's Saturday night.
>
> > Faron Young, "Saturday Night" (1956)

> I was working part time in a five-and-dime
> My boss was Mr. McGee
> He told me several times that he didn't like my kind
> 'Cause I was a bit 2 leisurely
>
> > Prince, "Raspberry Beret" (1985)

> Heard you singing in a Taco Bell bathroom
> Heard you singing a Cheap Trick song
>
> > Everclear, "Sunshine (The Acid Summer)" (2003)

"The View from the Cheap Seats"

When I was growing up in Baltimore, and the Orioles still played their home games in the old Memorial Stadium, the song played during the seventh-inning stretch was John Denver's "Thank God I'm a Country Boy." This was extremely important to the spectators in the bleachers. When "Thank God" came over the loudspeakers, they'd jump up on the benches with alacrity, sing along, even if the Orioles were losing, and holler out particular lines with an enthusiasm that seemed to go beyond their affection for the baseball team. This gleeful participation included both black and white fans. Once, for some reason, another song was played during the seventh-inning stretch. The people around me were pissed off. It was an alarming moment.

An admission up front: I hate John Denver—I always have—and I especially hate "Thank God I'm a Country Boy." But I have summoned Denver's song and those moments in the bleachers because I wanted deliberately to single out a cloying—even inauthentic—song so that I can start this essay by trying to show two things: First, the way people use popular music is complicated, contradictory, and not always predictable. Second, studying its many public and private functions as part of New Working-Class Studies is potentially very rewarding. In short, I wanted to open my thoughts on scholarship, class, and pop music with a moment in which those Americans Bill Malone likes to call "plain folk" used an insincere commercial song to articulate their own truth about class identity—and came together to wave it like a flag.

Baltimore in the 1970s was a big city, among the nation's Top 10 in population. (It's smaller now, due to deindustrialization, white flight, "free trade" job loss, and so on.) Its population of 780,000 was urban and dense, and it is likely that there were few, if any, country boys or girls in the stadium at most baseball games. But the families of many working-class Baltimoreans, black and white, had ended up there because previous generations had left the country and come to the city to work in the mills and factories. In Baltimore, to call someone "country" did not signify their being rural or even a rube; rather, it operated as a shorthand description for people who lived in certain blue-collar neighborhoods, worked at certain blue-collar jobs, frequented certain bars, and so on. A class-based insult when I was growing up was to call someone from a poor family a "grit," thereby expressing contempt for his or her cultural style while connecting it to the earlier generation's migration from the South in search of industrial jobs. Singing "Thank God I'm a Country Boy" at Memorial Stadium, then, worked as a statement of "grit" pride (though no one ever called it that). It didn't matter a whit that John Denver was not a "real" country boy or that "Thank God" was not a "real" country song.

There is a lot to be learned about the social and cultural history of Baltimore, Detroit, San Antonio, or any other American city that will help us to understand the precise ways in which economic class (and its range of attendant indicators) determines and is determined by the "way of life" that Americans experience—despite the fact that class mobility and mutability continue to lie at the heart of the myth of America. In this essay, I'd like to drop the undeserving John Denver (and other popular musicians) right into the center of that discussion. Keeping the music itself at center stage as much as possible, I am going to offer some thoughts on a two-part question: What are the special insights we can gain by examining music as a major way of understanding how working people have defined and comported themselves? And what does paying attention to class—using the toolkit of the cultural critic to pry into America's "dirty little secret"—bring to the still relatively new study of popular music? Here, I take under my purview the construction of work-based identity; the various manifestations of class consciousness and class struggle; the confluence (and contest) in music of race, class, gender, and region; and the ways music operates daily as industrial practice, aesthetic practice, and social practice. I urge that the history of popular music be conceived of as labor history and that working-class studies be conceived of as a home for a multifaceted consideration of the meanings of pop music in the material world. My title is taken from a song by country singer Aaron Tippin, in which the narrator instructs his listeners, with audible resentment about which kinds of knowledge get authorized, that there is more than one way to get an education. What, then, can we learn from a song?

"Jane, She Is a Clerk": Work and Identity in American Popular Music

In the postapocalyptic television series *Dark Angel,* which was (among other things) a meditation on the ownership of labor, a group of genetically enhanced worker-soldiers has been developed in a U.S. government research project. Believing that they and their work (and their particular abilities to perform certain tasks) should belong to themselves, one "sibling" group of "transgenics" escapes and is dispersed; their life on the run, and attempts to find and help each other, structure the show. One feature of the transgenics makes it easier for the escapees to identify one another—and also to be identified by their pursuers: transgenics have bar codes on the back of their necks, marking them permanently both as merchandise and as superworker.

This is meaningful fantasy: if people really did have bar codes (as good a pictorial representation of the marketplace as any) on their necks, then getting a grip on the meanings of "working class" would be so much easier that we might not need the apparatus of working-class studies to begin with. As it is, of course, "class" is a slippery concept that is differently understood, and applied, across a wide range of viewpoints. And what constitutes "class consciousness" is even slipperier. This is true in the ideological or scholarly sense—you can be a Marxist or a Weberian or a Durkheimian; you can believe that class is the source of all conflicts or that class mobility makes such distinctions irrelevant or temporary. This is just as true in the more individual sense, particularly with regard to self-identity. A person might or might not identify as a member of the working class, and once she or he does, what that means is certainly open for discussion. Does it have to do with the nature of the job you hold? The amount of money you earn?

What your parents did for a living? Your level of education? Whether you are salaried or paid by the hour? Whether you do "clean" or "dirty" work? Where you live? Your lifestyle? Further, a person can hold a particular class-based self-identity very dearly, only to have a different one imposed from without—as the bar codes remind us in *Dark Angel*. Of course, the whole equation must be adjusted constantly over time, because economies and the means of production change continuously: as the large number of industrial jobs emphasized by Marx, for instance, give way to growing numbers of jobs in the service economy or the new information technology industry.

I realize that I am rehearsing the obvious here as I try to set up "working class" as a terribly unfixed category. But the term works best when used to describe a meaningful, boisterous, highly motivated, frequently confrontational, and occasionally deadly conversation. Asserting this truism in a collection of writings by leading scholars of working-class studies may well be redundant and unnecessary. My reason for doing it anyway is motivated by my conviction that this noisy conversation has often been hosted by American popular music.

The pop song, in other words, is one of the most important forums wherein working Americans have made meaning out of the politics of their work. This has been true as long as there has been American music, and as long as laborers (performing under various levels of coercion imposed by slavery, wage capitalism, subsistence conditions, institutional racism and sexism, and so forth) have sung together words in the spirit of this gracefully knowing African American folk song from the Georgia Sea Islands: "If I were the bossman's son / Wouldn't have to work in the hot hot sun." In both black and white American song traditions, it is the work song that sits at the center of what is called "roots music" or more recently "Americana"—and therefore makes up the foundation of rhythm and blues, rock and roll, gospel, country, and hip hop.

Since music began to be recorded, music corporations have had to push constantly to protect and expand their control of music as a valuable commodity. In the twenty-first century, this push is visible all over the map, from the panic of music companies trying to stanch the (free) flow of music over the Internet to the plush success of shows such as *American Idol,* which daringly assert corporate puppeteering as part of the appeal. In the face of all this, it's striking that the producers, and especially the consumers, of popular music have continued to claim it as a space where work-based identity is processed. I don't just mean certain songwriters here, such as Woody Guthrie or Bruce Springsteen, who are well known for their politically engaged representations of working-class American lives. Nor do I refer only to particular genres of pop music, either, although certain ones, such as country music and rap, do present themselves as especially bound up with work as a theme.

One doesn't have to look hard for reasons why popular music is the cultural form most prominent for commenting on work-based identities. Most powerfully, access to popular music is practically universal. You need relatively few tools and no formal training to listen to it, and you even need relatively few tools and training to make it. Art Alexakis, with his West Coast rock band Everclear, makes clear the connection between access and working-class culture in his song "AM Radio" (as well as throughout his other songs). Recalling his youth in the 1970s, he sings, "Cruisin' with the windows rolled down, we'd listen to the radio station / We were too damn poor to buy the 8 track tapes . . . but you could hear it on the AM radio." On Everclear's albums, music accompanies their working-class protagonists through summers in housing projects, on Greyhound buses, to the unemployment office, walking home as the only white kid in a black neighborhood, and through dozens of lousy and temporary jobs in the service industry (including phone sex).

Music is one of the few cultural forms that can "follow" its practitioners in the course of their daily lives in that way, and perhaps the only form that some workers can partake of (listening *and* singing) while they are working. This makes music deeply connected to working lives, not sectioned off for leisure time the way, say, a movie would be. Members of painting crews, construction gangs, and assembly line workers have described to me the importance of having "their" music on the job—to the extent that listening to music while working as a battle between labor and management has become a recognizable trope in fictional representations of workplaces. For instance, in the 1976 movie *Car Wash* not only is listening to the radio presented as a significant working condition but who gets to choose the station is also figured as important.

Along slightly different lines, in the 2002 movie *8 Mile,* the protagonist Rabbit (played semi-autobiographically by the white rapper Eminem) and his coworkers at a stamping plant blow off steam during their lunch hour by holding impromptu rap battles (that take on, among other subjects, their working conditions). Because nothing is required besides the human voice, producing music at work in this way has also, along with listening to music at work, been an important way in which work identity and cultural identity merge in popular musical forms. Country megastar Buck Owens describes working as a cotton picker (before he became a star, of course): "The Mexicans would be picking cotton over here, and they'd be singing, great Mexican harmony that they sang. Over here the blacks would be singing, and they sang mostly blues and gospel songs, and you know, you hear all that, and here you are, a kid looking at all that."[1] Eventually Owens put these influences—along with the music of his own Texas family—together into what would come to be called the Bakersfield sound, a sound that would transform country music.

If, as scholars or teachers, we are looking for portraits of workers, concrete ones that show what they are doing and ones in which they can speak pretty much in their own voices (or "accents" as Michael Denning would call it), we'd do well to remember that for every *Roseanne, Rivethead* (by Ben Hamper), *The Circuit: Stories from the Life of a Migrant Child* (by Francisco Jimenez),[2] or painting by Ralph Fasanella (wonderful treasures that I don't mean to slight), there are hundreds of pop songs that picture working people working—and dozens more, I would argue, where work is encoded or referred to in various ways, just off screen, as it were. Rapper Shelley Thunder minced no words in 1989 when she proclaimed, "I'm a working girl / I don't waste my time, to get mine, in this world"; but more obliquely, how could the "hot fun in the summertime" promised by Sly and the Family Stone in 1969 happen until you got off your lousy summer job?

Working-class studies stands only to benefit from taking seriously such laden portraits as the many truck drivers of country music:

> The I.C.C. is checking on down the line.
> I'm a little overweight and my log's three days behind.
> But nothing bothers me tonight, I can dodge all the scales all right
> Six days on the road and I'm gonna make it home tonight.
>
> > Dave Dudley, "Six Days on the Road"

the stockyard and steel mill workers of the Chicago blues:

> I got a job at a steel mill, I'm shucking steel just like a slave
> Five long years, every Friday I went straight home with all my pay
> Yes, I've been mistreated
> And you got to, you got to know just what I'm talking about.
>
> > Eddie Boyd, "Five Long Years"

the fruit pickers of *conjunto:*

> Hombres, niños y mujeres
> Con el sol en las labores.
> ¿Cuanto se gana el ranchero,
> Cuanto los trabajadores?
>
> > Los Pinguinos del Norte,
> > "Corrido de César Chávez"

> (Men, women and children
> Labor beneath the sun.
> How much does the rancher profit?
> How much do the workers get paid?)
>
> > translation from *Chulas Fronteras
> > and Del Mero Corazon,* tran-
> > scribed and translated by Yolanda
> > and Guillermo Hernandez with
> > Zack and Juanita Salem, Maureen
> > Gosling, James Nicolopulos, and
> > Leticia Del Tora

the frustrated nine-to-fivers of rock and roll:

> He gets up each morning and he goes downtown
> where everyone's his boss and he's lost in an angry land
> he's a little man
>
> The Crystals, "Uptown"

not to mention the cowboys and prostitutes and teenaged lifeguards and sidemen and rail-splitters and drug dealers whose particular jobs serve a more symbolic function in what they evoke in listeners, but nonetheless are part of an important tapestry of popular song about who does what work, who sings about it, who gets credit—and who, of course, gets paid.

What these portraits accomplish, besides the creation of a certain class realism with a beat you can dance to, is the creation of a community—a community that, in the lyrics of Eddie Boyd quoted above, will "know just what I'm talking about." In other words, a major function of the music is to facilitate a sense of group identity, a commonality based on shared experience and shared economic interest—indeed, what could be called class consciousness.

Now, one could hardly argue that listening to pop songs about fictional characters who work is the same sort of self-interested activity as, say, becoming active in a trade union. But the sense of working-class community created by music has great symbolic importance, and it's worth our time as scholars to remember this. A good example of how wise and knowing this musical community building is can be teased out of the version the New York-based punk band the Del-Lords recorded in 1984 of "How Can a Poor Man Stand Such Times and Live." The song was originally recorded in 1929 by Blind Alfred Reed, a white street musician from Virginia. Reed's song is one of many Depression era protest songs that pit the "poor man" against the (relatively) wealthy, in Reed's case the grocer and the doctor:

> I remember a time when everything was cheap
> Now prices nearly puts a man to sleep
> Well, when we get our grocery bill
> We feel like making our will
> Tell me, how can a poor man stand such times and live?

When they recorded their cover version of the song, the Del-Lords updated its sound with powerfully effective punk vocals—punk being a form of rock music associated with working-class audiences and performers. They also added a verse:

> This poor boy's got some big plans of his own
> Gonna call up a couple of friends on the telephone

> Tell 'em bring some records and bring some beer
> We can just hang out down here
> Tell me, how can a poor man stand such times and live?

The added verse is wonderfully rich in its implications. Like Everclear, the Del-Lords are describing music as a crucial part of the working-class community ("bring some records and bring some beer"); by performing Reed's song, a class-based complaint that consistently uses the word "we," they are enacting this community building simultaneously with describing it—putting musicians into the working-class mix and putting their own efforts as musicians into a historical context of class resentment that spans a half century.

By adding the verse about records, the Del-Lords are taking some care to present themselves as listeners, not just performers. Indeed, music gives a huge amount of power to the audience, often blurring the lines between performer and artist to a degree that is unique (and likely to remain unique unless people find a literary or painterly equivalent of singing in the shower). Furthermore, because music is considerably unscripted in comparison to other cultural forms, there are gaps and invitations in which listeners can insert themselves and their values (starting with the five-year-old who revises Montell Jordan to suit his own needs by singing "This is how we do it / Pick your nose and chew it"). Dylan's quick-bake spiritual with the words "You're gonna have to serve somebody, it may be the devil and it may be the Lord, but you're gonna have to serve somebody" can very quickly become "You're gonna have to shoot somebody; it may be your landlord it may be your boss." Even such silly examples make a point about production and consumption, about big business and small listener.

"Let the Poor Man Live and the Rich Man Bust": Music as Location of Class Struggle

There are hundreds of songs like the ones I've quoted above that draw from a body of images of work and worker. But the popular economists who are writing and listening to these songs have more than inert illustration on their minds. Often in popular music, one can find the most naked representations of class difference and class resentment that you'll find on the American cultural landscape, which still often clings to an official cover story that class is an American secret—it exists, but we don't talk about it. Pretty much all my students (at urban, public UMass Boston) say, if asked, that they are from middle-class families; all but a few will tell you that they believe in, and have benefited from, class mobility. This alone is not surprising, for in the mass media as well as in recent academic work there has been a preoccupation with the term "middle class" and its cultures that has become so broad and nonspecific that it serves to blunt or elide a sense of class identity. But the musical lives of these same students—and it is a rare student who doesn't have one at all—reveal naked depictions of class divisions, class identifications, and even class struggle.

Class struggle crops up in the music in lots of ways. A trope of early rock and roll, as Jim Smethurst has pointed out, is the doomed (or at least threatened) love relationship between a poor boy and a rich girl or, somewhat less often, a poor girl and a rich boy ("Leader of the Pack," "Down at the Boondocks," "Dawn," "Rag Doll," "Hang on Sloopy," "Uptight," and many others).[3] In the teen-identified world of rock and roll (at least in its first few decades), class resentment was a structuring principle to the extent that camp king John Waters has organized more than one historical movie (*Hairspray,* made in 1988 about 1963, and *Cry-Baby,* made in 1990 about 1954) around struggles between the rich kids and the poor kids, which are resolved in musical cutting contests.[4] Waters's hormonally pumped teenaged "drapes" and "whiffles" may tussle and kiss, but in early country music the cost of these romantic class-crossings was generally death. Class difference hangs ominously over the many murder ballads, such as Ken Maynard's story of "Fair Fannie Moore" who chose a poor suitor over a rich one with the result that all three died at the "haughty" rich suitor's hand. The song's sympathy, of course, is all with the poor kids—as are Waters's movies. How could it not be? Country music and rock and roll (which partially descended from country music) are forms that have been associated with working-class audiences since their inception.

Class identification in popular music is cast in many ways—one of the most wonderful things about popular music studies is the number of levels at which it allows analysts to operate. Perhaps most evident is what gets said in the lyrics. Here there is often direct theorizing about the structures of class that could illustrate the most complex, canonical texts of economics. For example, Merle Haggard articulates the class-based structure of society in his 1969 "Hungry Eyes": "We kids were just too young to realize / That another class of people kept us somewhere just below / One more reason for my mama's hungry eyes." John Anderson sums up the whole concept of alienated labor in his Friday afternoon anthem "Quittin' Time": "I'm tired of making whatever it is we make / And having some fool tell me when to take a break." Country supergroup Alabama, in its "40 Hour Week," articulates the theory of surplus labor value: "There are people in this country who work hard every day / and not for fame and fortune do they strive / But the fruits of their labor are worth more than their pay / And it's time a few of them were recognized." Becky Hobbs explains the role of the family under capitalism in her song "Mama Was a Working Man," reminding us, "She made a living and a home / And if the truth be known / She worked twice as hard, for half the pay."

A particularly smart and layered example of music as class struggle is 1999's "Shove This Jay-Oh-Bee," by rappers Canibus and Biz Markie (from the soundtrack for the office revenge comedy *Office Space*). The song quotes, invokes, and revises country singer Johnny Paycheck's 1977 hit "Take This Job and Shove It," in which a worker on the factory floor imagines how gratifying it would be to tell his foolish foreman that he is quitting, in the most vivid language he can imagine. In his performance of this song (and in his self-presentation more generally), Paycheck took pains to style himself as a blue-collar worker. He took "Paycheck" as his stage name, abandoning an earlier one, Donny Young. He wore denim work clothes. He is pictured on the sheet music for "Shove It" amid a crowd of workers holding picket signs. His audiences seemed willing to see him this way, and in 1977 "Shove It" climbed to No. 1 on the *Billboard* country charts; because it mattered so much to listeners, the song became an anthem of working-class dissent even though the only action it advocates specifically is mouthing off.

On the face of it, it's fascinating that Canibus would choose Paycheck's country song as inspiration for his own rap song. It is generally understood (incorrectly, it appears) that country music and rap music speak for and to two entirely different audiences, divided by race (and also region) so completely that alliance would be unthinkable in this musical context. But in the case of "Shove This Jay-Oh-Bee," class resentment is clearly what has allowed the color line to be crossed, and while "Shove This Jay-Oh-Bee" is out to get laughs, it is not Johnny Paycheck, or pissed-off white workers, who are the butt of the joke. Rather, Canibus takes Paycheck's factory scenario and updates it to reflect the experiences of a low-level employee in the corporate environment:

> You wonder why your work load is so enormous
> Because your boss just laid off three-quarters of the whole office
> People get depressed, they get ulcers
> From the stress that the corporate environment causes

Canibus and Biz Markie are using Paycheck's song as a jumping-off place for a minihistory of work. In his version, Canibus invokes the postindustrial economy; he mentions cubicles and staplers and the like as opposed to Paycheck's factory and line boss. Since Paycheck's version is audible still in Canibus's—the chorus consists mainly of Biz Markie singing, over and over, the tag line of Paycheck's song, "Take this job and shove it / I ain't working here no more"—a commentary emerges about how one kind of exhausting work followed the other. (This intertextuality, a hallmark of rap music, has made it an important source of popular history, musical and otherwise. Here, a twenty-year-old song is introduced to new listeners.) Indeed, perhaps all that needs to be said is that the boss is the villain of both pieces.

Furthermore, Canibus's song is useful for the ways in which it challenges any simple notions of what kind of work is included in the category "working class"—he is talking about exploited office drones (they do punch time clocks) who probably have a dress code, but one that does not include hard hats. Here is an example whereby careful attention to these songs can broaden and deepen our practices as historians of the working-class experience.

The technology used to make "Shove This Jay-Oh-Bee" is the technology used in the kind of work that is being depicted. This is a song about working in an office, with telephones and computers and the kinds of electronic equipment that are used to produce rap music's wide kit of sounds: samples, distortions, superfast beats, overdubbing, and so forth. In other words "Good Morning, Mister Time Clock" (Pete Rowan) has become "Good Morning, Mister Motherboard." (Or should that be "Ms. Motherboard"?)

Finally, as well as invoking the new economy and the assembly line world, not to mention a decades-old song by a white country singer, Canibus and Biz Markie's version also can be seen to be making a sly nod (in a sly song) to more organized activism. They do give very specific instructions for how to give your boss the finger—close to his face, so he can see it clearly—but their decision to spell out the word "Job" in the title of the song also refers to the long-standing slogan "I need a J-O-B so I can E-A-T" that has been chanted for years at marches and rallies.

"Forget That You're a Lady and Give Them What They Deserve": Music as Social Practice

In the previous section, I have focused largely, though not exclusively, on the lyrical content of various songs—and indeed, all the tools of formal literary studies can usefully be brought to bear on the poetry of popular music. But one of the most compelling reasons to bring popular music into new working-class studies is that musical texts allow students and scholars to "have at" a topic in an unusually multilayered way, with the result that looking at class in music provides one of the most holistic pictures of the ways in which class makes meaning in American society.

Taking a cue from Graeme Turner's recognition of film as social practice,[5] we should more broadly adopt the notion of music as social practice. Because music is not just poetry set to a tune, we need to teach students to understand music as entertainment (which they do), as narrative, and as a cultural event. Discussing the major ideological issues surrounding the history of popular music, and using them to examine the cultural function of music and its place in our twenty-first-century popular culture, we can demonstrate the ways in which ideas about class have developed over time—and how these ideas have been popularly deployed, adopted, and challenged. For instance, students are generally amazed to learn how many racist songs from the minstrel stage—America's first form of popular culture—have found a sort of second life in the so-called American songbooks that are still frequently ensconced in elementary school classrooms. That the humorous misspeaking of "Oh! Susanna" was originally intended to mock the language and, by extension, the mental capacity of African Americans, for instance, or that "Turkey in the Straw" (which ice cream trucks play in my integrated neighborhood every summer) contained the hideous verse "I came to the river and I couldn't get across / So I jumped on a n——r cuz I thought he was a horse" offer plain lessons in how society can naturalize certain people to certain kinds of work. The fact that many college students remember singing these songs in school, and that school children still sing these songs, opens a discussion about how these naturalized ideas get handed down over the years and how the ideas survive or are moderated.

Fortunately, music can also be a tool of resistance and even revolution, and this capacity of songs to be weapons in struggle certainly extends to (working)-class interests. Florence Reece, wife of coal miner and organizer Sam Reece, wrote her well-known song "Which Side Are You On?" in 1931, during the coal-mining union struggle in Harlan County, Kentucky ("Bloody Harlan"). Reece scribbled the verses to "Which Side Are You On?" on the back of a calendar page she pulled hastily off the wall after her husband ran out the back door to elude a posse of sheriffs and thugs, hired by the coal company operators, who were coming in the front door. Her song was adapted and used in many other struggles, becoming a standard union protest song. (These uses included an "update" by English political rocker Billy Bragg, who used Reece's chorus in a song he recorded in 1984 about the British miners' strike of 1984–85; Bragg performed his version on the Labor MPs' Jobs for Youth Tour.) Reece's lyrics, by the way, insist that working-class identity depends on a simple choice of conscience, one that cannot be avoided or complicated:

> They say in Harlan County, there are no neutrals there
> You'll either be a union man or a thug for J. H. Blair.
> Which side are you on?
>
> Florence Reece, "Which Side Are You On?"

Likewise, in 1969 the rock and roll group Creedence Clearwater Revival, during the height of its popularity and at a time when its songs were climbing the charts, recorded "Fortunate Son," a bitter attack on the practice of members of the privileged classes sending working-class youth off to fight the war in Vietnam. Reece's song, and CCR's, were consciously written and taken up as part of cultural movements connected to immediate, ongoing political movements—the union's struggle for workers' rights in Harlan, the anti–Vietnam War movement (which from the beginning was powered by Vietnam veterans who were very aware of who was being sent to fight and who was receiving deferments).

But just as interesting are the songs taken up after the fact, perhaps after their whole first round of mainstream popularity, and connected by listeners' use to a political movement. This pattern is a long-standing one in American popular music history. For instance, "Weave Room Blues," recorded by the Dixon Brothers in 1932 as a Depression-era protest song, was taken up by striking Piedmont, North Carolina, textile workers following World War II, who sang it at their picket lines and considered the song to be a cultural part of their organizing strategy. Diana Ross's nonspecific self-esteem anthem of 1980, "I'm Coming Out," was immediately taken up by the largely working-class and nonwhite gay disco scene. The song's recent use in the movie *Maid in Manhattan* (2002), a vehicle for Jennifer Lopez (who had been desperately trying to reconnect with her working-class roots that year through her song "Jenny from the Block") to provide the soundtrack for a shy working mom coming out of her shell to recognize her inner ability to party with (and ultimately marry) the rich, puts an entirely different class-based spin on the song by bringing "coming out" back to its debutante meaning. More recently, star rapper Missy "Misdemeanor" Eliot's 2002 "Work It"—a song characterized by complex rhythms and celebratory, explicitly sexual lyrics—was adapted for use at a Boston march against the war in Iraq in early 2003.

"He Fired My Ass and He Fired Jerry Rivers": Music as Industrial Practice

Finally, there is much to be learned about class and culture from sustained industrial analysis of the music world, from its first manifestations as a sheet music business, through the consolidation of race-based styles and codes during the early recording period, to the handful of multibillion dollar corporations (and anticorporate file-sharing programs) that dominate it today—and those smaller producers and distributors who still manage to carve out some space. The groundwork has been laid by seminal writing on the music business by Russell Sanjek and David Sanjek (*American Popular Music Business in the Twentieth Century* [1991]) and Steve Chapple and Reebee Garofalo (*Rock 'N' Roll Is Here to Pay* [1977]). Still, this remains an area of sorely needed work, although some recent books, such as Sherrie Tucker's *Swing Shift: "All Girl" Bands of the 1940s* (2000) and Ruth Glasser's *My Music Is My Flag: Puerto Rican Musicians and Their New York Communities, 1917–1940* (1997), have tried to give full portraits of working musicians as people who are doing labor for other people.[6] Interviews, oral histories, autobiographies, and the like reveal that the musicians themselves frequently believe there is an important story to be told about the conditions of their labor—especially as it relates to their race, gender, and sexual identity. Indeed, this must have been at least part of what was on James Brown's mind when he dubbed himself "the hardest working man in show business." But too often, this story is left as conventional wisdom—white-owned recording industries ripping off "authentic" black performers—or, more recently, the corporate "creation" of an apparently endless stream of "inauthentic" teenaged stars—without the kind of vigorous institutional research that would show how the music itself is shaped and molded by the practices and mandates of industry. In short, how the categories of "authentic" and "inauthentic"—not to mention the tunes—have a class-based story to tell.

What I am suggesting here is that working-class studies could be an enormously fruitful place for popular music history to be written as labor history (in the way that Gerald Horne, James Lorence, and Paul Buhle have started to do for Hollywood). In this way, too, the materialist orientations of working-class studies could pose a productive challenge to our still-prevailing romantic notions of what goes into making great music—even great popular music. We'd have to let in the sweat, for instance, but even more difficult, we'd have to let in the money. It's still very hard to accept that a person who creates music could have getting paid in mind without necessarily being a "sellout" or lacking in artistic vision. We'd also have to sacrifice notions of musical performance as somehow natural—to abandon the lovely if corny idea that "the hills are alive with the sound of music"—to admit a more complicated, and contentious, picture of various social forces and economic interests coming together to create culture. The working-class history of popular music needs to include real analysis of contracts and royalty agreements. It needs to include in its purview salaries, hiring practices, health plans, and pensions (or lack thereof); union efforts (including the new one spearheaded in 2001 by Hole's Courtney Love, which calls for collective representation of the rights of recording artists); working conditions and hours; the relationship of musical output to the "day jobs" that most artists have had to maintain at least at the beginnings of their careers and the "fallback jobs" that many worked after their performing or recording careers ended or hit dry spells (such as R&B great Ruth Brown, who worked in domestic service).

Working-class studies could teach popular music studies that to keep up on the arts one has to read the business section of the local newspaper as well as the arts section. Lately, this has been easier than usual to see because digital distribution of music is changing the music business forever, and media coverage has been extensive. The recording industry succeeded in shutting down Napster, the first big file-swapping service, in 2000, on the grounds that it violated copyright agreements by distributing music, computer to computer, at no charge. But dozens of similar or replacement services have sprung up, and interested parties are scrambling to figure out how to deal with it. Recording companies and the Recording Industry Association of America are continuing to bring lawsuits against users. Colleges are fretting over the irreconcilable problem of pitting legal mandates against the free exchange of ideas and materials over their networks. Artists are responding in various ways: Prince, for instance, distributes his music primarily over the Internet now, while Billy Bragg handed out CD copies of his antiwar songs at concerts and urged people to upload them to file-sharing services. Some recording artists have taken the opportunity to point out that the money supposedly being lost in CD sales would not have reached them in the first place, while others have denounced the practice as stealing. The nonprofit Future of Music Coalition, which formed to address the new music and technology issues, points out that key decisions about the legality of trading music files online are being made without input from artists or listeners. In its manifesto, FMC uses the language of class to describe the position of artists in the digital age, claiming that a goal of their educational efforts is to help create a "musicians' middle class."[7]

"Poor Folks Stick Together": Class, Race, and Gender

Admitting business practices into the "arts" side of music studies has the potential to redefine our understanding of cultural expressivity. On the other hand, admitting cultural practices, such as the production and consumption of popular music, into our social histories will strengthen us as working-class historians. Music invariably brings the question of race into the picture, and gender, and sexual orientation, and regionalism, managing to show the way class commonalities can create a sense of community while not overlooking the special concerns facing women, say, or African Americans. Recently, the potential for a cross-racial class alliance through music was much discussed in the critical response to Eminem's movie *8 Mile,* in which class trumps race in a rap cutting contest. The crucial moment in the movie occurs when Eminem's white character triumphs in a black musical form by scornfully revealing that his African American opponent went to private school and drives a fancy car while he himself grew up poor in a trailer park. That sort of cross-racial give and take is actually the definitive story of American popular music. After all, American history has been defined by migration and immigration, causing culturally productive meetings among groups and cultures like the one described by Buck Owens earlier in this essay. And these new and older Americans were moving to and within the country for work-related reasons, giving a class context to both cultural confrontations and the music it ultimately produced. When African American workers were hired to build roads through the southern Appalachians, for instance, black and white workers shared musical styles that would change string band styles and blues styles. It also helped produce the many black string bands and white blues singers that have largely been forgotten with the help of racist institutions that would prefer for the former to be "white" music and the latter to be "black."

Popular music provides very rich moments for analysis of this process. African

American country singer Stoney Edwards worked as a janitor, gardener, and farmhand before beginning to perform in local clubs in Texas and California. In a supposedly "white" form, one deeply associated with the working-class experience, he sang in 1971 what starts out as a fairly standard song about being stranded on the highway in the rain. Expensive cars are passing him by:

> But yonder comes a diesel, and them's my kind of people
> They're the kind that never lets you down
> I can hear him shifting gears, in a minute he'll be here
> To take me down the road to where I'm bound.
>
> Stoney Edwards, "Poor Folks Stick Together"

In this song and many others, Edwards is making a point—utopian, perhaps, but moving in any event—about the potential for working people to depend on one another despite their racial backgrounds. Long before *8 Mile,* rap musicians imagined the act of listening as a way to create a multiracial community—as early as the first nationally released rap song, the Sugar Hill Gang's 1979 "Rapper's Delight," in which the group imagined making everybody dance with joy:

> Now what you hear is not a test—I'm rappin to the beat
> and me, the groove, and my friends are gonna try to move your feet
> See I am Wonder Mike and I like to say hello
> to the black, to the white, the red, and the brown, the purple and yellow

This utopian dream would be carried much further by the mischievous and outspoken Missy Eliot in her 2002 song "Work It," in which she lets it be known that she likes, and can please, "Boys, boys, all type of boys / Black, white, Puerto Rican, Chinese boys."

Popular music has also been attentive to the ways in which identity is more multiple or even fragmented than any simple definition of class can cover. Take, for example, Norma Jean's 1967 plaint "Heaven Help the Poor Working Girl," in which the narrator, a waitress, describes being propositioned by a (married) male customer, concluding, "Oh heaven help the working girl / In a world that's run by men." Norma Jean here is talking plainly (in a song that made the *Billboard* charts) about what came to be called sexual harassment and to be acknowledged as a special vulnerability faced by women workers.

These popular songs theorize class identity in a strikingly plain manner. Often, this identity is inflected in particular ways by race, region, gender, and the like—while "class" remains something that is pictured and theorized in ways that transcend these categories.

"Don Quixote Was a Steel-Driving Man": Class Aesthetics in Pop Music

I have only had space to hint at a few of the strategies that popular musicians and audiences have devised and employed to create a language of class: depictions of working people, expressions of economic injustice, appeals to cross-racial audiences, the use of music in social movements. These strategies and others combine to give us what I think we can call an aesthetics of class—as long as we are careful to ground that sense of aesthetics historically and materially, and keep it flexible enough to include both the tropes of blues about sharecropping and the tropes of girl group songs about dating.

It is crucial—and very rewarding—to look at class markers and arguments that exist in the pop music world in many different places. The persistent use of vernacular in lyrics, for instance, is an artistic choice that insists that no matter who's listening (or singing, for that matter) now, and no matter how much cash is being generated, popular music's roots and heart are not in the culture of the elite or the highly educated. At the same time, the use of vernacular (as simple as a dropped "g," a slang term, or the word "ain't") can express or encode an ambivalent or even hostile stance toward cultural forms associated with the bourgeoisie. A prime example here is the name of country music's traditional bedrock venue, the Grand Ole Opry.[8]

Although music is undeniably a primarily aural form, there are a range of visual gestures and stances, some familiar by now, that have to be considered as part of popular music's class consciousness. Worth particular mention is the cover of country super-group Alabama's 1985 album *40 Hour Week* (on which the song by the same title, mentioned earlier, appears). They are arranged in front of a time clock, wearing jeans, work boots, and hard hats, carrying lunch boxes, and so on—in other words, presenting themselves not just singing about workers but as workers, or at least as aligned symbolically with working-class men and women. Along similar lines, the irrepressible Dolly Parton has commented many times on her clothing—which has been the focus of much attention for its sexy, glitzy style—in relationship to her class background. When she was growing up in a poor mountain community, the only women she ever laid eyes on who dressed like she does now were prostitutes—and she always wanted to look glamorous, as they did to her child's eyes. Bruce Springsteen's onstage costumes notably changed from gangster/bohemian-styled suits to jeans and bandannas in a process that coincided with his singing more and more about work.[9]

In the songs themselves as well as in their packaging, I have found a "scavenger hunt" method quite useful in searching for a working-class aesthetic in popular music. It's often fascinating how recognizable objects are mentioned or invoked in the most conventional popular songs, as if to remind us who—or what—is being addressed. There are factory whistles blowing right in the middle of urban blues songs. There are country songs that mention lunch pails, and cheap pantyhose, and secondhand cars. There are rhythm and blues songs full of worn suitcases and kitchen tables. (The in-your-face "bling bling" consumerism of some current rap music drops in object clues in the same way—expensive ones, with brand names and numbers mentioned—but I think the intent is similar although the fantasy is leading in another direction.)

In other words, popular music provides an opportunity for aesthetic analysis that is so multileveled and so historically resonant that crossing disciplinary boundaries is the only way to "have at" it with sufficient attentiveness. Otherwise, we're going to miss the point—a combination of belligerence, exuberance, and complaint that is best summed up by the chorus to Sawyer Brown's 1995 song "Some Girls Do": "I ain't first class, but I ain't white trash / I'm wild, and a little crazy too / Some girls don't like boys like me / Ah, but some girls do."

Peaches and Figs

The quotation that forms the previous subhead ("Don Quixote was a steel-driving man") was taken from a song by the Moldy Peaches, a young antifolk duo from New York City. (All subhead quotations are identified in the endnotes.) The 2001 release of the Moldy Peaches' assertively lo-fi first album captured a re-markable amount of attention, and I'd like to end with a few words about them because the way they appeared on the scene, together with certain artistic choices they made on their album, seem to me to be at once summary and suggestive of the ways in which class has shaped popular music. The Moldy Peaches are Kimya Dawson, an African American singer who comes from, as music critic Robert Christgau has noted, "service-sector people on the poorer side of town,"[10] and Adam Green, the Jewish son of a professor and a psychiatrist. Although their self-presentation is relentlessly anticorporate, with a CD cover that consists of Do-It-Yourself black and white cutouts and handwritten track listings, they don't present themselves as working-class performers with gestures that are as familiar as Johnny Paycheck's persona. But I would argue that a working-class aesthetic has left its mark on their music—or perhaps more important, that their self-conscious, playful music makes a commentary on working-class consciousness that is instructive in its complexity.

Why would it occur to someone to bring Don Quixote, the bumbling quester from the earliest novel, together in song—a love song, no less—with John Henry, the steel-driving man of dozens and dozens of popular song versions? It's a joke, of course, one that changes earth (where John Henry was laying railroad track) to sky (where Don Quixote's head was stuck). It's also perfectly serious. The Moldy Peaches are mocking their own intellectual bent, but they are doing it by invoking one of the most famous "fake" songs in the American canon—"fake" because the song "John Henry" was a commercial product from its very beginning, which didn't stop it from becoming (in a reverse process from "popular" to "folk") a revered "roots" song in both black and white traditions, a standard for blues and bluegrass performers, and one of the best-known American songs about work. While the duo's name ridicules "moldy figs"—the kind of listener or scholar who thinks that culture of the "folk" should be untouched by time, commercialism, and the general messiness of living as social beings—the largeness of the John Henry tale in all its implications hints at a much more inclusive story about work, migration, and cultural production.

Finally, the line about Don Quixote and John Henry bridges the gap between art and labor so efficiently, it's downright elegant. Dreaming the right thing can be work, the Moldy Peaches insist. And work, never forget, can be noble.

Songs and Films Cited

Alabama. "40 Hour Week." 1985. *40 Hour Week.* RCA.

Anderson, John. "Quitting Time." 1994. *You Can't Keep a Good Memory Down.* MCA.

Blind Alfred Reed. "How Can a Poor Man Stand Such Times and Live." 1929. *Complete Recorded Works by Blind Alfred Reed.* Document, 1998.

Boyd, Eddie. "Five Long Years." 1952. *Blues Masters: The Essential Blues.* Volume 2: *Postwar Chicago Blues.* Rhino, 1992.

Bragg, Billy. "Which Side Are You On." 1983. *Back to Basics.* Elektra, 1987.

Canibus with Biz Markie. "Shove This Jay-Oh-Bee." 1999. *Office Space: The Motion Picture Soundtrack.* Interscope Records.

Car Wash. 1976. Dir. Michael Schultz. Perf. Franklyn Ajaye, Sully Boyer, and Ivan Dixon. Universal Pictures.

Creedence Clearwater Revival. "Fortunate Son." 1969. *Willy and the Poor Boys.* Fantasy Records.

Cry-Baby. 1990. Dir. John Waters. Perf. Johnny Depp, Amy Locane, Suzanne Tyrrell, and Polly Bergen. Universal Pictures.

Crystals. "Uptown." 1962. *Best of the Crystals.* Abkco, 1992.

Dark Angel. Fox TV. December 28, 2001–May 3, 2002.

Del-Lords. "How Can a Poor Man Stand Such Times and Live." 1984. *Frontier Days.* EMI America.

Denver, John. "Thank God I'm a Country Boy." 1974. *Back Home Again.* RCA.

Dudley, Dave. "Six Days on the Road." 1963. *Dave Dudley Hits.* Music Mill, 1999.

Dylan, Bob. "Gotta Serve Somebody." 1979. *Slow Train Coming.* Sony.

8 Mile. 2002. Dir. Curtis Hanson. Perf. Eminem, Kim Basinger, Mekhi Phifer, and Brittany Murphy. Imagine Entertainment.

Edwards, Stoney. "Poor Folks Stick Together." 1971. *Best of Stoney Edwards: Poor Folks Stick Together.* Razor & Tie, 1998.

Eliot, Missy. "Work It." 2002. *Under Construction.* Elektra/Asylum.

Everclear. "A.M. Radio." 2000. *Songs from an American Movie.* Volume 1:*Learning How to Smile.* Capitol.

Haggard, Merle. "Hungry Eyes." 1969. *Down Every Road.* Volume 2. Capitol, 1996.

Hairspray. 1988. Dir. John Waters. Perf. Sonny Bono, Ruth Brown, Divine, and Ricki Lake. New Line Cinema.

Hobbs, Becky. "Mama Was a Working Man." 1988. *All Keyed Up.* Capitol.

Isley Brothers, "Twist and Shout." 1962. *Shake It Up Baby: Shout, Twist and Shout.* Varese Records, 2000.

J-Lo. "Jenny from the Block." 2002. *This Is Me—Then.* Sony.

Los Pinguinos del Norte. "Corrido de César Chávez." 1976. *Chulas Fronteras and Del Mero Corazon: Soundtrack Recordings from Two Tex-Mex Classics.* Arhoolie, 1995.

Maid in Manhattan. 2002. Dir. Wayne Wang. Perf. Jennifer Lopez, Ralph Fiennes, Natasha Richardson, and Stanley Tucci. Hughes Entertainment/Columbia Pictures.

Maynard, Ken. "Fannie Moore." 1930. *Times Ain't Like They Used To Be: Early American Rural Music—Classic Recordings from the 1920s and 1930s,* vol. 1. Yazoo, 1997.

McCoys. "Hang on Sloopy." 1965. *Hang On Sloopy: The Best of the McCoys.* Sony, 1995.

Moldy Peaches. "Anyone Else But You." 2001. *Moldy Peaches.* Sanctuary Records.

Norma Jean. "Heaven Help the Poor Working Girl." 1967. *The Best of Norma Jean.* Collectors' Choice Music, 1999.

Paycheck, Johnny. "Take This Job and Shove It." 1977. *Take This Job and Shove It.* CBS.

Reece, Florence. 1931. "Which Side Are You On." *Songs of Work and Protest,* ed. Edith Fowke and Joe Glazer, 54–55 (New York: Dover Publications, 1973).

Ross, Diana. "I'm Coming Out." 1980. *The Disco Years.* Volume 4: *Lost in Music.* Rhino, 1992.

Rowan, Pete. "Good Morning, Mr. Time Clock." 1991. *All on a Rising Day.* Sugar Hill.

Royal, Billy Joe. "Down in the Boondocks." 1965. *The Very Best of Billy Joe Royal: The Columbia Years, 1965–1971.* Taragon, 2002.

Sawyer Brown. "Some Girls Do." 1992. *Greatest Hits, 1990–1995.* Curb, 1995.

Shangri-Las. "Leader of the Pack." 1964. *The Best of the Girl Groups.* Volume 1. Rhino, 1990.

Sly and the Family Stone. "Hot Fun in the Summertime." 1969. *Anthology.* Epic, 1981.

Sugar Hill Gang. "Rapper's Delight." 1979. *Hip Hop Greats: Classic Raps.* Rhino, 1990.

Thunder, Shelley. "Working Girl." 1989. *Fresh Out the Pack.* Island Records.

Tippin, Aaron. "Working Man's Ph.D." 1993. *The Essential Aaron Tippin.* RCA, 1998.

Valli, Frankie and the Four Seasons. "Dawn (Go Away)." 1964. *The Very Best of Frankie Valli and the Four Seasons.* Rhino, 2003.

———. "Rag Doll." 1964. *The Very Best of Frankie Valli and the Four Seasons.* Rhino, 2003.

Wonder, Stevie. "Uptight." 1966. *The Definitive Collection.* Universal, 2002.

PART FOUR

POLITICS AND EDUCATION

New Working-Class Studies emphasizes the vital connection between the academic study of working-class life and the real-world experience of being working class. Along with generating community projects and partnerships at working-class studies centers, the concern for the public implications of new working-class studies leads scholars to consider how our understanding of class can help us act on the world, whether through social activism or through education. The three essays in this section examine issues and strategies for taking new working-class studies public.

For Jack Metzgar, new working-class studies offers an analysis of class that can support political organizing. In "Politics and the American Class Vernacular," he argues that we must bring our understanding of how class works and our analysis of the widespread misunderstanding of class in American culture to bear in the political realm. By challenging the ordinary language that Americans use to talk about class, Metzgar suggests that we can develop an alternative view; offer a more complex, realistic alternative; and engage more working-class people in political involvement that reflects their own interests.

Renny Christopher explores the interventions in education, especially college teaching, being made by scholars in new working-class studies. In "New Working-Class Studies in Higher Education," she discusses the demographic changes that have led more working-class students into colleges and universities, and she surveys some of the arguments for and strategies of working-class pedagogy.

Robert Bruno and Lisa Jordan offer a model for critical teaching about social class, politics, and economics, drawn from their experience as labor educators. In "Building Class Identity: Lessons from Labor Education," they argue for an approach that combines students' experiences at work and in contemporary society with economic and political theory. This approach makes political and economic theory useable by students, but it may also generate greater student engagement with labor, political, and community organizing activities. As Bruno and Jordan suggest, thoughtful analysis by academics can lead to critical teaching that in turn leads students to action.

12

Politics and the American Class Vernacular

Jack Metzgar

During the summer of 2000, the "working class" as a demographic category made a brief but dramatic appearance at the heart of American politics. It transformed New Democrat Al Gore into a temporary populist, breathing new life into Democrats who at the time faced what seemed like a Bush juggernaut. Then the "working class," as is its tendency, quietly disappeared into the mists of the American class vernacular, the common language for American conversations about class.

The vernacular routinely forgets that there is a working class, and this leads to all kinds of mistakes and illusions—in politics, policy, economics, and cultural understanding. Envisioning American society as made up of a sprawling "middle class" that includes almost everyone, all those who are neither "rich" nor "poor," the vernacular cannot withstand the most superficial scrutiny, but as an everyday way of fitting oneself into a bigger picture, the vernacular is powerful. It is also cagey and resists direct frontal attacks, with richly shifting connotations that satisfy something deep and abiding in American culture. It can be momentarily startled by good social science, but its collective wisdom must be appreciated and respected if the working class—as concept and reality—is ever to be recognized as an essential part of American life.

Two works of politically savvy social science appeared in the spring of 2000 to point out (not for the first time) that the working class is a majority in the United

States. One—*America's Forgotten Majority* by Ruy Teixeira and Joel Rogers—
was a political science analysis of the 1990s American electorate by race, class,
gender (and union household). This one influenced a Gore adviser, who talked
Gore into trying to appeal to an actual majority rather than to a figment of the
New Democrat imagination. The other book—*The Working Class Majority* by
economist Michael Zweig—developed a delicate analysis of occupations and
economic power relations to articulate a comprehensive three-class model (working class, middle class, and capitalist class) as an alternative to the vernacular's
trinity of rich, poor, and middle class. Both books directly challenged the vernacular, showing its imprecision and the realities that imprecision obscures. Both, in
different ways, recognized the political significance of the words "working class"
and the reality they denote. Both also understood that part of the power of the vernacular is its simplicity—only three classes, not long strings of occupational, income, or cultural categories, as sociologists, economists, and marketers are wont
to do—and they kept the basic terms of their analyses clear and simple.[1]

Neither, unfortunately, made much of a dent in the power of the American
class vernacular to obscure our shared social reality. But each, with its clear division of the vernacular's "middle class" into a working class and a professional
middle class, has laid a foundation for New Working-Class Studies to chart an
agenda of research and debate that can provide a persistent, permanent challenge
to the vernacular.

Al Gore as Working-Class Hero

There must be several thousand people who make their livings as full-time "political analysts" at universities, think tanks, public opinion firms, and political
consulting companies. They pore over polling and voting data, using an incredibly sophisticated array of statistical tools. This kind of work can make your head
spin because of the complexity of the American electorate and the larger population that may or may not be part of that electorate at any given time. Demographics and public attitudes are constantly changing; what was indicates what might
be, but not without plenty of surprises. To be useful, political analysts have to
simplify, ignoring most of their data in order to present a picture that might be
strategically useful.

In the mid- and late 1990s, most political analysts concluded that the "typical"
or "swing" voters were "soccer moms" and their husbands, "wired workers." The
New York Times (May 4, 1999) characterized them as "affluent independent voters
and high-technology employees who work miles from any city." They are white,
college-educated, and "solidly middle class," usually professional or managerial
workers. They are also uniformly married with children, and the "soccer mom"
image is meant to capture the harried life of a working mother busy shuffling her

children to sporting events and other after-school activities, characteristically in a minivan. This group, polled and focus-grouped with regularity, is thought to have a distinctive political outlook that reflects their relatively privileged position and their optimism about the future.[2]

Though widely embraced across parties and ideologies, this picture of the American electorate was particularly pushed by New Democrats, who emphasized the "mom" because she was more likely to vote for Democrats; they were also wildly optimistic that executive and professional (white) dads could be talked out of their 2 to 1 century-long Republicanism. Traditional Democrats, the New Democrats argued, were hopelessly and increasingly out of date with their focus on the blue-collar working class (which is declining), union households (also declining), blacks and poor people (often seen as synonymous and neither of whom vote much). This old-fashioned focus, New Democrats said, alienates the forward-looking middle class that is busy pulling itself and its children up by its bootstraps.

Though contested, particularly by union and black leaders who (correctly) thought they could increase the turnout and Democratic proclivity of their constituencies, the "soccer mom—wired worker" image of the American electorate held sway until Teixeira and Rogers blew it up with a summary version of their analysis in the June 2000 *Atlantic Monthly*.

Using similar data to that presented below on occupation, income, and education, Teixeira and Rogers easily showed that a majority of all voters (55 percent) and three-fifths of suburbanites were properly categorized as the "white working class," which they dubbed "the forgotten majority." It gets more complicated from there, but to me the really valuable part of Teixeira and Rogers's analysis is the way they calculate the intersections of race, gender, and class to reveal an electorate that is very different from the picture that most of us carry around in our heads. Professional political analysts rarely do these kinds of cross-group tabulations because it requires a lot of work. Different voting demographics are reported one by one so that white suburban women will each get counted three times, but we can't determine how this three-category demographic group voted. We can guess, of course, but there's the rub. The science part of social science (basically, probability and statistics) is not about guessing, and when social scientists guess, they inevitably bring their own lived observation and experience into the guessing.

The error made by professional political analysts that was revealed by Teixeira and Rogers is colossal—something like the statistical equivalent of buying the Brooklyn Bridge. And it shows the power of the "middle-class" vernacular to confuse and befuddle even the most sophisticated and scientific among us. Here's how Teixeira and Rogers sum up their findings:

> The conventional view of the suburban electorate—affluent soccer moms, executive dads—is drawn from a few relatively wealthy towns like Bethesda, Maryland, and

Fair Lawn, New Jersey, and it doesn't come close to reflecting reality. The suburban electorate is in fact composed mostly of . . . two-earner families of low to moderate education and income, generally working in low-level white collar, service, and skilled blue collar jobs. . . . They are members of a white working class whose economic interests and experience diverge fundamentally—in terms of culture, class, and history—from those of soccer moms in Bethesda, suburban independents in Fair Lawn, and wired cyber professionals in Silicon Valley.[3]

How could sophisticated professionals make such a huge mistake, not once but persistently from June 1996 through June 2000? I'm a humanities professor, so guessing is a part of my job. Here's my guess: Political analysts almost uniformly come from or live in the Bethesdas and Fair Lawns, or the Oak Parks (where I live) and Evanstons of Illinois, or in-town enclaves such as DuPont Circle or Lincoln Park. Their everyday experience, at work, at home, traveling on business, eating out in the evening, is almost uniformly among middle-class professionals. When they guess, they rely on that observation and experience. And though they pore over the most complex and sophisticated demographic data ever assembled, they carry the vernacular conception of class in their heads, and when forced to guess, they fall into a crude syllogism that goes something like this:

Almost everybody in America is "middle class," neither "rich" nor "poor."
I'm "middle-class" myself.
Therefore, almost everybody in America must be like me.

The crudeness of this reasoning would be hard to believe if similar mistakes based on forgetting the working class hadn't consistently been made over the past four decades or so. But they have been and continue to be.

Teixeira and Rogers had an impact, however, when they helped convince Stanley Greenberg there was a working class. A Gore adviser, Greenberg was President Clinton's favorite pollster and had once famously and erroneously claimed that 90 percent of Americans think of themselves as "middle class."[4] At the time, Al Gore was looking for a strategy that could both energize the Democrats' traditional bases and appeal to suburban swing voters. Teixeira and Rogers advocated a nonracial, non-gendered economic social safety net strategy that would appeal to both the white nonunion working class (who reside mostly in the suburbs and are the true swing voters) and to the Democrats' black, Latino, and union household core. Gore was convinced. In August, using the AFL-CIO's "working families" rhetoric, Gore came out swinging with a program he claimed represented "the people" (versus "the powerful"), and he articulated a set of modest but potentially pathbreaking social democratic programs—gradual universal health insurance for children, prescription drug benefits for elders, and government-funded USA Accounts in addition to, rather than instead of, Social Security.

Those who think there is little difference between Democrats and Republicans usually refer to candidates' personal instincts and backgrounds, not to specific programs and policies. Gore and Bush, for example, are peas in a pod in their prep school, wealthy, political-class backgrounds, but they promised to take the country in dramatically opposite directions. Bush promised a huge tax cut mostly for the rich and a systematic program of public school and Social Security privatization. Gore promised to resist those antigovernment approaches and to extend what in any other political universe would be proudly referred to as "the welfare state."

So far as I know, the words "working class" never passed Gore's lips. In fact, he never used the word "class" except when preceded by "middle," but the recognition of the existence of a working-class majority was at the core of the Democrats' 2000 campaign strategy. When Republicans cried "class warfare," many Democrats were easily intimidated, pushing a none-too-steadfast Gore to make already fuzzy language even fuzzier. But the Teixeira-Rogers class approach passed the test of political pragmatism by, first, changing the dynamics of the election in August (helping Gore close a huge gap with Bush) and, then, because Gore had to continually return to it, in one form or another, to revive his campaign.

If Gore had had a consistent personality to go with his program, he would have won handily. But the mystifying power of the "middle-class" vernacular would have undermined the clarity of a much stronger, less synthetic candidate. If, on the other hand, we had a vernacular conception of class that routinely distinguished between "working class" and "professional middle class" (as both Teixeira-Rogers and Zweig do), even an all-too-human traditional Democrat could win office and move America in a much better direction than we're going now. But the vernacular is, as I have said, both cagey and powerful.

Nothing illustrates this better than the way class issues were center stage in the 2000 election in the form of Bush's and Gore's competing tax cut proposals. Both sought to appeal to the ubiquitous "middle class." This was bound to doom Gore in the long run because his entire package of proposals (including his tax cuts) benefited the working-class majority of all colors and genders (about two-thirds of all voters) but didn't do much for the professional middle class. Not being able to say so undoubtedly hurt his chances.

During the campaign's home stretch in October, for example, PBS economics reporter Paul Solman analyzed the Bush and Gore tax cut proposals in a fifteen–minute television segment on *The NewsHour with Jim Lehrer*. Solman is an economist with a puckish sense of humor and an inventive streak, and he is generally delighted to tackle complicated (math-related) subjects for a television audience. To illustrate the proposed tax cuts, he visited three Michigan families at different (1999) income levels:

Family 1: A 24-year-old black single mother of three who works in a factory and makes $18,440, a family income that puts her family right at the 10th percentile. Gore's tax cut was worth $1,200 to this family, while Bush's was insignificant.

Family 2: A 30-something white manager at United Parcel Service and his stay-at-home wife and four kids, with a family income of $69,000. This family would get nothing from Gore (until their kids went to college), but $3,100 from Bush.

Family 3: A 50-something white auto industry executive and his stay-at-home wife, with a family income of $113,000. Gore gave them nothing, Bush $3,500.

It was also mentioned that a family with an annual income of $1 million would get a $50,000 cut from Bush and nothing from Gore. The point of this analysis was that Gore was right when he claimed that the main beneficiaries of Bush's tax cut were the top 10 percent because, according to Solman, a family income of $113,000 was right at the 90th percentile. Bush was right, however, in claiming that the "middle class" would also benefit if you count the UPS manager and his family as "middle class." And you should have seen these folks—a good-looking white couple with four darling kids in their suburban Detroit backyard, complete with the breadwinner dad doing the talking and a minivan in the background![5]

You could devote a whole course in American studies to analyzing the iconography of Solman's choice of these three families to represent American taxpayers. Why is the factory worker black, and being so, why is she a single mother? How long did it take Solman to find two stay-at-home moms in the year 2000? But the question that interests me is why Solman chose a family with an annual income of $69,000 to represent the middle class? Why not choose a family near the median family income in 1999, $49,940?[6]

This may seem like a trivial difference, but it isn't. A family income of $69,000 puts the UPS manager and his family somewhere near the top 30 percent of families. Thus, two of the three families presented are in the top one-third, not the middle. The third family, the black single mother making $18,440, is not in the middle either; as a factory worker she might reasonably be called "working class," but with a family income at the 10th percentile, Solman is using her to illustrate what he calls a "lower income" family. What's missing, then, are the majority of families whose incomes in 1999 were between $18,440 and $69,000. Given the choices Solman has made, what's missing is *the majority of families* in the middle of the income distribution, all those from the 10th to the 67th percentiles. How did this group of families fare under the Bush and Gore tax cut proposals? Solman doesn't tell us, and so far as I know, nobody made a stink about it. Why not? After all, Solman starts off his report by explaining that the issue is that both candidates claim their proposal benefits "the middle class" better than the other guy's, but he ends up ignoring the majority of families actually in the middle. How could he make that mistake? How could he not be called on it?

By not starting at the median and going up and down from there, Solman's presentation made Bush's tax cut look better and Gore's worse (in fact, it showed Gore's as applying only to the "poor" and "black"). So maybe Solman is a Republican? Maybe—particularly because, unlike so many other journalists, he knew where the median was and chose not to use it. But here's the problem he faced. If you start at the median and take the 20 percent or 30 percent above and below it, you'll end up with lots of families who will not qualify as what most of your audience thinks of as "middle class." The middle 50 percent of families in 1999, for example, included those making as little as $25,000. Even those at the $50,000 median generally don't fulfill the strong connotation of "middle class" that includes "comfortable standard of living" with substantial discretionary income.

This depends on where you are in the income scale. People with family incomes of $25,000 usually think $50,000 would be "comfortable." But political analysts, professional journalists, university professors, and the PBS audience (often described as "upscale") are unlikely to think so. At the heart of the rich-poor-and-middle vernacular is a double meaning that is contradictory. The "middle class" that includes "almost everybody" is not the same group as the "middle class" that enjoys a "comfortable standard of living." Indeed, that second "middle class" has very specific connotative characteristics beyond income—they are "college educated" and are in "professional" (including managerial) occupations. By any measure—income, education, and occupation—this "middle class" is about 30 percent of the population, a large minority but a minority nonetheless, not even close to being "almost everybody," and, no matter how you configure it, not in the middle.

The American vernacular constantly shifts back and forth between these two meanings. And in doing so, it makes the professional middle class seem like almost everybody, all those who are neither rich nor poor. With only fifteen minutes of airtime, Paul Solman could not violate the vernacular by actually looking at a family in or near the middle. Instead, his visuals presented an American population two-thirds of which is either comfortable or well off, while the other third, though not officially poor, is getting by on what most of his audience (including me) could not imagine living on for four months, let alone an entire year. The UPS manager and family fulfill all the stereotypes of middle-classness, right down to their *Leave It to Beaver* manners and mores, but so does the auto executive and family. And though the factory worker is clearly not a welfare mom, she has an income and skin color that is associated more with "poor" than with "working class." The millionaire family is referred to, but not seen, to round out the iconography of classes—rich, poor, and middle, with the "middle" represented by two of the three families we see.

It is not uncommon in news reporting to present these kinds of families as representative. What's extraordinary and revealing about Solman's reporting is that he knows the numbers, and even reports some of them. As a result, with his words and his pictures, he literally says that the "middle class" is a minority yet almost everybody is like them.

The vernacular conception of classes in America can easily be shown to be ridiculous when exposed to the counting and classifying of demographic social science—as Teixeira and Rogers did in the spring of 2000. Working-class studies needs to do this over and over again because it works. There is no better evidence than the populist conversion of Al Gore, all of whose instincts and New Democrat ideology went against it. But by October, after Teixeira and Rogers had thoroughly educated the political and communications elite about the composition of the American electorate, the vernacular was still standing strong. Or, more accurately, it was cagily bobbing and weaving, working its magic to conceal the working class and confuse us about the realities of class in America.

Imagine if our vernacular routinely made the distinction between "middle class" and "working class" as Michael Zweig does, capped by a third class that Zweig dubs "the capitalist class." How would the Bush and Gore tax-cut proposals look then? What if PBS had chosen to show us one family from each of *these* three classes, while giving their proportions of the population as a whole? Gore would have won the election hands down, for one thing. More important, the character of American politics and the discourse around it would be completely different. This, and nothing less, is what's at stake for working-class studies.

Zweig's Challenge to the Vernacular

Zweig's conception defines the American class structure by occupations and the amount and kind of power people have in and around the workplace. In his schema, a "capitalist class" is defined by its ownership and control of giant profit-making enterprises; a very small group (Zweig says they could all fit in Yankee Stadium), this class has the overwhelming bulk of decision-making power in our society. Then, there's a "working class" defined by a lack of power at work and in society at large, despite the fact that they do the principal work in producing and reproducing the goods and services that make up our daily lives. Finally, there is a "middle class" of managers, professionals, and small-business owners who have a degree of autonomy and influence at work (and in the larger society) that makes them different from the working class but nowhere near as powerful as the capitalists.[7]

A restatement and updating of the classical Marxist view, Zweig's conception captures a core part of the original meaning of "middle class" as being *in the middle* between capital and labor—a meaning that still lingers within the American class vernacular. Outside America, this lineup of classes is familiar worldwide, and as such, competes with the American vernacular. In a sense, all modern politics is defined by the differences between these competing vernaculars. Zweig's contribution is that he looks carefully at the evidence in the homeland of the American vernacular, and though he finds a large and growing professional middle class, he can confidently report that the death of the working class has been greatly exaggerated.

Zweig is interested in proportions, and far from being "reductive," he uses his concepts of power in the workplace to carefully delineate the relative class sizes of occupational groupings as defined by the U.S. Department of Labor's Bureau of Labor Statistics. With the capitalist class representing far less than 1 percent, he finds a large middle class of 37 percent and a working-class majority of 62 percent.[8]

Zweig's rigor opens up a whole field of occupation-by-occupation analysis that should be invaluable to both labor and political organizers because it reads *class* interests from basic power relations at work. There is much else to admire in Zweig's analysis—not least of which is his subtle sketching of the possibilities for a grand cross-class alliance between the working and (segments of) the middle classes. But his very rigor in focusing only on occupations, eschewing any roles for education, income, or what he calls "lifestyle" in shaping social class in America, limits his ability to stay with the bobbing and weaving of the vernacular. What's more, his hierarchy of power relations misses some of the egalitarian attractiveness of the "middle class" vernacular as it is spoken and lived in twenty-first-century America.

Zweig's conception of the class structure is a classic pyramid, with a tiny ruling class at the top and a sprawling working class at the base:

capitalist class

middle class

working class

If this were the vernacular conception of classes, it would be clear for all to see that public policies should focus on improving (or, at least, not harming) the lives and prospects of the working-class majority, while maintaining a healthy middle class as well. While giving capitalists their due, government would necessarily be seen as a principal democratic counterforce (along with labor unions) against the inherent economic power of this class. As Zweig points out, this gives shape to an entirely different kind of politics than the current vernacular's pitting of "the poor" against a "middle class" that is envisioned as not only ubiquitous but prosperously comfortable. For this reason alone, a Zweigian vernacular would be preferable to the current one. But it's still not cagey enough to go head-to-head with the vernacular, which combines a seeming focus on income with various shifting connotations concerning education, culture, and even morality. If we were to diagram the American vernacular, it would be flat and nonhierarchical, and it is relatively generous in its moral and status inclusiveness:

poor/ # middle /rich

The "middle class" that includes "almost everybody" stigmatizes both "the poor" and "the rich" while honoring everybody who is not particularly distinguished but who works hard, looks out for others (particularly their families), pulls their own weight, and doesn't hold themselves out to be any better than anybody else. Though, as I point out below, the professional middle class is generally much more status conscious and achievement oriented than the working class, my sense is that huge majorities of each embrace the term "middle class" when it refers to "just ordinary people living ordinary lives," just "regular," "normal" folks doing the best they can. Although the rich, the celebrated, the powerful, and the gifted (all of whom are captured in the vernacular's sense of the deserved "rich") are "looked up to," they are also viewed as peculiarly subject to moral and happiness failings either because of excessive adulation or due to the lack of limits on their freedom from "playing by the rules." "The poor" are stigmatized for lacking classic "middle-class" values of hard work and self-discipline, but they are thought to be a very small group (like "the rich") who deserve some measure of compassion and at least "one more chance." "Middleness" itself is valued, including moderation in political views and moral judgments. The egalitarian ethos inherent in this notion of middleness has been seen as both peculiarly "American" and essential to democracy by political sociologists from Alexis de Tocqueville to Alan Wolfe.[9] I think there's something to that, and there's surely some element of it worth preserving even as we seek to eliminate the illusion of (roughly) equal power and life prospects that this conception fosters.

The principal problem with the vernacular is the way it first hides the working class (by including it within the ubiquitous middle) and then forgets it's there by assuming that almost everybody is college educated, professional, and has a reasonably comfortable standard of living. It mistakes the part for the whole, substituting the small "middle class" for the big, inclusive one. The immediate task of working-class studies should be to challenge this middle-class two-step every time it's performed, to constantly probe what users mean when *they* say "middle class," and to use "working class" consistently and rigorously to refer to all those purported members of the middle class who are not middle-class professionals.

When we do so, we need to clearly and emphatically avoid hierarchical uses that remove the "working class" from the vernacular's moral and status inclusiveness. The working class to which we refer is different from, not less than, the professional middle class. It refers to people, in Teixeira and Rogers's words, "whose economic interests and experience diverge fundamentally—in terms of culture, class, and history—from those of soccer moms in Bethesda." It's a complicated class with lots of differences within itself, but it's there in the middle with the rest of us, neither rich nor poor, but above all "working."

Such a conception can be diagrammed by simply dividing the vernacular's big "middle" in two, leaving everything else intact:

_{rich}/professional middle/working class/_{poor}

This is neither as politically desirable (to me) nor as ambitious as Zweig's alternative vernacular. "The rich" are not, as Zweig points out, a proper "target" in a democratic society the way "the powerful" (capitalists) are. And "poor" is not really a social class but more often a temporary condition, one that over a ten-year period "more than half of the working class experiences." Poverty, as Zweig says, is "something that happens to the working class," and it is a serious political mistake to divide "the poor from workers," as the vernacular routinely does.[10] But Zweig's conception is too ambitious and too political. For now, it will be quite enough to use and enrich his distinction between middle class and working class, building both on the vernacular's inclusiveness and on the actual practice of working class studies as it has thus far developed.

The existing vernacular, besides being relatively nonhierarchical, has one other advantage over Zweig's proposed alternative: it recognizes, as Zweig specifically and rigorously refuses to do, the sheer power of money, of wealth and income, in a capitalist society. Social classes are not all about power in the workplace. They are also about the distribution of status (of shame and honor), of freedom, of opportunities, of living standards and working conditions, and all these have to do with the distribution of money. The vernacular, with its crude stereotypes of "rich" and "poor," recognizes that. What it hides and confuses is the inequitable distribution of money—and of all the things it will buy, including freedom and opportunity. Focusing on money and on who is in the vernacular's big middle allows us to ask questions about who is contributing what to our society and what they are getting in return.

Sure, the capitalists are getting much more than they deserve or need. But so, in general, are we, the professional middle class—and as a class, we have a cultural power that even the capitalists envy. The working class, on the other hand, generally gets much less of everything compared to what its work contributes. I could be wrong about that. I'm not saying it's clear and obvious. Nor do I think it is easy to remedy, since I'm no longer willing to completely do away with the market's allocative role. But we can't see that this might be an issue, nor can we debate it, within either the existing vernacular or Zweig's alternative, which insists on a singular focus on power, not money. We could, however, ask such questions and debate such issues if we keep our attention focused on a revised vernacular, as proposed above, and are not restricted only to issues of power. Fortunately, there is no need to be so restrictive, since occupation, income, and education are intimately tied together. And though not without numerous complications, we have good numbers on all these things and how they relate to one another.

Working Class and Middle Class by Occupation, Education, and Income

A vernacular, any vernacular, is based on grossly simplifying reality. That's its value in helping us organize our perceptions and thoughts. The current American vernacular consistently overlooks the working class, a pattern we can trace back to the 1950s, when we declared ourselves "a middle-class society." But the vernacular has never been entirely consistent, and if you are referring to factory workers or other clearly recognizable "blue-collar" folks, you can use the forbidden term and everybody will know what you mean and a host of associations and connotations will arise. Thus, the "working class" (seen as small and decreasing, whether in 1954 or 2004) sometimes slides into the vernacular for brief appearances, usually to be pitied or blamed. Labor and social historians also can easily use the term, even extending it on occasion beyond blue collarness, because the vernacular grants that there once was a working class.

Although this permitted usage gives working-class studies something to build on, the "blue-collar" and "thing-of-the-past" connotations of "working class" (sometimes accompanied by stereotypes of a white, male Joe Six-Pack) also restricts us, both from talking sensibly and from challenging the existing vernacular. The clearly recognizable "blue-collar" group is still a fairly large part, probably 25 percent or more, of the workforce, and it includes men and women of all colors. But if that's what comes to mind when one says "working class," you miss the larger part of the working class that is not blue collar, most importantly the clerical, retail sales, and other kinds of "service" workers—all very large groups and growing mightily.[11] To win a place in the vernacular, we need a rough-and-ready concept of the "working class" that combines occupation, income, and education and that reflects the large majority of workers who are not now, never have been, and never will be "middle class." I think this can be done by using the vernacular's own principal contradiction and what social science statisticians call a "residual."

The middle-class two-step I referred to above has two contradictory definitions of "middle class"—the big middle class that includes almost everybody and the smaller middle class that is college-educated, professional (including managerial) and "comfortable" (referring to income or standard of living). The "working-class" residual, then, would be everybody who does not fully qualify for the smaller, more exclusive "middle class."

Basically, this is everybody who is not in the Bureau of Labor Statistics' "managerial and professional workers" category, as illustrated in Table 1. Admission to this broad occupational group usually (not always) requires at least a bachelor's degree and usually (not always) results in a substantially higher income than other workers. This rough–and-ready concept also grossly simplifies reality, though not as much as the current middle-class vernacular does. But it also captures some-

Table 1. Class as Defined by Occupation

Occupation	Percentage of workforce	Annualized median wage	BA degree required?	Middle-class wage premium[a] (%)
Middle Class				
Managerial and professional	30	$44,668	Yes	—
Working Class				
Precision production, craft, repair	10	$32,708	No	36
Technical, sales, admin. support	30	$27,092	No	65
Operators, fabricators, laborers	14	$24,284	No	84
Service	14	$19,604	No	128
Farming, forestry, fishing	1.5	$18,408	No	143

Source: Bureau of Labor Statistics, "Union Members in 2001," http://www.bls.gov/news.release /union2.t02.htm.

[a] The percentage that the median wage for this category would have to be increased to equal the median middle-class wage.

Table 2. Class as Defined by Education

Class	Highest level of education	Percentage of persons 25 and older (2000)	Mean annual earning ($) (1999)	Middle-class wage premium[a] (%)
Middle class				
	bachelor's or more	26	45,678[b]	—
Working class				
	associate's degree	8	32,152	42
	some college but no degree	18	26,958	69
	high school graduate	33	24,572	86
	not high school graduate	16	16,121	183

Source: U.S. Census Bureau *Statistical Abstract of the U.S., 2001*, tables 217 and 218 (p. 140) (Washington, D.C.: U.S. Government Printing Office, 2001).

[a] The percentage that the median wage for this category would have to be increased to equal the median middle-class wage.

[b] Mean includes only those with bachelor's degrees as their highest level of education; the means for those with master's, doctorate, and professional degrees range from $55,641 to $100,987.

thing "everybody knows." Income, wealth, status, life prospects, the kinds of vacations you can take, and lots of other things are usually (not always) firmly and clearly related to being a manager or professional and/or having at least a bachelor's degree. See, for example, Table 2 on the relation between education and income. So, if you go simply by occupation (in a much more gross and simplistic way than Zweig does), the residual "working class" is 70 percent. If you go simply by education (as Teixeira and Rogers do), the residual "working class" is 74 percent. And in both cases, the relation between class and income is clear and consistent.

The "comfortable" income or standard of living connotation is much more difficult because it is subjective, just as "rich" and "poor" are. Also, whether a level of income is "comfortable" or not depends on how many people are living off that income. A clerical worker making $27,000 married to a "repair worker" making $32,000—both working class by occupation—would have a family income of $59,000, and if they have no children, they could be living "comfortably" by most people's lights. Add even one child, however, and they're likely "struggling," though definitely not "poor." The same clerical worker as a single mother with one child, on the other hand, is definitely "struggling," and many people (depending on their own circumstances) would see her as "poor."

Although this discussion can quickly turn tedious or confusing, it is well worth having. Even a cursory look at income data will show an American population that is not nearly as "comfortable" as the vernacular assumes. It will also show the absurdity of the vernacular conception of "middleness," because the statistical middle, no matter how you define it, includes incomes that denote very different "lifestyles" across the middle, making it meaningless (Table 3). Such a division (and all other attempts to define rich, poor, and middle by income) makes it apparent how confused and confusing the vernacular is. People with household incomes of $90,000 will deny being "rich," and many people will insist that anybody making less than $30,000 (or $40,000) is "poor." And everybody will notice that it makes absolutely no sense to put households with $25,000 in the same income class as households with $70,000.

Discussions of class by income are best preceded by asking people how *they* would define a "middle class" income. In my experience teaching working adults, they almost uniformly begin the lower tier of the middle class above (usually well above) the median household income. After that, you can pretty much present any of the standard data on income to show that the "middle class" that is "comfort-

Table 3. Class as Defined by "Middleness" in Income

Class	Percentage of households	Income ($)
Poor	bottom 20	up to 17,950
Middle Class	middle 60	17,951 to 81,960
Rich	top 20	81,961 and up

Source: U.S. Census Bureau, *Money Income in the United States, 2000* (Washington, D.C.: U.S. Government Printing Office, 2001).

Table 4. Class as Defined by Level of Comfort

Class	Income ($)	Percentage of households
Poor	25,000 and below	29
Struggling working class	25,000–75,000	47
Comfortable middle class	75,000 and up	24

Source: U.S. Census Bureau, *Money Income in the United States, 2000* (Washington, D.C.: U.S. Government Printing Office, 2001).

able" is not the same as the one "in the middle." Thus, though this is infinitely variable depending on whom you're talking with, you can derive a "working-class" residual something like that shown in Table 4.

The "working class" by income is, thus, much smaller and much more variable than the "working class" by occupation or education. This reflects the fact that a couple with two working-class incomes (above the median) and not too many children can live comfortably on that combined income. It also reflects the fact that many more people are "poor" based on what most people think it takes to be not-poor than by the official definition of "poverty." But note that the "comfortable middle class" (at 24 percent in the illustration above) is about the same proportion as the "college educated" (at 26 percent) and "managerial and professional workers" (at 30 percent). These are all smaller than the vernacular routinely assumes, and getting people to look at actual numbers and proportions blocks the middle-class two-step, at least temporarily.

But blocking the two-step—making it difficult to confuse the big inclusive "middle class" with the small exclusive one—can easily be dissipated (or sidestepped) if you then insist on a univocal definition of "working class." Guardians of the middle-class vernacular will mention Bill Gates (who does not have a bachelor's degree) if your definition is based strictly on education. They'll mention the social worker with a master's degree who makes only $32,000 a year, and the UPS truck driver, an overtime hog, who makes $100,000 a year. Guardians insist on a precise definition of "working class," and then delight in pointing out the exceptions to the rule, attempting to make any discussion of class in America seem ridiculous or tedious.

Ask the guardians how *they* define "middle class." Make them be precise, and then bob and weave your definitions of "working class" among all the various ways that people think about class in America. If they want complexity and precision, welcome them to working-class studies, where they can learn how to stop doing the middle-class two-step that hides and ignores and overlooks the American working class.

Working Class and Middle Class by Self-Identification and Culture

Working-class studies has still other moves that undermine the vernacular—one more social science move involving how people identify themselves by class and one based on the observation and experience of people with roots in both classes or at the borders where the working class and middle class interact.

Clinton pollster and Gore adviser Stanley Greenberg probably knew there was a working class before Teixeira and Rogers reminded him of it in the spring of 2000. In the mid-1990s Greenberg claimed his polling had discovered that about 90 percent of Americans "think of themselves as middle class." S. M. Miller effectively debunked this claim in an article in the *American Prospect* (in whose orbit Greenberg travels) by pointing out that pollsters usually do not offer "working class" as a choice when asking people to identify their social class.[12] When offered this choice, Miller pointed out, about equal numbers self-identify as "working class" and as "middle class." Miller reviewed various studies, but he relied primarily on one of the most reputable, respected, and reliable of surveys, the General Social Survey (GSS) of the National Opinion Research Center at the University of Chicago. The GSS offers the choices of upper, middle, working, and lower class. The results of the most recent survey (1998) and a cumulative score for all GSS surveys that have asked the question since 1972 are shown in Table 5.

The low percentages of people who self-identify as "upper class" or "lower class" reflect, I think, the egalitarian stigma the vernacular attaches to "rich" and "poor." People generally do not want to identify themselves as "lower class" because of obvious moral and status connotations having nothing to do with income or life circumstances, but an even smaller group is willing to identify themselves as "upper class." In the Great Middle, those who identify themselves as "working class" may accurately assess their circumstances as not being those of the "com-

Table 5. Class as Defined by Self-Identification

Class	Percentage of respondents identifying themselves as belonging to class	
	Average, 1972–98	1998
Lower Class	5	5
Working Class	46	45
Middle Class	46	46
Upper Class	3	4

Source: National Opinion Research Center, http://www.norc.uchicago.edu; also available at http://www.icpsr.umich.edu/GSS//rnd1998/merged/cdbk/class.htm.

fortable middle class," but there's also likely some pride in being part of the group that actually does the work. There's a long-standing working-class tradition of seeing middle-class professionals as "all talk, no action," "afraid to get their hands dirty," and as lacking common sense because they never do the work they think they're overseeing. This is probably more of a blue-collar trait, but in my observation it is not uncommon among clerical and frontline sales workers, among others. In any case, "working class" does not have strong pejorative connotations and often has some honorific ones.

Checking a box among those offered by pollsters may not indicate much about class consciousness but, as Thurston Domina argues, this whole self-identification phenomenon deserves much more study.[13] Given the strength of the middle-class vernacular, and the often militant prohibition against using the term "working class" (particularly during the cold war), the fact that such a large group consistently identifies itself as "working class" may indicate that there is a vital working-class culture that does not define the world in quite the same way as the professional middle class does—and that the vernacular is not equally recognized and spoken in all parts of American society.

This perception of and respect for a separate and distinct working-class culture is, in fact, at the core of the working-class studies movement that has emerged out of a series of conferences beginning in 1995 at Youngstown State University. Janet Zandy, one of the pioneers, describes the initial purpose as "carrying the best of working-class values, ethos, and knowledge into the academy and . . . using that rich, complex, even discordant heritage to expand what constitutes knowledge."[14] Among the pioneers, there were two kinds of academics for whom working-class culture was a palpable presence in their lives, something they could not ignore, not something they had to remind themselves not to forget. One kind, like Zandy, were from working-class backgrounds they didn't want to give up or to dishonor in becoming middle-class professors—something the academy, and middle-class life more generally, tends to require. The other kind, like Sherry Linkon, were from solidly middle-class backgrounds and found themselves teaching students whose culture was palpably different from their own.[15] The initial impetus for working-class studies came out of this "lived experience" of a clash of cultures and of the need to talk about it and think about it—what the cultures are, what the clash is all about, and which side you are on. For conscientious teachers in the higher education industry, these are both practical and moral issues that cannot be ignored. And they open onto similar issues faced by labor and community organizers in working-class settings.

This part of working-class studies is not about counting and classifying people. It's about how to relate to your father and your sister or to a room full of students who bring a whole lot more to your classroom than the absence of professional middle-class values and skills. A lot of the work here is about gathering, creating, and analyzing working-class stories.[16] But a healthy and growing literature consists of memoirs of middle-class academics reflecting on their working-class roots and the clash of cultures they have experienced or continue to experience. Some of this literature is on the self-absorbed side and some of it is overly concerned with the special world of academia. But, as Carolyn Leste Law points out in introducing one of these collections, "ambivalence" is one of their consistent themes—uneasiness with (or sometimes outright hatred of) middle-class ways, and a nostalgia and sense of loss in leaving the working-class world. As Law quotes her mother as saying, "Education destroys something."[17] Law explains:

> In their heart of hearts, these [working-class] parents wanted their children to return home to them virtually unchanged by their sojourn in the academy, so mysterious and impenetrable a place they might as well have sent their kids up the Amazon. . . . Working-class families . . . know that a college degree has everything to do with class. . . . They know that somehow the very existence of a college degree undermines and actually threatens their children and, consequently, their own working-class identity. In the end, they do not want what they would wish for.[18]

Some of the memoirs reflect the middle-class view that working-class culture is an obstacle to overcome and occurs in a place to escape from.[19] Others are comfortable with middle-class culture, but value and honor working-class ways.[20] But the main theme is, as Law says, ambivalence—recognizing value in both working-class and middle-class cultures and trying to reconcile the irreconcilable.

Barbara Jensen, a counseling psychologist from a working-class background whose practice and teaching is heavily with working-class young people and adults, has attempted to describe and "theorize" the differences between what she sees as *competing cultures.* According to Jensen, middle-class culture, with its achievement orientation, emphasizes "doing and becoming," while working-class culture gives primary value to "being and belonging." Each culture has strengths and weaknesses, advantages and disadvantages, and many people who are crossing classes experience various kinds of "cognitive dissonance" that can be both disabling and enriching.[21] Jensen and I have attempted to chart these basic differences (see Table 6).[22] Fred Rose and Betsy Leondar-Wright, community organizers from middle-class backgrounds, have also attempted to describe the two class cultures and to draw lessons for building cross-class coalitions.[23] Others have attempted to derive culturally sensitive pedagogies from their teaching experience, which inevitably involves an evaluative reflection on the class cultures.[24]

All of this work is tentative, and though there is much agreement, there are also many differences between different descriptions and evaluations of the class cultures, all of which always reflect one's own class circumstances and background (which, refreshingly, everybody is consciously and comfortably aware of). As a result, this whole cultural discussion is unusually concrete, self-reflexive, and practical, with stories and anecdotes disciplining and enriching the theorizing. As

Table 6. Class as Defined by Cultural Difference

Professional Middle Class	Working Class
Doing and becoming	Being and belonging
—achievement-oriented	—character-oriented
—future-oriented	—present-oriented
—life as transformative	—life as tangled web of relationships
—status concerns	—anti-status
—individualistic	—solidaristic
Unintended Homogeneity	Unavoidable Diversity
—more cosmopolitan	—more parochial
—weaker loyalties to persons, places, groups, institutions	—stronger loyalties to persons, places, groups, institutions

Best Result
  individual achievement with positive
    human impact
	Best Result
	  secure community, collective action

Worst Result
  the lonely individual
	Worst Result
	  unachieved potential

such, with all kinds of imprecisions and contradictions, it practices and speaks something like the four-class vernacular I advocate above; it shows the superiority of that vernacular over the middle-class one; and while not directly political (in the pollsters' and politicians' sense), it speaks directly to people's varied experiences of class in America in a way that makes a whole different politics and political discourse not only possible but urgently necessary.

I teach working adults in a bachelor's degree program in downtown Chicago and suburban Schaumburg. All my students are working class by education, but they're in my classes to change that. Though they are sometimes factory and construction workers, cops and firefighters, most are technical or clerical workers. Many are already managerial workers who need a bachelor's degree to keep their jobs. Some, especially the techs, have family incomes in excess of $100,000, while some of the managers make peanuts and bash their corporate employers in ways that make some of the clerical workers uncomfortable. Some (particularly downtown) are "poor" by my lights, but none would define themselves that way. Most, using Jensen's terms, are culturally working class, but not without a lot of middle-class gloss and sometimes roots. There are more women than men. Downtown is more black, more Hispanic, and more Democratic. The suburbs are more conservative and Republican (particularly the white men), though every class has its liberal Democrats. But most are classic (and complicated) "swing voters," just as Teixeira and Rogers claim, adrift in a politics that for the most part does not speak to them.

I know that class and class identity are complicated in these United States. My father was a militant steelworker shop steward who, with an iron will and an aching heart, virtually herded my sister and me into the professional middle class, while my mother was a college graduate and a professional worker (a teacher) who steadfastly protected and nourished our working-class culture. I grew up thinking I was middle class because we were so much better off than kids from nonunion families, and I was surprised in college when I found out I had to *become* middle class.

Class and class identity are complicated in America, but not so complicated as to be meaningless. Americans already think in class terms, but the mainstream vernacular will not let us recognize, let alone think clearly about, this complexity. Working-class studies will. We don't need long strings of class permutations. Neither do we need one definition for all occasions. We simply need to make it harder and harder to speak in the existing vernacular; to ridicule the middle-class two-step every time it's performed; and to insist on the inclusion of the working class wherever and whenever our insistence might make a difference. Working-class studies has already shown how this can help us understand ourselves and our society better than we do now. For most of us, it's personal. It's time now to make it political.

13

New Working-Class Studies in Higher Education

Renny Christopher

New Working-Class Studies is growing at a time when higher education is undergoing dramatic changes in who its students are and what it prepares them for. As the U.S. economy has shifted from a manufacturing base to a service base and to what Robert Reich calls "symbolic manipulation," the role of universities has also changed. The meaning of higher education is shifting, even as old myths about it remain and new ones are formed. Earning a bachelor's degree is no longer, necessarily, a way out of the working class. Our stereotype of college students—as eighteen- to twenty-two-year-olds attending ivy-walled selective admissions schools—represents only a small proportion of today's actual students. Since the late twentieth century there has been a very widespread belief that a college degree is a necessary qualification for a "good" job. Although this is in part a myth, it is true that "minimum qualifications" for entry-level jobs have tended to be ratcheted upward, from a high school diploma to an associate's or a bachelor's degree (see Zweig, *The Working Class Majority*; for a different view of what constitutes a "good" job, see Sharon O'Dair).[1]

Just as the demographics of college students changed with the advent of the GI Bill and open admissions after World War II, those demographics have changed yet again since the 1980s, with the entry of displaced workers into higher education, and with wider college attendance than ever before (although the children of parents with bachelor's degrees remain overwhelmingly more likely to earn such degrees than the children of parents without higher education). According to a U.S. Department of Education report, "Between 1971 and 1998, the proportion of 25–29 year-olds who earned a bachelor's degree or higher rose (from 22 to 31 percent), as did the proportion who attended some college (from 44 to 66 percent)."[2] Because, as Zweig demonstrates, at least 60 percent of the U.S. population is working class, attending college is no longer a guaranteed road out of that class, and universities of the future will be training not only the professional middle class but sectors of the working class as well. Howard London puts it this way: "As technological advances have made many jobs obsolete and created others and as more occupations have sought to 'professionalize' by keeping their recruits in school longer, students have increasingly needed to exceed the educational level of their forebears to maintain their relative socioeconomic position. Like a column of marching soldiers, everyone has moved along without getting any closer to those in front."[3] Upward mobility is not necessarily the primary goal of all first-generation students, who "vary considerably in their feelings regarding mobility. Some cherish it, others are wary of it, and still others see it as incidental to their goals."[4]

In addition to more working-class students from the "traditional" age group, there are also more older and more female college students than ever before, and first-generation students are "more likely than others to be 24 years or older."[5] Regional campuses have grown in number and size to accommodate the growth in attendance. Faced with new student constituencies, universities have both changed to meet the new students' needs (in some ways) and failed to change (in fundamental ways).

New working-class studies has developed within this climate and has addressed it in a number of ways, including pedagogy, scholarship, and the development of centers and programs. I will address here some of the ways that new working-class studies has responded to and helped to shape developments within higher education as it has responded to the new student demographics.

Access and Service

In recent years some intriguing research has been done on who contemporary college students are and how they are distributed through our multitiered higher education system. However, this empirical research fails to grasp some qualitative issues that should be central to any exploration of higher education and social class.

Most college students today are in regional campuses and two-year universities, yet the "norm" of college education is still considered to be the selective admissions four-year university. First-generation students are more likely to be found in regional universities, yet publicly supported selective admissions schools receive a much higher level of support than do regional schools or two-year campuses (and private institutions have even greater resources). In 1995–96, "47 percent of all beginning postsecondary students were first generation—that is, neither of their parents had more than a high school education. . . . The proportion of students who were first generation declined as institution level increased—from 73 percent at less than 2-year institutions, to 53 percent at 2-year institutions, to 34 percent at 4-year institutions."[6] Figures from California show that first-generation students are more common in the California State University (CSU) system, the less prestigious of California's two four-year systems, than in the University of California (UC) system, the far more prestigious of the two. In the CSU system, approximately 20 percent of students are first generation. Data for the number of first-generation students in the UC system is harder to analyze, but the comparison is nonetheless clear. For 1999, 58.6 percent of the fathers of entering students had college degrees; 48.6 percent of students' mothers did; there is no way to merge the two numbers, but it is safe to say that at least 59 percent, if not more, of entering UC students are not first generation.[7] But the figures for UC and CSU are noncommensurate, since the UC figures measure four-year degrees while the CSU figures measure "some college"; thus, while an exact comparison is not possible, clearly there are far more first-generation students in the lower-prestige system, a result which is in all likelihood not unique to California.[8] The issue of equity needs to be carefully examined, and scholars in new working-class studies need to ask critical questions about how higher education is implicated in the maintenance of a class hierarchy in the United States.

John Alberti identifies as a class division the "gap between first-tier, selective admissions schools and second-tier, open registration, regional two- and four-year colleges."[9] He counts 24 percent of U.S. institutions as "elite," and 66 percent as "regional." As of 1994, "elite" campuses had 3.3 million students and "regional" campuses had 10.9 million students.[10] He notes that the purpose of the elite universities is to create "what we now think of as the professional managerial class," while the focus of the regional schools has been "mass education" to turn out " 'academically skilled' employees that would then be managed by the graduates of the more prestigious schools, a 'paper-working class.' "[11] Alberti suggests that we should view what he calls the "majority second-tier schools," not the elite schools, as the norm of college education. Doing so would give a clearer and more realistic picture of what's going on in higher education today; this shift of focus and understanding is already taking place in, and in part because of, new working-class studies.

A U.S. Department of Education report published in 2001, "Students Whose Parents Did Not Go to College," confidently states that "participation in postsecondary education has positive benefits for individuals and society."[12] The report's hard statistics paint a very clear picture of the access and service provided to first-generation students: "In 1999, 82 percent of students whose parents held a bachelor's degree or higher enrolled in college immediately after finishing high school. The rates were much lower for those whose parents had completed high school but not college (54 percent) and even lower for those whose parents had less than a high school diploma (36 percent)."[13] The report concludes that first-generation students "are at a distinct disadvantage when it comes to postsecondary access even after controlling for other important factors such as educational expectations, academic preparation, support from parents . . . and family income."[14] Further, first-generation students have a lower rate of "persistence" (that is, finishing a bachelor's degree), even after entering the university. First-generation students were twice as likely to leave four-year institutions before their second year, and less likely to return.[15] Interestingly, this difference did not exist at two-year institutions, suggesting that some factors that exist only at four-year institutions discourage first-generation students from continuing or that the greater number of first-generation students at two-year institutions has some effect on retention. The report thus suggests an area of study for those interested in working-class pedagogy.

Further, the report notes that a smaller percentage of first-generation students who receive bachelor's degrees do postgraduate work than do students whose parents have college degrees—25 percent vs. 34 percent.[16] While first-generation students were equally likely to enroll in MBA programs, they were far less likely to enroll in PhD programs (1 percent vs. 4 percent), indicating that the overall percentage of working-class academics is likely to remain low, and working-class academics will continue to feel the impact of their minority status.

The Department of Education report does not analyze why the attendance, and especially the persistence, of first-generation students does not match that of the children of the college educated, and even makes the following rather stunning statement:

> Readers should not interpret the findings in this essay as implying that the availability of student financial aid has no effect on the postsecondary enrollment and persistence of first-generation students. The availability and awareness of financial aid help remove the barriers to enrolling in college and remaining there. The independent effects of financial aid on the enrollment and persistence of first-generation students have not been explicitly considered in this analysis.[17]

This is roughly the equivalent of saying, "Financial aid removes barriers for first-generation students. There is no evidence to support this statement." The content of the experience of first-generation students is not taken into account in this government study—the time students must put in applying for aid, standing in line for aid, and waiting for overdue disbursements, the humiliation of being known as a financial aid student, and so forth.

As Lee Warren, who has studied the class background of students at Harvard, says, working-class students don't know how to "work the system. . . . They feel unwelcome . . . They are afraid of being found out."[18] Further, working-class students' identities and family relations are subject to great stresses when they enter college. As Howard London notes, the first-generation community college students he has studied "reported having to renegotiate relations with family members, friends, and in a fundamental way, with themselves. These negotiations are not always accomplished easily or with a happy ending, for such passages inevitably call into question the very meaning of allegiance and love, over which people can intensely disagree."[19]

To understand the situation of working-class students in higher education, scholars in working-class pedagogy have focused not only on empirical data but on qualitative information as well, both observational and autobiographical. They have, in other words, sought to explicate what Department of Education reports simply identify. This work must continue if we are to understand, and intervene in, the development of higher education in the twenty-first century.

The Scholarship of Pedagogy

Just as the question "what is feminist pedagogy?" arose in the 1970s, the question "what is working-class pedagogy?" reemerged in the 1980s and 1990s (having virtually disappeared from public discourse after having been a subject of much attention, scholarship, and praxis during the 1930s). With the entry of increasing numbers of first-generation college students into universities, professors trained to deal with students from privileged backgrounds found themselves teaching students with different worldviews, and thus they needed to develop a pedagogy relevant to these students. Simultaneously, scholars in new working-class studies began questioning their own educational experiences and developing ideas about alternative educational strategies that might foster the inclusion of first-generation students within the academic community. In a 1995 issue of *Women's Studies Quarterly* dedicated to working-class studies, Janet Zandy asked, "Let us imagine what it would be like if the history and culture of working-class people were at the center of educational practices. What would students learn?"[20] The questions of what they would learn and how they would learn are central to working-class pedagogy.

In his article in the journal *College English,* John Alberti writes:

> The term "first-generation" itself potentially obscures the class implications of being such a student in order to minimize the potentially radical significance of these differences, differences that signify a level of conflict and change beyond the capacity of most traditional institutional structures to handle.[21]

Scholarship in working-class pedagogy has made it clear that many of the problems encountered by reentry women students and by students of color are problems shared by all first-generation college students across lines of race and gender. As Alberti suggests, the presence of first-generation students represents a crisis that institutional structures have handled poorly, largely by allowing the wholesale marginalization of these students, perhaps because to do otherwise would transform the academy itself. Working-class pedagogy calls for no less than that institutional transformation, even while making smaller and more local changes.

A number of publications have described the scope and direction of working-class pedagogy. In 1990 a volume of articles from the journal *Radical Teacher* was published under the title *Politics of Education*.[22] Several authors endeavored to bring social class into the curriculum as a way of helping students understand their own positioning within the academy and the world. The collection provides a framework for teachers looking for ways to transform their curricula and pedagogical methods to fit student constituencies made up of those conveniently called "nontraditional" by the institution.

In 1995 *Women's Studies Quarterly* published the first of two special issues on working-class studies. The 1995 issue, edited by Janet Zandy, included, along with personal essays, autobiography, and oral history, an article with syllabi by Linda Strom, "Reclaiming our Working-Class Identities: Teaching Working-Class Studies in a Blue-Collar Community." The second special issue, published in 1998 and edited by Renny Christopher, Lisa Orr, and Linda Strom, also featured articles on pedagogy.[23] In 2001, the Feminist Press published a revised and expanded version of the 1995 special issue of *Women's Studies Quarterly* under the title *What We Hold in Common: An Introduction to Working-Class Studies*.[24] The book includes an extended section, "New Initiatives, Syllabi, and Resources," that contains articles, sample syllabi, and bibliographies that demonstrate the state of development of the field.

Coming to Class: Pedagogy and the Social Class of Teachers contains personal narratives by teachers of writing and literature in which they explore "the effects of their own class histories on their teaching."[25] The editors call this "the first book to focus on how social class shapes the way a teacher works in the classroom or in a particular course," and the book illustrates one of the major themes of working-class pedagogy: the need for the instructor to be self-conscious about her or his own class position and aware of her or his students' class backgrounds. The editors note that several writers called their contributions "the most difficult writing assignments they had ever accepted—difficult because class is still so invisible in higher education."[26] Volumes like this one are beginning to make class increasingly visible, to the benefit of both instructors and students.

A measure of the impact of new working-class studies is the journal *Lingua Franca*'s naming Sherry Lee Linkon's *Teaching Working Class* one of the most important academic books of the 1990s.[27] The essays in her book address what pedagogical methods best suit first-generation students; how to integrate working-class material into the curriculum; taking university education off campus and into a working-class arena; the dynamics of classrooms with mixed populations of working- and middle-class students; and the intersections of race and class in the classroom. Linkon's book has been cited regularly by other scholars and has helped to firmly establish working-class pedagogy as a central concern of future research.

The greatest dialogue about working-class pedagogy has occurred in the field of composition. Because "freshman composition" is a near-universal requirement, the vast majority of working- and middle-class students must pass through such a course, often having had to work their way into it through one or more "remedial" or "basic skills" pre-baccalaureate-level classes. Although it is impossible to tell what percentage of these students might be first-generation, the U.S. Department of Education report suggests that there is "some evidence that first-generation students who began at 4-year institutions in 1995–96 were less well prepared academically than their peers whose parents had bachelor's or advanced degrees."[28] Thus, Composition has been heavily affected by the entry of nontraditional students into the academy, and has responded by developing an extensive literature on the subject. A Listserv called the "working-class-students-study-group" was first established in the late 1990s; its members have conducted special programs at the Conference on College Composition and Communication each year, including outreach programs and book donations to the local communities in the cities where the conference is held.[29]

Another organization, Pedagogy and Theatre of the Oppressed, grew out of a series of conferences held in Omaha, Nebraska, from 1995 through 1998 based on the work of Paulo Freire, the Brazilian educator. The organization's mission statement reads: "To challenge oppressive systems by promoting critical thinking and social justice. We organize an annual meeting that focuses on the work of liberatory educators, activists, and artists; and community organizers."[30] The inclusion of "community organizers" is typical of working-class pedagogies, which frequently look beyond the bounds of the academy.

All these works share two overarching questions: What is the best way to teach first-generation students and to overcome the culture shock they experience when they enter the academic world? And how can we transform the content of the curriculum to represent the majority population of the country, the working class, which now makes up almost half the student population in higher education?

For many people interested in working-class pedagogy those questions come not only out of their dealings with first-generation students in their classrooms but out of their own experiences as first-generation students. In a growing subgenre of autobiographical work, working-class academics write about their experiences traveling from the working class to the academic world. Many of these writers question the methodology and value of their education, characterizing their experiences as "miseducation." Their experiences have led many of them to look for ways to pass on a different kind of education to their students and to change the institution itself to make it more responsive to first-generation students and to working-class issues.

In addition to autobiographical essays in the collections mentioned above, a number of major works have appeared, thus legitimizing the subgenre in the most respectable of forums, including the Modern Language Association.[31] These works include Jake Ryan and Charles Sackrey's *Strangers in Paradise* (the first to appear), *Working-Class Women in the Academy, Liberating Memory,* and *This Fine Place So Far from Home,* all collections of essays.[32] Also in this genre are the memoirs *Hunger of Memory, Bootstraps,* and *Crossing Ocean Parkway.*[33] There is also an association of Working-Class Academics that sponsors an e-mail list and an annual conference.[34]

What all these writers share is a perception that the academic world is at best indifferent and at worst openly hostile to first-generation students, and that it demands that students from the working class deny their past, dissociate themselves from their families, and remake themselves in its own image in order to "earn" a place within it. Many of them tell stories of loss and nostalgia, and they question the institution and the participation of working-class academics in it, looking for ways future generations of working-class students can enter and find a place in the academy without betraying their origins or denying their working-class identities.

Pedagogy within the Classroom and the Institution

Given the presence of first-generation students in colleges and universities, and given the changing role of a university education in our social structure and economy, how, then, can we transform the classroom and the institution?

At the 2003 Youngstown Center for Working-Class Studies conference, psychologist Barbara Jensen discussed the "survivor psychology" of first-generation students and talked about the psychological damage that many first-generation students suffer in higher education. She said, "We can change this, and changing it might change entirely what higher education looks like." I pose this question: How would it change? What would it look like? Another participant at the conference said that we should educate people not to leave the working class but to serve the working class. I think that's a good starting point.

Increasing the numbers of first-generation students means increasing the numbers of students of color. We need to bring together the fields of working-class studies and ethnic studies (along with women's studies) to assess realistically what issues are common to working-class students across lines of race and gender, as well as what issues are specific to particular groups. By recognizing that first-generation students (both white and of color) share pedagogical issues, we've taken a great step forward, because we've redefined a new majority. In *Educating a New Majority,* Laura Rendón and Richard Hope address issues of significance to students of color, but much of their discussion is relevant to all first-generation students. For example, they call for rethinking the way classes are taught:

> College classes tend to be competitive as opposed to collaborative in nature, and faculty tend to use lecture as opposed to active learning techniques. However, the most used practices may have a detrimental effect on students with divergent ways of learning. While more research is needed to assess how students of color learn best, active learning strategies and group activities such as collaborative learning and learning communities have a positive impact on students of color.[35]

I believe the strategies Rendón and Hope refer to benefit all first-generation students, and that studies on "how students of color learn best" would reveal class-based differences within racial groups, something that Rendón and Hope don't discuss but which I think we must discuss. Knowing more about the ways class and race cut across each other is vital not only to our own scholarly projects but also to the well-being of our students.

In "From the Barrio to the Academy," Rendón writes that "higher education must begin to think in new ways about what constitutes intellectual development and about whether the traditional manner with which education prepares new students is appropriate for people of color as well as for white women and men." I would reframe her question to ask whether traditional educational strategies are appropriate for first-generation students, both white and students of color.[36] She notes that a "great lesson" students learn is that "separation [from one's past] leads to academic power" and argues that this model is not appropriate for women and students of color. Rather, for those students (as first-generation students), "it is important that from the beginning of our college career, our professors express their sincere belief that we are capable of learning and can be taught to learn."[37] That last phrase, "taught to learn," deserves careful attention; I would rephrase it to "can be taught to learn in an academic context." All too much of what working-class people do isn't looked at as "learning," and therefore educators don't see that first-generation students already possess transferable skills. We just need to show students how to transfer them.

First, in the classroom, we have to take big risks, and we should encourage our colleagues to take risks as well. Whenever we have institutional power, we need to work to change how teaching is evaluated, to free ourselves and our colleagues to try methods that are more effective for working-class students—methods that might be frowned on by our more traditional colleagues, whose methods might be all right for well-assimilated students with professional middle-class origins but are an obstacle for first-generation students. We need to argue that these risks—these "deviations" from the standard gatekeeper model of classroom teaching and grading—will lead to broader and deeper educational gains for nontraditional students and do not constitute a "watering down" of the curriculum. (I also believe we must be careful not to engage in "watering down," because our duty to our nontraditional students is to give them a rigorous, meaningful, and useful education.) Besides, these methods might be more beneficial for professional middle-class students as well.

These practices center around empowering students' learning by bringing the academic environment of the classroom into a sphere where the students already feel empowered, orality; deemphasizing the authority of the instructor, allowing students to engage in teaching and learning from one another; meeting students where they are; and allowing them to perform out of strengths, rather than out of disadvantages. Further, these practices demonstrate that students are active and valuable participants in one another's learning and that relationships within the classroom are part of a horizontal network, rather than a vertical hierarchy in which the expert instructor imparts knowledge to the ignorant, passive, and un-skilled audience of students.

David Brodsky suggests that we need to teach our students basic "political literacy," starting with "knowledge of political economy and the UN Universal Declaration of Human Rights."[38] I would add that we need to do that no matter what our discipline is. I teach literature courses, but nonetheless I try to teach my students about the structure of the university they're attending, even though that would not traditionally be considered "relevant" to the course. But to empower them and to demystify the conditions of their own learning, I think it's important that they start by understanding the institution they are enrolled in (something I never understood as an undergraduate, and only began hazily to understand as a graduate student).

Beyond the classroom, institutional initiatives such as learning communities can do much to produce a greater sense of self-efficacy in students, to enable them to be learners who are part of a network, a formally recognized group, so that less emphasis is put on individualism, an emphasis that produces a serious value conflict for many working-class students. Other programs can also help to increase students' sense of self-efficacy, such as directed self-placement for freshman composition, a program pioneered by Grand Valley State University in Michigan that has been adopted at a number of campuses, including my own, California State University, Channel Islands, whose mission includes the education of first-generation students.

One thing selective admissions universities can do is to recognize what they're preparing their PhD students to do. Because second-tier institutions outnumber selective admissions schools, most PhD graduates will spend all or part of their careers in those institutions. This is certainly true of the people with whom I went to graduate school. Yet one of our professors, a Harvard-educated white male of upper-middle-class origin, once told us explicitly, "I'm preparing you to be scholars, not teachers." Of the people sitting in the classroom when he made this statement, only two are now at research universities. Of the rest of us, some are at community colleges or state universities, some are in adjunct positions, some have left academia, and some have gone overseas to teach when they couldn't find jobs in the United States. I am a scholar, yes, as he tried to train me to be, but I make my living as a teacher. I could spend only 10 percent of my time on scholarship and still do very well in my career at the state university where I teach. Further, that professor was preparing us not only to be scholars but to be a certain kind of scholar—the ivory tower kind, not the kind who write and publish articles like this one and attend Center for Working-Class Studies conferences at which union activists appear side by side with PhDs. As John Alberti points out, we are the majority, but our voices are not the loudest. They can be, though, and they need to be. I needed to hear someone like Alberti when I was in graduate school, not just my former professor who disdains what my career has become. The more vocal working-class studies becomes as a discipline, the more opportunities people like me will have to hear them.

And this is vital, since we must, unfortunately, carry out our classroom strategies in an institutional setting that is designed to replicate, not overturn, the existing social class structure. The combination of lower resources allocated to second-tier schools with the class prejudice against working-class students at selective admissions schools results in a bad situation for students no matter which branch of higher education they find themselves in.[39] But there are activist strategies we can use to deal with this.

David Brodsky argues that public education "belongs to the much broader realm of the public domain, which benefits the vast majority of the population,"[40] and because the majority of the population is working class, we must foreground this point of view for ourselves, our colleagues, and the public, in order to work against the outcome that Brodsky predicts:

> Education for the great majority, however, the non-elite and the underprivileged, the student body that public institutions were created to serve, will be increasingly limited in duration, scope, and quality. The content and conditions of working and learning will be degraded further. . . . The dystopian model currently being proposed and imposed promises to mass-produce beasts of burden content with their blinders and routines, harboring the lowest life expectations, and conditioned into obedience and loyalty to their "managers," "betters," and "benefactors."[41]

Because the university has descended from an arcane medieval institution designed only for power elites and is surrounded by a veil of mystique, and because elite institutions and their graduates have done much over the centuries to preserve this mystique, and, further, because the majority of the population does not have a college degree, these issues are either invisible to, or very obfuscated for, the public. As academics we must put aside our jargon, especially in times of budgetary crisis, to speak plain English to our students and their families, to make plain what the system of higher education is, what it does, whom it serves and how, so that the institutions that most first-generation students attend will be given both the respect and the resources they need and deserve. Brodsky sees "potential sources of resistance" in the "changing class composition of academic labor" and "public disenchantment with corporate behavior."[42] We need to explore and encourage these sources of resistance, in order to create a new vision of higher education, one which works for, instead of against, social justice.

The Future of Working-Class Pedagogy

The Youngstown State University Center for Working-Class Studies Web site calls for four areas of future development in working-class studies: "the intersection of class with other aspects of identity; the expansion of its historical and cultural studies foundation; renewed attention to teaching of and about the working class; the links between academic study of working-class culture and political and social activism on behalf of the working class."[43] With the entry of more and more working-class students into higher education, the third goal becomes increasingly important. We need to continue to think about and write about pedagogical strategies that will be most effective for first-generation students, as well as thinking about changes in institutional structures, such as the promotion of ideas like learning communities, which will be of use to first-generation students. At the same time we need to continue to transform the content of the curriculum by introducing a focus on the history, culture, and cultural productions of the working class. By so doing, we can transform higher education into something that works for, instead of against, the working class.

14

Building Class Identity: Lessons from Labor Education

Robert Bruno and Lisa Jordan

As many in both the labor movement and New Working-Class Studies understand, education can serve as a tool for building class consciousness. Union-based training programs that use politics and economics to foster class identification and solidarity have a long history. During the 1920s and 1930s union members from around the country regularly attended educational sessions in union halls and community centers, and such programs positioned organized labor as the vanguard of a working-class movement—united in a conceptual frame that critiqued capitalism, political power, and inequality. However, by the end of World War II, labor education increasingly focused on contract interpretation, labor negotiations, and grievance handling. It was not only the unions and their approach to education that changed. The social context in which unions operated and the popular discourse around political and economic issues shifted over the years. By the end of the twentieth century, not only had debates about socialism and laborite New Dealism vanished but workers had also been left with a popular economic discourse focused on the stock market, industrial competition, and globalization. Moreover, workers had been left without a framework through which to analyze the impact of these variables on their own lives.

American workers know "something" has been going on and that at least since 1970 it has not been good for them. By all economic indicators a deregulated and unbounded capitalism has triumphed over labor-led efforts to maintain a credible state-enforced social safety net for all workers. By 1980, workers, even union members, were voting more conservatively, and they were taking less seriously their often self-proclaimed identity as members of the working class. To counter these trends, we believe that workers' education should reintroduce class analysis as a viable way of understanding the reality of contemporary life.

To fulfill this goal, we have developed a political economy curriculum for union members that, unlike the standard paycheck orientation of many workers' economic education classes, draws heavily from radical political economy and addresses "root" causes of economic inequality. Our objective is to make visible and understandable the structural conditions that most determine economic reality. We emphasize the role of labor markets, public policy, workplace and political power, and racism and sexism over individual and moral qualities to explain socioeconomic circumstances. In short, our program prioritizes class distinctions and class struggle. The course links politics and economics in a unified approach that helps to deepen workers' understanding of *how* and perhaps more importantly *why* the world has changed around them. A class-based approach to teaching political economy provides the language workers need to describe their own experience and to consider creative forms of resistance.

We contend that theory is critical to defining the political and social context in which learning occurs and in constructing the content of every curriculum. In short, while the student brings his or her own knowledge of the work world and relations of production to the class, theory offers the student a road map to discovering the common basis of seemingly disparate phenomena operating within an "identifiable process with identifiable actors, structures and directions."[1] This essay provides a rationale for our course "Working-Class Struggle and the Politics of Power," and a brief overview of the strategies we use to raise the class consciousness of working-class students.

Although we designed the course for union members, the core themes and strategies we present will, we hope, prove useful to anyone who wishes to incorporate greater attention to political economy and class analysis in their academic courses and to build on students' economic and political experience. If one of the goals of new working-class studies is to generate more critical understanding of class in America, and if education is one way of moving toward that goal, then the field must develop models for working-class education. Our approach offers one such model.

Working-Class Struggle and the Politics of Power examines the development and structure of the American economy and the importance of political action and organizing to protect workers' economic interests. The course uses class as an analytic tool to examine social structures and social relationships from different angles. What values dominate American political beliefs? Where do the contemporary conservative threats to union workers come from? Who is behind the drive to "globalize," "downsize," "privatize," "contract out," and "deregulate"? Are there alternatives to this neoliberal agenda? What happened to the politics of the

New Deal? The goal of this analysis is to integrate the everyday experience of the students with an understanding of the socially constructed nature of the market. We use their material conditions and a discussion of various theoretical perspectives to help workers develop a language to describe their own experiences and critique the way in which others describe them. As part of this process, throughout the course students define and redefine what they mean by "working class," including the historical tensions created by race, gender, sexual orientation, and national identities.

From Class Culture to Radical Political Economy

The fact that Working-Class Struggle and the Politics of Power has become a popular course testifies to both a surge in workers' class resentment and a changing economic class landscape. As the economic destruction caused by neoliberalism continued into the twenty-first century, average workers not only saw their material conditions worsen but they became less accepting of the conventional business cycle explanation of downturns. In class discussions workers heartily condemned the inequities of capitalism—at least a grossly unfair capitalism—and we never encountered a single defender of the economic system.

Contrary to what much mainstream and left class scholarship had declared, union workers were not suffering from false consciousness. Workers knew that because they sold their labor they were being marginalized by the political system. So when given the chance to take a course that promised an analysis of the difficulties they were living through, workers enthusiastically enrolled. To a large extent, capital had already provided the material groundwork for radicalizing workers' consciousness. Before we had constructed a course curriculum, economic devastation had been shaping places and relationships that working people embraced.

Job loss meant that working-class neighborhoods lost neighbors. Less money meant fewer car repairs and home improvements, and too many signs of an economic "falling down." Underfunded and failing schools, where working-class children learned the "three Rs," produced kids who were more likely than ever to fail to fulfill their parents' dreams of a better life. Dance halls pulled up their rugs, amusement parks padlocked the gates, working-class bars and restaurants became antique "junk" stores; public pools dried up, and working-class cultural life appeared to morph into something dark and dangerous. But of course working-class culture had not disappeared or transformed into predatory behavior or even suffered from a lapse of memory.

Working-class men and women continued to live and work beside one another. Together they routinely experienced abuse and witnessed firsthand the inequities of capitalism. This was nothing new. But what was different was how they interpreted their experiences. Our teaching experiences with both union and nonunion students revealed that instead of conservative workers fully supportive of a free market economy, we were now teaching angry critics of the economic system, though they often seemed unsure where to focus that anger. Most lacked a historical context and political language for their hard-earned awareness, but their righteous antagonism toward the boss brought our class, Working-Class Struggle and the Politics of Power, into being. In other words, in defense of a working-class way of life—inside and outside of the workplace—union workers turned to the classroom for help in political mobilization, organizing new members, waging creative contract fights, and preserving the places where they lived.

The study of political economy mattered more now than ever because corporate behavior was not only incredibly exploitive but, according to our workers, it unfolded without a decent measure of government control. Bad business and weak state regulation led workers to seek another way to understand their reality. The old ways of knowing had proven false. Our course showed that workers had a heightened level of class consciousness and were ready to do something constructive with it. Being more class-conscious, however, did not mean that workers were speaking in leftist tongues or envisioning alternative ways to create and distribute wealth.

We created a "structured space for reflection on class as it relates to their lives"[2] in order to provide a place to examine what was happening in their lives and to develop the language to name it. As labor educators we recognized that while workers objectively experienced their class status, we had to make visible the narratives and ideas that nurture solidarity with workers' issues, struggles, and perspectives across race and gender differences. Here, then, was an opportunity for a course on political economy and working-class fortunes—an opportunity to move beyond blaming individual "others" and instead analyze the system in which they live. A structured classroom environment was precisely what was needed to move the workers from "pissed off" to activist. This transition from acted upon to actor was central in our construction of the class.

As labor educators, we wanted to bring class analysis back into the conversation. With worker identities up for grabs between "class and its others," worker education focusing on the political economy of power can present class as the principal axis of social transformation. The accompanying shift in authority can empower working men and women to understand their experiences as valid interpretations of the economic system. However, to properly situate the class process in identity development, we first had to introduce political and economic theory into the discussion.

Structure and Substance Cannot Be Divided

The educational goal of the course is for our students to move beyond a reflective understanding of the material covered in the class toward a more theoretical, analytical, and critical perspective. Toward this end, workers' personal experiences (that is, their work, family, health, and community histories, their racial, ethnic, and gender identities, and their life expectations and dreams) become the core of the class discussion, but they are consistently considered in the context of public discourse and knowledge. In other words, we try to move the student from the personal to the broader political structure and to focus analysis on the relationship between the two. The individual is not seen simply as someone who is acted upon but also as a potential agent for change. Feminist pedagogy helped us develop strategies to challenge the students to see ideas and institutions as socially constructed. Feminist pedagogy explicitly works to build community, to empower students, and to facilitate their recognition of their own ability to lead and create. It is our goal to move students beyond mere understanding to action.

To move workers to challenge the language and ideology of the neoliberal understanding of political economy, the course aims to deconstruct the positivist neoclassical approach to economic thinking and to expose it as only one way of viewing the world. Students are reintroduced to the principal tenets of mainstream economics with the express purpose of revealing how economic theory is socially constructed around class and power relations. This activity challenges students' belief that the reliance of neoclassical economics on the rational actor and deductive reasoning is powerful, logical, and complete. In the current political environment, with both Republicans and Democrats touting profit margins, deregulation, low inflation, balanced budgets, lower taxes, globalization, and competition, students see little intellectual space to challenge conventional economics.

How could we empower workers to challenge the language and premise of a neoliberal political economy? By encouraging them to tell their personal stories. As a mode of learning and thinking about economic reality, storytelling can transform a seemingly "objective" course on political economy into an effective critique of class relations. Personal and collective accounts of work, home, family, and community bring out alternative interpretations of how capitalism affects workers. The result, according to feminist economist Diana Strassman, is that students stop thinking that there are "heroes who, aided by superior understanding, lead the way to economic truths or laws."[3] Storytelling also demonstrates, as rhetorician James Berlin contends, that our economic and political choices are based on "competing ideologies, competing discursive interpretations" and not on choosing "between truth and ideology."[4] We aim to encourage our students to renounce Wall Street positivism and help them instead understand the economic system as a Main Street battlefield. In addition to calling specific attention to the class-constructed nature of economic rhetoric and analysis, we challenge students to develop their own understanding of the political and economic environment in which they operate.

Feminist pedagogy, especially storytelling, works because it reduces the *distance* between the worker and the "market," it shifts *authority* back to the worker, and it *disrupts* the students' safe modes of understanding.

Distance

In economics, the subject (that is, the market) is often seen to be very distant from the worker-student's life and thus nearly impossible to affect. Outcomes simply happen; the market adjusts; no one is responsible. Economic behavior appears magically, as if the system exists naturally and no alternatives exist. This also erases complexities, such as how class, race, and gender shape political and economic structures and behavior. Charles Bazerman has argued that writing within all disciplines emphasizes "rhetorical perception" as a means to distance people from the everyday practice of the world's business in order to maintain a popular dependency on "experts" to impart seemingly scientific truths.[5] Thus, in order to help students realize the constructed nature of economic theory, the distance between the worker's life and the "invisible hand" must be reduced. As in the land of Oz, we need to reveal the actor behind the curtain. But unlike the Emerald City, the bad wizard is not actually a good man.

Workers' stories of economic destruction, discriminatory work practices, unsafe working conditions, growing inequities in the workplace, and unjust dismissals make economics personal and highlight the inconsistencies between their lives and the neoliberal theory of individual merit and reward. Their stories also reveal the direct impact of broader sociopolitical changes. Moreover, workers' stories of successful collective action both at the work site and politically show that the system is not impenetrable.

Authority

Often, because of the nature of work and work relations, students enter our classes with specific expectations about how knowledge will be bestowed. However, in a classroom structured on feminist ideas, students' storytelling may not only challenge class assumptions but may create new understanding. Such a pedagogy builds community in the classroom by engaging students in a constructive conversation and by encouraging them to challenge their own ideologies. This community or class-building orientation to the instruction relies on atypical sources for legitimate "data" on politics and economics. For instance, instead of a narrow focus on supply and demand theory students examine the contradictions between democracy and capitalism, equality and poverty, their lives and notions of the American Dream. As this example shows, sharing authority with students can liberate the instructor as well as the students.

Notice how the social outcome of this teaching methodology differs from the rationalist approaches to political economy. By studying the literature, stories, and histories of work (texts that are often viewed as personal, subjective, expressive, and poetic) in conjunction with materials that are traditionally viewed as objective and transactional (as merely transferring and conferring truths, ideas, and knowledge), students can redefine the science of economics as less rational and as not value-free.

The immediate objective here is to illustrate that economics evolved as a response to pragmatic problems and popular ideas in specific historical and linguistic contexts. When students understand that economics grows out of people's experiences, authority then shifts away from professionals, economists, bankers, and television commentators and moves toward homeowners, workers, parents, and citizens. Authority is also layered by racial and "gendered modes" of identification.[6] In addition, although mainstream economics provides some historical perspective in which to place questions of inequality and power, considering specific social contradictions makes clear that Alan Greenspan's economy is really capital's creation. When viewed this way, authority is transferred from economics as a holy script to economics as class struggle.

Disruption

In order to get students to not only envision a different world but also believe in their power to create that world, a space must be created for new ways of understanding. To create that space we have to intentionally draw out contradictions in workers' worldviews. By disrupting their comfortable ways of thinking, by forcing them to ask increasingly difficult questions about their own lives, we challenge the students' tendency to fall back on nonclass interpretations of economic relations.

This can be a difficult process because people often do not want to think differently. Students do not want facts to get in the way of a perfectly good myth about the way America works. Often students will express anger and disbelief: "You must have made the statistics up!" In essence the class challenges the culture of the American Dream. For example, as workers tell their stories, we point to places where capitalist institutions are more powerful than the individual. To a degree the aim is to anger students and then to direct the focus of that anger. Too often in political economics courses, the economic evidence disheartens workers. We, instead, push our students to move from near depression to anger and from anger to action.

One example of how the course pierces conventional, sacred myths is the class's review of the origins of the "new right" conservative political movement.

Typically our labor union students are rightfully primed to vilify the economic politics of the Republican Party. But how should the class interpret the policy stances of the Democrats? If capitalism has not "captured" both parties, then the Democrats can potentially be pro-working class in their orientation. The question, however, needs to be raised and answered. To disrupt the class's comfort with political reality, students learn that it was, according to William Grieder, "not Ronald Reagan, for instance, who opened the floodgates of tax giveaways for business interests but Representative Dan Rostenkowski, Democratic chairman of the House Ways and Means Committee." Further, "It was the Democrats, not the Republicans, who first proposed bringing down the top tax rate on unearned income."[7] In light of labor's battle with President George W. Bush's tax and budget plans, this information disrupts our students' settled beliefs. Pointing to the flaws of Democratic Party politics does not absolve years of Republican hostility to organized labor, but it does raise questions about the possibility of political independence within a capitalist system.

The Course

To illustrate these ideas more clearly, we will briefly describe the class sessions and readings for Working-Class Struggle and the Politics of Power. Although we cannot discuss the specifics of the entire class, the following outline summarizes the material discussed in each section and our primary interest in developing each issue.

Session I. Class Structure and American Values

At the beginning of the session, students debate the definition of "the/or a working class." To assist them in this task, we rely on Michael Zweig's *The Working Class Majority* (2000) to present a reasonable national picture of working-class demographics. Following the discussion, students discuss a commonly agreed on list of basic American values (e.g., individualism, freedom, equality, sanctity of contracts and law, property rights, and hard work). Although these values nominally have broad generic public support, their meaning is typically contested. In this session, students explore the various ways "conservatives," "liberals," "radicals," and others understand these values. The class then considers what a working-class perspective on these values would require and begins deconstructing the way the students talk about the economy and politics. Unlike the AFL-CIO's "Common Sense Economics" curriculum, we consider and discuss "the Left" and the Marxist critique of capitalism and government.

Session II. Two Sides of the Same Coin

This session begins by acknowledging that while Democrats and Republicans disagree about how capitalism should be administered, most are in full ideological agreement that capitalism is the best system, thus little if any public discourse takes place concerning alternative political economic systems or theories. From this opening vantage point, we introduce a brief history of economic thought. In a discussion that moves through Adam Smith, Karl Marx, Thorstein Veblen, John Maynard Keynes, and a variety of more contemporary theorists, we give special attention to the sociopolitical times in which they were writing. This connection between theory and context draws attention to the created nature of understanding and interpretation.

At this point, the stories shared by workers earlier in the class are exposed to economic analysis. For example, free trade issues touch the lives of many of the workers in class, so we encourage the students to analyze trade from a variety of perspectives. First, we examine the role of trade with its focus on comparative advantage and efficient use of resources. Students identify this approach as a "conservative" one, which is often referred to in the media as a neoliberal or neoclassical analysis. Students then consider a more "center" or "liberal" analysis of trade with its emphasis on maximizing efficiency while acknowledging that laws may be needed to protect those hurt by global exchange. Finally, a "left" or "radical" prospective that trade can and often does hurt both those workers in the developed and developing countries, and that trade policy serves primarily to support corporate profits and not workers' needs, is discussed. Throughout the discussion, we pose the following questions: "Which analysis makes the most sense to you? What are the strengths and weakness of each? Which analysis do you most often hear in the media?" The goal is to help students to see how issues can be analyzed in a variety of ways and that all facts are indeed theory-laden.

Session III. Gays, Guns, Government, and God: The Rise of the New Right

American politics has been dominated by two political theories: liberalism and conservatism. Since the dawn of the twentieth century conservative thought has been a mixture of different intellectual elements. However, beginning in the late 1960s, right-wing beliefs and movements within conservatism have come to strongly define the American political landscape. This session focuses on how diverse groups and uncommon values and trends were brought together around a common conservative currency, producing the "New Right." In brief, students examine the diverse ways that class conflict has been waged by capital against working people.

This session often angers students as we touch on politically sensitive social issues such as crime, affirmative action, gun control, school prayer, family values, and abortion. The degree of anger expressed here and the level of disruption created becomes a powerful teaching tool in the later sessions. In no case, however, do we take a stand, other than to demonstrate how these issues have been used to divide and confuse the working class. To provide a context and history of why these "wedge" issues have become dominant in modern political discourse, students read and discuss E. J. Dionne's *They Only Look Dead* (1995), which provides a very concise and readable description of the forces that have created an "anxious" working-class voting public.

This section concludes with a more focused examination of the beginnings of "backlash" politics as best sculpted and practiced by Georgia governor and two-time presidential candidate George Wallace. Wallace's political career and political strategy, as described in Dan Carter's *The Politics of Rage* (1995), establishes the importance of the Southern segregationist as the father of post-1970s conservative populist movements. In essence, the lesson argues that contrary to conservative defamation of government activism, to be right wing has meant to support the state in its capacity as enforcer of order and to oppose the state as distributor of wealth and power downward and more equitably in society.

Session IV. Who Gets What, When, and How

A political system can be best understood as the interaction of several related dynamic elements designed to determine how authoritative decisions are made about "who gets what, when, and how." The work of Karl Marx, Max Weber, Robert Dahl, Benjamin Barber, David Held, and David Eaton presents the students with different ways of understanding basic principles of American political behavior and the functional attributes that sustain the political system. This engages the workers in a discussion about their belief in or commitment to notions of American political pluralism.

This session, along with the following one, also provides an opportunity to address the "outcomes" of the political system in gender- and race-based terms. Exploring how gender, ethnic, and racial identification has structured layers of opportunity and advantage for American workers helps our students to take seriously a meaningful political and economic class analysis. Labor education students are typically a very diverse population (though the racial and gender mix varies by workforce). Union-sponsored classrooms provide an ideal environment for an inclusionary discussion of the merits of a "who gets what" approach to politics and the labor movement. In this respect, Robin Kelley's *Race Rebels* (1994) and Dan Georgakas and Marvin Surkin's *Detroit: I Do Mind Dying* (1998) provide a number of interesting departures for a discussion of black workers and their inclusion in a broader working-class political movement. For similar reasons, Dennis Deslippe's *Rights Not Roses* (2000) and Jacqueline Ellis's *Silent Witnesses* (1998) are helpful in talking about the juncture of politics and working-class feminism. Another powerful resource that provides a wide variety of short readings on class, race, gender, and sexual orientation is *Reading for Social Justice and Diversity,* edited by Maurianne Adams et al. (2000).

Session V. A Working-Class Economic Analysis

What has happened over the last twenty years to wages, taxes, corporate investments, corporate profits, pension plans, stock values, job security, foreign trade, union density, and government spending? Donald Barlett's and James Steel's Pulitzer Prize–winning work, *America: What Went Wrong?* (1992), is an excellent "reader" on the economic destruction of the 1980s. The AFL-CIO's "Common Sense Economics" has served as a good resource, but the Economic Policy Institute's annual, *The State of Working America,* provides most of the data used in this section. Students examine how economic changes and trends have created class winners and class losers. This session also addresses the ways that gender and race handicap resource distribution. Special attention is given to the effects of globalization as a joint corporate-state trade, investment, and currency speculation strategy. On the spread of international capital, resource material from the AFL-CIO and from industrial unions such as the United Steelworkers of America also emphasizes the disparate economic effects of national trade policy.

Session VI. Politics as an Act of Will

This final session has two principal objectives: to recommend a strategic plan for creating a working-class or union-derived issue agenda and to establish a set of rules for class-based political action. The session begins with the question, "So what is to be done?" We ask students to create a political action plan around a set of issues. Before they generate their plans, they engage in a brief discussion designed to answer two underlying fundamental questions. First, how can a movement of class-informed union leaders engage a political system dominated by two capitalist parties? Second, what political message is required to mobilize rank-and-file workers around class issues? Before attempting to answer these questions, the class reads sections of Ruy Teixeira's and Joel Rogers's (2000) analysis of national voting trends and issue polls, in *America's Forgotten Majority: Why the White Working Class Still Matters.* Teixeira and Rogers put forward the idea of an issue agenda around which progressive class-based political action can be successfully built.

In the interplay of student comments a number of principles and activities emerge. Students discuss the importance of exposing and denouncing excessive corporate political power and the corporate political agenda: They grapple with the need and difficulty of educating, organizing, and mobilizing all workers now outside of the labor movement and the political system. Students typically agree that it is paramount to construct and endorse an independent labor agenda and not simply a Democratic Party–defined agenda. Students also argue for basing a political and social vision on the issues of class fairness and class equality. We remind students of the need to preserve a strong and independent labor movement as a condition of a free, democratic, egalitarian, and prosperous society. Finally, we ask union workers to develop their political strategies, tactics, and goals democratically with other rank-and-file members.

In this session, we provide both historical and contemporary examples of workers exerting themselves and winning, sometimes with government protections and sometimes without. The message is that legislation is one way to protect workers, but the most important protection workers have is in organizing "as a class" with a consciousness of class struggle.

The breathtaking acceleration of capital flows and "creative destruction" in the early twenty-first century makes labor educators and worker-students painfully aware of the temporary and contingent nature of all capitalist arrangements. Between the contemporary configuration of political power in Washington, D.C., and global capital's latest dismemberment of the manufacturing sector of the economy, the labor movement may seem to have little time for education. Labor has all it can handle simply trying to survive. But if we have arrived at a world in which capitalism has become economically and politically unassailable, then a debunking education is more necessary then ever.

Time and resources may be stretched thin but the intellectual field is ripe for a root-and-branch critique of everything workers have taken as harmful but given. The power of an economic and political education centered in a theory of capitalism is linked to the real-world threats against organized labor and to the fears workers carry with them from paycheck to paycheck. In principle (if not precisely), the same deteriorating material and psychological conditions experienced in the 1930s inspired radical workers' education classes in union halls. In the formative days of industrial unionism an analytical class education went hand-in-hand with building strong unions. But for all the progressive activity of today's labor movement, it does not prominently feature the word *class* in its rhetorical arsenal.[8] Political and economic agendas are for "working people" or "working families," and labor is fighting for "middle-class" America. The result of this universal middling or nonclass discourse is that class analysis has been dropped from the labor curriculum.

But the cost of speaking the language of bourgeois economics and politics has been high. Without a radical education informing the political economy of workers, the power of class identity to provide resistance not only to capitalism but also to other entrenched structures of power has been diminished. Still, the working class (as a concept) has disappeared only from the classroom. The working class as Marx described it and projected it is now everywhere, and because of neoliberal politics and globalized markets it is everywhere more alike. Material conditions are once again, as in an earlier era, contributing to a radical theoretical framework for understanding politics and economics. With unionization of the private sector workforce in the United States at less than 10 percent, it is now appropriate for labor education to think and act like a new movement yet to be born.

This kind of education needs to happen not only within the labor movement but in other educational settings, and we encourage our colleagues in new working-class studies to learn from our experience as labor educators. The vast majority of America's workers do not belong to unions, but a significant proportion of young adults go to college, and most of them work while they are in school. And despite their best hopes, very few will ever find a way to make a living that is free of the exploitation that shapes the lives of workers under capitalism. Although students in college classrooms may not think of themselves primarily as workers, and their teachers may not place building a class-based movement at the top of their lists of course goals, the strategies we've outlined here can bring a more critical and political perspective to discussions of class, economics, and politics in American culture. Such an approach might well spark labor, political, and community organizing activities by students. It will certainly deepen the analysis of politics and economics in the classroom.

Notes

What's New about New Working-Class Studies?

1. Cobble made this argument in a roundtable discussion about the connections between labor studies, labor history, and working-class studies that was sponsored by the journal *International Labor and Working Class History* at the New School for Social Research in October 2000.

2. Roy Rosenzwieg, *Eight Hours for What We Will: Workers and Leisure in an Industrial City, 1870–1920* (New York: Cambridge University Press, 1983); Kathy Peiss, *Cheap Amusements: Working Women and Leisure in Turn-of-the-Century New York* (Philadelphia: Temple University Press, 1986).

3. Michael Denning, *Mechanic Accents: Dime Novels and Working-Class Culture in America* (London: Verso, 1987).

4. John Russo, "The Crisis in the Servicing Model and Alternative Labor Education Approaches," plenary address at Joint AFL-CIO Education Departments/University and College Labor Education Association annual meeting, 1990; John Russo and Andy Banks, "Applications of the Organizing Model of Labor Education," Joint AFL-CIO Education Departments/University and College Labor Education Association annual meeting, 1991. In addition, between 1988 and 1991, editor Jack Metzgar devoted four issues of the journal *Labor Research Review* to discussions of the organizing model.

5. Bruno and Jordan explain their approach fully in their article "To Know, to Remember, to Realize: *Illinois Labor Works*—A History Workers Can Use," in Sherry Lee Linkon, *Teaching Working Class* (Amherst: University of Massachusetts Press, 1999), 145–59.

6. David Roediger, *The Wages of Whiteness: Race and the Making of the American Working Class* (London: Verso, 1991); Robin D. G. Kelley, *Hammer and Hoe: Alabama Communists during the Great Depression* (Chapel Hill: University of North Carolina Press, 1990); Alessandro Portelli, *The Death of Luigi Trastulli and Other Stories: Form and Meaning in Oral History* (Albany: State University of New York Press, 1991); Michael Frisch and Milton Rogovin, *Portraits in Steel* (Ithaca: Cornell University Press, 1993).

7. George Lipsitz, *Rainbow at Midnight: Labor and Culture in the 1940s* (Urbana: University of Illinois Press, 1994) and *Time Passages: Collective Memory and American Popular Culture* (Minneapolis: University of Minnesota Press, 1990); Nan Enstad, *Ladies of Labor, Girls of Adventure: Working Women, Popular Culture, and Labor Politics at the Turn of the Twentieth Century* (New York: Columbia University Press, 1999).

8. "Education and Scholarship," Ford Foundation, 2003, http://www.fordfound.org/program/edu_units.cfm?unit_name=education_and_scholarship (accessed June 26, 2003).

9. Paul Lauter, "Working Class Women's Literature—An Introduction to Study," *Radical Teacher* 15 (1980): 16; Janet Zandy, ed., *Calling Home: Working-Class Women's Writings: An Anthology* (New Brunswick, N.J.: Rutgers University Press, 1990); Janet Zandy, ed., *Liberating Memory: Our Work and Our Working-Class Consciousness* (New Brunswick, N.J.: Rutgers University Press, 1995); Peter Oresick and Nicholas Coles, *Working Classics: Poems on Industrial Life* (Urbana: University of Illinois Press, 1990); Bottom Dog Press, http://members.aol.com/lsmithdog/bottomdog/; Constance Coiner, *Better Red: The Writing and Resistance of Tillie Olsen and Meridel Le Sueur* (New York: Oxford University Press, 1995); Paul Lauter and Ann Fitzgerald, introduction to *Literature, Class, and Culture: An Anthology* (New York: Longman, 2001); Renny Christopher and Carolyn Whitson, "Toward a Theory of Working-Class Literature," *Thought and Action* 71 (spring 1999): 71–81.

10. Ira Shor, *Empowering Education: Critical Teaching for Social Change* (Chicago: University of Chicago Press, 1992); Mike Rose, *Lives on the Boundary: The Struggles and Achievements of America's Underprepared* (New York: Free Press, 1989).

11. Don Mitchell, *The Lie of the Land: Migrant Workers and the California Landscape* (Minneapolis: University of Minnesota Press, 1996); Andrew Herod, ed., *Organizing the Landscape: Geographical Perspectives on Labor Unionism* (Minneapolis: University of Minnesota Press, 1998).

12. Stanley Aronowitz, *False Promises: The Shaping of American Working-Class Consciousness* (New York: McGraw-Hill, 1973), and *How Class Works: Power and Social Movement* (New Haven: Yale University Press, 2003); William Julius Wilson, *When Work Disappears: The World of the New Urban Poor* (New York: Knopf, 1996).

13. Kathryn Marie Dudley, *The End of the Line: Lost Jobs, New Lives in Postindustrial America* (Chicago: University of Chicago Press, 1994); Maria Kefalas, *Working-Class Heroes: Protecting Home, Community, and Nation in a Chicago Neighborhood* (Berkeley: University of California Press, 2003); Dimitra Doukas, *Worked Over: The Corporate Sabotage of an American Community* (Ithaca: Cornell University Press, 2003).

14. Michael Zweig, *The Working-Class Majority: America's Best Kept Secret* (Ithaca: Cornell University Press, 2000).

15. Janet Zandy, *What We Hold in Common: An Introduction to Working-Class Studies* (New York: Feminist Press, 2001); Michael Zweig, *What's Class Got to Do with It? American Society in the Twenty-first Century* (Ithaca: Cornell University Press, 2004).

16. National Opinion Research Center, University of Chicago. *General Social Survey: Social Class-Subjective,* General Social Survey Data Information and Retrieval System, http://www.icpsr.umich.edu:8080/GSS/homepage.htm (accessed Jan. 22, 2004).

17. bell hooks, *Where We Stand: Class Matters* (New York: Routledge, 2000), 8.

18. Radio interview, with Evelyn Hu-DeHart and Sherry Lee Linkon, "Focus," recorded May 15, 2003.

19. Kwadwo Agymah Kamau, *Flickering Shadows: A Novel* (Minneapolis, MN: Coffee House Press, 1996) and *Pictures of a Dying Man* (Minneapolis, MN: Coffee House Press, 1999).

20. Stephen J. Ross, *Working-Class Hollywood: Silent Film and the Shaping of Class in America* (Princeton: Princeton University Press, 1998).

21. For more information on Bread and Roses, see http://www.bread-and-roses.com/1199.html.

22. C. L. Barney Dews and Carolyn Leste Law, eds., *This Fine Place So Far from Home: Voices of Academics from the Working Class* (Philadelphia: Temple University Press, 1995); Janet Zandy, ed., *Liberating Memory: Our Work and Our Working-Class Consciousness* (New Brunswick, N.J.: Rutgers University Press, 1995). Other examples include Michelle M. Tokarczyk and Elizabeth A. Fay, *Working-Class Women in the Academy: Laborers in the Knowledge Factory* (Amherst: Univer-

sity of Massachusetts Press, 1993) and Jake Ryan and Charles Sackrey, *Strangers in Paradise: Academics from the Working Class* (Lanham, Md.: University Press of America, 1996).

23. Jeff Crump, "The End of Public Housing as We Know It: Public Housing Policy, Labor Regulation, and the U.S. City," *International Journal of Urban and Regional Research* 27 (May 2003): 179–87; Mary Romero, *Maid in the U.S.A.* (New York: Routledge, 1992); Dudley, *The End of the Line*; Sherry Lee Linkon and John Russo, *Steeltown U.S.A.: Work and Memory in Youngstown* (Lawrence: University Press of Kansas, 2002).

24. Jefferson Cowie, *Capital Moves: RCA's Seventy-Year Quest for Cheap Labor* (Ithaca: Cornell University Press, 1999).

Chapter 1. Gender, Class, and History

1. See David Brody, "The Old Labor History and the New," *Labor History* 20 (1979), 11–26, for an introduction.

2. For overviews, see Ava Baron, "Gender and Labor History: Learning from the Past, Looking to the Future," in *Work Engendered: Toward a New History of American Labor,* ed. Ava Baron (Ithaca: Cornell University Press, 1992), 1–46; Alice Kessler-Harris, "Treating the Male as 'Other': Re-defining the Parameters of Labor History," *Labor History* 34 (spring-summer 1993): 190–204; Elizabeth Faue, "Reproducing the Class Struggle: Class, Gender, and Social Reproduction in U.S. Labor History," in *Amerikanische Arbeitergeschichte heute,* ed. Irmgard Steinisch, Mitteilungsblatt des Instituts für soziale Bewegungen 25 (Essen: Klartext, 2001), 47–66; Sonya Rose, "Gender and Labor History: The Nineteenth-Century Legacy," supplement to *International Review of Social History* 38 (1993): 145–62.

3. See, for example, Howard Kimeldorf, "Bringing the Unions Back In (Or Why We Need a New Old Labor History)," *Labor History* 32 (winter 1991); Ira Katznelson, "The 'Bourgeois' Dimension: A Provocation about Institutions, Politics, and the Future of Labor History," *International Labor and Working Class History* 46 (fall 1994): 7–32.

4. See essays in *Perspectives on American Labor History: Toward a Synthesis,* ed. J. Carroll Moody and Alice Kessler-Harris (DeKalb: Northern Illinois University Press, 1989); Bryan Palmer, *Descent into Discourse: The Reification of Language and the Writing of Social History* (Philadelphia: Temple University Press, 1990).

5. See, for example, David Halle, *America's Working Man: Work, Home, and Politics among Blue-Collar Property Owners* (Chicago: University of Chicago Press, 1984); Rick Fantasia, *Cultures of Solidarity: Consciousness, Action, and Contemporary American Workers* (Berkeley: University of California Press, 1988); Lillian B. Rubin, *Families on the Fault Line: America's Working-Class Families Speak about the Family, the Economy, Race, and Ethnicity* (New York: Harper Collins, 1994); Ruth Milkman, *Farewell to the Factory: Auto Workers in the Late Twentieth Century* (Berkeley: University of California Press, 1997).

6. See, among others, Michael Denning, *The Cultural Front: The Laboring of American Culture in the Twentieth Century* (New York: Verso, 1996); Bill Mullen and Sherry Lee Linkon, eds., *Radical Revisions: Rereading 1930s Culture* (Urbana: University of Illinois Press, 1996); Constance Coiner, *Better Red: The Writing and Resistance of Tillie Olsen and Meridel Le Sueur* (New York: Oxford University Press, 1995).

7. Much of the early work appeared originally as articles and was later republished. See David Brody, *Steelworkers in America: The Nonunion Era* (New York: Harper and Row, 1960); idem, *Labor in Crisis: The Steel Strike of 1919* (Philadelphia: Lippincott, 1965); idem, *Workers in Industrial America: Essays on the Twentieth Century Struggle* (New York: Oxford University Press, 1980); Herbert G. Gutman, *Work, Culture, and Society in Industrializing America* (New York: Random House, 1976); idem, *The Black Family in Slavery and Freedom, 1750–1925* (New York: Pantheon, 1976); idem, *Power and Culture: Essays on the American Working Class,* ed. Ira Berlin (New York: Pantheon Books, 1987); David Montgomery, *Workers' Control in America: Studies in the History of Work, Technology, and Labor Struggles* (Cambridge, Cambridge University Press, 1979). David Montgomery, *The Fall of the House of Labor: The Workplace, the State, and Labor Activism, 1865–1925* (New York: Cambridge University Press, 1987) synthesizes much of the new labor history.

8. This essay focuses on women and gender. For how labor history has ignored race as well, see Robin D. G. Kelley, " 'We Are Not What We Seem': Rethinking Black Working-Class Opposition in the Jim Crow South," *Journal of American History* 80 (June 1993): 75–112; David Roediger, "Race and the Working-Class Past in the United States: Multiple Identities and the Future of Labor History," in supplement to *International Review of Social History* 38 (1993): 127–43; idem, "What if Labor Were Not White and Male? Recentering Working-Class History and Reconstructing the Debates on Unions and Race," *International Labor and Working Class History* 51 (spring 1997): 72–95.

9. Barry Goldberg, "Slavery, Race, and the Language of Class: 'Wage Slaves' and 'White Niggers,' " *New Politics* 3 (summer 1991): 64–83; Lawrence Glickman, *A Living Wage: American Workers and the Making of Consumer Society* (Ithaca: Cornell University Press, 1997).

10. For a synthesis, see Elizabeth Faue, *Writing the Wrongs: Eva Valesh and the Rise of Labor Journalism* (Ithaca: Cornell University Press, 2002), 143–63.

11. The literature is voluminous here. See, for example, Stanley Aronowitz, *False Promises: The Shaping of American Working Class Consciousness* (New York: McGraw-Hill, 1973), and Mike Davis, *Prisoners of the American Dream: Politics and Economy in the History of the U.S. Working Class* (London: Verso, 1986). See also Thomas Goebel, "Becoming American: Ethnic Workers and the Rise of the CIO," *Labor History* 29 (spring 1988): 173–98; Gary Gerstle, *Working-Class Americanism: The Politics of Labor in a Textile City, 1914–1960* (Cambridge: Cambridge University Press, 1989); Lizabeth Cohen, *Making a New Deal: Industrial Workers in Chicago, 1919–1939* (New York: Cambridge University Press, 1990); Michael K. Honey, *Southern Workers and Civil Rights: Organizing Memphis Workers* (Urbana: University of Illinois Press, 1993); Michael Goldfield, "Race and the CIO: The Possibilities for Racial Egalitarianism during the 1930s and 1940s," *International Labor and Working Class History* 44 (1993): 1–32; Rick Halpern, *Down on the Killing Floor: Black and White Workers in Chicago's Packinghouses, 1904–1954* (Urbana: University of Illinois Press, 1997); Kevin Boyle, *The UAW and the Heyday of American Liberalism, 1945–1968* (Ithaca: Cornell University Press, 1995); Thomas Sugrue, *The Origins of the Urban Crisis: Race and Inequality in Postwar Detroit* (Princeton: Princeton University Press, 1996); Heather Thompson, *Whose Detroit? Politics, Labor, and Race in a Modern American City* (Ithaca: Cornell University Press, 2002); Robert Rodgers Korstad, *Civil Rights Unionism: Tobacco Workers and the Struggle for Democracy in the Mid-Twentieth-Century South* (Chapel Hill: University of North Carolina Press, 2003), among others.

12. Philip S. Foner, *Women and the American Labor Movement,* 2 vols., (New York: Free Press, 1979–1980); Barbara Wertheimer, *We Were There: The Story of Working Women in America* (New York: Pantheon, 1977); Alice Kessler-Harris, *Out to Work: A History of Wage-Earning Women in the United States* (New York: Oxford University Press, 1982); Elyce Rotella, *From Home to Office: U.S. Women at Work, 1870–1930* (Ann Arbor: University of Michigan Press, 1981); Lynn Weiner, *From Working Girl to Working Mother: The Female Labor Force in the United States, 1820–1980* (Chapel Hill: University of North Carolina Press, 1985); Claudia Goldin, *Understanding the Gender Gap: An Economic History of American Women* (New York: Oxford University Press, 1990).

13. Early discussions were James Kenneally, "Women in Trade Unions, 1870–1920," *Labor History* 14 (winter 1973): 45–55; Alice Kessler-Harris, "Where Are the Organized Women Workers?" *Feminist Studies* 3 (fall 1975): 92–110; Milton Cantor and Bruce Laurie, eds., *Class, Sex, and the Woman Worker* (Westport, Conn.: Greenwood, 1977); James Kenneally, *Women and American Trade Unions* (St. Albans, N.Y.: Eden Press Women's Publications, 1978); Nancy Gabin, "Women Workers and the U.A.W. in the Post-World War II Period," *Labor History* 21 (winter 1979–1980): 373–98; Ruth Milkman, "Organizing the Sexual Division of Labor: Historical Perspectives on Women's Work and the American Labor Movement," *Socialist Review* 49 (Jan.–Feb. 1980): 95–150; Ann Schofield, "Rebel Girl and Union Maids: The Woman Question in the Journals of the A.F.L. and I.W.W., 1905–1920," *Feminist Studies* 9 (summer 1983): 335–58; Sharon Hartman Strom, "Challenging 'Woman's Place': Feminism, the Left, and Industrial Unionism in the 1930s," *Feminist Studies* 9 (summer 1983): 359–86; Susan Levine, "Labor's True Woman: Domesticity and Equal Rights in the Knights of Labor," *Journal of American History* 70 (Sept. 1983): 323–39; Lisa Kannenberg, "The Impact of the Cold War on Women's Trade Union Activism: The UE Experience," *Labor History* 34 (spring-summer 1993): 309–23.

14. Daniel J. Walkowitz, *Worker City, Company Town: Iron and Cotton Workers' Protest in Co-*

hoes, New York, 1855–1885 (Urbana: University of Illinois Press, 1978); Thomas Dublin, *Women at Work: The Transformation of Work and Community in Lowell, Massachusetts, 1826–1860* (New York: Columbia University Press, 1979); Christine Stansell, *City of Women: Sex and Class in New York, 1789–1860* (New York: Knopf, 1986); Mary Blewett, *Men, Women, and Work: Class, Gender, and Protest in the New England Shoe Industry, 1780–1910* (Urbana: University of Illinois Press, 1988); Elizabeth Faue, *Community of Suffering and Struggle: Men, Women, and the Labor Movement in Minneapolis, 1915–1945* (Chapel Hill: University of North Carolina Press, 1991); Ardis Cameron, *Radicals of the Worst Sort: Laboring Women in Lawrence, Massachusetts, 1860–1912* (Urbana: University of Illinois Press, 1993); Mary Murphy, *Mining Cultures: Men, Women, and Leisure in Butte, 1914–1941* (Urbana: University of Illinois Press, 1997; Elizabeth Jameson, *All That Glitters: Class, Conflict, and Community in Cripple Creek* (Urbana: University of Illinois Press, 1998); Laurie Mercier, *Anaconda: Labor, Community, and Culture in a Montana Smelter City* (Urbana: University of Illinois Press, 2001).

15. Louise Tilly, "Paths of Proletarianization: Organization of Production, Sexual Division of Labor, and Women's Collective Action," *Signs* 7 (winter 1981): 400–417; Carole Turbin, "Reconceptualizing Family, Work, and Labor Organizing in Troy, 1860–1890," *Review of Radical Political Economics* 16 (spring 1984): 1–16; Harold Benenson, "The Community and Family Bases of U.S. Working Class Protest, 1880–1920: A Critique of the 'Skill Degradation' and 'Ecological' Perspectives," *Research in Social Movements, Conflict, and Change* 8 (1985): 109–32.

16. Some representative studies are Barbara Melosh, *The Physician's Hand: Work Culture and Conflict in American Nursing* (Philadelphia: Temple University Press, 1982); Margery W. Davies, *Woman's Place Is at the Typewriter: Office Work and Office Workers, 1870–1930* (Philadelphia: Temple University Press, 1982); Susan Porter Benson, *Counter Cultures: Saleswomen, Managers, and Customers in American Department Stores, 1890–1940* (Urbana: University of Illinois Press, 1986); Vicki Ruiz, *Cannery Women, Cannery Lives: Mexican Women, Unionization, and the California Food Processing Industry, 1930–1950* (Albuquerque: University of New Mexico Press, 1986); Patricia A. Cooper, *Once a Cigar Maker: Men, Women, and Work Culture in American Cigar Factories, 1900–1919* (Urbana: University of Illinois Press, 1987); Darlene Clark Hine, *Black Women in White: Racial Conflict and Cooperation in the Nursing Profession, 1890–1950* (Bloomington: Indiana University Press, 1989); Sharon H. Strom, *Beyond the Typewriter: Gender, Class, and the Origins of Modern American Office Work, 1900–1939* (Urbana: University of Illinois Press, 1992); Angel Kwolek-Folland, *Engendering Business: Men and Women in the Corporate Office, 1870–1930* (Baltimore: Johns Hopkins University Press, 1994); Dorothy Sue Cobble, *Dishing It Out: Waitresses and Their Unions in the Twentieth Century* (Urbana: University of Illinois Press, 1991). For race and gender in the workplace, see Venus Green, *Race on the Line: Gender, Labor, and Technology in the Bell System, 1880–1980* (Durham, N.C.: Duke University Press, 2001).

17. See Montgomery, *Workers' Control in America*; David Bensman, *The Practice of Solidarity: American Hat Finishers in the Nineteenth Century* (Urbana: University of Illinois Press, 1985).

18. For feminist approaches to masculinity and skill, see Anne Phillips and Barbara Taylor, "Sex and Skill: Notes toward a Feminist Economics," *Feminist Review* 6 (Oct. 1980): 79–88 Cooper, *Once a Cigar Maker*; Mary Blewett, "Manhood and the Market: The Politics of Gender and Class among the Textile Workers of Fall River, Massachusetts, 1870–1880," in *Work Engendered*, ed. Baron, 92–113; Nancy A. Hewitt, " 'The Voice of Virile Labor': Labor Militancy, Community Solidarity, and Gender Identity among Tampa's Latin Workers, 1880–1921," in ibid., 142–67; Andrew Edward Neather, "Popular Republicanism, Americanism, and the Roots of Anti-Communism, 1890–1925," PhD diss., Duke University, 1994; Ileen DeVault, " 'To Sit among Men': Skill, Gender, and Craft Unionism in the Early American Federation of Labor," in *Labor Histories: Class, Politics, and the Working-Class Experience*, ed. Eric Arnesen, Julie Greene, and Bruce Laurie (Urbana: University of Illinois Press, 1998), 259–283; Daniel Bender, " 'A Hero . . . for the Weak': Work, Consumption, and the Enfeebled Jewish Worker, 1881–1924," *International Labor and Working Class History* 56 (fall 1999): 1–22; essays by Stephen Meyer, Paul Taillon, Nancy Quam-Wickham, and Lisa Fine, among others, in *Boys and Their Toys? Masculinity, Technology, and Class in America*, ed. Roger Horowitz (New York: Routledge, 2001).

19. For early work, see Gerda Lerner, *Black Women in White America: A Documentary History* (New York, Random House, 1972); Claudia Goldin, "Female Labor Force Participation: The Origin of Black and White Differences, 1870–1880," *Journal of Economic History* 37 (Mar. 1977):

87–108; Jacquelyn Jones, *Labor of Love, Labor of Sorrow: Black Women, Work, and the Family from Slavery to the Present* (New York: Basic Books, 1985); Teresa Amott and Julie Matthaei, *Race, Gender, and Work: A Multicultural History of Women in the Unite States* (Boston: South End, 1991).

20. David M. Katzman, *Seven Days a Week: Women and Domestic Service in Industrial America* (New York: Oxford University Press, 1978); Phyllis M. Palmer, *Domesticity and Dirt: Housewives and Domestic Servants in the United States, 1920–1945* (Philadelphia: Temple University Press, 1989); Mary Romero, *Maid in the U.S.A.* (New York: Routledge, 1992).

21. Julia Kirk Blackwelder, *Women of the Depression: Caste and Culture in San Antonio, 1930–1940* (College Station: Texas A&M University Press, 1984); Karen T. Anderson, "Last Hired, First Fired: Black Women Workers in World War II," *Journal of American History* 69 (summer 1982): 82–97; Lois Helmbold, "Beyond the Family Economy: Black and White Working Class Women during the Great Depression," *Feminist Studies* 13 (fall 1987): 629–56; idem, "Downward Occupational Mobility during the Great Depression: Urban Black and White Working Women," *Labor History* 29 (spring 1988): 135–72.

22. David Roediger, *The Wages of Whiteness: Race and the Making of the American Working Class* (New York: Verso, 1991), inspired much of the discussion. See "Whiteness and the Historians' Imagination," special section, *International Labor and Working Class History* 60 (fall 2001): 1–92. Dana Frank, "White Working-Class Women and the Race Question," *International Labor and Working Class History* 54 (fall 1998): 80–102, applies the model to working-class women; most of her evidence, however, is anecdotal. On issues of racial difference, see Dolores E. Janiewski, *Sisterhood Denied: Race, Gender, and Class in a New South Community* (Philadelphia: Temple University Press, 1985); Tera Hunter, *To 'Joy My Freedom': Southern Black Women's Lives and Labors after the Civil War* (Cambridge: Harvard University Press, 1997); Georgina Hickey, *Hope and Danger in the New South City: Working-Class Women and Urban Development in Atlanta, 1890–1940* (Athens: University of Georgia Press, 2003).

23. Christopher L. Tomlins, *Law, Labor, and Ideology in the Early American Republic* (Cambridge: Cambridge University Press, 1993); William Forbath, *Law and the Shaping of the American Labor Movement* (Cambridge: Harvard University Press, 1991); Victoria C. Hattam, *Labor Visions and State Power: Origins of Business Unionism in the United States* (Princeton: Princeton University Press, 1993); Karen Orren, *Belated Feudalism: Labor, the Law, and Liberal Development in the United States* (Cambridge: Cambridge University Press, 1991).

24. Christopher L. Tomlins, *The State and the Unions: Labor Relations, Law, and the Organized Labor Movement in America, 1880–1960* (New York: Cambridge University Press, 1985); Staughton Lynd, ed., *'We Are All Leaders': The Alternative Unionism of the Early 1930s* (Urbana: University of Illinois Press, 1996); Nelson Lichtenstein, *The Most Dangerous Man in Detroit: Walter Reuther and the Fate of American Labor* (New York: Basic Books, 1995); Jennifer Klein, *For All These Rights: Business, Labor, and the Shaping of America's Public-Private Welfare State* (Princeton: Princeton University Press, 2003), among others.

25. Judith Baer, *The Chains of Protection* (Westport, Conn.: Greenwood, 1978). Theda Skocpol, *Protecting Soldiers and Mothers: The Political Origins of Social Policy in the United States* (Cambridge: Harvard University Press, 1992), synthesizes the protective legislation literature.

26. Colin J. Davis, *Power at Odds: The 1922 National Railroad Shopmen's Strike* (Urbana: University of Illinois Press, 1997); Julie Greene, *Pure and Simple Politics: The American Federation of Labor and Political Activism, 1881–1917* (Cambridge: Cambridge University Press, 1998); Joseph McCartin, *Labor's Great War* (Chapel Hill: University of North Carolina Press, 1998); Joshua B. Freeman, *Working-Class New York: Life and Labor since World War II* (New York: Metropolitan Books, 2000); Nelson Lichtenstein, *State of the Union: A Century of American Labor* (Princeton: Princeton University Press, 2002).

27. M. Patricia Fernandez Kelly, *For We Are Sold, I and My People: Women and Industry on Mexico's Frontier* (Albany: State University of New York Press, 1983); Jefferson Cowie, *Capital Moves: RCA's Seventy-Year Quest for Cheap Labor* (Ithaca: Cornell University Press, 1999).

28. Kelley, "We Are Not What We Seem"; Kessler-Harris, "Treating the Male as 'Other' "; Faue, "Reproducing the Class Struggle."

29. Elizabeth Ewen, *Immigrant Women in the Land of Dollars: Life and Culture on the Lower East Side, 1890–1925* (New York: Monthly Review, 1985); Kathy Peiss, *Cheap Amusements: Work-*

ing Women and Leisure in New York City, 1880 to 1920 (Philadelphia: Temple University Press, 1986); Joanne J. Meyerowitz, *Women Adrift: Independent Wage Earners in Chicago, 1880–1930* (Chicago: University of Chicago Press, 1988); Miriam Cohen, *Workshop to Office: Two Generations of Italian Women in New York City, 1900–1950* (Ithaca: Cornell University Press, 1993); Donna R. Gabaccia, *From the Other Side: Women, Gender, and Immigrant Life in the U.S., 1820–1990* (Bloomington: Indiana University Press, 1994). See also George Chauncey, *Gay New York: Gender, Urban Culture, and the Making of the Gay Male World, 1890–1940* (New York: Basic Books, 1994), on sexuality and class.

30. See Joan W. Scott, *Gender and the Politics of History* (New York: Columbia University Press, 1988). For important case studies, see Ann Schofield, "An 'Army of Amazons': The Language of Protest in a Kansas Mining Community, 1921–22," *American Quarterly* 37 (winter 1985): 686–701; Jacquelyn Dowd Hall, "Disorderly Women: Gender and Labor Militancy in the Appalachian South," *Journal of American History* 73 (Sept. 1986): 354–82; idem, "Private Eyes, Public Women: Images of Class and Sex in the Urban South, Atlanta, Georgia, 1913–1915," in *Work Engendered*, ed. Baron, 216–42; Elizabeth Faue, " 'The Dynamo of Change': Gender and Solidarity in the American Labour Movement of the 1930s," *Gender and History* 1 (summer 1989): 138–58; Nan Enstad, *Ladies of Labor, Girls of Adventure: Working Women, Popular Culture, and Labor Politics at the Turn of the Twentieth Century* (New York: Columbia University Press, 1999).

31. For the earlier period, see Robin Miller Jacoby, "The Women's Trade Union League and American Feminism," *Feminist Studies* 3 (1975): 126–40; Nancy Schrom Dye, *As Equals and As Sisters: Feminism, the Labor Movement, and the Women's Trade Union League* (Columbia: University of Missouri Press, 1980); Mari Jo Buhle, *Women and American Socialism, 1870–1920* (Urbana: University of Illinois Press, 1981); Annelise Orleck, *Common Sense and a Little Fire: Women and Working-Class Politics in the United States, 1900–1965* (Chapel Hill: University of North Carolina Press, 1995); Jennifer Guglielmo, "Italian Women's Proletarian Feminism in New York City Garment Trades, 1890s–1940s," in *Women, Gender and Transnational Lives*, in Donna R. Gabaccia and Franca Iacovetta, ed., 247–98. Nancy Gabin, *Feminism in the Labor Movement: Women and the United Auto Workers, 1935–1975* (Ithaca: Cornell University Press, 1990), did pioneering work on the postwar period; see also Dennis A. Deslippe, "Organized Labor, National Politics, and Second Wave Feminism in the U.S., 1965–1975," *International Labor and Working Class History* 49 (1996): 143–65; idem, *'Rights, Not Roses': Unions and the Rise of Working-Class Feminism, 1945–1960* (Urbana: University of Illinois Press, 2000); Dorothy Sue Cobble, "Recapturing Working-Class Feminism: Union Women in the Postwar Era," in *Not June Cleaver: Women and Gender in Postwar America*, ed. Joanne Meyerowitz (Philadelphia: Temple University Press, 1994); idem, " 'A Spontaneous Loss of Enthusiasm': Workplace Feminism and the Transformation of Women's Service Jobs in the 1970s," *International Labor and Working Class History* 56 (fall 1999): 23–44; Nancy Maclean, "The Hidden History of Affirmative Action: Working Women's Struggles in the 1970s and the Gender of Class," *Feminist Studies* 25 (1999): 43–78.

32. Recent labor and working-class biographies include Paula F. Pfeffer, *A. Philip Randolph, Pioneer of the Civil Rights Movement* (Baton Rouge: Louisiana State University Press, 1990); Steve Fraser, *Labor Will Rule: Sidney Hillman and the Rise of American Labor* (New York: Free Press, 1991); Diane Kirkby, *Alice Henry: The Power of Pen and Voice; The Life of an Australian American Labor Reformer* (Cambridge: Cambridge University Press, 1991); Richard Griswold del Castillo and Richard A. Garcia, *Cesar Chavez: A Triumph of Spirit* (Norman: University of Oklahoma Press, 1995); James R. Barrett, *William Z. Foster and the Tragedy of American Communism* (Urbana: University of Illinois Press, 1999); Robert Bussel, *From Harvard to the Ranks of Labor: Powers Hapgood and the American Working Class* (University Park: Pennsylvania State University Press, 1999); Craig Phelan, *Grand Master Workman: Terence Powderly and the Knights of Labor* (Westport, Conn.: Greenwood, 2000); Yvette Richards, *Maida Springer, Pan-Africanist and International Labor Leader* (Pittsburgh: University of Pittsburgh Press, 2000); Elliott Gorn, *Mother Jones, the Most Dangerous Woman in America* (New York: Hill and Wang, 2001); Thaddeus Russell, *Out of the Jungle: Jimmy Hoffa and the Remaking of the American Working Class* (New York: Knopf, 2001).

33. See Mary Jo Maynes, *Taking the Hard Road: Life Course in French and German Workers' Autobiographies in the Era of Industrialization* (Chapel Hill: University of North Carolina, 1995); "Narratives and Social Identities," *Social Science History* 16 (fall–winter 1992), special issue intro-

duced by William H. Sewell; "Identity Formation and Class," special issue, *International Labor and Working Class History* 49 (spring 1996); Elizabeth Faue, "Retooling the Class Factory: The Future of Labor History after Montgomery, Marx, and Postmodernism," *Labour History* 82 (May 2002): 109–19.

34. Fran Leeper Buss, ed., *Forged under the Sun: The Life of Maria Elena Lucas* (Ann Arbor: University of Michigan Press, 1993); Robert Bruno, *Steelworker Alley: How Class Works in Youngstown* (Ithaca: Cornell University Press, 1999); Cheri Register, *Packinghouse Daughter, a Memoir* (St. Paul: Minnesota Historical Society, 2000); Jack Metzgar, *Striking Steel: Solidarity Remembered* (Philadelphia: Temple University Press, 2000); Faue, *Writing the Wrongs*.

35. Kathleen A. Brown and Elizabeth Faue, "Social Bonds, Sexual Politics, and Political Community on the U.S. Left, 1920s–1940s," *Left History* 7 (spring 2001): 7–42; idem, "Revolutionary Desire: Redefining the Politics of Sexuality among American Radicals, 1919–1945," in *Sexual Borderlands: Constructing an American Sexual Past,* ed. Kathleen Kennedy and Sharon Ullman (Columbus: Ohio State University Press, 2003), 273–302.

Chapter 2. "More Than Two Things"

1. Alexander Saxton, *The Rise and Fall of the White Republic: Class Politics and Mass Culture in Nineteenth-Century America* (London: Verso, 1990); Matthew Jacobson, *Whiteness of a Different Color: European Immigrants and the Alchemy of Race* (Cambridge: Harvard University Press, 1998); Cheryl Harris, "Whiteness as Property," *Harvard Law Review* 106 (June 1993), 1710–91, and "Finding Sojourner's Truth," *Cordozo Law Review* (November 1998), 309–410; Allan Bérubé, "How Gay Stays White" (paper delivered at "The Making and Unmaking of Whiteness" conference, Berkeley, Apr. 1997); Thandeka, *Learning to Be White: Money, Race, and God in America* (New York: Continuum, 1999); Maurice Berger, *White Lies: Race and the Myths of Whiteness* (New York: Farrar, Straus and Giroux, 1999); Theodore Allen, *The Invention of the White Race,* 2 vols. (New York: Verso, 1994 and 1997); Bruce Nelson, *Divided We Stand: American Workers and the Struggle for Black Equality* (Princeton: Princeton University Press, 2001); Linda Gordon, *The Great Arizona Orphan Abduction* (Cambridge: Harvard University Press, 1999); Toni Morrison, *Playing in the Dark: Whiteness and the Literary Imagination* (Cambridge: Harvard University Press, 1990); Neil Foley, *The White Scourge: Mexicans, Blacks, and Poor Whites in Texas Cotton Culture* (Berkeley: University of California Press, 1997); Karen Brodkin, *How Jews Became White Folks* (New Brunswick, N.J.: Rutgers University Press, 1998); Noel Ignatiev, *How the Irish Became White* (New York: Routledge, 1995). Among several fine collections on the subject, the best is Richard Delgado and Jean Stefancic, eds., *Critical White Studies: Looking beyond the Mirror* (Philadelphia: Temple University Press, 1997). Thanks to Sterling Stuckey, for exposing me to Sterling Brown's genius, and to Aprel Thomas and Karen Rodriguez for their help with this manuscript.

2. For discussions of these figures and of the naming and trajectory of critical studies of whiteness, see David R. Roediger, *Colored White: Transcending the Racial Past* (Berkeley: University of California Press, 2002), 18–26; Roediger, ed., *Black on White: Black Writers on What It Means to Be White* (New York: Schocken, 1998), 1–26; and Roediger, "Defending Critical Studies of Whiteness, But Not Whiteness Studies," *Souls* 4 (fall 2002): 57–59.

3. Rose Brewer, "Theorizing Race, Class, and Gender," in *Theorizing Black Feminisms: The Visionary Pragmatism of Black Women,* ed. Abena Busia and Stanlie James (London: Routledge, 1993), 16.

4. Tera Hunter, *To 'Joy My Freedom: Southern Black Women's Lives and Labors after the Civil War* (Cambridge: Harvard University Press, 1997).

5. Steven Watts, "The Idiocy of American Studies: Poststructuralism, Language, and Politics in the Age of Self-Fulfillment," *American Quarterly* 43 (Dec. 1991): 653.

6. Julie Willett, *Permanent Waves: The Making of the American Beauty Shop* (New York: New York University Press, 2000); Gordon, *Orphan Abduction*; Elsa Barkley-Brown, "Negotiating and Transforming the Public Sphere: African American Political Life in the Transition from Slavery to Freedom," *Public Culture* 7 (fall 1994): 107–46; *Rootedness,* Patterson's study of Hurston and social history, is forthcoming from Temple University Press; Evelyn Nakano Glenn, *Unequal Freedom: How Race and Gender Shaped American Citizenship and Labor* (Cambridge: Harvard University Press, 2002); Venus Green, *Race on the Line: Gender, Labor, and Technology in the Bell*

System, 1880–1980 (Durham, N.C.: Duke University Press, 2001); Robert Lee, *Orientals: Asian Americans in Popular Culture* (Philadelphia: Temple University Press, 1999); Vicki Ruiz, *Cannery Women, Cannery Lives: Mexican Women, Unionization, and the California Food Processing Industry, 1930–1950* (Albuquerque: University of New Mexico Press, 1987); George Lipsitz, *Rainbow at Midnight: Labor and Culture in the 1940s* (Urbana: University of Illinois Press, 1994).

7. Edward Said in a 1999 lecture at Macalaster College and Archie Green in a 1995 conversation with the author. For Marx, see his 1844 *The Economic and Philosophical Manuscripts* in *Karl Marx: Early Writings*, ed. T. B. Bottomore (New York: McGraw-Hill, 1963) and Karl Marx, *Grundrisse: Foundations of the Critique of Political Economy*, trans. Martin Nicolaus (New York: Vintage, 1973), 325. On the comparison with the young Karl Marx, I am indebted to conversations with Robin Kelley. For Cooper, see his "Back to Work: Categories, Boundaries, and Connections in the Study of Labour," in *Racializing Class, Classifying Race: Labour and Difference in Britain, the USA, and Africa*, ed. Peter Alexander and Rick Halpern (New York: St. Martin's, 2000), 216–17.

8. John R. Commons and others, *History of Labour in the United States*, 4 vols. (New York: 1918–35), 2:252–53 and passim; Bari J. Watkins, "The Professors and the Unions: American Academic Social Theory and Labor Reform, 1883–1915" (PhD diss., Yale University, 1976).

9. See, for example, Caroline Ware, *Greenwich Village, 1920–1930* (Boston: Houghton Mifflin, 1935); W. E. B. Du Bois, *Black Reconstruction in America, 1860–1880* (New York: Atheneum, 1992 [1935]); Philip S. Foner, *American Labor Songs of the Nineteenth Century* (Urbana: University of Illinois Press, 1974).

10. For Gutman's sweeping concerns, see Ira Berlin's fine editor's introduction to the posthumous collection of Gutman essays, *Power and Culture: Essays on the American Working Class* (New York: Pantheon, 1997); cf. Nan Enstad, *Ladies of Labor, Girls of Adventure: Working Women, Popular Culture, and Labor Politics at the Turn of the Twentieth Century* (New York: Columbia University Press, 1999); Peter Linebaugh and Marcus Rediker, *The Many-Headed Hydra: Sailors, Slaves, Commoners, and the Hidden History of the Revolutionary Atlantic* (Boston: Beacon, 2000); Robin Kelley, *Hammer and Hoe: Alabama Communists during the Great Depression* (Chapel Hill: University of North Carolina Press, 1990); Rachleff and Cleary's work focuses on Buffalo and is forthcoming.

11. To greatly shorten a very long list: Joe William Trotter, *Coal, Class, and Color: Blacks in Southern West Virginia, 1915–1932* (Urbana: University of Illinois Press, 1990); Chris Friday, *Organizing Asian-American Workers: The Pacific Coast Salmon Industry, 1870–1942* (Philadelphia: Temple University Press, 1994); Susan Porter Benson, *Counter Cultures: Saleswomen, Managers, and Customers in American Department Stores, 1890–1910* (Urbana: University of Illinois Press, 1986); Mary Blewett, *Men, Women, and Work: Class, Gender and Protest in the New England Shoe Industry, 1780–1860* (Urbana: University of Illinois Press, 1988); David M. Emmons, *The Butte Irish: Class and Ethnicity in an American Mining Town, 1875–1925* (Urbana: University of Illinois Press, 1989); Gunther Peck, *Reinventing Free Labor: Padrones and Immigrant Workers in the North American West* (Cambridge: Cambridge University Press, 2000); George Chauncey, *Gay New York: Gender, Urban Culture, and the Making of an Urban Gay Male World, 1890–1940* (New York: Basic, 1994); Madeline Davis and Elizabeth Lapovsky Kennedy, *Boots of Leather, Slippers of Gold: The History of a Lesbian Community* (New York: Routledge, 1993); William Sutton, *Journeymen for Jesus: Evangelical Artisans Confront Capitalism in Jacksonian Baltimore* (University Park: Pennsylvania State University Press, 1998); Ken Fones-Wolf, *Trade Union Gospel: Christianity and Labor in Industrial Philadelphia, 1865–1915* (Philadelphia: Temple University Press, 1989).

12. Howard Kimeldorf, "Bringing Unions Back In (Or Why We Need a New, Old Labor History)," *Labor History* 32 *(winter 1991)*, 99, and passim, provides the quoted phrase in a measured discussion; cf. Eric Arnesen, "Whiteness and the Historian's Imagination," *International Labor and Working Class History* 60 (fall 2001): 3–32; see also Daniel Letwin, "Response to Symposium on *The Challenge of Interracial Unionism*," *Labor History* 41 (February 2000), 89, for a sophisticated union-centeredness that nonetheless suggests that union sources, almost alone, can enable us to know the "workers' sense of who they are"; Richard Schneirov, "Labor and the New Liberalism in the Wake of the Pullman Strike," in *The Pullman Strike and the Crisis of the 1890s*, ed. Schneirov, Shelton Stromquist, and Nick Salvatore (Urbana: University of Illinois Press, 1999), 204–5; Roediger, *Colored White*, 192–94.

13. Naomi Wallace's scintillating *In the Heart of America and Other Plays* (New York: Theatre Communications Group, 2001), includes *Slaughter City* at 197–274, with the bibliography at 275–76; Mark Nowak, "$00, Line/Steel/Train," *xcp* (November 9, 2001), 66–84. See also Kate Manning, *Whitegirl* (New York: Dial Press, 2002), 403.

14. Ruiz, *Cannery Women,* 10, 51, 199–20, and 125–28; Kelley, *Hammer and Hoe,* 105–7 and 149–51; Elsa Barkley-Brown, "African American Women's Quilting: A Framework for Conceptualizing and Teaching African American Women's History," in *Black Women in America: Social Science Perspectives,* ed. Micheline Malson (Chicago: University of Chicago Press, 1990), 9–18, and idem, "Polyrhythms and Improvisation: Lessons for Women's History," *History Workshop Journal* 31 (spring 1991): 85–90; Lee, *Orientals*; Lipsitz, *Rainbow at Midnight,* 19– Enstad, *Ladies of Labor,* 18–20 and 48–83; Gordon, *Orphan Abduction,* 45, 50, and 118; Hunter, *To 'Joy My Freedom,* 4–5 and 245; Linebaugh and Rediker, *Many-Headed Hydra,* 16–31; Saxton, *White Republic, The Great Midland* (Urbana: University of Illinois Press, 1997 [1948]), and *Bright Web in the Darkness* (New York: St. Martin's, 1958).

15. On Brown, see the preface by Michael S. Harper and the introductions by Sterling Stuckey and James Weldon Johnson to Harper, ed., *The Collected Poems of Sterling A. Brown* (Chicago: Triquarterly Books, 1989), xiii–17; see also John Edgar Tidwell's account of his life in *The Oxford Companion to African American Literature* (New York: Oxford University Press, 1997); Joanne Gabbin, *Sterling A. Brown: Building the Black Aesthetic Tradition* (Westport, Conn.: Greenwood, 1985); Robert Stepto, "'When de Saints Go Ma'chin' Home': Sterling Brown's Blueprint for a New Negro Poetry," *Kunapipi* 4 (1982): 94–105; Mark A. Sanders, *Afro-Modernist Aesthetics and the Poetry of Sterling Brown* (Athens: University of Georgia Press, 1999). James Smethurst, *The New Red Negro: The Literary Left and African American Poetry, 1930–1946* (New York: Oxford University Press, 1999), 60–62, sees a Communist attraction to Brown even under and after the Popular Front but also shows that his approaches were at odds with the reigning political emphases of the party. Sterling A. Brown, *A Son's Return: Selected Essays of Sterling A. Brown* (Boston: Northeastern University Press, 1996); for the historical poems mentioned, see Harper, ed., *Collected Poems,* 197–210.

16. Harper, ed., *Collected Poems,* 156; for race-based hate strikes and terror in railroading, see Eric Arnesen, *Brotherhoods of Color: Black Railroad Workers and the Struggle for Black Equality* (Cambridge: Harvard University Press, 2001), 34–39, 66–71, and 118–22, especially 1 Herbert Hill, *Black Labor and the American Legal System* (Madison: University of Wisconsin Press, 1985), 342–46.

17. Harper, ed., *Collected Poems,* 35.

18. Harper, ed., *Collected Poems,* 182 and 187; Matthew Lessig, "On 'Sharecroppers,'" on the Modern American Poetry Web site at http://www.english.uiuc.edu/maps/poets/a_f/brown/onshare.htm.

19. Harper, ed., *Collected Poems,* 214–15 and 218–22.

20. Sanders, *Afro-Modernist Aesthetics,* 111 and 143–48.

21. Arnesen, *Brotherhoods of Color,* 322–32; equally reductive is Judith Stein, *Running Steel, Running America: Race, Economic Policy, and the Decline of Liberalism* (Chapel Hill: University of North Carolina Press, 1998), 99–100 and 346, n. 36; for alternatives, see Herbert Hill, "Race and the Steelworkers Union: White Privilege and Black Struggle," *New Politics* 8 (winter 2002), 172–205; Ruth Needleman, *Black Freedom Fighters in Steel: The Struggle for Democratic Unionism* (Ithaca: Cornell University Press, 2003) and Paul Taillon, *Brothers and Breadwinners in the U.S. Railroad Industry, 1877–1924,* forthcoming.

22. Cf. Sanders, *Afro-Modernist Aesthetics,* 148–49, with Du Bois, *Black Reconstruction,* 727.

23. Sanders, *Afro-Modernist Aesthetics,* 148, and Raymond Williams, *Modern Tragedy* (Stanford: Stanford University Press, 1966); see also Stuckey's important remarks on Brown and tragedy in Harper, ed., *Collected Poems,* 12. Stuckey (p. 6) is also the source of the "desire to shout" wisdom.

24. Harper, ed., *Collected Poems,* 219.

25. Lessig, "'On Sharecroppers.'"

26. Sanders, *Afro-Modernist Aesthetics,* 111.

Chapter 3. "All I Wanted Was a Steady Job"

1. Willie Ruff, *A Call to Assembly: An American Success Story* (New York: Penguin Books, 1991), 104–5.

2. Washington, D.C. Research Division, *State and County Veteran Population, Mar. 31, 1983* (Washington, D.C., 1983); "Powell Testifies that Blacks Join Military for Those Opportunities That Are Denied Elsewhere," *Jet* (Mar. 1991), 34; James E. Ellis, "Where Troop Cuts Will be Cruelest: For Blacks, the Services Have Been the Best Employer Around," *Business Week* (June 8, 1992), 72–73; "Looking for a Few Good (Black) Men," *The Nation* (Oct. 16, 1995), 428.

3. Christian G. Appy, *Working-Class War: American Combat Soldiers and Vietnam* (Chapel Hill: University of North Carolina Press, 1993); James E. Westheider, *Fighting on Two Fronts: African Americans and the Vietnam War* (New York: New York University Press, 1997); Gerald Astor, *The Right to Fight: A History of African Americans in the Military* (Novato, Calif.: Presidio Press, 1998).

4. "Private First Class Reginald 'Malik' Edwards," in *Bloods: An Oral History of the Vietnam War by Black Veterans*, ed. Wallace Terry (New York: Ballantine, 1984), 4.

5. Ruff, *A Call to Assembly;* Curtis James Morrow, *What's a Commie Ever Done to Black People* (Jefferson, N.C.: McFarland, 1997); Debra J. Dickerson, *An American Story* (New York: Anchor, 2000); Timothy Tyson, *Radio Free Dixie: Robert F. Williams and the Roots of Black Power* (Chapel Hill: University of North Carolina Press, 2000); Harry Shapiro and Caesar Glebbeck, *Jimi Hendrix: Electric Gypsy* (New York: St. Martin's, 1995), 408, 423–27; Rubin "Hurricane" Carter, *The 16th Round: From Number 1 Contender to Number 45472* (New York: Penguin, 1974), 106. Vietnam War narratives include David Parks, *GI Diary* (Washington, D.C.: Howard University Press, 1984 [1968]); Samuel L. Vance, *The Courageous and the Proud* (New York: W. W. Norton, 1970); Terry Whitmore, *Memphis Nam Sweden: The Story of a Black Deserter* (Jackson: University Press of Mississippi, 1997 [1971]); Fenton Williams, *Just before Dawn: A Doctor's Experiences in Vietnam* (1971); James A. Daly, *A Hero's Welcome: The Conscience of Sergeant James Daly versus the United States Army* (Indianapolis: Bobbs-Merrill, 1975); and Norman A. McDaniel, *Yet Another Voice* (New York: Hawthorn Books, 1975). Collections of oral narratives include Terry, ed., *Bloods*, and Stanley Goff and Robert Sanders, *Brothers: Black Soldiers in the Nam* (New York: Berkley Books, 1985). Recent autobiographies include Antwone Quenton Fisher, *Finding Fish: A Memoir* (New York: Perennial, 2001), and Colin L. Powell, *My American Journey* (New York: Random House, 1995).

6. Notable exceptions include David E. Bernstein, *Only One Place of Redress: African Americans, Labor Regulations, and the Courts from Reconstruction to the New Deal* (Durham, N.C.: Duke University Press), 200; Daniel Kryder, *Divided Arsenal: Race and the American State during World War II* (Cambridge: Cambridge University Press, 2000); Alex Lichtenstein, *Twice the Work of Free Labor: The Political Economy of Convict Labor in the New South* (New York: Verso, 1996); Desmond S. King, *Separate and Unequal: Black Americans and the US Federal Government* (Oxford: Clarendon, 1995); Norma M. Riccucci, *Women, Minorities, and Unions in the Public Sector* (Westport, Conn.: Greenwood, 1990); Darlene Clark Hine, *Black Women in White: Racial Conflict and Cooperation in the Nursing Profession, 1890–1950* (Bloomington: Indiana University Press, 1987), esp. 153–59; Joe William Trotter Jr., *Black Milwaukee: The Making of an Industrial Proletariat, 1915–45* (Urbana: University of Illinois Press, 1985), 147–95; August Meier and Elliot Rudwick, "The Rise of Segregation in the Federal Bureaucracy, 1900–1930," *Phylon* 28 (1967): 178–84.

7. In *Servants of the State: Managing Diversity and Democracy* (Athens: University of Georgia Press, 2002), Margaret C. Rung considers the activist hiring policies of New Deal and World War II federal agencies from the perspective of managers, but it is nonetheless illuminating for the discussion of the United Federal Workers of America. Excluding military and postal workers (where percentages of black employees range from 20 to 25%), since 1969 African Americans have held 15–16% of federal jobs, with the majority in clerical, craft, and service positions. See King, 228–42. In contrast to gains made in civilian employment on military bases, African Americans have made relatively limited gains in the civilian agencies dealing with military technology. See Bristow Hardin, "Race and Poverty in the Militarized Welfare State," *Poverty and Race Research Action Council* (Jan.–Feb. 1999), http://www.prrac.org/topics/jan99/hardin.htm.

8. Debra Dickerson, "The Martial Melting Pot: How the Military Encourages and Promotes Blacks without Lowering Its Standards," *U.S. News & World Report* (Dec. 23, 1996), 32.

9. Eric Arnesen, *Brotherhoods Of Color: Black Railroad Workers and the Struggle For Equality* (Cambridge: Harvard University Press, 2001); Melinda Chateauvert, *Marching Together: Women of the Brotherhood of Sleeping Car Porters* (Urbana: University of Illinois Press, 1998); David D. Perata, *Those Pullman Blues: An Oral History of the African American Railroad Attendant* (New York: Twayne, 1996).

10. Brian Kelly, *Race, Class, and Power in the Alabama Coalfields* (Urbana: University of Illinois Press, 2001); Daniel Letwin, *The Challenge of Interracial Unionism: Alabama Coal Miners, 1878–1921* (Chapel Hill: University of North Carolina Press, 1998); Karin A. Shapiro, *A New South Rebellion: The Battle against Convict Labor in the Tennessee Coalfields, 1871–1896* (Chapel Hill: University of North Carolina Press, 1998); Joe William Trotter Jr., *Coal, Class, and Color: Blacks in Southern West Virginia, 1915–32* (Urbana: University of Illinois Press, 1995).

11. Ruth Needleman, *Black Freedom Fighters in Steel: The Struggle for Democratic Unionism* (Ithaca: Cornell University Press, 2003); John Hinshaw, *Steel and Steelworkers: Race and Class Struggle in Twentieth-Century Pittsburgh* (Albany: State University of New York Press, 2002); Bruce Nelson, *Divided We Stand: American Workers and the Struggle for Black Equality* (Princeton, N.J.: Princeton University Press, 2001); Judith Stein, *Running Steel, Running America: Race, Economic Policy, and the Decline of Liberalism* (Chapel Hill: University of North Carolina Press, 1998); Henry McKiven Jr., *Iron and Steel: Class, Race, and Community in Birmingham, Alabama, 1875–1920* (Chapel Hill: University of North Carolina Press, 1995).

12. Heather Ann Thompson, *Whose Detroit? Politics, Labor, and Race in a Modern American City* (Ithaca: Cornell University Press, 2001); Rick Halpern and Roger Horowitz, *Meatpackers: An Oral History of Black Packinghouse Workers and Their Struggle for Racial and Economic Equality* (New York: Twayne, 1996); Rick Halpern, *Down on the Killing Floor: Black and White Workers in Chicago's Packinghouses, 1904–1954* (Urbana: University of Illinois Press, 1997); Roger Horowitz, *"Negro and White, Unite and Fight": A Social History of Industrial Unionism in Meatpacking, 1930–1990* (Urbana: University of Illinois Press, 1997); Shelton Stromquist and Marvin Bergman, eds., *Unionizing the Jungles: Labor and Community in the Twentieth-Century Meatpacking Industry* (Iowa City: University of Iowa Press, 1997); Timothy Minchin, *Hiring the Black Worker: The Racial Integration of the Southern Textile Industry, 1960–1980* (Chapel Hill: University of North Carolina Press, 1999).

13. Most of these new studies include a discussion of the civil rights movement. Of note, however, are the following: Arnesen, *Brotherhoods of Color;* Nelson, *Divided We Stand;* Suzanne E. Smith, *Dancing in the Streets: Motown and the Cultural Politics of Detroit* (Cambridge: Harvard University Press, 2000); Timothy Minchin, *The Color of Work: The Struggle for Civil Rights in the Southern Paper Industry, 1945–1980* (Chapel Hill: University of North Carolina Press, 2001); Michael K. Honey, *Southern Labor and Black Civil Rights* (Urbana: University of Illinois Press, 1993).

14. Minchin, *Color of Work;* Ernest Obadele-Sparks, *Black Unionism in the Industrial South* (College Station: Texas A&M University Press, 2000).

15. Tera Hunter, *To 'Joy My Freedom: Southern Black Women's Lives and Labors after the Civil War* (Cambridge: Harvard University Press, 1997); Elizabeth Clark-Lewis, *Living In, Living Out: African-American Domestics and the Great Migration* (Washington, D.C.: Smithsonian Institution Press, 1994); Donald Holley, *The Second Great Emancipation;* Sharon Ann Holt, *Making Freedom Pay: North Carolina Freedpeople Working for Themselves, 1865–1900* (Athens: University of Georgia Press, 2000); Geta LeSeur, *Not All Okies Are White: The Lives of Black Cotton Pickers in Arizona* (Columbia: University of Missouri Press, 2000); Stewart E. Tolnay, *The Bottom Rung: African American Family Life on Southern Farms* (Urbana: University of Illinois Press, 1999); Cindy Hahamovitch, *The Fruits of Their Labor: Atlantic Coast Farmworkers and the Making of Migrant Poverty, 1870–1945* (Chapel Hill: University of North Carolina Press, 1997); Venus Greene, *Race on the Line: Gender, Labor, and Technology in the Bell System* (Durham, N.C.: Duke University Press, 2001).

16. The literature is rich. See Victoria W. Wolcott, *Remaking Respectability: African American Women in Interwar Detroit* (Chapel Hill: University of North Carolina Press, 2001); Shirley Ann Wilson Moore, *To Place Our Deeds: The African American Community in Richmond, California,*

1910–1963 (Berkeley: University of California Press, 2000); Smith, *Dancing in the Streets;* Kimberley L. Phillips, *Alabama North: African-American Migrants, Community, and Working-Class Activism in Cleveland, 1915–1945* (Urbana: University of Illinois Press, 1999); Gretchen Lemke-Santangelo, *Abiding Courage: African-American Migrant Women and the East Bay Community* (Chapel Hill: University of North Carolina Press, 1996); Quintard Taylor, *The Forging of a Black Community: Seattle's Central District from 1870 through the Civil Rights Era* (Seattle: University of Washington Press, 1994); Richard W. Thomas, *Life for Us Is What We Make It: Building Black Community in Detroit, 1915–1945* (Bloomington: Indiana University Press, 1992); Earl Lewis, *In Their Own Interests: Race, Class, and Power in Twentieth-Century Norfolk, Virginia* (Berkeley: University of California Press, 1991); Joe William Trotter Jr., ed., *The Great Migration in Critical Perspective: New Dimensions of Race, Class, and Gender* (Bloomington: Indiana University Press, 1991).

17. Sharon Kurtz, *Workplace Justice: Organizing Multi-Identity Movements* (Minneapolis: University of Minnesota Press, 2002).

18. Daniel M. Johnson and Rex R. Campbell, *Black Migration in America: A Social Demographic History* (Durham, N.C.: Duke University Press, 1981), 142; 101–69.

19. Robert C. Weaver, *The Negro Ghetto* (New York: Harcourt Brace, 1948); August Meier and Elliot M. Rudwick, *From Plantation to Ghetto* (New York: Hill and Wang, 1966); Kenneth Goings and Raymond A. Mohl, *The New African American Urban History* (Thousand Oaks, Calif.: Sage, 1996); Neil R. McMillen, ed., *Remaking Dixie: The Impact of World War II on the American South* (Jackson: University Press of Mississippi, 1997); Holley, *The Second Great Emancipation: The Mechanical Cotton Picker, Black Migration, and How They Shaped the Modern South* (Fayetteville: University of Arkansas Press, 2000); Josh Sides, *L.A. City Limits: African Americans from the Great Depression to the Present* (Berkeley: University of California Press, 2003); Moore, *To Place Our Deeds;* Lawrence B. De Graff, Kevin Mulroy, and Quintard Taylor, eds., *Seeking El Dorado: African Americans in California* (Seattle: University of Seattle Press, 2001); Quintard Taylor, "Blacks and Asians in a White City: Japanese Americans and African Americans in Seattle, 1890–1940," in *Racial Encounters in the Multi-Cultural West,* ed. Gordon Morris Bakken and Brenda Farrington (New York: Garland, 2000), 187–215; and idem, *Forging of a Black Community.* A controversial account from a journalist is Nicholas Lemann, *The Promised Land: The Great Black Migration and How It Changed America* (New York: Knopf, 1991).

20. Johnson and Campbell, *Black Migration in America,* 101–69.

21. Moore, *To Place Our Deeds;* Taylor, *Forging of a Black Community;* Dickerson, *An American Story;* Annelise Orleck, "I Decided I'd Marry the First Man Who Asked: Gendering Black Migration from Cotton Country to the Desert Southwest," paper presented at the conference on "Repositioning North American Migration History: New Directions in Modern Continental Migration and Citizenship," Princeton University, Mar. 15, 2003, in author's possession.

22. Clifton L. Taulbert, *Watching Our Crops Come In* (New York: Penguin, 1997).

23. Ibid., 142.

24. Abram J. Jaffe and Seymour L. Wolfbein, "Postwar Migration Plans of Army Enlisted Men," *Annals of the American Academy of Political and Social Science* 238 (Mar. 1941): 8–10.

25. Ibid.; Ruff, *Call to Assembly,* 189.

26. Moore, *To Place Our Deeds;* DeGraff, Mulroy, and Taylor, eds., *Seeking El Dorado.*

27. Walter R. Allen and Reynolds Farley, "The Shifting Social and Economic Tides of Black Americans, 1950–1980," *Annual Review of Sociology* 12 (1986): 2 William Julius Wilson, *The Declining Significance of Race: Blacks and Changing American Institutions* (Chicago: University of Chicago Press, 1978); Douglas Glasgow, *The Black Underclass: Poverty, Unemployment, and Entrapment of Ghetto Youth* (San Francisco: Jossey-Bass, 1980); Manning Marable, *How Capitalism Underdeveloped Black America: Problems in Race, Political Economy, and Society* (Boston: South End Press, 1983); Thomas J. Sugrue, *Origins of the Urban Crisis: Race and Inequality in Postwar Detroit* (Princeton, N.J.: Princeton University Press, 1996).

28. Arnesen, *Brotherhoods of Color,* 231.

29. Leo Bogart, ed., *Social Research and the Desegregation of the U.S. Army* (Chicago: Markham, 1969); Bernard C. Nalty, *Strength for the Fight: A History of Black Americans in the Military* (New York: Free Press, 1986); Ruff, *Call to Assembly,* 111–85; Richard M. Dalfiume, *Desegregation of the U.S. Armed Forces* (Columbus: University of Missouri Press, 1969).

30. Paula Pfeffer, *A. Philip Randolph: Pioneer of the Civil Rights Movement,* 136, 133–68. The NAACP papers are rich with accounts of resistance by African American soldiers. For late war and postwar riots and resistance on military bases, see Jean Byers, "A Study of the Negro in Military Service," (unpublished study, 1946).

31. This phrase received repeated attention by soldiers and organizations.

32. Thurgood Marshall, "Summary Justice: The Negro GI in Korea," *Crisis* 58 (May 1951): 297–304; Richard J. Stillman II, *Integration of the Negro in the U.S. Armed Forces* (New York: Praeger, 1968), 41–56; Bogart, *Social Research and Desegregation,* 43–185; Alan L. Gropman, *The Air Force Integrates, 1945–1964,* 2nd ed. (Washington, D.C.: Smithsonian Institution Press, 1998).

33. See, for example, D. Hepburn, "U.S. Armed Forces in 1950: Record of Integration," *Our World* 5 (June 1950), 10–35; J. H. Thomson, "It's a No Race Army Now," *Negro Digest* 9 (Apr. 1951), 56–57; "Marine Corps Now Follows Race Policies of Navy," *Ebony* 7 (July 1952), 16–23; "Every GI a King in Japan," *Ebony* 8 (Apr. 1953), 36–40.

34. John C. O'Brien, "All Blood Is Red," *The Sign* (Mar. 2, 1951), 23–25.

35. "Statement by Senator Herbert H. Lehman on the Ending of Segregation in the Far East Command in the Army," July 27, 1951, in "Integration in the Armed Services, 1940–1955," Records of the National Association for the Advancement of Colored People, General Office File, Group II, Box A647, Manuscript Division, Library of Congress.

36. "Does Integration Work in the Armed Forces?" *U.S. News and World Report* 40 (May 1956), 54.

37. James C. Evans, "Integration in the Armed Services," *New South* 7 (1955), 75–78.

38. Letter from James C. Evans to Roy Wilkins, May 8, 1953, "Integration in the Armed Services, 1940–1955," Records of the NAACP, General Office File, Group II, Box A647, Manuscript Division, Library of Congress.

39. News release, NAACP, Aug. 22, 1953, "Integration in the Armed Services, 1940–1955," Records of the NAACP, General Office File, Group II, Box A647, Manuscript Division, Library of Congress.

40. Morton Puner, "What the Armed Forces Taught Us about Integration," *Coronet* (June 1960), 110. For an important examination of segregation's impact on national and foreign policy, see Mary Dudziak, *Cold War Civil Rights: Race and the Image of American Democracy* (Princeton, N.J.: Princeton University Press, 2000), esp. 81–88.

41. David R. Segal, *Recruiting for Uncle Sam* (Lawrence: University Press of Kansas, 1989), 32.

42. Stillman, *Integration of the Negro,* 49– Bogart, ed., *Social Research and Desegregation.*

43. Carter, *The 16th Round,* 106.

44. Ibid., 116.

45. Quoted in Tony Brown, *Jimi Hendrix: In His Own Words* (London, 1994), 15.

46. Appy, *Working-Class War,* 28–30; Segal, *Recruiting for Uncle Sam,* 34–35, 110– Harry A Marmion, "Historical Background of Selective Service in the United States," in *Selective Service and American Society,* ed. Roger W. Little (New York: Russell Sage, 1969), 38–40; John Whiteclay Chambers, *To Raise an Army* (New York: Free Press, 1987), 103–51; Neil D. Fligstein, "Who Served in the Military, 1940–73," *Armed Forces and Society* 6 (winter 1980): 297–312.

47. Appy, *Working-Class War,* 29.

48. Robert D. Mare and Christopher Winship, "The Paradox of Lessening Racial Inequality and Joblessness among Black Youth: Enrollment, Enlistment, and Employment, 1964–1981," *American Sociological Review* 49 (Feb. 1984): 39– John F. Cogan, "The Decline in Black Teenage Employment: 1950–1970," *American Economic Review* 72 (1982): 621–38.

49. Mark A. Fossett, Omer R. Galle, and Jeffrey A. Burr, "Racial Occupational Inequality, 1940–1980: A Research Note on the Impact of the Changing Regional Distribution of the Black Population," *Social Forces* 68 (Dec. 1989): 418–22.

50. Taulbert, *Watching Our Crops Come In,* 10.

51. Appy, *Working-Class War,* 28.

52. "Specialist 5 Harold 'Light Bulb' Bryant," *Bloods,* 18. Volunteers made up the bulk of the enlistment in the Marines, though it did draft twenty thousand men during the Vietnam War.

53. Quoted in Appy, *Working-Class War,* 49.

54. Whitmore, *Memphis Nam Sweden,* 37–38.

55. Eli Ginzberg, *The Negro Potential* (New York: Columbia University Press, 1956), 61.

56. Stillman, *Integration of the Negro,* 122.

57. Kathleen Maas Weigert, "Stratification, Ideology, and Opportunity Beliefs among Black Soldiers," *Public Opinion Quarterly* 38 (spring 1974): 63– Morris Janowitz, "The Logic of National Service," in *The Draft: A Handbook of Facts and Alternatives,* ed. Sol Tax (Chicago: University of Chicago Press, 1967), 77. Although some airborne recruiters used subterfuge to get black men to enlist for combat, many black men volunteered for airborne and other combat units. Col. Don Phillips, interview with author, Mar. 17, 2003; Goff and Sanders, *Brothers,* 17.

58. Weigert, "Stratification, Equality, and Opportunity."

59. "One War," *The Nation* (Oct. 14, 1968), 357.

60. Westheider, *Fighting on Two Fronts,* examines black soldiers' rising resentment of racism in Vietnam and the military generally. See also Alvin J. Schexnider, "The Development of Racial Solidarity in the Armed Forces," *Journal of Black Studies* 5 (June 1975): 425–30. The correlation between high combat mortality rates and lower black enlistment rates has not been well established.

61. Bruce K. Chapman, "Policies and Conscription: A Proposal to Replace the Draft," in *The Draft,* ed. Tax, 217.

62. Ellis, "Where Troop Cuts Will Be Cruelest," 72.

63. Charles N. Jamison, "The Cannon Fodder Myth," *Forbes* 152 (July 19, 1992), 82.

64. Melissa S. Herbert, *Camouflage Isn't Only for Combat: Gender, Sexuality, and Women in the Military* (New York: New York University Press, 1998).

65. Mark Thompson, "The Food-Stamp G.I.? Enlisted Turn to Food Stamps," *Time* (May 8, 2000), 43.

Chapter 4. "This Mill Won't Run No More"

1. William Jint, Kildav, Harlan Co., Kentucky, Oct. 6, 1996; Annie Napier, Cranks Creek, Harlan Co., Oct. 6, 1986. All interviews are by the author and are located in the Franco Coggiola Sound Archive of the Circolo Gianni Bosio in Rome; copies of Harlan County interviews previous to 1999 are also located at the Margaret R. E. King Library, Special Collection, University of Kentucky, Lexington.

2. Bill Winters, Ypsilanti, Michigan, Mar. 17, 2001.

3. Bruce Springsteen, "Youngstown," on *The Ghost of Tom Joad,* Columbia CD 481650 2.

4. E. Y. Harburg and Jay Gorney, as sung by Barbara Dane on her record *When We Make It Through,* Paredon P-1046; Bernie Abel, "Song of My Hands," as sung by Barbara Dane on the record *I Hate the Capitalist System,* Paredon P-1014; Tom Russell, "U.S. Steel," on the CD *The Long Way Around,* Hightone HCD 8081.

5. Umberto Catana, b. 1915, steelworker, Terni, Dec. 29, 1982; also quoted in Alessandro Portelli, *Biografia di una città: Storia e racocnto, Terni, 1830–1985* (Turin: Einaudi, 1985), 77.

6. Umberto Martinelli, b. 1913, steelworker, Terni, May 3, 1983; see Portelli, *Biografia di una città,* 72–73.

7. Settimio Piemonti, b. 1903, steelworker, Terni, July 9, 1980; Ida Sbarzella, b. 1906, textile worker, Terni, Jan. 30, 1980 (interviewed by Tina Moretti Antonucci and Settimio Berarducci); both quoted in Portelli, *Biografia di una città,* 77.

8. Pete Anderson, "Working Class" (1994), on the CD *Working Class,* Little Dog Records, LDR-94001–2.

9. Collected by the author from Calabrian migrants at a sit-in, Mar. 27, 1970; folk revival versions by Canzoniere del Lazio, on the CD *Qundo nascesti tune* (Bravo Records 070; originally issued as a Dischi del Sole LP in 1972), and by Valentino Santagati, on the CD *Vent'anni e più,* edited by Circolo Gianni Bosio, *il manifesto* CD 091.

10. Gualtiero Berteli, "Nina" (1966), as sung by Giovanna Marini and Francesco De Gregori in the 2003 CD *Sento il fischio del vapore,* Sony COL 510218 2.

11. Antonio Ruggieri, b. 1938, disabled steelworker, Terni, Jan. 26, 1976 (interview by Valentino Paparelli); see *Biografia di una città,* 77.

Chapter 5. Under Construction

1. Raymond Williams, *Culture and Society, 1780–1950* (New York: Columbia University Press, 1958), 325–26.

2. Vicinus wrote mainly about music hall and amateur British performance in the Victorian era (*The Industrial Muse* [New York: Barnes and Noble, 1974]); Tannacito about some fairly obscure miner's poetry ("Poetry of the Colorado Miners, 1903–1906," *Radical Teacher* 15 [Dec. 1979]: 1–15); and I mostly about songs and other oral forms ("Working-Class Women's Literature: An Introduction to Study," *Women in Print*, vol. 1, ed. J. Hartman and E. Messer-Davidow [New York: Modern Language Association, 1982]).

3. See, for example, Janet Zandy, ed., *Liberating Memory: Our Work and Our Working-class Consciousness* (New Brunswick, N.J.: Rutgers University Press, 1995). A comment about Hannah Craft on the e-list of the Society for the Study of American Women Writers, for example, reads as follows: "Black artists are often operating out of a cultural tradition that is invisible, and therefore easily misunderstood, to most white people, and often which is invisible to those of color who are not trained in the history and literary traditions that are specific to African American experience." Lori J. Askeland, Society for the Study of American Women Writers e-list, Apr. 29, 2002. Here, it seems to me, the claims of the Black Arts movement of the 1960s are being recycled in a more nuanced way, having less to do with identity and authenticity—problematic categories in any case—than with study and learning.

4. "The Orange Bears" by Kenneth Patchen, from *The Collected Poems of Kenneth Patchen*, copyright 1949 by New Directions Publishing Corporation, reprinted by permission of New Directions Publishing Corporation. The full texts of most of the poems cited in this chapter, and some information about the writers, may be found in Paul Lauter and Ann Fitzgerald, eds., *Literature, Class, and Culture: An Anthology* (New York: Longman, 2001).

5. "Filling Station" from Elizabeth Bishop, *The Complete Poems: 1927–1979* (New York: Farrar, Straus and Giroux, 1983), copyright 1979, 1983 by Alice Helen Methfessel. Reprinted by permission of the Farrar, Straus and Giroux, LLC.

6. Robert Tressell, *The Ragged Trousered Philanthropists* (New York: Monthly Review Press, 1955 [1914]).

7. Quoted in Igor Webb, " 'What Culture Is Appropriate to the Worker?' Two English Working-Class Novelists: Robert Tressell and Jack Common," *Radical Teacher* 1 (Dec. 1975): 11.

8. Upton Sinclair, *The Jungle* (New York: Doubleday, Page, 1906); Tillie Olsen, *Yonnondio: From the Thirties* (New York: Delacorte Press, 1974).

9. Studs Terkel, *Working* (New York: Avon, 1975), xiii. Quoted in Leonard Vogt, "The Literature of Work," *Radical Teacher* 9 (Sept. 1978): 39.

10. Toni Morrison, *Playing in the Dark: Whiteness and the Literary Imagination* (Cambridge: Harvard University Press, 1992).

11. John Gilgun, "Counting Tips," in Paul Lauter and Ann Fitzgerald, eds., *Literature, Class, and Culture, An Anthology* (New York: Longman, 2001). Used by permission of the author.

12. William Butler Yeats, "The Lake Isle of Innisfree," lines 1–4. Linguistically, Gilgun picks up on Yeats's deployment of the word *and* in "Innisfree," but turns it here into a mechanism for emphasizing the piled-up burdens his people face instead of the accumulation of grace, peace, and the "evening full of the linnet's wings" that Yeats's speaker can enjoy.

13. Olsen, *Yonnondio*, pp. 63–64. Pietro Di Donato, *Christ in Concrete; A Novel* (Indianapolis: Bobbs-Merrill, 1939).

14. Elmo Mondragon, "Why I Am a Poet," *XY Files: Poems on the Male Experience* (Santa Fe, N.M.: Sherman Asher Publishing, 1997), 92. Used by permission of Elmo Mondragon.

15. From *The Collected Poems of Langston Hughes* by Langston Hughes, copyright 1994 by The Estate of Langston Hughes. Used by permission of Alfred A. Knopf, a division of Random House, Inc.

16. Jack London, *The People of the Abyss* (New York: Lawrence Hill, 1995 [1903]); "The Apostate" in *When God Laughs and Other Stories* (New York: Macmillan Co., 1911).

17. "The working-class novelist . . . lives in what is effectively an alien territory, rarely explored, and thus his or her impulse when writing assumes an inevitable documentary turn." Webb, " 'What Culture Is Appropriate to the Worker?' ," 11.

18. William Attaway, *Blood on the Forge* (Garden City, N.Y.: Doubleday, Doran & Co., 1941); Thomas Bell, *Out of This Furnace* (Pittsburgh: University of Pittsburgh Press, 1976 [1941]); Tillie Olsen, "I Want You Women Up North to Know," *Partisan,* Mar. 1934, rpt. in *Heath Anthology of American Literature,* vol. II, 4th edition (Boston: Houghton Mifflin, 2002), pp. 1324–1327.

19. From Patricia Dobler, "Field Trip to the Mill" in *Talking to Strangers,* copyright 1986. Winner of the 1986 Brittingham Prize in Poetry. Reprinted by permission of The University of Wisconsin Press.

20. Susan Eisenberg, *Pioneering: Poems from the Construction Site* (Ithaca: Cornell University Press, 1998).

21. Meridel Le Sueur, "Women on the Breadlines," *New Masses,* Jan. 1932, rpt. in *Harvest Song: Collected Essays and Stories* (Albuquerque: West End Press, 1960), pp. 166–171; *The Girl* (Cambridge, Mass.: West End Press, 1978).

22. T. S. Eliot, "Tradition and the Individual Talent," *Selected Essays* (New York: Harcourt, Brace, 1950), 9: "The poet has, not a 'personality' to express, but a particular medium, which is only a medium and not a personality, in which impressions and experiences combine in peculiar and unexpected ways."

23. Gilgun has written (e-mail of Jan. 30, 2004): "I taught Levine's 'You Can Have It' . . . for ten years in my creative writing classes. I honor Philip Levine as one of the few poets in my time who's written on working-class themes. I consider his work essential and I always taught 'You Can Have It' each semester because Missouri Western College is an Open Door, working-class, community college. My students needed to know that poems on work and working-class people were being written and that these poems applied to their lives as working-class people. *'This is your life and here it is in poetry.' 'Can we write like that?' 'Why not? Levine does.'*

However, there are a few things I disagree with in Levine's 'You Can Have It' and my poem 'Counting Tips' is my way of 'getting it right,' that is, specifically, it is my way of writing a working-class poem in which no moonlight shines through a window to put a poetic gloss on the gritty, dirt-under-the-fingernails 'reality' of what work really means to a working-class person."

24. H. H. Lewis, *Road to Utterly* (Holt, Minn.: B. C. Hagglund, 1935), 5.

25. From *Pioneering: Poems from the Construction Site,* 42. Used by permission of Susan Eisenberg.

26. " 'Bourgeois' is a significant term because it marks that version of social relationship which we usually call individualism: that is to say, an idea of society as a neutral area within which each individual is free to pursue his own development and his own advantage as a natural right. . . . The individualist idea can be sharply contrasted with the idea that we properly associate with the working class: an idea which, whether it is called communism, socialism or cooperation, regards society neither as neutral nor as protective, but as the positive means for all kinds of development, including individual development. Development and advantage are not individually but commonly interpreted. The provision of the means of life will, alike in production and distribution, be collective and mutual. Improvement is sought, not in the opportunity to escape from one's class, or to make a career, but in the general and controlled advance of all. The human fund is regarded as in all respects common, and freedom of access to it a right constituted by one's humanity; yet such access, in whatever kind, is common or it is nothing. Not the individual, but the whole society, will move." Raymond Williams, *Culture and Society, 1780–1950,* 325–26.

27. Tom Wayman, *Introducing Tom Wayman: Selected Poems, 1973–1980* (Princeton, N.J.: Ontario Review Press, 1980).

28. "Our fathers were only acquainted with *égoïsme* (selfishness). Selfishness is a passionate and exaggerated love of self, which leads a man to connect everything with himself and to prefer himself to everything in the world. Individualism is a mature and calm feeling, which disposes each member of the community to sever himself from the masses of his fellows and to draw apart with his family and his friends, so that after he has thus formed a little circle of his own, he willingly leaves society at large to itself. . . . Selfishness blights the germ of all virtue; individualism, at first, only saps the virtues of public life; but in the long run it attacks and destroys all others and is at length absorbed in downright selfishness." Alexis de Tocqueville, *Democracy in America* (New York: Vintage, 1956), 2: 104.

29. *The Industrial Muse,* 1.

30. Tannacito, "Poetry of the Colorado Miners," 1.

31. Walter Rideout, *The Radical Novel in the United States, 1900–1954* (New York: Hill and Wang, 1966 [1956]), 170: "And just as literature during the years of capitalist domination had reflected bourgeois values, had attempted, while reassuring the middle classes, to disarm the worker and alienate him from his class, so the new literature would reflect proletarian values, would bring the worker to class-consciousness, steel him for the coming revolution, prepare him for the role he would play in the next stage of history. Art was a form of politics; it was a weapon in the class war."

32. June Jordan, "Poem About My Rights," *Naming Our Destiny: New and Selected Poems* (New York: Thunder's Mouth Press, 1989); Rodolfo Gonzales, *I Am Joaquín/Yo Soy Joaquín* (New York: Bantam, 1972); Joy Harjo, "The Woman Hanging from the 13th Floor Window," *She Had Some Horses* (New York: Thunder's Mouth Press, 1983).

33. Jeanne Bryner, "For Maude Callen: Nurse Midwife, Pineville, N.C., 1951," *Breathless* (Kent, Ohio: Kent State University Press, 1995); Judy Grahn, "Ella, in a square apron, along Highway 80," *The Common Woman* (Oakland, Calif.: Women's Press Collective, 1973).

34. Meridel Le Sueur, *The Girl* (Cambridge, Mass.: West End Press, 1978); idem, *I Hear Men Talking and Other Stories,* edited with an afterword by Linda Ray Pratt (Minneapolis: West End Press, 1984); Tillie Olsen, *Yonnondio: From the Thirties* (New York: Delacorte, 1974); Robert Cantwell, *The Land of Plenty* (New York: Farrar and Rinehart, 1934); Clara Weatherwax, *Marching! Marching!* (New York: John Day, 1935); Kenneth Patchen, *The Journal of Albion Moonlight* (New York: United Book Guild, 1944), and *Sleepers Awake* (New York: Padell Book Company, 1946), among other works.

35. See Constance Coiner, *Better Red: The Writing and Resistance of Tillie Olsen and Meridel Le Sueur* (New York: Oxford University Press, 1995).

36. Though they are of intense historical interest. Quite differing takes on politics and style in the '30s are presented by Alan M. Wald, *The New York Intellectuals: The Rise and Decline of the Anti-Stalinist Left from the 1930s to the 1980s* (Chapel Hill: University of North Carolina Press, 1987); Barbara Foley, *Radical Representations: Politics and Form in U.S. Proletarian Fiction, 1929–1941* (Durham, N.C.: Duke University Press, 1993); Michael Denning, *The Cultural Front: The Laboring of American Culture in the Twentieth Century* (New York: Verso, 1997).

37. The title of Renny Christopher's book is nicely indicative: *Longing Fervently for Revolution* (Niagara Falls, N.Y.: Slipstream, 1998).

38. Dwight Macdonald, "A Theory of Mass Culture," *Diogenes* 3 (summer 1953): 1–17.

Chapter 6. Working-Class Geographies

1. The classic history is Dan Georgakas and Marvin Surkin, *Detroit, I Do Mind Dying: A Study in Urban Revolution* (Boston: South End Press, 1998 [1975]).

2. Quoted in ibid.

3. William Bunge, *Theoretical Geography* (Lund: Royal University of Lund, 1962); Bunge, *FitzGerald: Geography of a Revolution* (Cambridge, Mass.: Schenkman, 1971); Ronald Horvath, "The 'Detroit Geographical Expeditions and Institute' Experience," *Antipode* 3 (1971): 73–85; for an excellent history of the "geographical expedition" movement, see Andy Merrifield, "Situated Knowledge through Exploration: Reflections on Bunge's 'Geographical Expeditions,' " *Antipode* 27 (1995): 49–70.

4. William Bunge and Ronald Bordessa, *The Canadian Alternative: Survival, Expeditions, and Urban Change* (Department of Geography, York University: Geographical Monographs, 1975).

5. David Harvey, *Explanation in Geography* (London: Edward Arnold, 1969); idem, *Social Justice and the City* (London: Edward Arnold, 1973).

6. M. Elliot Hurst, "Establishment Geography: Or How to Be Irrelevant in Three Easy Lessons," *Antipode* 5, no. 2 (1972): 40–59; Richard Peet, ed., *Radical Geography* (Chicago: Maaroufa, 1977); Richard Peet, *Modern Geographical Thought* (Oxford: Blackwell, 1998).

7. David Harvey and Neil Smith, "From Capitals to Capital," in Bertell Ollman and Edward Vernoff, eds., *The Left Academy: Marxist Scholarship on American Campuses,* vol. 2 (New York: Praeger, 1982), 99–121; see also Noel Castree, "Professionalism, Activism, and the University: Whither 'Critical Geography'?" *Environment and Planning A* 32 (2000): 955–70.

8. David Harvey, "On the History and Present Condition of Geography: An Historical Materi-

alist Manifesto," in *Spaces of Capital: Towards a Critical Geography* (New York: Routledge, 2001 [1984]), 108–20.

9. David Harvey, *The Limits to Capital* (London: Verso, 1999 [1982]), xiii–xiv; see also David Harvey, *Consciousness and the Urban Experience* (Baltimore: Johns Hopkins University Press, 1985), and *The Urbanization of Capital* (Baltimore: Johns Hopkins University Press, 1985); and for a contemporary evaluation of its importance, see the "Symposium on David Harvey's *Limits to Capital*" in *Antipode* 36, no. 3 (2004): 401–549.

10. Harvey, *Limits,* chaps. 9–10.

11. Ibid., 354.

12. Ibid., 368.

13. George Henderson, *California and the Fictions of Capital* (Oxford: Oxford University Press, 1999), 39; see also Felicity Callard, "The Body in Theory," *Environment and Planning D: Society and Space* 16 (1998): 387–400; David Harvey, "The Body as Accumulation Strategy," *Environment and Planning D: Society and Space* 16 (1998): 401–21.

14. Karl Marx, *Capital,* vol. 1 (New York, International Publishers, 1987), 168; David Harvey, "Labor, Capital, and Class Struggle around the Built Environment in Advanced Capitalist Societies," in Kevin Cox, ed., *Urbanization and Conflict in Market Societies* (Chicago: Maaroufa, 1978), 9–37.

15. Harvey, *Limits,* 380, 381.

16. Frances Fox Piven and Richard Cloward, *Regulating the Poor: The Functions of Public Welfare,* rev. ed. (New York: Vintage, 1992); see Peter Andreas, *Border Games: Policing the U.S.-Mexico Divide* (Ithaca: Cornell University Press, 2000); J. Nevins, *Operation Gatekeeper: The Rise of the "Illegal Alien" and the Making of the U.S.-Mexico Boundary* (New York: Routledge, 2001).

17. Harvey, *Limits,* 284.

18. Vera Chouinard, "Structure and Agency: Contested Concepts in Human Geography," in Carville Earle, Kent Mathewson, and Martin Kenzer, eds., *Concepts in Human Geography* (Lanham, Md.: Rowman and Littlefield, 1996), 383–410, quotation from 392; Linda McDowell, "Towards an Understanding of the Gender Division of Urban Space," *Environment and Planning D: Society and Space* 1 (1983): 59–72, quotation from 62; see also Cindi Katz, "Lost and Found in the Posts: Addressing Critical Human Geography," *Environment and Planning D: Society and Space* 16 (1998): 257–78; Cindi Katz, "Vagabond Capitalism," *Antipode* 33 (2001): 709–78; Doreen Massey, "Reflections on the Debate: Thoughts on Feminism, Marxism, and Theory," *Environment and Planning A* 21 (1989): 692–97; Doreen Massey, *Spatial Divisions of Labour,* 2nd ed. (London: Macmillan, 1995 [1984]); K. Nelson, "Labor Demand, Labor Supply, and the Suburbanization of Low-Wage Office Work," in Allen Scott and Michael Storper, eds., *Production, Work, Territory: The Geographical Anatomy of Industrial Capitalism* (Boston: Allen and Unwin, 1986), 149–71; S. MacKenzie and D. Rose, "Industrial Change, the Domestic Economy, and Home Life," in J. Anderson, S. Duncan, and R. Hudson, eds., *Redundant Spaces in Cities and Regions* (New York: Academic Press, 1983).

19. Marx, *Capital,* vol. 1, 537.

20. Nelson, "Labor Demand, Labor Supply"; Massey, *Spatial Divisions;* on social reproduction see Katz, "Vagabond Capitalism" and "Whose Nature, Whose Culture? Private Productions of Space and the 'Preservation of Nature,' " in Bruce Braun and Noel Castree, eds., *Remaking Reality: Nature at the Millennium* (New York: Routledge, 1998), 46–63; on Mexico, see, e.g., Patrick Fernandez-Kelly, *For We Are Sold, I and My People: Women and Industry in Mexico's Frontier* (Albany: State University of New York Press, 1983); June Nash and Patricia Fernandez-Kelly, eds., *Women, Men, and the International Division of Labor* (Albany: State University of New York Press, 1983); Altha Cravey, "The Politics of Reproduction: Households in the Mexican Industrial Transition," *Economic Geography* 73 (1997): 166–87; Melissa Wright, "Feminine Villains, Masculine Heroes, and the Reproduction of Ciudad, Juarez," *Social Text* 19, no. 4 (2001): 93–113; and "A Manifesto against Femicide," *Antipode* 33 (2001): 550–66.

21. Katz, "Vagabond Capitalism," 711.

22. Massey, *Spatial Divisions,* 3, 289, 288.

23. Ibid., 114.

24. Alan Warde, "Spatial Change, Politics, and the Division of Labour," in D. Gregory and J.

Urrey, eds., *Social Relations and Spatial Structures* (London: Macmillan, 1985), 190–212; Massey, *Spatial Divisions,* 116.

25. Neil Smith, *Uneven Development: Nature, Capital, and the Production of Space,* 2nd ed. (Oxford: Blackwell, 1990 [1984]), 151, 99.

26. Ibid., 148.

27. Ibid.; see also Smith, "Contours of a Spatialized Politics: Homeless Vehicles and the Production of Geographical Scale," *Social Text* 33 (1992): 55–81; and "Homeless/Global: Scaling Places," in John Bird, Barry Curtis, Tim Putnam, George Robertson, and Lisa Tucker, eds., *Mapping the Futures: Local Culture, Global Change* (New York: Routledge, 1993), 87–119; and Andrew Herod, "The Production of Scale in United States Labour Relations," *Area* 23 (1991): 82–88.

28. Neil Smith, "Dangers of the Empirical Turn: Some Comments on the CURS Initiative," *Antipode* 19 (1989): 59–68; and in general, the special issue of *Environment and Planning A* 23 (1991) on the locality debates.

29. Doreen Massey, *Space, Place, and Gender* (Minneapolis: University of Minnesota Press, 1994).

30. Andrew Herod, *Labor Geographies: Workers and Landscapes of Capitalism* (New York: Guilford, 2001), see also Herod, "Production of Scale"; "Local Political Practice in Response to a Manufacturing Plant Closure: How Geography Complicates Class Analysis," *Antipode* 23 (1991): 385–402; "The Practice of International Labor Solidarity and the Geography of the Global Economy," *Economic Geography* 71 (1995): 341–63; "Labor as an Agent of Globalization and as a Global Agent," in Kevin Cox, ed., *Spaces of Globalization: Reasserting the Power of the Local* (New York: Guilford, 1997), 167–200; and "Labor's Spatial Praxis and the Geography of Contract Bargaining in the U.S. East Coast Longshore Industry, 1953–1989," *Political Geography* 16 (1997): 145–69.

31. Herod, *Labor Geographies,* 34, 35, 36 (emphasis in original), 37.

32. Andrew Herod, "Towards a Labor Geography: The Production of Space and the Politics of Scale in the East Coast Longshore Industry, 1950–1990," PhD diss., Department of Geography, Rutgers University, 1992; Rebecca Johns, "International Solidarity: Space and Class in the U.S. Labor Movement," PhD diss., Department of Geography, Rutgers University, 1992; Leyla Vural, "Unionism as a Way of Life: The Community Orientation of the International Ladies Garment Workers' Union and the Amalgamated Clothing Workers of America," PhD diss., Department of Geography, Rutgers University, 1994; Don Mitchell, "Land and Labor: Worker Resistance and the Production of Landscape in Agricultural California before World War II," PhD diss., Department of Geography, Rutgers University, 1992; see also Rebecca Johns and Leyla Vural, "Class, Geography, and the Consumerist Turn: UNITE and the Stop Sweatshops Campaign," *Environment and Planning A* 32 (2000): 1193–1213; Don Mitchell, *The Lie of the Land: Migrant Workers and the California Landscape* (Minneapolis: University of Minnesota Press, 1996).

33. Ruth Wilson Gilmore, "From Military Keynesianism to Post-Keynesian Militarism: Finance Capital, Land, Labor, and Opposition in the Rising California Prison State," PhD diss., Department of Geography, Rutgers University, 1998; and *The Golden Gulag: Labor, Land, State, and Opposition in Globalizing California* (Berkeley: University of California Press, forthcoming); see also Carey McWilliams, *Factories in the Field* (Boston: Little, Brown, 1939).

34. Herod, *Labor Geographies,* 48–49.

35. See Andrew Herod, ed., *Organizing the Landscape: Geographical Perspectives on Labor Unionism* (Minneapolis: University of Minnesota Press, 1998); Jane Wills, "Geographies of Trade Unionism: Translating across Space and Time," *Antipode* 28 (1996): 352–78; "Space, Place, and Tradition in Working-Class Organization," in Herod, ed., *Organizing the Landscape,* 129–58; "Taking on the Cosmo Corps? Experiments in Transnational Labor Organization," *Economic Geography* 74 (1998): 111–30; Jane Wills and Peter Waterman, *Place, Space, and the New Labour Internationalisms* (Oxford: Blackwell, 2001); and Ron Martin, Peter Sunley, and Jane Wills, *Union Retreat and the Regions: The Shrinking Landscape of Organized Labour* (London: J. Kingsley, 1996).

36. General Baker, "DRUM Veteran General Baker at the Black Radical Congress: Listen to the Past, Anticipate the Future," *The People's Tribune,* Aug. 1998, http://www.lrna.org.org/league/PT/PT.1998.08/PT.1998.08.6.html (accessed Oct. 21, 2002). On the history of Detroit's deindustrialization, and its striking unevenness, see Thomas Sugrue, *The Origins of the Urban Crisis: Race*

and Inequality in Postwar Detroit (Princeton: Princeton University Press, 1996). As Sugrue makes clear, Detroit's decline began immediately after World War II and was well advanced by the time the league began its work—these were part of the conditions the league, and the Revolutionary Union Movement, struggled over (as, for example, in its analysis of "niggermation"—their word for the speed-up in old inner-city factories that had to complete with new suburban ones).

37. For one of those exceptions see Brian Page, "Charting the Middle Ground: History, Geography, and City-Hinterland Relations in the Great West," *Ecumene* 5 (1998): 81–104.

38. See Herod, *Labor Geographies,* 48; J. K. Gibson-Graham, *The End of Capitalism (As We Knew It)* (Oxford: Blackwell, 1998).

39. David Harvey, "On the History and Present Condition of Geography: An Historical Materialist Manifesto," in *Spaces of Capital: Towards a Critical Geography* (New York: Routledge, 2001 [1984]), 108–20, quotation from 116–17.

Chapter 7. Class as a Question in Economics

1. For a detailed presentation of class definitions and empirical findings on the class composition of the United States, see Michael Zweig, *The Working Class Majority: America's Best Kept Secret* (Ithaca: Cornell University Press, 2000), chap. 1.

2. Adam Smith, *An Inquiry into the Nature and Causes of the Wealth of Nations* (New York: Modern Library, 1937 [1776]).

3. Ibid., 48.

4. Karl Marx, "Letter to J. Weydemeyer," Mar. 5, 1852, in Robert C. Tucker, ed., *The Marx-Engels Reader,* 2nd ed. (New York: W. W. Norton, 1978), 220, original emphasis.

5. Karl Marx, *Capital,* 3 vols. (New York: International Publishers, 1967); *Theories of Surplus Value,* 3 vols. (New York: International Publishers, 1952). Volume one of *TSV* is mostly devoted to Marx's critique and elaboration of Adam Smith's economics.

6. See Mark Blaug, *Economic Theory in Retrospect,* 4th ed. (Cambridge: Cambridge University Press, 1985), 294–327; Ronald L. Meek, *Smith, Marx, and After* (London: Chapman and Hall, 1977), 163–75; William K. Tabb, *Reconstructing Political Economy* (London: Routledge, 1999), 91–110.

7. Meek, *Smith, Marx, and After,* 166–67.

8. Joseph Schumpeter, *History of Economic Analysis* (London: Routledge, 1994 [1954]), 886–87.

9. This problem was the center of what was called in the 1960s the "Cambridge controversy," pitting economists at Harvard and MIT (Cambridge, Mass.) against economists at Cambridge University in England who discovered the problem. For a brief summary, see Tabb, *Reconstructing Political Economy,* 155–56; Howard Wachtel, *Labor Economics,* 3rd ed. (Ft. Worth, Texas: Dryden Press, 1993), 91–93. For a technical investigation, see Piero Sraffa, *Production of Commodities by Means of Commodities: Prelude to a Critique of Economic Theory* (Cambridge: Cambridge University Press, 1960).

10. Zweig, *Working Class Majority,* 62–65; Larry Mishel et al., *The State of Working America, 2002–2003* (Ithaca: Cornell University Press, 2003), 156–58.

11. Nelson Lichtenstein, *The State of the Union: A Century of American Labor* (Princeton: Princeton University Press, 2003); Joshua B. Freeman, *Working Class New York* (New York: New Press, 2000); Michael Zweig, "The Challenge of Working-Class Studies," in Zweig, ed., *What's Class Got to Do with It? American Society in the Twenty-first Century* (Ithaca: Cornell University Press, 2004), 1–17.

12. U.S. States Census Bureau, *Current Population Reports P60–209, Money Income in the United States: 1999* (Washington, D.C., 2000), table B-3, updated at http://www.census.gov/hhcs/income/histinc/ie1.html; Edward N. Wolff, *Top Heavy: The Increasing Inequality of Wealth in America and What Can Be Done about It* (New York: New Press, 2002).

13. Steven Greenhouse, "Verizon Is Told It Must Reinstate 2,300 Workers Let Go Last Year," *New York Times* (July 12, 2003), C4.

14. Steven Greenhouse, "Transit Strike Averted after Tentative Deal Is Reached," *New York Times* (Dec. 17, 2002), A1; Steven Greenhouse, "Contract Gains Won't Finance Higher Wages:

M.T.A. Failed to Get Main Productivity Goal," *New York Times* (Dec. 18, 2002), B1; Randy Kennedy and Steven Greenhouse, "To Move Ahead, Each Side's Negotiators Had to Loosen Grip on the Past," *New York Times* (Dec. 18, 2002), B10.

15. Mishel et al., *State of Working America,* 189–96.

16. Richard B. Freeman and James L. Medoff, *What Do Unions Do?* (New York: Basic Books, 1984).

17. William K. Tabb, *The Amoral Elephant: Globalization and the Struggle for Social Justice in the Twenty-first Century* (New York: Monthly Review, 2001).

18. Jeff Madrick, "Regardless of Progress of a Few, Many Nations Still Face Economic Despair," *New York Times* (Aug. 7, 2003), C2; Joseph E. Stiglitz, *Globalization and Its Discontents* (New York: W. W. Norton, 2003).

19. Harry Magdoff, *Imperialism: From the Colonial Age to the Present* (New York: Monthly Review, 1978), 154–59.

20. National Agricultural Statistics Service, *1997 Census of Agriculture,* AC97–A-51 (Washington, D.C.: United States Department of Agriculture), vol. 1, pt. 51, table 5.

21. *The National Security Strategy of the United States of America* (Falls Village, Conn.: Winterhouse Editions, 2002), issued by President George W. Bush on Sept. 19, 2002 at http://www.whitehouse.gov. See also David E. Sanger, "Bush to Outline Doctrine of Striking Foes First," *New York Times* (Sept. 20, 2002), A1, and related stories on A14.

22. United States Space Command, *Vision for 2020,* Feb. 1997 (contains no pagination as downloaded from http://www.spacecom.mil/visbook.pdf).

23. Ibid.

24. Meek, *Smith, Marx, and After,* 187–88.

25. This distinction originated with the economist Neville Keynes and got its fullest contemporary treatment in Milton Friedman, *Essays in Positive Economics* (Chicago: University of Chicago Press, 1966), pt. 1.

26. E. H. Carr, *What Is History?* (New York: Vintage, 1961), 3–35.

27. Meek, *Smith, Marx, and After,* 187.

28. Zweig, ed., *What's Class Got to Do with It?,* pt. 1.

Chapter 8. Work Poetry and Working-Class Poetry

1. Richard Price in "Up North, Down South: The Birth of a Novel," Peter Applebome. *New York Times* (May 19, 1998), E1.

2. Tom Wayman, *Inside Job: Essays on the New Work Writing* (Madeira Park, B.C., Canada: Harbour Publishing, 1983), 24.

3. *The Grievance: Poems from the Shop Floor* (San Pedro, Calif.: Singlejack Books, 1980), inside front cover.

4. Tom Wayman, *Going for Coffee* (Madeira Park, B.C., Canada: Harbour, 1987), introduction to the 2nd ed.

5. Nicholas Coles and Peter Oresick, *For a Living: The Poetry of Work* (Urbana: University of Illinois Press, 1995), xv.

6. Ibid., xvi.

7. "Poetry Is for Everybody: Introduce Poetry to a Wider Audience" (Iowa City: University of Iowa Press, 2003).

8. Karen Blomain, *Coalseam: Poems from the Anthracite Region* (Scranton, Penn.: University of Scranton Press, 1996), 7.

9. Harry Humes, "The Bootleg Coal Hole," in *Coalseam,* 106. Reprinted by permission of author.

10. Ben Hamper, "Psychedelics," in *Labor Pains: Poetry from South East Michigan Workers* (Roseville, Mich.: Ridgeway Press, 1991), 71. Reprinted by permission of Ridgeway Press.

11. Lolita Hernandez, "diamonds on the pads of my hands," in *Labor Pains,* 14. Reprinted by permission of Ridgeway Press.

12. Donna Langston, "Down on the Strike Line with My Children," in *Calling Home: Working-Class Women's Writing,* ed. Janet Zandy (New Brunswick, N.J.: Rutgers University Press, 1990), 282.

13. Rina Ferrarelli, "I'm Standing in Line," from *Home Is a Foreign Country* (Greensburg, Penn.: Eadmer Press, 1996). The poem first appeared in *Laurel Review*. Reprinted with permission.

14. Larry Evans, "The Mill Hunk Anthology: An Organizer's Odyssey," in *Overtime: Punchin' Out with the* Mill Hunk Herald, eds. Beatty, Begandy, Becker, Daniels, Dyen, Evans, Ferlo, Gallaway, Meyer, Oresick (Pittsburgh: Piece of the Hunk Publishers, and Albuquerque, N.M.: West End Press, 1990), viii.

15. Mike Basinksi, "Priorities," in *Overtime,* 175. Reprinted by permission of author.

16. Ron De La Houssaye, "Corporatania," in *Bad Attitude: The Processed World Anthology,* ed. Chris Carlsson, with Mark Leger (New York: Verso, 1990), 175. Reprinted by permission of *Processed World.*

17. Editorial statement, *Blue Collar Review* 5, no. 2 (winter 2001–2002): inside front cover.

18. Meridel Le Sueur, *Blue Collar Review* 5, no. 2: back cover.

19. Leona Gom, "The Work Issue," *event* 11, no. 1 (1982): 3.

20. Grant Tracey, "About This Issue," *North American Review* 286, no. 5 (Sept.–Oct. 2001): 2.

21. Bob Hicok, "What We Say," *Witness* 10, no. 2 (1996): 55.

22. Herb Scott, "Boss," in *Groceries* (Pittsburgh: University of Pittsburgh Press, 1976), 8.

23. Richard Martin, "Room 212," in *Dream of Long Headdresses* (Bellingham, Wash.: Signpost Press, 1988), 55. Reprinted by permission of author.

24. Cortney Davis, "What the Nurse Likes," in *Details of Flesh* (Corvallis, Ore.: Calyx Books, 1997), 25.

25. Antler, *Factory* (San Francisco: City Lights Books, 1980), 34. Reprinted by permission of author.

26. Ibid., 34.

27. Ibid., 41.

28. Peter Oresick, "The Story of Glass," *Definitions* (Albuquerque: West End Press, 1990), 5. © 1977 by Peter Oresick. Reprinted by permission of author.

29. Christian Thomas, "Sprawl," *Mòly & Manganese* (Harrisburg, Penn.: Two Doors Down Press, 1997), 20.

30. Michael Casey, "the company pool," *Millrat* (Easthampton, Mass.: Adastra Press, 1996), 10. Reprinted by permission of author.

31. Denise Levertov, foreword to *It's a Good Thing I'm Not Macho* (Boston: Whetstone Press, 1984), vii.

32. Peter Blair, "Last Heat," *Last Heat* (Washington, D.C.: Word Works, 1999), 71. Reprinted by permission of author.

33. Jeanne Bryner, "How to Say It," *Blind Horse: Poems* (Huron, Ohio: Bottom Dog Press, 1999), 79. © Bottom Dog Press/Jeanne Bryner. Reprinted by permission of Bottom Dog Press.

34. David Brooks, "What the Slogan Means," *Right Livelihood* (Scotia, N.Y.: Pavement Saw Press, 1998), 17. Reprinted by permission of author.

35. Martin Glaberman, "Ecology," *The Grievance: Poems from the Shop Floor* (San Pedro, Calif.: Singlejack Books, 1980), 26.

36. Michael S. Weaver [Afaa M. Weaver], "Bethlehem," *My Father's Geography* (Pittsburgh: University of Pittsburgh Press, 1992), 15.

37. Philip Levine, "What Work Is," *What Work Is* (New York: Knopf, 1992), 18.

38. Tom Wayman, "What the Writing Students of Detroit State Think of Philip Levine," *Counting the Hours* (Toronto: McClelland and Stewart, 1983), 43. Reprinted by permission of author.

39. Aurora Harris, "Dream 1:10–1:25 a.m., August 22, 1997," in *Brooding the Heartlands,* ed. M. L. Liebler (Huron, Ohio: Bottom Dog Press, 1998), 72–73. © Bottom Dog Press/Aurora Harris, 1998. Reprinted by permission of Bottom Dog Press.

40. Gary Soto, "Mexicans Begin Jogging," *New and Selected Poems* (San Francisco: Chronicle Books, 1995), 51. © 1985 by Gary Soto. Used by permission of author.

41. Patricia Dobler, "Steelmark Day Parade, 1961," *Talking to Strangers* (Madison: University of Wisconsin Press, 1986), 23. © 1986 by the University of Wisconsin Press. Reprinted with permission.

42. Susan Eisenberg, "Past the Finish Line," *Pioneering: Poems from the Construction Site* (Ithaca: Cornell University Press, 1998), 58–59. © 1998 by Susan Eisenberg. Reprinted by permission of author.

43. Kate Braid, "Sister in the United Brotherhood of Carpenters & Joiners of America," *Covering Rough Ground* (Vancouver, B.C., Canada: Polestar, 1991), 35. Reprinted by permission of author.

44. Susan Eisenberg, "First Day on a New Jobsite," *Pioneering: Poems from the Construction Site* (Ithaca: Cornell University Press, 1998), 48. © 1998 by Susan Eisenberg. Reprinted by permission of author.

45. Kate Braid, "Saw," *Covering Rough Ground,* 23. Reprinted by permission of author.

46. Chris Llewellyn, "Author's Note," *Steam Dummy / Fragments from the Fire: The Triangle Shirtwaist Company Fire of March 25, 1911: Poems* (Huron, Ohio: Bottom Dog Press, 1993), vii.

47. Chris Llewellyn, "Sear," *Steam Dummy / Fragments from the Fire,* 68. © Bottom Dog Press/Chris Llewellyn 1989. Reprinted by permission of Bottom Dog Press.

48. Chris Llewellyn, "Scraps," *Steam Dummy / Fragments from the Fire,* 13. © Bottom Dog Press/Chris Llewellyn 1989. Reprinted by permission of Bottom Dog Press.

49. Ruth Daigon, "Watchers Down Below," *Payday at the Triangle* (Concord, Calif.: Small Poetry Press, 2001), 12.

50. Sean Thomas Dougherty, "Labor Day," *The Body's Precarious Balance* (Lancaster, Calif.: Red Dancefloor Press, 1997), 35.

51. Joseph Millar, *Overtime* (Spokane: Eastern Washington University Press, 2001), 64 (author biography note).

52. Gerald Locklin, comment on back cover of Fred Voss's *Goodstone Aircraft Company* (Long Beach, Calif.: P.O. Press, 1988).

53. Fred Voss, "Asleep," *Goodstone Aircraft Company,* 27. Reprinted by permission of author.

54. Harry E. Northup, "it's a time," *Reunions* (Los Angeles: Cahuenga Press, 2001), 220. Reprinted by permission of author.

55. Harry E. Northup, "time passage," *Reunions,* 251. Reprinted by permission of author.

56. Joseph Millar, "Telephone Repairman," *Overtime,* 3. Reprinted by permission of Eastern Washington University Press. © 2001.

57. Karen Blomain, introduction to *Coalseam,* 8.

58. Timothy Russell, "In Re," *Adversaria* (Evanston, Ill.: Northwestern University Press, 1993), 1. Reprinted by permission of author.

59. Arlitia Jones, "Shit Job," *The Bandsaw Riots* (Cohasset, Calif.: Bear Star Press, 2001), 9–10. Reprinted by permission of Bear Star Press.

60. Sue Doro, "Muscle," *Heart, Home & Hard Hats* (Minneapolis: Midwest Villages and Voices, 1986), 21.

61. Tom Wayman, "The Factory Hour," *Did I Miss Anything?* (Madeira Park, B.C., Canada: Harbour, 1993), 68. Reprinted by permission of author.

62. Tom Wayman, "Afterword: Work, Money, Authenticity," *In a Small House on the Outskirts of Heaven* (Madeira Park, B.C., Canada: Harbour, 1989), 117. Reprinted by permission of author.

Chapter 9. Class Memory

1. Grade refers to a category of workers.

2. John Burnett, ed., *Useful Toil: Autobiographies of Working People from the 1820s to the 1920s* (London: Routledge, 1994), ix.

3. Ibid., x.

4. There are a number of autobiographies from railway workers in North America and Australia, but not on the scale of those from the United Kingdom.

5. Paul Thompson, *The Voice of the Past: Oral History,* 2nd ed. (Oxford: Oxford University Press, 1988), 125.

6. Michael Reynolds, *Engine-Driving Life: Stirring Adventures and Incidents in the Lives of Locomotive Engine-Drivers* (London: Hugh Evelyn, 1968 [1881]).

7. Albert Hooker, *Bert Hooker: Legendary Railwayman* (Sparkford: Oxford Publishing, 1994); Frank Mason, *Life Adventure in Steam: A Merseyside Driver Remembers* (Birkenhead: Countyvise, 1992); Stan Symes, *55 Years on the Footplate* (Oxford: Oakwood Press, 1995); David Newbould, *Yesterday's Railwayman* (Poole: Oxford Publishing, 1985); Ron Bradshaw, *Railway Lines and Levers* (Paddock Wood: Unicorn Books, 1993).

8. See, for example, Charles Taylor, *Life in a Loco Works: First-hand Experiences of a Crewe Engineering Apprentice in Wartime* (Sparkford: Oxford Publishing, 1995); Brian Grant, *Home and Distant: A 40-year Railway Career from Apprentice Fitter to BRB Headquarters, 1952–93* (Kettering: Silver Link, 1998); Charles Hewison, *From Shedmaster to the Railway Inspectorate* (Newton Abbot: David Charles, 1981); Frank Hick, *That Was My Railway: From Ploughman's Kid to Railway Boss, 1922–1969* (Kettering: Silver Link, 1991); Peter Kirton, *Proceed at Caution* (Nottingham: Challenger, 1998); Peter Rayner, *On and Off the Rails* (Stratford-upon-Avon: Novelangle, 1997).

9. John Kellett, "Writing on Victorian Railways: An Essay in Nostalgia," *Victorian Studies* 13, no. 1 (1968): 90–96, 92.

10. David Howell, "Railway Safety and Labour Unrest: The Aisgill Railway Disaster of 1913," in *On the Move: Essays in Labour and Transport History,* ed. C. Wrigley and J. Shepherd (London: Hambledon Press, 1991), 130.

11. David Wilson, *Forward! The Revolution in the Lives of the Footplatemen, 1962–1996* (Sutton: Far Thrupp, 1996), 3.

12. Raphael Samuel and Paul Thompson, eds., *The Myths We Live By* (London: Routledge, 1983), 1.

13. Michael Robbins, *Points and Signals: A Railway Historian at Work* (London: George Allen and Unwin, 1967), 26.

14. Kellett, "Writing on Victorian Railways," 92.

15. Taylor, *Life in a Loco Works,* 11.

16. Ken Gibbs, *Swindon Works: Apprenticeship in Steam* (Poole: Oxford Publishing, 1986), 15.

17. Ibid., 15.

18. Frank McKenna, *The Railway Workers, 1840–1970* (London: Faber, 1980), 118.

19. Ron Spedding, *Shildon Wagon Works: A Working Man's Life* (Durham: County Durham, 1988), 32–33.

20. Taylor, *Life in a Loco Works,* 21.

21. Bradshaw, *Railway Lines and Levers,* 25.

22. Ibid., 21.

23. Susan Faludi, *Stiffed: The Betrayal of Modern Man* (London: Vintage, 1999), 72.

24. Bradshaw, *Railway Lines and Levers,* 29–30.

25. Samuel and Thompson, eds., *Myths We Live By.*

26. E. P. Thompson, *The Making of the English Working Class* (London: Penguin, 1980), 12.

27. Raphael Samuel, ed., *History Workshop: A Collectanea, 1967–1991* (Oxford: History Workshop, 1991), iii.

28. Samuel and Thompson, *Myths We Live By,* 6. Emphasis in the original.

29. Ibid.

30. Richard Sennett and Jonathan Cobb, *The Hidden Injuries of Class* (London: Norton, 1972).

31. See Zygmunt Bauman, *Work, Consumerism, and the New Poor* (Buckingham: Open University Press, 1998); Ulrich Beck, *The Brave New World of Work* (Cambridge: Polity, 2000); André Gorz, *Reclaiming Work: Beyond the Wage-Based Society* (Cambridge: Polity, 1999).

32. Jeremy Rifkin, *The End of Work: The Decline of the Global Labor Force and the Dawn of the Post-Market Era* (New York: Putnam, 1996).

33. Bauman, *Work, Consumerism,* 17.

34. Ibid., 27.

35. Beck, *Brave New World,* 2–3.

36. Stanley Aronowitz and William DiFazio, *The Jobless Future: Sci-Tech and the Dogma of Work* (Minneapolis: University of Minneapolis, 1994).

37. Gorz, *Reclaiming Work,* 1.

38. Ibid., 55.

39. Bauman, *Work, Consumerism,* 18.

40. Beck, *Brave New World,* 7.

41. Kathryn Dudley, *The End of the Line: Lost Jobs, New Lives in Postindustrial America* (Chicago: University of Chicago Press, 1994), 179.

42. Spedding, *Shildon Wagon Works,* 72.

Chapter 11. "Working Man's Ph.D."

The chapter subheads are from the following songs:

"The View from the Cheap Seats," Alabama, *Cheap Seats,* 1993.

"Jane, She Is a Clerk," *Lou Reed and the Velvet Underground, Sweet Jane,* 1974.

"Let the Poor Man Live and the Rich Man Bust," Dave McCarn, *Rich Man, Poor Man,* 1930.

"Forget That You're a Lady and Give Them What They Deserve," Salt-N-Pepa, *Somebody's Getting' on My Nerves,* 1993.

"He Fired My Ass and He Fired Jerry Rivers," Hank Williams Jr., *The Ballad of Hank Williams,* 1981.

"Poor Folks Stick Together," Stoney Edwards, *Poor Folks Stick Together,* 1971.

"Don Quixote Was a Steel-Driving Man," The Moldy Peaches, *Anyone Else But You,* 2001.

1. *Bakersfield Country!* Prod. Paula Mazur. KCET Arts and Culture, Los Angeles, Nov. 15, 1991.

2. Ben Hamper, *Rivethead: Tales from the Assembly Line* (New York: Warner Books, 1991); Francisco Jimenez, *The Circuit: Stories in the Life of a Migrant Child* (Albuquerque: University of New Mexico Press, 1997).

3. James Smethurst, "Everyday People: Popular Music, Race, and the Articulation and Formation of Class Identity." Paper presented at the American Studies Association annual meeting, Houston, Texas, Nov. 2002.

4. Director John Hughes's "brat pack" movies (*Pretty in Pink* [1986], *Sixteen Candles* [1984], *The Breakfast Club* [1985]) also often turn on class conflict between groups of high-school kids, organized around music tastes and the styles (or cliques) that accompany them.

5. Graeme Turner, *Film as Social Practice* (New York: Routledge, 1997).

6. Russell Sanjek and David Sanjek, *American Popular Music Business in the Twentieth Century* (New York: Oxford University Press, 1991); Steve Chapple and Reebee Garofalo, *Rock 'N' Roll Is Here to Pay: The History and Politics of the Music Industry* (Chicago: Nelson-Hall, 1977); Sherrie Tucker, *Swing Shift: "All Girl" Bands of the 1940s* (Durham, N.C.: Duke University Press, 2000); Ruth Glasser, *My Music Is My Flag: Puerto Rican Musicians and Their New York Communities, 1917–1940* (Berkeley: University of California Press, 1995).

7. Posted on Future of Music Coalition, "Welcome to the Future of Music Coalition," http://www.futureofmusic.org.

8. This usage of vernacular or nonstandard English certainly includes, and is extended by, the inclusion in songs of languages other than English—an important aspect of some American popular music that space doesn't permit me to explore fully here.

9. This insight about Bruce Springsteen is Jeffrey Melnick's.

10. Robert Christgau, "Outer Children: The Moldy Peaches Slip You a Roofie," *Village Voice* (Dec. 11, 2002), available online at http//robertchristgau.com/xg/rock/moldy-01.php.

Chapter 12. Politics and the American Class Vernacular

An earlier version of this essay appeared in *Working USA: The Journal of Labor and Society* 7, no. 2 (summer 2003).

1. Ruy Teixeira and Joel Rogers, *America's Forgotten Majority: Why the White Working Class Still Matters* (New York: Basic Books, 2000), and Michael Zweig, *The Working Class Majority: America's Best Kept Secret* (Ithaca: Cornell University Press, 2000).

2. See Rogers and Teixeira, "America's Forgotten Majority," *Atlantic Monthly* (June 2000), pt. 1, 1, at http://www.theatlantic.com/issues/2000/06/rogers.htm.

3. Ibid., pt. 2, 2.

4. For the Greenberg connection, see Thomas Byrne Edsall, "Class Doesn't Trump Culture," *Dissent* (spring 2001), 105; and Ruy Teixeira, "Gore's Tenuous Bond with Workers," *American Prospect* (November 20, 2000), 15.

5. See "Competing Tax Plans," *Online NewsHour,* Oct. 17, 2000, at http://www.pbs.org/newshour/bb/election/july-dec00/taxplans_10–17.html.

6. U.S. Census Bureau, *Money Income in the United States: 1999.* (Washington, D.C.: U.S. Government Printing Office, 2000).

7. Zweig, *Working Class Majority,* 1–4 and 9–37.

8. For a summary of Zweig's full analysis, see his table 1 on p. 29, which uses 1996 labor force data.

9. Alan Wolfe, *One Nation, After All: What Middle-Class Americans Really Think* (New York: Penguin, 1998).

10. Zweig, *Working Class Majority,* 86, 89.

11. See Bureau of Labor Statistics, "Occupations with the Largest Job Growth, 2000–2010," *Monthly Labor Review,* Nov. 2001, http://www.bls.gov/emp/emptab4.htm. Of the top twenty-five occupations listed, only five require a bachelor's degree. Some of the occupations with the largest projected growth are food service workers (#1), customer service representatives (2), retail salespersons (4), cashiers (6), office clerks (7), security guards (8), and waiters and waitresses (10). Most of these jobs will pay less than $18,491 on a full-time yearly basis, according to the BLS.

12. S. M. Miller, "Class Dismissed?" *American Prospect* 6, no. 21 (Mar. 21, 1995).

13. Thurston Domina, "Class and the American Consensus: Predictors of Working-Class Identity, 1972–2000," paper presented at "How Class Works" conference, SUNY–Stony Brook, June 8, 2002.

14. Janet Zandy, ed., *What We Hold in Common: An Introduction to Working-Class Studies* (New York: Feminist Press, 2001), ix.

15. Sherry Lee Linkon, ed., *Teaching Working Class* (Amherst: University of Massachusetts Press, 1999).

16. See, for example, Janet Zandy, ed., *Liberating Memory: Our Work and Our Working-Class Consciousness* (New Brunswick, N.J.: Rutgers University Press, 1995); "Working-Class Studies," special issue of *Women's Studies Quarterly* 13, nos. 1–2 (spring–summer 1995); David Shevin et al., *Writing Work: Writers on Working-Class Writing* (Huron, Ohio: Bottom Dog Press, 1999); and *The Heat: Steelworker Lives and Legends,* with introduction by Jimmy Santiago Baca (Mena, Ark.: Cedar Hill Publications, 2001).

17. C. L. Barney Dews and Carolyn Leste Law, eds., *This Fine Place So Far from Home: Voices of Academics from the Working Class* (Philadelphia: Temple University Press, 1995), 1. Also see the earlier collection edited by Jake Ryan and Charles Sackrey, *Strangers in Paradise: Academics from the Working Class* (Boston: South End Press, 1984).

18. Dews and Law, *This Fine Place,* 5.

19. See, for example, Marianna De Marco Torgovnick, *Crossing Ocean Parkway: Readings by an Italian American Daughter* (Chicago: University of Chicago Press, 1994), and Alfred Lubrano, *Limbo: Blue-Collar Roots, White-Collar Dreams* (New York: John Wiley, 2004).

20. See bell hooks, *where we stand: class matters* (New York: Routledge, 2000); Cheri Register, *Packinghouse Daughter: A Memoir* (St. Paul: Minnesota Historical Society Press, 2000); and Richard Rodriguez, *Hunger of Memory* (New York: Bantam, 1983). For eloquent hostility to middle-class ways, see Renny Christopher, *A Carpenter's Daughter: A Working-Class Woman in Higher Education* (forthcoming).

21. Jensen has presented a series of papers at working-class studies conferences that she is now developing into a book. The ones I've read are "The Silent Psychology" (Youngstown, 1995), "Becoming versus Belonging: Psychology, Speech, and Social Class" (Youngstown, 1997), "Post-Traumatic Lives: Identity and Invisible Injury in the Working Class" (Youngstown, 1999), and "Across the Great Divide: Cultural and Psychological Dynamics from the Working Class to the Middle Class" (SUNY–Stony Brook, 2002).

22. Joint presentation titled "Working Class and Middle Class as Competing Cultures" at Youngstown State University Working-Class Studies Conference, May 2001.

23. Fred Rose, *Coalitions across the Class Divide: Lessons from the Labor, Peace, and Environmental Movements* (Ithaca: Cornell University Press, 2000), and Betsy Leondar-Wright, *Class Matters* (Philadelphia: New Society, forthcoming).

24. In addition to Linkon's collection cited above, see Sharon O'Dair, *Class, Critics, and Shakespeare: Bottom Lines on the Culture Wars* (Ann Arbor: University of Michigan Press, 2000).

Chapter 13. New Working-Class Studies in Higher Education

1. Michael Zweig, *The Working Class Majority: America's Best Kept Secret* (Ithaca: Cornell University Press, 2000); Sharon O'Dair, *Class, Critics, and Shakespeare: Bottom Lines on the Culture Wars* (2001).

2. Susan Choy, "Students Whose Parents Did Not Go to College: Postsecondary Access, Persistence, and Attainment" (Washington, D.C.: U.S. Department of Education, National Center for Education Statistics, 2001), 30.

3. Howard B. London, "Transformations: Cultural Challenges Faced by First-Generation Students," *New Directions for Community Colleges* 80 (1992): 6.

4. Ibid., 7–8.

5. Choy, "Students Whose Parents Did Not Go to College," 20.

6. Ibid., 19. See Renny Christopher, "Working-Class Students in Elite and Regional Institutions: Damned If You Do, Damned If You Don't," *Academe* 89, no. 4 (2003), for a further discussion of how this works in the California system of public higher education.

7. University of California, news release (Nov. 16, 2000 [accessed Dec. 2001]), http://www.ucop.edu/news/archives/2000/budgetplan111600.html.

8. See Christopher, "Working-Class Students in Elite and Regional Institutions."

9. John Alberti, "Returning to Class: Creating Opportunities for Multicultural Reform at Majority Second-Tier Schools," *College English* 63, no. 5 (2001): 563.

10. Ibid., 564.

11. Ibid., 565–66.

12. Choy, "Students Whose Parents Did Not Go to College," 3.

13. Ibid.

14. Ibid., 4.

15. Ibid., 22–23.

16. Ibid., 28.

17. Ibid., 30.

18. James Rhem, "Social Class and Student Learning," *National Teaching and Learning Forum* 7, no. 5 (1998): 2.

19. London, "Transformations," 6.

20. Janet Zandy, ed., special issue on "Working Class Studies," *Women's Studies Quarterly* 23, nos. 1–2: 3.

21. Alberti, "Returning to Class," 581.

22. Susan O'Malley, Robert C. Rosen, and Leonard Vogt, eds., *Politics of Education: Essays from* Radical Teacher (Albany: State University of New York Press, 1990).

23. Renny Christopher, Lisa Orr, and Linda Strom, eds., special issue on "Working-Class Lives and Cultures," *Women's Studies Quarterly* 26, nos. 1–2 (1998).

24. Janet Zandy, ed., *What We Hold in Common: An Introduction to Working-Class Studies* (New York: Feminist Press, 2001).

25. Alan Shepard, John McMillan, and Gary Tate, eds., *Coming to Class: Pedagogy and the Social Class of Teachers* (Portsmouth, N.H.: Boynton/Cook, 1998), vii.

26. Ibid., viii.

27. Sherry Lee Linkon, *Teaching Working Class* (Amherst: University of Massachusetts Press, 1999).

28. Choy, "Students Whose Parents Did Not Go to College," 21.

29. The Listserv is wcs-1@umn.edu.

30. The Web site is at http://www.unomaha.edu/pto/.

31. Christine Launius coined this term in her paper, "Biting the Hand That Feeds Them: Working-Class Academics and Cross-Class Identity," presented at the Modern Language Association conference, New Orleans, 2001.

32. Jake Ryan and Charles Sackrey, *Strangers in Paradise: Academics from the Working Class,* rpt. (Lanham, Md.: University Press of America, 1996 [1984]); Michelle M. Tokarczyk and Elizabeth A. Fay, ed., *Working-Class Women in the Academy: Laborers in the Knowledge Factory* (Amherst: University of Massachusetts Press, 1993); Janet Zandy, ed., *Liberating Memory: Our*

Work and Our Working-Class Consciousness (New Brunswick, N.J.: Rutgers University Press, 1995); C. L. Barney and Carolyn Leste Law Dews, eds., *This Fine Place So Far from Home: Voices of Academics from the Working Class* (Philadelphia: Temple University Press, 1995).

33. Richard Rodriguez, *Hunger of Memory: The Education of Richard Rodriguez* (New York: Bantam, 1982); Victor Villanueva Jr., *Bootstraps: From an American Academic of Color* (Urbana, Ill.: National Council of Teachers of English, 1993); Marianna de Marco Torgovnick, *Crossing Ocean Parkway* (Chicago: University of Chicago Press, 1994).

34. The Web site is http://stingray.liu.edu/wca/wca.htm.

35. Laura Rendón and Richard Hope, *Educating a New Majority: Transforming America's Educational System for Diversity* (San Francisco: Jossey-Bass, 1996), 26.

36. Laura Rendón, "From the Barrio to the Academy: Revelations of a Mexican American 'Scholarship Girl'," *New Directions for Community Colleges* 80 (1992): 61.

37. Ibid.

38. David Brodsky, "Democracy against Corporatism in Education," *Workplace* 4, no. 2 (2002): 2.19.

39. See Christopher, "Damned If You Do."

40. Brodsky, "Democracy against Corporatism in Education," 1.2.

41. Ibid., 2.12–2.13.

42. Ibid., 3.1.

43. See ;owhttp://www.as.ysu.edu/~cwcs/Whyhow.html.;ew

Chapter 14. Building Class Identity

1. Dan Kalb, "Class (in Place) without Capitalism (in Space)?" *International Labor and Working Class History* 57 (2000): 31–39.

2. Fred Glass, "Amplifying the Voices of Workers: An Organizing Model for Labor Communications," *Labor Studies Journal* 27 (2003): 1–16.

3. Diana Strassman, "The Stories of Economics and the Power of the Storyteller," *History of Political Economy* 25 (1993): 147–65.

4. James Berlin, "Rhetoric and Ideology in the Writing Class," *College English* 50 (1988): 477–94.

5. Charles Bazerman, "From Cultural Criticism to Disciplinary Participation: Living with Powerful Words," in *Writing, Teaching, Learning in the Disciplines,* ed. Anne Herrington and Charles Moran (New York: Modern Language Association, 1992), 61–68.

6. Dale M. Bauer, "The Other 'F' Word," *College English* 50 (1988): 477–94.

7. William Greider, *Who Will Tell the People: The Betrayal of American Democracy* (New York: Touchstone, 1992), 91.

8. For instance, the AFL-CIO's Web site home page is full of informative links about the labor movement and important work-related issues, but not a single use of the words "class" or "working class."

Contributors

Robert Bruno is Associate Professor of Labor and Industrial Relations at the University of Illinois. He is the author of two books, *Steelworker Alley: How Class Works in Youngstown* (Cornell University Press 1999) and *Reforming the Chicago Teamsters: The Story of Local 705* (Northern Illinois University Press 2003). Bruno is the coauthor and presenter, with Lisa Jordan, of a labor play, *Illinois Labor Works,* and is cochair of the Chicago Center for Working-Class Studies.

Renny Christopher is Associate Professor of English at California State University–Channel Islands. She is working on an autobiography, *A Carpenter's Daughter: A Working-Class Woman in Higher Education,* which addresses her experiences as the first in her family to attend college. Before she earned her PhD, she worked as a printing press operator, typesetter, carpenter, and horse wrangler.

Jim Daniels's most recent books are *Show and Tell: New and Selected Poems* (University of Wisconsin Press) and *Detroit Tales,* a book of short fiction from Michigan State University Press, both published in 2003. He directs the Creative Writing Program at Carnegie Mellon University in Pittsburgh.

Elizabeth Faue is Professor of History at Wayne State University. She is the author of *Writing the Wrongs: Eva Valesh and the Rise of Labor Journalism* (2002), *Community of Suffering and Struggle: Women, Men, and the Labor Move-*

ment in Minneapolis, 1915–1945 (1991), and essays on gender, labor, and politics. She is working on a family memoir and on a study called "Citizens and Clients: A History of the U.S. Welfare State in the 20th Century." Since 1991, she has directed the North American Labor History Conference.

Lisa Jordan is Director of Women's and Diversity Programming in the Labor Education Service at the University of Minnesota. She is coauthor and presenter, with Robert Bruno, of *Illinois Labor Works*.

Paul Lauter is the Allan K. and Gwendolyn Miles Smith Professor of Literature at Trinity College and General Editor of the *Heath Anthology of American Literature*. He is author of *Canons & Contexts* (1991) and *From Walden Pond to Jurassic Park: Activism, Culture, and American Studies* (2001). Lauter is a past president of the American Studies Association and a longtime member of the collective that publishes the journal *Radical Teacher*. In 2001, he received the Hubbell Award, which is given annually by the American Literature Section of the Modern Language Association of America in recognition of his lifetime of scholarly work in the field.

Sherry Lee Linkon is a founder and codirector of the Center for Working-Class Studies at Youngstown State University, where she also teaches American Studies and is a Professor of English. She is the editor of *Teaching Working Class* (University of Massachusetts Press, 1999) and coauthor, with John Russo, of *Steeltown U.S.A.: Work and Memory in Youngstown* (University Press of Kansas, 2002).

Jack Metzgar is Professor of Humanities at Roosevelt University in Chicago, where he has taught general education courses for working adults for the past twenty-five years. Metzgar has published numerous articles, mostly on the American labor movement, in both scholarly publications such as the *Industrial Relations Research Association Journal* and *Relations Industrielles/Industrial Relations* and in progressive political journals such as *The Nation, Dissent, Socialist Review,* and *In These Times*. His most recent book is *Striking Steel: Solidarity Remembered*, a memoir and history of the 1959 steel strike. Published in 2000 by Temple University Press, *Striking Steel* won the Sidney Hillman Foundation Award for best book of the year (the Hillman Foundation is a project of the Union of Needletrades, Industrial and Textile Employees—UNITE!). Metzgar helped found the Chicago Center for Working-Class Studies, a group of faculty from several Chicago-area universities dedicated to "making class visible" in the study of American social reality.

Don Mitchell is Professor and Chair of the Geography Department of the Maxwell School, Syracuse University. He is the author, most recently, of *The Right to the City: Social Justice and the Fight for Public Space* (Guilford Press 2003). A recipient of a MacArthur Fellowship, he is the founder and director of the People's Geography Project, Web site at http://www.peoplesgeography.org.

Kimberley L. Phillips is Associate Professor of History and Black Studies at the College of William and Mary. She is the author of *Alabama North: African-American Migrants, Community, and Working-Class Activism in Cleveland, 1915–1945* (University of Illinois Press 2000). Her current research focuses on African American cultural production and the military.

Alessandro Portelli is Professor of American Literature at the University of Rome La Sapienza and is the author of a number of essays and books on oral culture and oral history. His work published in English includes *The Death of Luigi Trastulli and Other Stories: Form and Meaning in Oral History* (State University of New York Press 1990); *The Text and the Voice: Speaking, Writing, and Democracy in American Literature* (Columbia University Press 1994); and *The Battle of Valle Giulia: Oral History and the Art of Dialogue* (State University of New York Press 1990).

David Roediger directs the Center on Democracy in a Multiracial Society at the University of Illinois, where he teaches in the Afro-American Studies Program. A longtime labor activist, his books include *Wages of Whiteness: Race and the Making of the American Working Class* (Verso 1999), *Colored White: Transcending the Racial Past* (University of California Press 2003), and (with Philip S. Foner) *Our Own Time: A History of American Labor and the Working Day* (W. W. Norton 1989). Books he has recently edited include *Black on White: Black Writers on What It Means to Be White*, Covington Hall's *Labor Struggles in the Deep South and Other Writings*, and W. E. B. Du Bois's *John Brown*.

Rachel Lee Rubin is Associate Professor of American Studies at the University of Massachusetts–Boston. She is the author of *Jewish Gangsters of Modern Literature* (University of Illinois Press 2000) and coeditor of *American Popular Music: New Approaches to the Twentieth Century* (University of Massachusetts Press 2001). Rubin is a member of the editorial collective of the *Journal of Popular Music Studies* and a general editor of a series of books (with University of Massachusetts Press) on American Popular Music. She has written and spoken widely on country music.

John Russo is a founder and the codirector of the Center for Working-Class Studies at Youngstown State University where he also serves as the Coordinator of the Labor Studies Program. He has written widely on labor and social issues and is recognized as a national expert on labor unions and working-class issues. His most recent work is a book coauthored with Sherry Lee Linkon, *Steeltown, U.S.A.: Work and Memory in Youngstown* (University Press of Kansas 2003). He has been recognized as a Distinguished Professor in three areas: research and scholarship, teaching, and public service.

Tim Strangleman is Senior Research Fellow and Institute Manager at the Working Lives Research Institute, London Metropolitan University. A sociologist by training, he has previously taught and done research at the Universities of Durham, Manchester, and Nottingham. He has carried out studies in the railway, construction, engineering, and coal mining industries. His PhD was on the experience of privatization in the British railways. His interests center on labor history, oral history, working-class autobiography, workplace culture, nostalgia, and the experience of organizational change.

Tom Zaniello is director of the Honors Program at Northern Kentucky University and Adjunct Professor at the National Labor College of the George Meany Center for Labor Studies. He is the author of *Working Stiffs, Union Maids, Reds, and Riffraff: An Expanded Guide to Films about Labor* (Cornell University Press, 2003).

Michael Zweig is Professor of Economics at the State University of New York at Stony Brook, where he has received the SUNY Chancellor's Award for Excellence in Teaching and is the director of the Center for the Study of Working Class Life. His most recent book is *The Working Class Majority: America's Best Kept Secret* (Cornell University Press, 2000). He is also the editor of *What's Class Got to Do with It? American Society in the Twenty-first Century* (Cornell University Press, 2004).

Index